A Wilder West

A Wilder West

Rodeo in Western Canada

Mary-Ellen Kelm

UBCPress · Vancouver · Toronto

20 19 18 17 16 15 14 13 12 11   5 4 3 2 1

Printed in Canada on FSC-certified ancient-forest-free paper (100% post-consumer recycled) that is processed chlorine- and acid-free.

Library and Archives Canada Cataloguing in Publication

Kelm, Mary-Ellen
   A wilder West : rodeo in Western Canada / Mary-Ellen Kelm.

Includes bibliographical references and index.
Also issued in electronic format.
ISBN 978-0-7748-2029-5 (cloth); 978-0-7748-2030-1 (pbk)

  1. Rodeos – Alberta – History. 2. Rodeos – British Columbia – History. 3. Rodeos – Social aspects – Alberta – History. 4. Rodeos – Social aspects – British Columbia – History. I. Title.

GV1834.56.C2K44 2011   791.8'409711   C2011-906193-7

Canadä

UBC Press gratefully acknowledges the financial support for our publishing program of the Government of Canada (through the Canada Book Fund), the Canada Council for the Arts, and the British Columbia Arts Council.

This book has been published with the help of a grant from the Canadian Federation for the Humanities and Social Sciences, through the Aid to Scholarly Publications Programme, using funds provided by the Social Sciences and Humanities Research Council of Canada.

Illustration and indexing of this book were made possible by a Single Event Publication grant from the Simon Fraser University Publications Fund.

UBC Press
The University of British Columbia
2029 West Mall
Vancouver, BC V6T 1Z2
www.ubcpress.ca

For Don

Contents

Illustrations

Acknowledgments

This project began on a hot day in May 1993 as I travelled north to take part in the founding of what was then Canada's first new university in a generation – the University of Northern British Columbia. Driving out of the Fraser Canyon, with my two cats in a small crate on the seat next to me, I passed through small towns and reserves along Highway 97. As I entered towns such as Clinton and Williams Lake, and reserves such as Bonaparte and Soda Creek, I started noticing signs for upcoming rodeos. I grew up in Windsor, Ontario, so I knew nothing about rodeos. My dad, a native Californian born and raised in Visalia, had once taken me to a travelling rodeo that came to the Windsor Stockcar Racetrack. A typical teenager, I was unimpressed. Now it seemed to me, on that day in 1993, I was in real cowboy country. But what did that mean in this very Canadian West?

Answering that question has taken some considerable time. A seed grant from the University of Northern British Columbia (UNBC) and a standard research grant in 2000 from the Social Sciences and Humanities Research Council funded the work. A team of research assistants at both UNBC and Simon Fraser University (SFU) gathered piles and piles of newspaper clippings, rodeo programs, and photographs, and conducted some of the interviews. So I wish to thank Dan Watt, Rhys Pugh, Mark Sarrazin, Lorna Townsend, Greg Sell, Sarah Carr-Locke, Megan Prins, Kathy McKay, and Corinne George. Staff at a great many archives large and small have also generously given of their time, especially Jim Bowman of the Glenbow Museum Archives, Diana French of the Rodeo and Ranching Museum at Williams Lake, the Esplanade Arts and Heritage Centre in Medicine Hat, the Galt Museum and Archives in Lethbridge, the Museum of the Highwood in High River, the Kamloops Museum and Archives, the Secwepemc Heritage Centre Archives, the Dawson Creek Archives, the Oliver and District Heritage Society, the Surrey Archives, the Vancouver Archives, the Provincial Archives of Alberta, the British Columbia Archives, and

Library and Archives Canada. Individuals much better versed in rodeo than I generously gave of their time both in formal interviews and conversation; these include Mike LeBourdais, Pete "Duke" LeBourdais, Ron, Joan, Ted, and Garry Gottfriedson, Monty Palmantier, Joan (Palmantier) Gentles, Dick Ardill, Gwen Johansson, Deb Fleet, Jean Palmer, Terry Cook, the Linnell family, Ron West, Garry and Johnny Oker, and Maureen Richter. Over the years, colleagues and students have read, heard, or discussed various sections of this work, including Jacqueline Holler, Ted Binnema, Jonathan Swainger, Gordon Martel, Bill Morrison, Elise Chenier, Jay Taylor, Jeremy Brown, Thomas Kuehn, Dimitri Krallis, Nicolas Kenny, Ilya Vinkovetsky, Jennifer Spear, Willeen Keough, and participants of the panel in honour of Sylvia Van Kirk at the Canadian Historical Association meetings in Saskatoon, the Print Culture Lecture Series at SFU, and the American Society for Ethnohistory meetings in Quebec City and Chicago. Jean Barman, Ted Binnema, Jay Taylor, Christine Obansawin, Dave Poulsen, and Rod Day read the manuscript and offered important and helpful commentary. Jean Wilson and Darcy Cullen warmly welcomed me back to UBC Press, and Darcy, Laraine Coates, and Anna Eberhard Friedlander skilfully shepherded the manuscript through the processes involved in publishing. Deborah Kerr did the copy editing with patience and great attention to detail. An SFU publication grant paid for the reproduction of photographs. Finally, I want to especially thank my husband, Don McLean, who walked with me through nearly the whole process that brought this book to fruition. He brought a photo of a rodeo rider to one of our first dates and told me stories of the Mt. Currie Rodeo and the Calgary Stampede of the 1970s. Little did he know that he would be going to rodeos every summer for nearly the next ten years as I researched this book. But he did so with an insurmountable sense of adventure and good spirit. Don is truly my best friend, and it is to him that I dedicate this book.

A Wilder West

Introduction

Riders were warming up their horses when I arrived at the Whispering Pines Reserve, near Kamloops, British Columbia, for the National Aboriginal Achievement Day rodeo that clear, hot morning in June 2004. The contestants were both settlers and Aboriginal people, defined here as First Nations, Métis, and mixed-heritage people, local men and women from ranches, reserves, and small towns.[1] Singly and in groups of two, they walked their horses in wide circles in the outdoor arena. As they did they talked, catching up on news and gossip, asking more serious questions of each other: How close had the fires of the previous summer come to their property? Had they lost buildings, rangeland, or stock?[2] As they moved their horses into a trot, the conversations continued, groups split apart, and new ones formed. Circles widened as the horses began to canter. Riders peeled off on their own to work with their horses, reminding the horses of the specific skills they would need that day: the abrupt halt of the calf-roping horse, the sudden burst of speed required for steer wrestling. (A glossary at the end of this book provides definitions of rodeo events and terms.) As they began to cool down their horses, the riders grouped again, joking, challenging each other, until it was time to leave the arena and prepare for the day's events. Such fleeting encounters, moments when camaraderie challenges the differences and antipathies created by racialization and gender, are at the heart of this book.

Such ephemeral moments as these are not easy to find in the historical record. Nearly twenty years ago, Richard White encouraged us to seek them out, to go beyond histories of the West that depict Aboriginal people and settlers as either attracting or repelling each other.[3] Rodeo may seem a poor topic in which to search for more nuanced views. Some historians have dismissed popular culture, like rodeos, as an "extension of capitalist manipulation of the West as an icon of individualism ... a 'twilight zone' of myth and denial."[4] Like much of the culture of the West, they contend, rodeo celebrated what Richard Slotkin called the myth of the frontier, which grounded American national identity in conquest of Aboriginal peoples and nature, and provided the justification for American power internationally. Rodeo acted out these ideas and in so doing supported white male dominance – or so the standard academic interpretation has gone. Canadian and American scholars have found this interpretation compelling at least in part because, like cowboying itself, rodeo has a hemispheric history: American immigrants brought the sport, and its values, to Canada in the early twentieth century, and Canadians have adapted the standard scripts to their own purposes.[5] Rodeo truly is a transnational topic, and thought of in the broadest terms, it does seem to do little more than glorify conquest.

But focusing on the big transnational picture denies careful attention to the details in which the everyday interactions in the rodeo arena, and in the more extended celebrations that became known as stampedes (see glossary), challenged and modified the standard storyline of conquest. So this book strikes a balance between this broader history and micro-histories of rodeo in small towns and rural and Aboriginal communities in three regions of Western Canada: southern Alberta; the BC Interior, located between the eastern slopes of the Coastal Range and the western slopes of the Rockies; and the Peace River country, east of the Rockies in northern BC and Alberta. All these regions are historical ranching districts, though many communities that eventually staged rodeos had moved on to other economic modes, mainly grain farming or fruit growing, by the twentieth century when the bulk of our story takes place. Many shared commonalities, not just between themselves but also with other groups of people who embraced rodeo across the transborder West. They shared an attraction to the myth of the frontier, lauding early pioneers dubbed "old-timers" and celebrating the pacification of Aboriginal people, though in Canada this was more often conceived as a process of benevolent containment rather than conquest, a distinction few Aboriginal people care much about. But there were important variations too. For example, Alberta's First Nations used stampedes to remind settlers and governments of their treaty rights, whereas Aboriginal people in BC, with a few exceptions, had no treaties. Government officials laid out reserves in Alberta of a size intended to render the First Nations there self-sufficient; in British Columbia, reserve size was kept small in order to force residents into wage labour, ensuring that BC ranches would rely, for many years, on Aboriginal

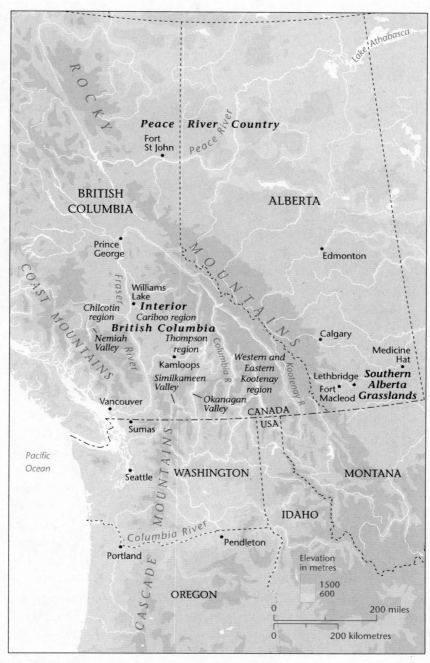

MAP 1   The regions discussed in this book.

workers. The specific social relations of a particular setting shaped what went on at a rodeo even while the broader transborder history of the event encouraged consistent forms and structures to develop over time. This book attends to both the general patterns of that history and how those patterns played out in small communities in Western Canada.

By the early twentieth century, rodeos had developed a predictable set of contests, and what follows is a generalized overview of rodeo events as they existed in the 1930s. Bucking horse, steer, and bull riding, known as the roughstock events, tested the agility and toughness of both rider and mount. Calf roping, steer wrestling, and the other timed events demonstrated the teamwork of horse and rider. In this way, rodeos played and replayed, often dozens of times in a single rodeo, the relationships between humans and animals inherent to ranching life. Parades, grand-stand events, and historical re-enactments all taught spectators about the progression of the West into modernity. And yet, even these recurrent stagings, these endless repetitions, could not foreclose the possibility that things might get out of hand. That possibility is what put the wild in the Wild West Show.

Still, by the 1930s, people expected that rodeos would have certain features. A parade announced the beginning of festivities. For travelling performances, such as Wild West Shows and circuses, the parade was a form of advertising: it tempted onlookers with a glimpse of the exciting sights and dramatic features awaiting them. Rodeo built on this tradition, as famous cowboys and cowgirls rode through town exhibiting feats of riding or roping. Since many small towns and rural enclaves were not always secure settlements, rodeos and their parades offered a chance for communities to demonstrate orderly stability and to perform historical narratives that might convey legitimacy.[6] Much like the early nineteenth-century parades in American cities in which the desired social order was envisioned, rodeo parades told a certain kind of story.[7] Aboriginal people often led them, demonstrating their indigeneity and, in the minds of or-ganizers, their pre-modern place in an unfolding history of settlement. Then came the cowboys and cowgirls, dressed, in the early part of the century, in woolly chaps, brightly coloured shirts, and high-crowned hats. They represented open-range ranching, considered at the time to be a rudimentary form of settlement. Then came the floats organized and constructed by local clubs, farmers and town-dwellers, businesses and churches, all a testament to the productivity, the success, the civilized

Tsuu T'ina people on parade in Lethbridge, 1910s. *Glenbow Museum Archives,
NA-1105-78*

modernity of the place. Intermingled throughout were marching bands,
demonstrating discipline and unity, hallmarks of rational masculinity.[8]

The grand entry brought organizers, civic elites, honoured guests,
cowboys, and Aboriginal people into the arena. Bands played national
anthems, and a minister prayed, opening the rodeo with a reminder that
God granted man dominion over the animals. A master of ceremonies,
usually a local community leader but sometimes a celebrity from out of
town, mounted the stage and introduced that year's rodeo queen and her
entourage. Sometimes, local rodeo cowboys who had died during the past
year were honoured in the opening ceremonies.

As they waited for the rodeo to begin, spectators could peruse their
programs. Here too the story of conquest was often repeated. Programs
recounted town histories and regaled readers with investment opportunities in the region. Advertisements from local businesses competed to
attract visitors. The programs explained the various events, often linking
them to the working life of the cowboy but also elucidating the rules and
procedures of what increasingly became sporting events rather than exhibitions of cowboy skills. Rodeo programs included ethnographic tidbits
about local First Nations, especially if the stampede also included an
Indian village, as it did at Fort Macleod, Alberta, and Williams Lake,

BC, in the early twentieth century. The schedule often featured cowboy and cowgirl events, and "Indian" and "squaw" races as they were called – competitions in which contestants vied within their own gendered and racialized categories. Finally, programs included a dictionary of terms, offering visitors access to the world of rodeo by teaching them its specialized language. All of this – the parade, the program, and the schedule of events – seemed to constitute a kind of ritual in which the values and the social structures of the North American West were displayed and where settler hegemony was legitimized.

Then the contests began. In some of the signature rodeo events, such as bronc riding and calf roping, men and women, Aboriginal people and settlers all competed against each other. Here the careful staging of rodeos as masculinist celebrations of settlement encountered the unpredictable. Rodeo parades and programs extolled settler ascendancy, but the contests themselves could lead to other outcomes. As Peter Iverson and others have shown, Aboriginal men were expert riders and ropers, and they took their share of prize money, becoming local, and eventually international, rodeo heroes. Both settler and Aboriginal women proved their courage and skill in riding roughstock or standing astride two horses hurtling down the track in Roman racing at early twentieth-century stampedes.[9] Even the animals stood a chance of winning. Horses could buck off their riders; calves might escape the rope.[10] Cowboys and cowgirls sometimes lost their lives in the ring. By midcentury, rodeo became somewhat less chaotic as managers and cowboys crafted new rules and standards, but it was not worth watching if the outcome were guaranteed. Rodeo was about risk – including the risk that events would challenge dominant narratives about settler ascendancy. In this sense, it was always wilder than a study of its forms and structures would suggest.

Similarly, there were moments of encounter outside the arena that went beyond local stampede scripts. These are harder to document, for often they exist only in photographs and reminiscences. In British Columbia, where Aboriginal men were a significant part of the ranching workforce, they also shared leisure time with settler cowboys. In some cases, the emerging elites of BC's early twentieth-century rodeos, men such as the Similkameen Valley's Harry Shuttleworth, were mixed-heritage offspring of unions between ranchers and Aboriginal women, and as such, they could not be neatly categorized as either "cowboy" or "Indian." Rodeo in BC, then, was an expression as much of hybridity as of settler hegemony.

Tillie Baldwin (right) in the Roman race, Winnipeg Stampede, 1913. *Glenbow Museum Archives, NA-1029-18*

In Alberta, rodeo emerged in the often underappreciated alliances between reserve communities and small towns against more powerful entities such as the federal government or big-city media. Organizers fought government prohibitions on Aboriginal attendance at small-town rodeos. When Calgary papers pilloried Kainai bronc-rider Tom Three Persons in 1912, the town elites of Fort Macleod, Alberta, came to his defence, demanding a retraction. Rodeo visitors, many of whom were tourists, had their first encounters with Aboriginal people in the Indian encampments at small-town stampedes, purchasing beadwork and paying to take photographs. And Aboriginal people used these moments of encounter to raise awareness of their cultures, their histories, and their current concerns. In Lethbridge and Medicine Hat, Mike Mountain Horse found in stampede-goers an audience for his writing on contemporary Kainai issues. Finally, a shared interest in the sport brought settler spectators to reserve rodeos across southern Alberta and in the BC Interior. Both the in-arena encounters between Aboriginal people and settlers, and those that occurred in the Indian villages, the grandstands, the midways, and the food concessions, suggest that seeing rodeo only as an institution of settler hegemony, as scholars such as Elizabeth Furniss and Elizabeth Atwood Lawrence have done, misses some important points.

Left to right: Garney Willis, Cyclone Smith, Hans Richter, Herb Matier, and Harry Shuttleworth, winners of the 1926 Sumas, Washington, Rodeo. The five BC cowboys were reputed to have won all the money that year and had this photo printed as a postcard. Although all five friends hailed from BC at the time, Smith and Matier were originally from the US. *British Columbia Cowboy Heritage Society*

The first of these is that rodeo was a place of encounter, or to borrow Mary Louise Pratt's useful concept, a "contact zone." Pratt coined the term to impart a sense of the unpredictable and the chaotic, that which slips beyond controlling impulses of organization and discourse, when peoples interacted with one another. Certainly rodeos, as suggested above, were heavily structured both materially and discursively, but they were never fully contained by those formations. Thinking about rodeo as a contact zone allows us to fully explore those extraneous, surprising, subverting strands without ignoring the larger socio-economic, political, and cultural arrangements in which it was staged and to which it contributed.[11]

Rodeos, as we will see, were contact zones precisely because they were venues at which the improvisational coexisted with the staged, where hybridity rubbed shoulders with racial and gendered segmentation, and where colonial power infused events but did not overdetermine how people would behave or indeed how they would ascribe meaning to what they saw or experienced. Moreover, as James Clifford reminds us, "contact approaches presuppose not sociocultural wholes subsequently brought into relationship, but rather systems already constituted relationally, entering new relations through historical processes of displacement."[12] Rodeo contributed to those "new relations," created histories, built communities, and crafted new identities as both settlers and First Nations grappled with modernity, in varying ways and with varying levels of control and intensity.

Accordingly, it was a site of struggle for both settler and Aboriginal communities, and this is my second point. The growth of the sport over the last century tends to obscure the fact that some small towns in British Columbia and Alberta were quite ambivalent about staging rodeos. Whereas some, such as Raymond, Alberta, and Williams Lake, BC, embraced it from the outset, Medicine Hat and Kamloops wondered if it were worth the expense. Some, such as Lethbridge, worried that it brought Aboriginal people to town and into contact with unscrupulous whites; others found that stampedes were not money-makers unless Aboriginal people attended. The federal government was certainly opposed to Aboriginal people going to stampedes, especially if that meant dressing in traditional clothing and performing outlawed dances. Indeed, the Department of Indian Affairs under Duncan Campbell Scott amended the Indian Act in 1914 precisely to prohibit such attendance, putting government in conflict with settlers as well as First Nations. For their part, Aboriginal people were not united on the value of rodeos. Aboriginal youth in southern Alberta eagerly attended them, and elders worried that this distracted them from the spiritual gatherings of the spring and summer, particularly the sun dance. Like other celebrations, rodeo brought division as well as commonality to the surface, multiple perspectives that are lost in an interpretation that finds only settler dominance in its effects. In the sense that rodeo was not entirely predictable, it was wilder than anyone planned, and it reflected a wilder history of relationships between Aboriginal people and settlers.

Further, rodeos did not simply reflect communities – they actively constituted them in particular ways, and this is the third argument put forward in this book. For small towns and rural communities, rodeo helped pay the bills of less financially viable events such as fairs and exhibitions. As rodeo became a sport, it required purpose-built facilities, and committees ran fundraising campaigns that resulted in new arenas, racetracks, and grandstands in small towns and rural communities across the West. When Tommy Wilde and Jack Lawless staged their rodeos at Taylor Flats in the Peace River country at the end of the Second World War, they built the region's first dance hall, illuminated by strings of electric lights. In First Nations today, rodeo provides the focus for infrastructural renewal. At Whispering Pines, near Kamloops, the arena is one venue in a larger recreational park that also includes a motocross course. Rodeos, then, provided the focus for efforts to build structures that often had multiple uses and that contributed to the leisure opportunities for rural people.

They constituted community in more subtle ways as well. Much like the exhibitions and pageants studied by Elsbeth Heaman and H.V. Nelles, rodeo did more than reflect community values; communities came to define themselves by the values they thought rodeo expressed.[13] Organizers encouraged volunteer labour by calling on local men and women to live up to the mythic standards of pioneer voluntarism and hospitality. The *High River Times* reminded townsfolk of the cooperative spirit of the pioneer generation when it asked them to help build the chutes and corrals necessary for the High River Rodeo of 1946. The 1950 rodeo committee at Kamloops encouraged women to open their homes to visitors just as their foremothers had done in the early years of settlement. Swinging a hammer, accommodating a visitor, or donating a trophy thus gave the people of small-town Alberta and BC a chance to demonstrate that they were the true descendants of the much-lauded pioneer generation. Just as the Canadian West became increasingly modern, with better roads and communication networks, the development of megaprojects, and economic diversification, small towns such as High River and Williams Lake sought out and celebrated surviving old-timers, defined as settlers from the first or second generation of settlement. Lauding their "pioneer history" became one of the selling points of small-town stampedes, and in the process, they commodified that history as heritage to be consumed by tourists and locals alike.[14] The focus on old-timers, moreover, highlighted whiteness – defined, demonstrated, and feted it – as the keystone to heritage in Western Canada. In this, the small towns of BC and Alberta linked themselves to the broader mythic constructions of the transborder West, with all the legitimacy and internal ambivalence that entailed.[15]

All participants could use rodeo to define and display identity. Even in the early decades of the twentieth century, when Aboriginal people seldom

Welcoming Princess Margaret to Secwepemc land at the Williams Lake Stampede, 1958. *Courtesy of Royal BC Museum, BC Archives, H-05839*

controlled the staging of public celebrations, they used them to communicate directly to visiting dignitaries about their concerns over treaty rights (or lack of treaties) and access to land and resources. Riding in parades, setting up Indian villages, or dancing before dignitaries forcefully demonstrated to both spectators and Aboriginal people themselves that they were not just remnants of the past but very much had a place in a modernizing Canada, combining old and new cultural expressions to exhibit that fact.[16] They also rode to express pride in themselves. As one elder described his participation in the 1958 Williams Lake Stampede held in honour of Princess Margaret's BC visit, "we showed her and the people of Canada that we have royalty too."[17] Aboriginal involvement in settler and reserve rodeos at the turn of the twenty-first century retained its political edge while honouring elders and families of First Nations communities. Dakelh (Carrier) families took their place in the 2001 Anahim Lake Stampede parade, and at the 2002 Nemiah Stampede on the Chilcotin Plateau, announcers honoured the "great Tsilhquot'in warriors" of the past, personified that day by the riders assembled for the mountain race. Such displays point to a long history of occupation of the land, of cultural persistence and adaptation, and of families and masculinities emergent despite all government attempts to destroy aboriginality throughout the twentieth century. Simultaneously, they are both cultural production and political activism.[18]

Moreover, rodeos have become deeply embedded in some First Nations' sense of themselves. "It's part of our tradition: horses and rodeo," declares the narrator of one documentary film. The ways in which Aboriginal people have incorporated rodeo as part of both specific (Kainai, for example) and broadly defined Aboriginal culture constitute a process that neither escaped nor was completely bounded by colonial legacies of exoticism and commodification.[19] Scholars agree that the relationship between communities, memories, cultural production, and commemoration is a negotiated one that must cope with ambivalence and divergent epistemologies of the past. Aboriginal engagements with rodeo are no exception. Just as public celebrations contained change, ambivalence, and multiple perspectives in settler societies, so too did Aboriginal performances emerge from division as well as agreement.[20] Rodeo engaged with old rivalries in southern Alberta between the Cree at Hobbema, the Nakoda at Morley, and the Kainai at Standoff as well as among signatories of Treaty 7.[21] At the same time, it fed into emerging pan-Indian definitions of aboriginality by contributing images such as the Indian cowboy of Buffy Sainte-Marie's song "He's an Indian Cowboy at the Rodeo," written, in her words, "to celebrate the beauty of Indian reality."[22] What is important to remember, in all of this, is not that some version of authenticity was either staged or negated, a tradition invented or commodified, but rather that new authenticities, identities, and relationships arose in the contact zone where audiences and performers interacted, as Julie Cruikshank has so persuasively argued.[23] In the late twentieth century, in the context of monumental land-claim litigation, new treaty negotiations, and intensifying Aboriginal protest, cultural performance and interaction bear considerable political weight. Therefore, *A Wilder West* offers new perspectives on the history of Aboriginal activism, demonstrating the palpable linkages between cultural display and political action.[24]

Rodeo also formed a community where none had existed before: specifically, that of the "on the road" professional cowboy. As rodeo's popularity grew in the 1920s, circuits developed across the transborder West. As contestants and their families travelled together, a new community developed. A sense of common cause grew, and by the 1930s and 1940s, rodeo cowboy organizations emerged – the Cowboys' Turtle Association in the United States, which was eventually renamed the Professional Rodeo Cowboys Association (PRCA), and in Canada the Cowboys' Protective Association, which was renamed the Canadian Professional Rodeo Association (CPRA). In Canada, the CPRA recognized the import-ance of Aboriginal cowboys by setting aside two "Indian representative" positions on its executive. More importantly, Aboriginal communities across BC and Alberta produced elite rodeo cowboys such as Kenny McLean, Fred Gladstone, and Dave Perry. During the 1950s and 1960s, the on-the-road community of professional cowboys to which they be-longed became a kind of liminal contact zone in which Aboriginal and non-Aboriginal people lived and worked together. As the CPRA developed its rules and standards of conduct, it quite deliberately avoided defining "The Rodeo Cowboy" as white. Its official rhetoric and the testimonies of pro rodeo cowboys all downplayed racialization in favour of a professional identity highlighting masculinities and grounded in the right to make a living at rodeo, the responsibility to behave in ways that put rodeo in a good light before the media and the public, in an emphasis on rodeo as a family sport, and in precepts of fair play and open competition. In this way, rodeo joined other sports in reflecting and constituting masculinities, emerging and varying, over the course of the twentieth century.[25] It was this community that so intrigued Clifford Westermeier, rodeo's first histor-ian, who wrote in the 1940s; subsequent historians, such as Kristine Fredriksson and Michael Allen, have focused on the rise of professional rodeo and the ways in which the rodeo cowboy, as a particular image of masculinity, resonates with American culture. Only Max Foran has ques-tioned how and why Western Canadians embraced the sport.[26]

At first, the definition of the rodeo cowboy did not include women. Though women had performed and competed at rodeos early in the twentieth century, the rise of professional organizations and pro rodeo sidelined them for two decades, until they too formed their own associa-tion. Established in 1957, the Canadian Barrel Racing Association worked hard to win acceptance for female participation in rodeos staged in Western Canada. Women too deployed the rhetoric of the pro cowboy community, depicting themselves as members of the rodeo family. They did not challenge the dominant values of the sport, even those that lauded masculinity. Though their efforts to demand re-entry coincided with women's movements of the late twentieth century, few cowgirls reported an affinity with feminism. The women who demanded space at rodeos in small Canadian towns did so from within a community that defined femininity as including both competence around horses and stock and the mental, emotional, and physical toughness required to flourish in the pro rodeo world. The travelling rodeo community emerged in the second half of the twentieth century with its own processes of forming racialized and gendered categories.

Rodeo constituted community in one further way. Because not all Aboriginal people had access to the pro community or found it congenial, several Aboriginal rodeo organizations developed, as did a circuit of reserve rodeos. Here too they developed their own definition of the rodeo cowboy, one that emphasized a commitment to acting as role models for young men and women in their communities. Rather than simply reflecting pre-existing social groupings and their values, rodeo represented a set of overlapping communities in which individuals found a sense of belonging and self-definition. This surplus of meanings is exemplified by people such as Joan (Palmantier) Gentles of Williams Lake, who, as a Tsilhquot'in woman, former rodeo queen, barrel-racer, and CPRA-approved judge, belonged in several of these communities simultaneously.

Throughout, this book attends to discourses of difference and the pathways used by individuals and communities to navigate within and around them. We know from the "new" imperial history that difference was produced not just through law or spatial segregation but through the regulation of sex, through domesticity, and through exhibition and performance.[27] The scholars who have focused on rodeo as ritual make plain that it produced binaries, such as cowboy and Indian, that were grounded in popular perceptions of history, race, and gender. Equally important to historical cartographies of difference is the scholarship that marks out thresholds that opened racialized boundaries. As Louis B. Warren has shown for the Wild West Show, friendships, rivalries, fleeting love affairs, and lifelong marriages developed when the many cultures of the American West found themselves living and travelling together.[28] Yet emotions that strayed across racialized lines could come with a cost. Intimacy offered opportunities, but it also exposed the recesses of human lives to colonial surveillance, division, and disapprobation. Indeed, as Ann Laura Stoler has reminded historians, the racial taxonomies of colonialism were not solely rational but affective as well. And just as sexual desire could lead to transgression, so too could other emotions, such as parental and filial love in mixed-heritage families. Friendships and collaborations that crossed racialized lines could be equally challenging.[29] Assimilation's putative success stories – missionary converts, educated colonial subjects, even, perhaps, Indian cowboys – offered object lessons in the *im*permanence of difference.[30] As Nicholas Thomas writes, "the products of assimilation were taken to be subversive as often as they attested to the successes of civilizing missions."[31] For "mimic men," to use Homi Bhabha's term, demonstrated the very artificiality of the colonial project, its ambivalence, and in so doing, undercut its authority.[32] So this book seeks out both difference and ambivalence, building on a burgeoning scholarship that closely examines the subtle nuances in specific relationships and local dynamics in small towns, rural communities, and reserves in Western Canada.[33]

Attention to the "microphysics of daily lives," to use Stoler's phrase, brings new sources and new methods to the fore that read "for discrepant tone, tacit knowledge, stray emotions, extravagant details, 'minor' events" and highlight the ephemeral moments such as those observed at the Whispering Pines Rodeo.[34] As Richard Slatta suggested years ago, studying cowboy culture requires the use of a variety of sources.[35] This book is based on just such an array. The records of the Canadian Professional Rodeo Association were the largest archival collection, but organizational and administrative records existed for a few rodeos as well. Most were run on a shoestring budget by a handful of volunteers, and their records, when they exist, are in basements, barns, and garages. Newspaper coverage helped set rodeos into the context of small-town, rural, and reserve life, reported on the work of rodeo committees, and offered glimpses of how they responded to rodeos. Given the "boosterism" of much Western Canadian press, I tried, wherever possible, to triangulate its accounts with autobiographies and oral histories. The proliferation of small presses in British Columbia that foster local histories has meant that people from Dog Creek to Dawson Creek have published their own accounts. The Glenbow Museum in Alberta and the various oral history projects of the BC Archives produced thousands of hours of testimony from Aboriginal people and from settlers speaking of life in early twentieth-century Western Canada. The Dorothy Calverley Collection of the South

Peace Archives covers life in the Peace River country. Placing announce-
ments on CBC Radio and in local newspapers introduced me to a delight-
ful assortment of cowboys and cowgirls, stock contractors, and rodeo
promoters who agreed to talk with me about their experiences. Finally,
the records of the Department of Indian Affairs and police and court
accounts rounded out the sources used to research this book. With their
intriguing contradictions and loose ends, they called out for interpretations that would give full play to the "wildness" and the surprising social
relations that emerged at rodeos in the Canadian West.

As this book explores rodeo as a contact zone, it does not deny the
structures of rodeo, the regional forces of colonization, the specific local
mappings of difference that settlers and First Nations constructed and
with which they contended when they met at a rodeo. But it also wishes
to explore other affective relationships – family ties, friendships and
rivalries, professional identities, and associations – that crossed or reaffirmed racialized, gendered, and classed lines. And so this book begins
in the next chapter with a history of rodeo as it developed in small towns,
rural communities, and reserves in southern Alberta and the BC Interior.
As small-town elites worked to advertise their districts, competing for settlers and investment, they turned to rodeos and stampedes to attract
attention. Here visitors and residents could take pride in the modernity
of their settlements while they praised the past, embodied by both "cowboys and Indians" who were placed in competitions that were segmented
by race and gender. Yet even as they celebrated settlement, they honoured
a more mixed past when, as the Pincher Creek organizing committee put
it, "Indians were very much a part of the scene."[36] Moreover, organizers
did not fully enforce the rules that separated cowboys from Indians, so
Aboriginal cowboys emerged as an integral part of rodeo history. Federal
government attempts to keep Aboriginal people away from these festivities
constituted a particular point of conflict between settlers and Ottawa.
Government restrictions nearly curtailed stampede organizing in Alberta
during the 1910s, but the persistent pressure of both settlers and First
Nations effectively circumvented them. Aboriginal people, for the most
part, incorporated southern Alberta and BC Interior rodeos into annual
seasonal economic, cultural, and spiritual rounds. They organized rodeos
themselves on reserves, and rodeo cowboys embodied new articulations
of Aboriginal masculinity. Stampedes at Fort Macleod in the 1920s, for
example, became an opportunity for Aboriginal leaders from across the

region to meet and discuss common concerns, and to involve settler supporters in their efforts. Although the intended message of southern Alberta rodeos was one of settler dominance, a much more mixed experience was available to those who attended them. Men and women, Aboriginal people and settlers also interacted at rodeos in British Columbia and, especially for women, with much greater latitude. In these ways, rodeo quite clearly was a significant contact zone for settlers and Aboriginal people, men and women.

Chapter 2 explores the idea that rodeo as a contact zone shaped subjects as well as structures by examining the role it played in crafting identities, affinities, and relationships in and between rural and reserve communities, settlers, and Aboriginal people. In particular, this chapter tracks the masculinities and femininities associated with rodeo and the specific and overlapping influences of regional contexts and of the conditions of settlement and colonization. As increasing numbers of small centres in Alberta and British Columbia staged rodeos, the cowboy became a popular icon of self-sufficiency in the desperate Depression years. In BC, provincial-government-assisted settlement schemes put people on the land in more and more isolated places, and they found that community festivities, such as rodeos, made life more bearable.

By the end of the 1920s, a rodeo circuit, which is the focus of Chapter 3, spanned Alberta and BC and crossed the border into the United States. Greater divisions along racialized, classed, and gendered lines appeared. The pressure of Indian Agents and the costs of riding the large transborder circuits excluded many Aboriginal cowboys. Women too found themselves sidelined as, by the 1930s, organizers began to eliminate their events at the larger shows, bringing in women mainly as paid-per-ride performers. Meanwhile, the settler cowboys who rode the circuit started to see themselves as a community, formed associations, and began to craft for themselves a new normative category of masculinity – the professional rodeo cowboy.

The next chapter examines the growth of the Canadian pro rodeo community as it materialized after the Second World War. Organized as the Cowboys' Protective Association (which was later renamed the Canadian Professional Rodeo Association), members worked together to standardize rodeos, to increase the winnings so that individuals could make a living at the sport, and to improve the public image of rodeo cowboys. To this end, the CPRA devised and enforced a code of conduct that sought to make the cowboys respectable. Fitting in with the mascu-linities that developed during the Cold War, the cowboys were tough, not averse to physical risk but rational and responsible, as evidenced by their participation in a CPRA insurance plan that would help defray medical and funeral costs should they be injured or killed in the arena. The CPRA set out to portray them as respectable family men, willing and capable of paying their bills, knowledgeable (not sentimental) protectors of animals. The CPRA held places on its executive for Aboriginal men, but women struggled to re-enter the sport after the Second World War. Still, as families, both Aboriginal and settler travelled the pro circuit together, where they became a kind of liminal contact zone.

Chapter 5 then traces the effects of professionalization on small-town rodeos. As before the war, local organizers relied on nearby residents, both settler and Aboriginal, to do the work of staging a rodeo. But it was increasingly difficult to make money at these events, for professional rodeos, with their guaranteed prize money for riders and guaranteed entry fees for organizers, competed with small-scale ventures. So, many small towns from Cremona, Alberta, to Williams Lake, BC, agreed to put on CPRA-sanctioned rodeos. This meant higher entry fees and fewer events but assured numbers of travelling professional cowboys. The im-mediate effect was to eliminate many local competitors from the main events. And yet, as a sport, rodeo did not have a large following in many quarters. Thus, small-town organizers scrambled to add "local" features: some of these, such as barrel racing, were particular to women, and others, such as tipi villages, to Aboriginal people, repeating the gendered and racialized segmentation of previous decades. Although it was still possible, of course, for a professional Aboriginal cowboy to enter and win the pro competitions, the signature events became largely associated with white cowboys, whereas the amateur contests such as the Williams Lake moun-tain race became connected with local and Aboriginal men. For many, the world of rodeo had become increasingly masculine and increasingly white. Some small towns avoided professional rodeo altogether, con-structing images for themselves that directly countered those of pro rodeo. When Williams Lake went professional, the Anahim Lake Rodeo advertised itself with the slogan "the west just got wilder," signalling that the efforts of pro rodeo organizations to make the sport respectable were not without detractors.

Some Aboriginal cowboys also challenged the idea that pro rodeo in Canada had created a competitive world that was free of discrimination. They started their own organizations and continued to stage rodeos on reserves. The Indian rodeo circuit developed much more along the lines of the pro rodeo cowboy organizations; indeed, the Aboriginal cowboys who formed it came from the ranks of the professional circuit, adapted the CPRA rulebook, and governed reserve rodeos with the same rules. In these last two chapters, we watch the contact zone that was rodeo fragment as professional, small-town, and reserve rodeos celebrated very different communities.

The Whispering Pines Rodeo that I attended in June 2004 was a reserve rodeo held in honour of National Aboriginal Achievement Day. The arena, grandstand, chutes, and corrals were all built by Aboriginal labour as part of a larger plan to provide economic opportunities on the reserve. Yet on that day, under the hot southern Interior sun, settlers and Aboriginal people competed against each other and combined in teams for roping. Husbands and wives, fathers and sons rode and roped together. And when I interviewed Secwepemc elder and rodeo veteran Pete "Duke" LeBourdais, he told me of men from all across southern Alberta and BC, both Aboriginal and settler, who competed against each other, got into trouble together, travelled alongside each other with their families, and raised children on the rodeo circuit of the mid-twentieth century. For him, instances of camaraderie among rodeo people were not fleeting moments of encounter but the core of a life spent rodeoing in the Canadian West.

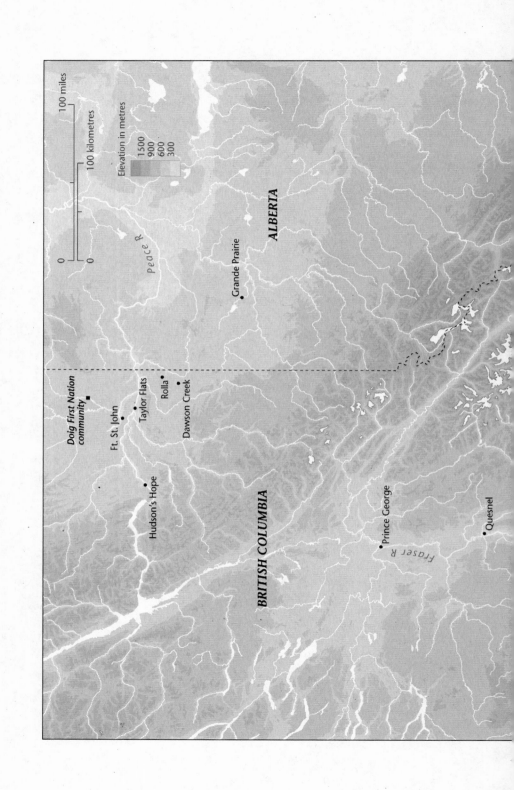

100 miles

100 kilometres

Elevation in metres

1500
900
600
300

Peace R

ALBERTA

Grande Prairie

Doig First Nation community

Ft. St. John

Taylor Flats

Rolla

Dawson Creek

Hudson's Hope

BRITISH COLUMBIA

Prince George

Fraser R

Quesnel

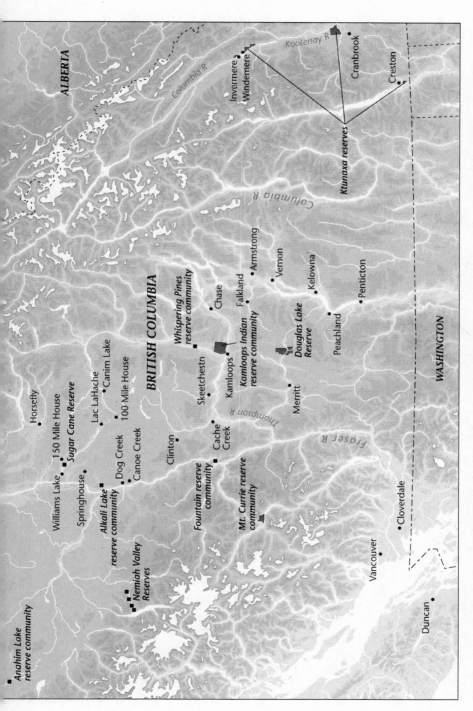

MAP 2   Communities in British Columbia that had rodeos. Locations in the far southeast of the province appear in Map 3.

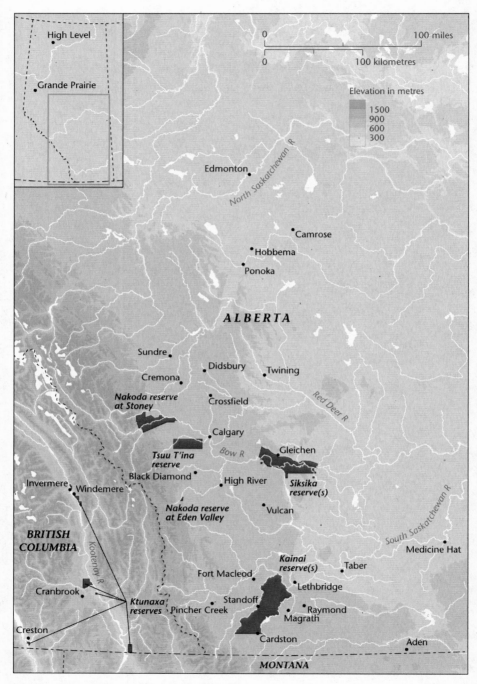

MAP 3 Communities in Alberta that had rodeos.

1
An Old-Timers' Town
Western Communities, Performance, and Contact Zones

Supposing "antiquity" were, at a certain historical juncture, the necessary consequence of "novelty"?
          – *Benedict Anderson,* Imagined Communities

In 1906 thirty-two women journalists from Canada and the United States arrived in Cardston, Alberta, one stop on an across-the-West tour that brought them to Winnipeg, Regina, Calgary, Edmonton, and Banff. They were the very vision of modernity – professional women, wielding cameras and pens – rendering their opinions about the prospects of settlement and investment in the Canadian West for prestigious newspapers of the American Midwest and Eastern Canada. In Cardston, they were met not with a display of equal modernity but with something quite different:

> The mayor of the town was on the platform to welcome us, and soon we were hurried into the rigs that were in waiting. "You are going out to see a bucking contest," said someone, and immediately our new found dignity fled. Everyone was in a flutter and all talked at once. Cameras were hurriedly got in readiness and it was an excited crowd of women that drove behind the gorgeous band wagon which led the way to the corral. We had all read of the roping and break-ing of wild horses but had never seen it outside of a wild west show. Here we were to see the real thing and the fever of the plains was upon us. We forgot that the horses might be hurt in the contest, forgot everything except the won-derful display of pluck and horsemanship. We climbed the bar fence to get a better view, sat on top of it to take snap shots and did many foolish things beneath the dignity of "literary" women.[1]

A bucking contest was a surprising but effective choice of introduction. Cardston, a Mormon settlement founded by Charles Ora Card in 1887, was showing signs of prosperity and permanence by 1906. It had been

Bronc riding at the Gleichen Stampede, 1916. *Glenbow Museum Archives, NA-446-77*

selected as the site of the region's Mormon temple and was establishing itself as a key commercial centre. It had weathered the scrutiny of law-makers and police attuned to discovering polygamy among its residents and, by the turn of the twentieth century, was proclaiming itself to be a "patriotic community."[2] A bucking contest was clearly not a simple rep-resentation of the town of Cardston. However, it did capture what many rural communities wanted to portray as their essence – the "fever of the plains" – a palpable sense of optimism, determination, and collective goodwill. To this end, they staged rodeos to enact these values, to perform their communities even as they built them. Across southern Alberta and the BC Interior in the first decades of the twentieth century, rodeos be-came a major promotional activity for small towns.

They did important work for communities. As John Walsh and Steven High remind us, communities are forged through interaction and im-agination; rodeos encouraged both.[3] They brought people to town, both settlers and Aboriginal people, to spend their money, by paying admission to the staged events but also to shop, eat in restaurants, stay in hotels, and camp nearby. As with the bucking contest in Cardston, rodeos attracted the attention of media, tourists, and investors, enhancing the material forecast of settlements in an era of competition between small towns. Rodeos did more sophisticated and complicated work as well. Settler communities, relatively new in the context of Western Canada, used them as an expression of their cultural heritage. As Benedict Anderson suggests, this was not the florescence of a long tradition but rather the result of change and novelty.[4] Rodeo had its roots in a hemispheric ranching history of the transborder West, but the decline of that economic mode signalled the region's transition to modernity. That was what small towns celebrated. Rodeos promised that, in the West, modernity would not bring the worries it appeared to carry with it elsewhere – emasculated men, emancipated women, enervated familial relations, atomism. Rather, the cowboy spirit, the "spirit of the Plains," would endure. Small towns in Alberta and British Columbia commodified this past through rodeos to perform the social relations and identities they were in the process of creating. They did so both through the production of texts, such as rodeo programs, and through performances including pageants, parades, and, of course, the contests themselves.

Scholars describe rodeo as a ritual of conquest, of settlers ascendant over nature and, as Elizabeth Furniss and Joan Burbick contend, over Aboriginal people. And yet, small towns in Alberta and BC invited Aboriginal people to participate in their rodeos, and they responded in large numbers. If, as James Clifford argues, such events constitute "insiders and outsiders," with the former sharing in the "symbolic wealth" of the community while either excluding or partially integrating others, where did Aboriginal peoples find themselves on that continuum? As Clifford puts it, "This is the stuff of contemporary cultural politics, creative and virulent, enacted in the overlapping historical contexts of colonization/decolonization, nation formation/minority assertions, capitalist market expansion/consumer strategies."[5] A contact perspective allows attention to the uneven relations of power inherent in rodeo without disavowing Aboriginal spaces within it or the possibility of creative interactions.[6] Small towns in Alberta and BC included "cowboys and Indians" in their events because they believed that *both* were essential to them. Aboriginal people participated because they found value in doing so, as communities and as individuals, but perhaps not as much value as they had hoped. This chapter looks at the early history of rodeos in the Canadian West, why small towns staged them, how they became contact zones, and what happened when settler and Aboriginal communities converged at them.

Small-town rodeo committees, of course, did not invent leisure activities in the rural Canadian West. Dances, sports days, and rodeo contests all broke the monotony and isolation of life on the edge of settlement. Holidays such as Victoria Day or Dominion Day provided a focus for organizing events, and towns from Dawson Creek in the Peace River country to Cardston in southern Alberta hosted rodeos, horse races, and gymkhanas on 1 July.[7] In Alberta, the popularity of Dominion Day events prompted railway companies to offer reduced fares between towns.[8] Polo and fox hunts brought settlers together at Lethbridge, High River, and Kamloops in sporting traditions that reminded them of home.[9] Such celebrations were not confined to settler communities. First Nations in Alberta gathered for treaty days and put on horse races and rodeos as well as outlawed ceremonial dances. These attracted settler audiences, which frustrated Indian Affairs officials.[10] Partly in order to counter the appeal of traditional ceremony, some officials helped stage rodeos on reserves. In 1896, for example, government workers organized a rodeo on the Siksika reserve, specifically to distract residents from the sun dance.[11] The Siksika remained interested in drawing the attention and commerce of local settlers, and in 1898 they put on a fair, advertising exhibitions of their produce, horse races, and sports to the surrounding community.[12] Ranchers held events to entertain their cowboys and their neighbours during the slack midsummer season between calving and roundup. At such impromptu contests, Aboriginal and settler working cowboys honed their skills and demonstrated their courage before appreciative audiences of their peers.[13] Canada's first and longest-running rodeo owed its origins to such a ranch-based contest. In 1902, Ray Knight, sheep-rancher, sugar beet entrepreneur, and founder of the town of Raymond, Alberta, challenged local ranchers to enter their cowboys in steer-roping and bucking-horse competitions.[14] Other events were added over the years, and during a 1939 interview, Knight stated that he had organized over sixty shows for more than 300,000 fans.[15] Ranch rodeos continued to be popular throughout the twentieth century. In 1914 the Calder brothers of Aden, Alberta, staged a Dominion Day rodeo on their ranch, which drew six hundred people from Alberta and Montana.[16] Wild West Shows offered historical pageants, cowboy sports, and trick riding and roping to small-town audiences. Although big

Stastia Carry trick riding, 1926. *Glenbow Museum Archives, PA-3457-18*

American touring companies such as the Miller Brothers' 101 Ranch Wild West Show included western Canadian cities on their circuits, local entrepreneurs offered their own Wild West Shows. Peter Welsh, Jim and Stastia Carry, Milt Dowker, Buff Larkin, and Addison P. Day ran touring companies that organized some of the first rodeos in small-town Western Canada. Although most were Americans and veterans of the Wild West Show circuit, they presented shows that put a Canadian spin on the format, offering fewer battle re-enactments and more roping and riding tricks.[17] By the first decades of the twentieth century, small towns and rural and reserve communities shared an appreciation for cowboy sports that encouraged the growth of rodeo.

Most annual small-town rodeos were first organized by agricultural exhibition committees trying to keep their own events financially afloat. As Elsbeth Heaman has shown, agricultural exhibitions began in the nineteenth century as an attempt to educate and improve farmers and their techniques.[18] As settlers moved west, government encouraged them to offer fairs and exhibitions as soon as there was produce worth displaying. Fort Macleod held its first fair in 1886, intent on demonstrating the possibility of mixed farming in the district.[19] Certainly, town and regional boosters believed that exhibitions were, in the words of the *Kamloops Telegram* editor, "a visual object lesson [to the visitor of] the possibilities of this particular section of the province. [And] to the local farmer and the local professional and amateur gardener it is also of value, giving each an opportunity to see the best fruits of his neighbor's skill and industry."[20] Fairs advertised economic incentives to investors and eulogized the character of small-town residents, praising the productive landscape of the region and generally attracting as much positive attention as possible.[21] As the *High River Times* crowed in 1907, "We have been watching the development of High River for some time past and judging from the wonderful progress it has made, the character of the men who are taking their part in its construction and the splendid country of which it is the center, we are confident that it is destined to rank among the leading cities of Alberta ... One dare not assume to limit its possibilities."[22]

Government offered grants to small-town agricultural fairs and stressed the educational nature of the events.[23] Despite this support, the fairs struggled in the early decades of the twentieth century. Fort Macleod's Agricultural Society was embarrassed when local banks would not advance the funds to carry out horse races at its 1914 fair. Instead, the society announced that it would offer open events for local sportsmen and novelty races, hoping to cover expenses through entry fees.[24] Lethbridge banded together with Cardston, Magrath, and Raymond to stage its exhibition in 1918. Organizers offered new trophies to generate interest and encourage competition.[25] As Elsbeth Heaman found for Eastern Canada, fairs were more successful if they combined other attractions with agricultural exhibits. The Kamloops Agricultural Association, which formed in 1895, built on a short history of exhibitions in the area and included representation from communities throughout the North Thompson region. Graphic arts and wood carving, floral displays and taxidermy, cast-iron stoves and bottled beer soon accompanied the display of fruit, crops, and livestock, but the fair remained impecunious. In 1901 the association purchased land formerly held by the Hudson's Bay Company in order to build a racetrack, but costs drove it to sell the land to the city. The fair's fortunes did not improve until the mid-1920s when rodeos started generating revenue for the association. In 1925, renamed the Kamloops Exhibition

Association, it cooperated with the BC Stockbreeders Association to build an arena for rodeo events, after which it began to grow.[26]

Few fairgoers actually wanted to be educated, whatever earnest government bureaucrats might hope. As one Lethbridge observer put it,

> I understand there was a difference of opinion about giving sports a prominent place in the coming fair. Some argued for the purely agricultural features while others maintained that the fair in order to be a success should have some attractions like horse racing, athletic events, etc, etc. We don't want to get into any argument, but believe it is worth mentioning that in Ontario, many a country fair went to the dogs for the very reason that the sports were cut out. It is very commendable to encourage agriculture but a fair will not draw a crowd unless there is some greater attraction than cattle, sheep, pigs, [and] pumpkins.[27]

So, most fair committees found that they had to supplement the fair with more entertaining features. At first they turned to the local entrepreneurs who were experienced in putting on Wild West Shows. In 1917 the Medicine Hat Agricultural Society agreed to pay Addison Day $8,000 to hold a stampede in its city in conjunction with the fair. The society also agreed to pay Pendleton cowboy Del Blancett $1,700 to bring his string of cowboys, cowgirls, and horses to rodeo. It built a grandstand to hold nine thousand people and cleared $10,000 when all accounts were paid.[28] The following year, the amalgamated fair board representing Lethbridge, Cardston, Magrath, and Raymond also contracted with Day to stage a rodeo featuring riders testing the "worst bucking broncos in the country." The fair committee borrowed money to build new corrals and grandstands to ensure that the audience got up close to the action. Despite these efforts, or perhaps because of their cost, the Lethbridge Fair did not break even that year, but it claimed gate and grandstand receipts of nearly $20,000.[29] In 1918, after Medicine Hat learned that, due to his commitment to Lethbridge, Day would be putting on a smaller show for them, it turned to rodeo promoter Ray Knight for assistance. The Medicine Hat Agricultural Society declared its stampede a roaring success. For its efforts, the town earned praise for its public spirit and hearty cooperation.[30]

Using an outside entrepreneur, however, did not always sit well with local spectators. In 1924 the Kamloops City Council and Board of Trade approached Peter Welsh's Alberta Stampede Company to stage a stampede the following year as a fundraiser for the fair.[31] Strawberry Red

Wall, collaborating with Welsh, promised an event that would put the town on the map just as the Pendleton Rodeo had done for that Oregon town.[32] Wall and Welsh brought riders and stock from southern Alberta, and opened events to local competitors as well. Though the newspaper reported "thrills of a lifetime," the crowds of six to seven hundred were disappointingly small.[33] Ultimately, as one commentator pointed out, paying Wall and Welsh $3,000 for their work made no sense if they then took the money out of Kamloops. Wouldn't it be better to put on a rodeo where the money stayed with local people?[34]

Of course many communities had no interest in paying a promoter to stage a rodeo for them. When Wild West Show veteran Jake Yeager made Rolla in the Peace River District his home, he invited his neighbours to participate in that region's first rodeo, in 1919. The following year, Yeager organized the bucking-horse, steer-riding, and wild-cow-milking contests at Dawson Creek's first fall fair, drawing entirely on local talent.[35] The Williams Lake Stampede, initiated in 1919, did not contract with professionals, relying instead on recent American immigrants such as Joe Fleiger, Arnie Madden, and Leonard Palmantier to organize events and on the willingness of Cariboo ranch and reserve families to compete in them. As rider Dave Twan put it, "We, the local cowboys, used to enter everything in those days. We'd do anything, try anything."[36] First Nations in Alberta and British Columbia saw no reason to pay others to ride for their enjoyment. Nakoda, Kainai, and Pikuni organizers staged rodeos on reserves in the 1920s, some open only to Aboriginal riders. These were tremendously popular: in 1926 the four hundred Pikuni on the reserve near Brocket welcomed over twenty-five hundred spectators to their rodeo, including a thousand settlers.[37] The Canim Lake, Clinton, and Canoe Creek Bands of BC collaboratively staged rodeos at Green Lake in the 1920s, pulling riders and ropers from reserves across the Cariboo.[38] Johnny Star organized a rodeo on his home Ktunaxa reserve in 1928, bringing in about forty dollars in revenue and a hundred spectators.[39]

Small-town organizers soon learned that local contestants, recognizable to spectators as neighbours, friends, or family, brought greater excitement than big-name cowboys imported to ride in performance. As the *High River Times* wrote, "it gave great zest to the performance to hear familiar names called from the megaphone."[40] Fans in Kamloops gasped when Secwepemc cowboy Alex Thomas was forced from his horse Shoofly in a hotly contested point-to-point race in 1925. The *Kamloops Sentinel* reported

Joe Fleiger, arena director, Williams Lake Stampede, 1923. *Courtesy of Royal BC Museum, BC Archives, E-01435*

on the "much-liked cowboy's" transportation to hospital, his injuries, and his recovery as front page news.[41] During the Lethbridge Stampede in 1918, crowds leapt to their feet when Kainai rider Tom Three Persons neatly dismounted in the bucking bronc competition by landing on the top rail of the corral fence.[42] Lethbridge local Rollo Kinsey became a crowd favourite when he won the calf-branding contest, branding twenty-five calves in nine minutes.[43] Other stampedes ran "Maverick" races open only to Alberta residents.[44] During the 1920s, rodeos in Lethbridge, High River, and Cardston increasingly featured local riders and found that they attracted audiences in the thousands.[45]

Small-town stampedes soon laid particular claims to authenticity because of their local connections. As the Williams Lake Stampede boasted,

The contestants who take part in the Stampede at Williams Lake are first and foremost the Real Thing. We have no professional exhibition riders, showmen, trick-riders, circus performers, or acrobats displaying their "specialities" at so much a night. The vaudeville element is non-existent. No – our contestants are the good everyday Citizens of the Rangeland – the ranchers, cowboys and range-riders of the Cariboo, assembled to make holiday for themselves and their friends from all over the Provinces, and to exhibit not vaudeville acts and specialty

Tom Three Persons riding at the Lethbridge Stampede, 1918. *Glenbow Museum Archives, NA-1943-25*

turns, but the wonderful feats of skill, daring and endurance learned on the wide plateaus and among the wild cattle of the Cariboo – feats which, wonderfull [sic] as they seem when performed before the Grandstand are after all but the everyday life of these men, to whom the risk of life and limb is "all in a day's work."[46]

Similarly, High River asserted its position as the "Oldest Cowtown in the West" because the contestants who competed in its annual roundup during the 1920s were not performers engaged in "fake stuff" but experienced cowboys, real ranchers who roped calves and rode wild horses.[47] Medicine Hat Stampede promoters claimed that their event "recreates the life of the west as it once existed, without being a professional circus with actors dressed up to play the part. It is an exhibition staged by the foremost exponents, now living, of a rugged way of life that is fast declining and a skill which will soon be a thing of the past."[48] Cardston too claimed that it offered an authentic stampede because so many well-known cowboys hailed from the town and its environs, men such as Herman Linder, Tom Three Persons, Pete Bruisehead, Floyd Peters, and Al Faulkner.[49]

The language of authenticity permeated the way in which communities talked about stampedes, which included trick riding and roping, horse races, and pageants and parades, along with rodeo events. This was so for two reasons. First, stampedes provided important financial opportunities for small towns and big cities alike. With thousands of visitors attending a successful stampede, businesses boomed for the duration of the event, competing against each other for trade by advertising special deals for stampede guests.[50] But as population growth slowed in southern Alberta during the early 1920s, small-town exhibitions and stampedes competed for a finite number of visitors whose spending power was increasingly limited. Some did not survive; others faltered. Lethbridge amalgamated with four other small towns to pool resources, whereas Cardston delayed its stampede twice at the end of the 1920s because other towns had scheduled their events on the popular summer holiday dates.[51] Claims of authenticity were one way for stampede committees to demonstrate that their event had greater value than the one down the road.

These claims of genuineness also distinguished the stampede – as a relatively new form of entertainment – from the touring Wild West Show, which was declining in popularity. It is clear that the point of comparison for many stampede publicists was the touring company, with its "professional exhibition riders, showmen, trick-riders, circus performers, or acrobats."[52] Ironically, stampede organizers used the Wild West Show's own definition of authenticity to valorize their own events. Buffalo Bill Cody's entourage set the standard for the genre, seeking out performers who were not actors but actual participants in the historical events that were re-enacted or recollected.[53] Over time, however, Wild West Shows recruited an array of performers, some of whom had range experience, though many did not. Miller Brothers, for example, trained its performers on its Oklahoma ranch, and though some, such as Flores LaDue, were westerners with riding and roping experience, others, such as Guy Weadick, were easterners who came with little more than a love of all things cowboy.[54] As Wild West Show veterans settled in the Canadian West, they brought this sense that a real stampede should employ "real cowboys and real Indians." As they advertised their events and sought to assert their local stampede's superiority to the touring show, they fell back on the old rhetoric of the Wild West Show.

The notion that Aboriginal people could themselves be an attraction was something that local event committees understood by the beginning of the twentieth century. As early as 1905, citizens of Fort Macleod and Lethbridge invited local Kainai men, women, and children to come to their fair and to parade dressed in traditional regalia, offering prizes to the best attired. The Kainai responded enthusiastically, and soon they became the "leading attractions of the fairs."[55] The 1906 report on the Lethbridge Fair announced that over six hundred Kainai people had paraded at the fair, camped on-site, gone shopping in Lethbridge, and been sad to leave when it was over. All in all, the report concluded, "it had been a big success."[56] The Indian Agent for the Blood Agency went so far as to remark that "at Fort Macleod [in 1907] the Indian show was practically the whole thing, the ordinary fair features of the white people were quite insignificant."[57] That same year in Lethbridge, some three hundred Siksika, Pikuni, and Kainai men and women walked in the parade to the delight of onlookers.[58]

The federal government opposed such displays. Amendments to the Indian Act in 1885 and 1894 had outlawed ceremonial dancing, but agents found it difficult to get the point across that such forms of cultural expression had no place in the new West when local businessmen and town promoters were paying Aboriginal people to present them. Ottawa pressured towns, particularly on the prairies (less so in British Columbia where the potlatch was the focus of concern), to stop inviting First Nations.[59] When that failed, the Department of Indian Affairs put forward an amendment to section 49 of the Indian Act, prohibiting ceremonial dancing off-reserve and requiring that any Indian going to a stampede must receive the consent of the Indian Agent to do so.[60] A roar of protest ensued from small towns in southern Alberta. From Brocket to Fort Macleod to Lethbridge, fair organizers denounced the law and pressured local Indian Agents to grant permission for Aboriginal people to attend, prompting one official to conclude that "it seems to me that the Indian is being exploited and people have gone Stampede crazy."[61] Even foreign journalists weighed into the debate as one opined in 1914, "I know I tread on debatable ground when I mention the Indians, and I am sure the Indian agent has very good reasons for thinking it better the Indians should remain on their reserves, but from the public point of view they are infinitely preferable to some of the side shows which take up space and dollars at your Exhibition. They, at all events, are a characteristically local product – if anything is local and native born – they are."[62] Few, it seemed, supported the government's position.

Some had doubts of their own. Aboriginal elders in southern Alberta worried that rodeos were drawing young people away from summer rituals such as the sun dance but soon found that both could be incorporated into seasonal ceremonial cycles.[63] The Alberta Indian Commission of the Methodist Church alleged that "when the Indians took part in fairs, they licked up fire water in such copious fashion that they were useless for the rest of the year. In addition to the aftereffects of their exhibition jags, they also became swollen up with false ideas of their importance, and as a consequence mission workers found them almost unmanageable."[64] Southern Alberta fair committees countered by stating that the man most responsible for ensuring that Aboriginal people went to stampedes was the Methodist missionary John McDougall. Moreover, some, such as the Lethbridge Agricultural Society, issued notarized statements to the press asserting that only a handful of arrests for drunkenness were made and that, in fact, most of the men who ended up in the drunk tank were white, not Aboriginal. And, as J.W. McNichol of Lethbridge wrote, police reported that stampedes were remarkable for their "freedom from drunkenness, disorder and vice."[65] The Department of Indian Affairs held the power to prevent Aboriginal participation in stampedes, and small-town committees knew that they were worse off financially without that participation. The unwillingness of agents to permit Aboriginal people to attend the Lethbridge Stampede, for example, contributed to its financial failure in 1918. Indeed, the pecuniary difficulties of the fall fairs in the 1910s were undoubtedly made worse by the work of Indian Agents who opposed Aboriginal participation.[66]

In the face of persistent protest from settler fair and stampede committees, the government faltered, and this changed the fortunes of many small-town fairs. When the Lethbridge Stampede re-emerged in 1921, "Indian Events" were the backbone of its program. At eleven in the morning, the Grand Indian Parade opened the day's events, offering ten-dollar prizes for the best-dressed Indian man and woman. After lunch, horse and foot races for Aboriginal men and women promised "plenty of excitement," since, according to the promotional press, "Indian races ... are always for blood ... and the grandstand is always sure of an honest-to-goodness race when the red men cut loose."[67] In 1921, when Taber, Alberta, sought to improve its fair, it announced that three hundred Indians were planning to attend, to parade, give a "war dance," and take part in special pony races.[68] Upon reviewing the event, Taber's fair board concluded that the Indian village, providing as it did a particularly "unique" feature, had been a major reason for success.[69] Pincher Creek also advertised "Indian events" as part of its fall fair lineup.[70] Indeed, one way to signal the antici-pated presence of First Nations was to design events that were segmented by race. The Pincher Creek Natal Day celebration in 1921 offered a "squaw race" and an "Indian race."[71] The Fort Macleod Jubilee Stampede in 1924 held tipi races and travois races open to Aboriginal women that combined ethnographic display with competition.[72] Nanton's fair and stampede advertised an "Indian Pow-wow in Regalia." Its organizers credited a sub-stantial Aboriginal presence for the success of their events.[73]

As rodeo gained popularity, organizing committees stressed that their contests were "open to all." In an attempt to make its intentions abundantly clear, the 1926 Cardston Stampede committee wrote, "The Management this year wants it understood that our friends from the Blood Indian Re-serve are open to enter any event, on par with any other contestant" and concluded that "All Events [are] Open To Indians." The mayor of Cardston went even further, announcing that the Kainai could attend the stampede for free.[74] Later, when it was over, Manager Jack Galbraith made this state-ment: "Cardston's Indian friends from the B.I. [Blood Indian] Reserve were of great assistance too, for entering in the spirit of the day with energy and finest friendliness, the Indian cowboys took their full share of the burden of entertainment for the great crowd of spectators and incident-ally captured several of the leading prizes of the day."[75] All across southern Alberta, small-town stampedes worked hard to draw First Nations, both as grandstand attractions and to compete in rodeos.[76] They included them in planning committees. At Cardston, two positions on the stampede's sports committee were reserved for Kainai representatives of the band's own choosing.[77] Lethbridge's Golden Jubilee committee (1935) included a number of local Aboriginal leaders. Chiefs Fred Tail Feathers, Cross Shield, Shot on Both Sides, Frank Red Crow, Owns Different Horses, and John Crow Eagle joined the usual array of businessmen and town fathers. The 27 July 1935 *Lethbridge Daily Herald* printed a portrait of the group on its front page, which showed the chiefs side by side in the front row, all in well-worn cowboy hats, their hands placed squarely on their knees.[78] The enthusiasm of small-town planning committees for Aboriginal participa-tion made it exceedingly difficult for Indian Agents to deny their requests, though some did. Even the tough-minded deputy-superintendent Duncan Campbell Scott reported that he found the situation "very difficult to

Lethbridge Golden Jubilee committee and guests, 1935. *Back row, left to right:* William H. Ripley, William D. Hay, Penrose Melvin Sauder, Albert Edward Dupen, Charles Parry. *Second row, left to right:* Edward Davis, Thomas G. Bates, George Watson, Charles E. Cameron, John Stanley Kirkham (Chairman, Jubilee Committee), John T. Watson (City Manager), David Horton Elton K.C. (Mayor of Lethbridge), John G. Hutchings, Charles Roland Daniel, Dr. William Harmon Fairfield (President, Lethbridge Exhibition Board). *Front row, left to right:* Adrian E. Russell (Secretary-treasurer, Lethbridge Exhibition Board), William [Billy] Lamb (President, Lethbridge Old Timers Association), Chief Fred Tail Feathers, Chief Cross Shield, High Chief Shot Both Sides, Chief Frank Red Crow and Chief Own Different Horses all of the Blood Tribe, and Chief John Crow Eagle of the Peigans. *Galt Museum, Acc #19754226018*

control."[79] Brian Titley has argued that the growth of stampedes in Western Canada seriously undermined Department of Indian Affairs efforts at cultural suppression.

The experience of BC stampede-goers and organizers differed slightly from that in Alberta. In BC, Aboriginal participation in rodeos grew without interference from Indian Agents. Indeed, they supported sports in general on reserves.[80] The Indian Agent at Williams Lake and the missionary at the nearby St. Joseph's Mission both served on the stampede association's board of directors and occasionally acted as judges for events. Aboriginal people, including Métis and mixed-heritage individuals, participated in community events wherever these were organized in the BC Interior, from Dawson Creek in the north to Windermere in the south. Johnny Napoleon (Métis) in the Peace River country, Johnny Smillie and Andy Manuel (Secwepemc) in the Kamloops area, Joe Elkins (Tsilhquot'in) and Nels Chelsea (Secwepemc) in the Cariboo-Chilcotin, Harry Shuttleworth (mixed heritage) of the Similkameen, and Jim Baptiste (Syilx) of Inkameep – every region had its share of Aboriginal cowboy heroes. In 1918 the first Armstrong Fair invited Aboriginal people to race.[81] Inkameep First Nation rode in the parade of Oliver's first rodeo, in 1924.[82] Secwepemc and Tsilhquot'in people paraded and camped at the Williams Lake Stampede, where they dominated its mountain race.[83] They dressed up and vied for best-dressed Indian cowboy and cowgirl at the Kamloops Rodeo. They provided stock and helped organize events.[84] Like the cowboys, they made community-building stampedes happen.

Across the West, and at the most basic level, stampedes helped build communities by attracting visiting shoppers, encouraging infrastructure development, and promoting investment.[85] Small-town merchants eagerly awaited the thousands of visitors drawn to their shops during stampedes.[86] Restaurants, in particular, did a lively trade.[87] Kamloops restaurants were reportedly full during the 1925 stampede.[88] The success of stampedes was measured by the number of visitors who brought cash and left with positive impressions of the district. Organizers of the Lethbridge Fair boasted that fifteen thousand people passed through its turnstiles for Dominion Day 1926, visitors who came from all over Canada.[89] Cardston merchants were particularly pleased when a Montreal tourist attended their rodeo and wrote about it favourably in the *Montreal Herald*. The *Cardston News* reported that a thousand cars brought five thousand visitors to the stampede that year.[90] Stampedes also circulated money through communities as the latter paid wages and prizes, and purchased goods and services for the event. Medicine Hat's 1923 stampede earned nearly $1,500 for the local Rotary Club, and just over $800 went back into the community to pay for supplies and wages.[91] Fort Macleod's Fiftieth Jubilee Stampede lasted three days and cost $16,000.[92] The 1929 Williams Lake Stampede redistributed $4,208.27 to workers, contestants, and suppliers of stock and decorations.[93] Organizers of Lethbridge's 1935 jubilee stampede contributed to the local economy: $15,000 in wages, contracts, supplies, and prize money. A hundred and fifty temporary workers were hired and paid a total of $4,000 in wages, where preference was given to married jobless men and unemployed veterans from Lethbridge. Lethbridge merchants, it was asserted, "made substantial profits" through the sale of lumber, hardware, decorations, food, and drink. Moreover, these merchants then made payments on the taxes they owed the city so that it too benefited from the infusion of cash. Tourists flocked to the town and contributed their share to the financial success of the event.[94] In the Okanagan, Penticton started rodeos in the late 1930s, inspired by the mayor's visit to take in Lethbridge's successful jubilee stampede.[95] In some cases, by being able to attract large numbers of Aboriginal people, stampedes redirected the flow of cash from one town to another. Cardston's stampede helped make it the principal beneficiary of increased buying power among the Kainai in the 1920s, eclipsing Fort Macleod in the process.[96] In BC, the Williams Lake Stampede drew First Nations from across the Cariboo and Chilcotin to the relatively new settlement of Williams Lake, shifting their attention from the more historical entrepôt of Quesnel.[97]

Merchants capitalized on civic interest in stampedes by pressing for infrastructure improvements both within and between towns. In the early years, Lethbridge merchants worked with the stampede committee to better hotel and livery accommodation, and the railway offered cheap excursion fares to bring shoppers from outlying districts to town for the stampede.[98] The introduction of the automobile extended the reach of local travellers. Alberta's first car arrived in 1901, and the number of vehicles remained small until after the First World War, when car ownership increased dramatically. There were about 40,000 cars in 1921 and over 100,000 in 1930; by 1931, 42 percent of farm families owned a car or truck.[99] In British Columbia, where the economy boomed after 1923, car ownership grew from 15,000 in 1918 to 100,000 in 1930.[100] Urban business people launched campaigns to improve the road system, eyeing the prospective American tourist but intent on encouraging more regional traffic. They set up "auto camps" near the downtown business district to attract tourist dollars into local hands. Fair and rodeo circuits prompted both competitors and spectators to take in a number of events at locations linked by road. During the 1920s, small-town rodeos, such as those at Cardston and High River, scheduled their events near the date of the Calgary Stampede to capitalize on that show's draw of automobile tourists.[101] In the 1930s, merchants encouraged stampedes to continue through

Stampedes brought new infrastructure. The Lethbridge grandstand, 1918. *Glenbow Museum Archives, PA-3331-15*

the lean years, hoping that they would attract American tourists and bring "a few additional dollars to the little towns and cities."[102] New venues, built for stampedes, advanced a town's image.[103] Constructing grandstands and racetracks was considered extremely important to the successful running of an event.[104] Improving the grounds and grandstand at Lethbridge taxed the finances of the stampede organizing committee in 1918, but when the work was complete, organizers boasted that they had "one of the finest racetracks and grandstands in Western Canada."[105] Kamloops invested in chutes and corrals in 1925, hoping to make its stampede a regular feature.[106] New buildings, such as those completed at Cardston in 1914 or renovated at Magrath in 1921, could also be used for other events throughout the year.[107] The ability of a town to offer an array of entertainment was a selling point and added a competitive advantage over other towns.[108]

Stampedes contributed to the general boosterism of the age.[109] They sought to attract investment and, in relatively unpopulated districts, to promote migration to the area. Medicine Hat used the opportunity of its 1917 stampede to let *Calgary Herald* readers know that it sat in the midst

of one of the largest and most successful ranching districts on the continent, a statement clearly designed to encourage continued American immigration to a region calling itself "the last best west."[110] By the 1920s and
1930s, the "last best west" had moved again, now to the Cariboo-Chilcotin
region of British Columbia. Merchants, large landowners, and ranchers
collaborated to organize the Williams Lake Stampede to focus attention
on the investment and settlement opportunities of the district. Trucking
entrepreneur Thomas "Jack" Hodgson, hotel and saloon owner Alexander
Meiss from Horsefly, cowboss (manager) James Newman of 150 Mile
House, ranchers Antoine Boitano (Springhouse), G.W. Moore (Chimney
Creek Ranch), and James Stuart (River Ranch) comprised the organizing
committee in 1923.[111] When the Cariboo Stampede Association registered
as a company in 1926, merchants Roderick Mackenzie (later MLA), Thomas
Allen Moore, and John Smedley came forward as directors and invested
$250 each, as did Dr. F.V. Agnew and clerk James Stuart Smith.[112] Their
objectives were to promote good animal husbandry and stock rearing, to
put on a stampede, and to support "the business of cattle dealers, race-track
proprietors, horse and cattle breeders, livery keepers, theatrical agents,
variety and opera managers, restaurant keepers, grocers, tobacco and spirit
merchants, dance and athletic hall proprietors and any other business
which can be conveniently carried on in connection with any of these
objects and to produce, show, advertise, prepare and to give prizes either
in cash or otherwise at, any rodeo, Stampede, dance, athletic meet or other
entertainment to encourage competition therein or otherwise."[113]

Early programs advertised the region's natural resources, rangelands
said to constitute the "Last Great West," mineral riches, timber, furs, and
the "wonderful scenery and historic value [that] will be a Mecca of thousands of tourists."[114] Furthermore, the 1923 program told readers, all the
highways and the new Pacific Great Eastern Railway now converged at
Williams Lake, a thriving "business point for ranchers, miners, trappers,
tourists and lumbermen, with fine modern business accommodations and
a prosperous, contented population."[115] Stampedes advertised the region
to investors, settlers, and tourists.

That the Williams Lake Stampede directors would advertise their population as "prosperous" and "contented" marks a shift in boosterism that
occurred during the 1920s. As Donald Wetherell and Irene Kmet put it,
the old "boosterism," now considered garish, was replaced in that decade

by more specific marketing that sold community cohesion, positive thinking, self-reliance, and initiative instead.[116] By celebrating these attributes,
stampedes did not simply reflect community values: they engaged in creating them. Settler communities were new and changing. There was little
that was solid, little that grounded identity, so when communities turned
to events such as rodeos, they did so with creative rather than simply reflexive energy. When small towns commodified a version of their past
through the stampedes they staged, they constructed, as Stuart Hall argues,
a "self-legitimating social memory."[117] Given the presence of both settlers
and Aboriginal people at these events, inevitably what got performed was
something of the contact zone. As the Wild West Show had done, stampedes in Western Canadian small towns often enacted conquest, whether
through the simple ordering of the parade, through pageants and performances, or through the designation of some contests as "Indian" and
others as "white." But this process of staging, ordering, and segmenting
was not as simple as some scholars have suggested. For one thing, embedded in the very people who attended stampedes were memories and
identities that spoke of other, more tangled pasts. Moreover, the presence
of Aboriginal people, acting of their own accord, with their own agendas
and sometimes self-consciously in dialogue with the storyline of the stampede, complicated the message that emerged from such events. The
histories and cultures that were articulated at stampedes were not static:
like histories and cultures everywhere, they were changing in concert with
the communities and the people who embraced stampedes in the first
decades of the twentieth century.[118]

As Benedict Anderson alerts us, novelty cries out for a past. Within two
generations of settlement, towns across the Canadian West had begun the
process of defining themselves by looking back. No longer solely reliant
on the nearby collieries for economic force, Lethbridge was in the midst
of reinventing itself as an agricultural community when it introduced
rodeo contests to its annual fair.[119] The largest town in southern Alberta,
with a population of over eleven thousand in 1921, Lethbridge typified
some of the trends. The dominance of Anglo-Canadian culture in the
region was slipping as increasing numbers of Americans crossed the border
to settle. By the 1920s, half the farmers in southern Alberta were American
in origin.[120] Ranching declined in the region, usurped by farming, a transition aided by government land policy and spurred on by disastrous winters
in which thousands of cattle perished. Towns such as Medicine Hat, which

would later look back nostalgically on the ranching era, did not mourn the change, commenting in 1906 that the "rancher's loss was the country's gain."[121] By 1913 southern Alberta was on the cusp of moving from an isolated region of settlement to an integrated community of successful farms and agricultural service centres of prosperous businesses.[122] Drought and tumbling wheat prices brought economic downturn to the region in the late 1910s and early 1920s, depleting the coffers of local stampede committees along with those of everyone else. Lethbridge's 1918 stampede, for example, which drew thousands of spectators, lifted the spirits of weary townsfolk and neighbouring farmers.[123] Despite troubling economic times, Howard and Tamara Palmer argue that the 1920s were the heyday of small-town Alberta as mechanization allowed more time for leisure, automobiles increased mobility, and towns offered an widening array of entertainments.[124] Growing Americanization saw rodeo eclipse polo and baseball edge out cricket as southern Albertans developed a new sense of their own culture.[125]

Migration away from southern Alberta brought settlers west across the Rockies to British Columbia and north to the Peace River country. BC's settler population grew in the years leading up to 1914, demographically overwhelming First Nations. Settler communities staged fairs, races, and regattas, "giving support, both symbolic and real, to a growing sense of community."[126] These were boom years for BC as world demand soared for its natural resources, the provincial government realized surpluses, and immigrants brought capital, skills, and the value of their labour, hopes, and dreams to the fledgling province.[127] Entrepreneurs extended transportation networks as rail lines penetrated the BC Interior and steamboats plied coastal and riparian waters.[128] The worldwide post-war recession eased in BC by 1923, and as real wages grew, British Columbians began to explore their province as tourists and welcomed Americans and others to do the same.[129] They ventured beyond the cities to the rural interior where, as Jean Barman puts it, agriculture was the poor cousin in the BC economy. Most farms were small-scale family enterprises, few of them larger than two hundred acres. The net value of agricultural production peaked in 1928 at $45 million but plummeted thereafter.[130] Nonetheless, the agrarian dream remained strong, and in 1915 the provincial government established the Agricultural Credit Commission, later renamed the Land Settlement Board. With the help of grants, the government encouraged irrigation in the Okanagan, the West Kootenay, and around Kamloops, and it looked north to the Bulkley and Nechako Valleys as the "New British Columbia." The land board paid $500 to any returned soldier or his widow who took up land for agricultural purposes.[131] Surveyed before the First World War, the Peace River District was thrown open to settlement. By the end of the 1920s, seven thousand people were living there.[132] Many, such as Jake Yeager in Rolla, or Jim and Stastia Carry at High Level (on the Alberta side of the line), were Americans pursuing the dream of owning land and running cattle. Government revived assisted settlement in the 1930s to relocate unemployed men and their families on the land. The backwoods of the central Interior are dotted with the collapsed cabins of Depression-era homesteads, encouraged but inadequately supported by a desperate government.[133] For poor families in remote regions, small-town entertainments, including rodeos, helped ease isolation.

Some economic opportunities were realized in the 1930s. As Rich Hobson found, there was "grass beyond the mountains," and immigrants, Americans and British both, started new lives ranching or living off the land.[134] Tourism promoters redoubled their efforts in the 1930s, and provincial politicians supported established stampedes and helped fund new ones in the Okanagan.[135] As Michael Dawson and others have pointed out, the depressed economy of the 1930s did not kill tourism. Price reductions, for some, meant more disposable income, and event promoters actively courted local audiences by reducing fares.[136] In the Nicola Valley, the struggling town of Merritt hosted its first rodeo in 1934 and attracted two thousand visitors.[137] Rodeos in Kamloops remained popular throughout the 1930s, and in 1935, 2,545 adults and 836 children paid admission fees and bought 1,649 grandstand tickets.[138] Government, health reformers, and business advocated physical recreation to combat the enervating effects of unemployment on men. The 1930s saw an increased appetite for entertainment of all kinds, and the radio brought American popular culture to even the most distant homesteads.[139]

It was in this context of careening economics and shifting demographics that stampedes emerged as one way of expressing community identity. History and modernity walked together somewhat awkwardly in parades and pageants orchestrated to demonstrate the progression of the region from primitivism to prosperity. Organizers staged performances that put Aboriginal people and cowboys at centre stage – playing out myths of conquest and collaboration – acting and enacting a contact zone in the process. Programs relayed the narrative of place, one that did more than simply eulogize the past, but asserted that this noble past lived in the cowboy ethos that permeated stampedes. In this way, stampedes enabled small towns in Western Canada to see themselves as modern while containing what they feared might be the baleful effects of modernity. They offered pride and hope to communities in the face of daunting challenges. This was true for Aboriginal people as well, for there were certain benefits to be had from participating in stampedes, including asserting an identity that embraced both enduring cultural forms and the opportunities presented by modernity. In so doing, they temporarily eluded the stultifying grasp of Indian Agents and Indian policy, even blurred the categories of cowboy and Indian. Stampedes also provided a chance to speak directly to a settler audience who, stirred by its own nostalgia, might be prepared to listen. In a time when conflicts between Aboriginal people and small towns were not uncommon, stampedes presented a vision of what life might be like if Aboriginal people were fully welcomed into the new modernizing West.

Parades and pageants had long been a part of community events in Western Canada. Itinerant entertainment, such as circuses and Wild West Shows, used parades to advertise their events, providing glimpses of what they had to offer – elephants and acrobats, trick riders and stately chiefs – to prospective audiences who lined the streets to watch them arrive. Communities too used parades to advertise their attributes, often, as Mary Ryan has suggested, performing the social structures they were in the process of building.[140] Small-town stampede organizers used their parades to visually situate their progressive and well-serviced community in an illustrious past of Aboriginal people and pioneers, and the order of the parade told the story of advancing civilization. Some organizers placed First Nations at the head of their parades in honour of their indigeneity, of their "being the original dwellers in this country," but most deployed them as exotic remnants of a foregoing time and a "good drawing card for a good cause" – namely, the promotion of their town.[141] Although Indian Agents across southern Alberta disapproved of such events, hundreds of Aboriginal people walked in parades nonetheless. In 1906 four hundred Kainai and Pikuni people progressed through the streets of Lethbridge in what the *Lethbridge Daily Herald* described as "the greatest parade of Indians ever seen in Alberta."[142] As the century progressed, organizers used Aboriginal people, dressed in "gawdy [sic] native costumes and war paint," in their parades to help provide the "connecting link between the old west, which is rapidly passing, and the new."[143] Lethbridge's parade of 1926, titled "From Redman and Buffalo to Joyous Present," began with Kainai and Pikuni on foot and horseback who were followed by Red River carts, representing the Métis. After these came North West Mounted Police riding in their red serge and early missionaries and fur traders. Next came the floats built by businesses, churches, and service organizations that completed the three-mile exhibition of the "passage of time."[144] Events across North America in the early decades of the twentieth century often used Aboriginal people as foils to modernity, to demonstrate by contrast the superiority of the progressive age. Nonetheless, this ran the risk of diluting the message that the West was safe, open for settlement, and advanced beyond the "Old West."[145] By the 1920s, stampede parades, though still relying on Aboriginal people in "paint and feathers," also included First Nations participants who more clearly represented the contemporary period and demonstrated to visitors, as the *Lethbridge Daily Herald* explained in 1926, that "today on their reservations, they are rapidly discarding the dress and customs of their forefathers and adopting those of the white neighbour. They are now successful farmers and stockmen ... and not a few of them are driving cars."[146] Fort Macleod's jubilee stampede of 1924 included Aboriginal men and women riding "polka dot" steeds and drawing children on travois, followed by the Blood reserve marching band displaying rational, organized masculinity, with the nattily dressed cadets and Girl Guides from the reserve bringing up the rear.[147] In stampede parades, Aboriginal people were not entirely constrained by scripts in which they portrayed the past.

Nor were they pastoralism's sole representatives. Settler cowboys were also called upon to be authentic reminders of the past. Fort Macleod's 1924 parade featured cowboys riding in wagons, "bringing up the rear with a whoop and a yell."[148] They were the living symbols of the past, but like Aboriginal people, they too were brought in to show how life in the West blurred the line between past and present. The 1926 Raymond Stampede featured an exhibition of cowboys roping a calf from the hood of a car.[149] At the Williams Lake Stampede the following year, cowboys represented the lure of the open range now made accessible by a new system of road and rail that made the town the centre of ranching in the district.[150] Stampede parades told stories of progress where particular portions of the population – "cowboys and Indians" – simultaneously represented both past and present.

They also used pageants to perform the founding narratives of place. The Williams Lake Stampede staged one in 1928, something called "an exact reproduction of an actual Indian massacre," which was a loose representation of the Chilcotin War. The program gave a muddled account of the events of 1864 in which Tsilhquot'in warriors killed a crew of road builders who were intent on connecting the Cariboo goldfields with a sea route from Bute Inlet. Mistaking Hudson's Bay Company factor Donald McLean for a "scout" and inaccurately describing the company's ill-fated Fort Chilcotin as a hastily erected outpost, the Williams Lake Stampede version of the Chilcotin War did get one thing right – the Tsilhquot'in were tricked into surrendering. The pageant featured six scenes including an Indian attack on a stagecoach, a "Sun Dance" (not something Tsilhquot'in people did historically) in which the Indians celebrated their victory, and a final scene that was to include the "presentation of three Indians who took actual part in the above massacre."[151] Ollie Curtis played a passenger in the stagecoach. Her role involved being dragged from the coach onto the horse of an attacking "Indian" and then being dragged onto the horse of her rescuer, local cowboy Fred Chuchholz. All the while, the "war party of Indians" burned the makeshift fort to the ground. Reminiscing about the pageant, Curtis smiled and said, "It must have been quite a show and a real crowdpleaser."[152] Whatever lessons spectators may have drawn from it, the pageant had a brief tenure at the stampede. Two years later, it was gone, replaced in 1930 by a stage performance arranged in two scenes, one of a cowboy campfire and one in an "Indian Teepee," featuring an "Indian Love Song" performed by "Princess Pokahunta." This was followed by daredevil aerial stunts and the initiation of Premier S.F. Tolmie as "Chief Cariboo" by local Secwepemc people.[153]

Lethbridge staged its own pageant as part of its golden jubilee stampede in 1935. Called the Fort Whoop-Up Days pageant, it was cobbled together from three scripts that had been awarded first, second, and third place in the *Lethbridge Daily Herald*'s script contest that year. Running to five episodes (or scenes), it began with an "allegorical Indian legend" about first contact between a white man and First Nations. In a tale clearly reminiscent of the Pocahontas myth, the white man was initially feted by the Aboriginal people as a harbinger of the long-awaited buffalo and given "the most beautiful of the Indian maidens" to marry. When jealousy and the dispersal of the buffalo prompted the chief to murder the white man, his "faithful little Indian wife" rushed forward to protect him and was killed. In a reversal of the usual connection between aboriginality and superstition, it was the white man who uttered a curse, a curse, the audience was told, that was "destined to bring everlasting destruction upon the Indian." The theme of honourable white men dealing with treacherous "Indians" continued through the next two episodes. In Episode 2, the latter inexplicably burned Fort Whoop-Up, and as the heroic A.B. Hamilton, trader, attempted to save an Aboriginal woman left behind in the fort, he was informed that she had already been shot. The second scene of Episode 2, however, brought together "colorful Indians and Traders" to celebrate the first white wedding at the rebuilt fort in 1877. Episodes 3 and 4 performed the discovery of coal and the coming of the railway. The final episode was a display of the "well-dressed ladies and gentlemen of 1885," and the whole pageant closed with a dance number executed by the pupils of Miss Bernadette Fisher's School of Dance and a rousing rendition of "O Canada" sung by the audience and performers.[154] Such pageants enacted versions of the past that became common sense, part of the social memory of place.[155]

If visitors did not entirely catch the meaning of such parades and pageants, stampede programs helped convey it. In a sense, the pageants and parades were a prologue to the main story of the stampede – that which demonstrated the special modernity of the community in which it was staged. The program for the Lethbridge Golden Jubilee Stampede ended its history of the city by stating confidently that it was celebrating its past, "secure in the knowledge that its founders built well, and conscious that the natural resources which first gave it life are capable of development into a greater city in the services of Southern Alberta."[156] Cardston too claimed that it was a "good place to live" because its "people are thrifty, [and] industrious, and the growth of the Town and district has been steady and healthy, with no severe setbacks."[157] Williams Lake said what others only implied. It was a modern town without the ailments of modernity. Stampede publicists extolled the virtues of manly men who clung to self-sufficiency and cleared the land of predators and nuisances that impeded the expansion of settlement. The stampede, programs claimed, reinvigorated masculine responses dulled by "automobiles and white collars, morris chairs and Mah Jong." Presenting the roughstock events as a "titanic contest ... wherein the principal pits his muscle and sinews and heart's blood against the cyclonic forces of nature," stampede publicists such as C.H. Dodwell made the rodeo cowboy the embodiment of conquest, a man who could make use of the wild untapped resources of the region: "Keen-eyed, careless, self-reliant, tuned to vast solitudes, calmly facing dangers and enduring hardships alone and unsung, lording it over horse and brute on the fringe of the world, taking life in one hand and rolling a cigarette in the other, sweating on roundups and freezing on the feeding grounds from daylight to dark for forty dollars a month, the Cowboy has a definite place in the march of Western civilization."[158] In the words of Louis LeBourdais, amateur historian and later MLA for the Cariboo, they were "real men," the true descendants of those who survived the awful trek to the Cariboo in the 1860s and went on the thrive in the region.[159] It was white men who made the range safe for cattle and who pushed back species that got in the way of prosperity, whether predator or prey. Indeed, in stampede programs, man emerged as the supreme predator. If the prose itself were not sufficiently picturesque, the 1927 program included a photograph of cougar bounty hunter G.G. Hamilton sitting on a Russell fence, snowshoes at his side, a neat log cabin in the background, with the bodies of four dead cougars arrayed in front of him. The caption went on to congratulate local cowboys Tom Carolan, Don Weir, and Eddy Ross for successfully gunning down a thousand wild horses to save the rangeland from overgrazing, to preserve the land for cattle. The continued emphasis placed on pacifying the frontier in the Williams Lake Stampedes of the late 1920s put conquest in all its forms at centre stage.

The sense that the stampede was about "cowboys and Indians," plucky women, and self-sufficient men was further reinforced by the order in which rodeo events were scheduled. Gendered and racialized segmentation was standard fare; the Williams Lake Stampede was no exception. Its 23 June 1928 program featured these events in order:

1   Cowboy Camp
2   Cowboy Novelty Race
3   Bronk Riding Championship (trophy presented by P. Burns & Co.)
4   Cowgirls Steer Riding
5   Boys Steer Riding
6   Indian Derby

7   Stage Coach Race

8   Relay Championship of BC Event (One and a half miles)

9   Half mile Ladies Race (Trophy presented by Hon. Dr. S.F. Tolmie)

10 Reproduction of the Chilcoten [sic] Massacre, 1864

11 Cariboo Derby 3/4 of a mile, open (Trophy presented by the Vancouver Racing Ass.)

12 Roman Race

13 Wild Horse Race Championship of BC (Trophy presented by Great West Saddlery)

14 Cowgirls Pony Express Championship of BC (Trophy presented by John A. Fraser, MP)

15 Trick Riding

16 Mountain Race (Trophy presented by Native Sons of Canada)[160]

Similarly, Pincher Creek's 1921 stampede featured contests set aside for Aboriginal men and women, cowboys and "ladies".[161] Such gender segregation reified and produced difference as much as it reflected it. Novelty races went further to playfully perform masculinity, femininity, cowboys, and Indians. In the "drunken ride," a favourite of the 1920s, riders hooked their stirrups over the saddle horn and stood in the loops that formed on either side of the saddle. As they swayed back and forth, they brandished a bottle and at a certain point appeared to fall from the horse, but, one foot in a loop, they finished the race with head and shoulders just inches above the ground. While demonstrating riding skills, flexibility, and dexterity, the drunken ride also played upon a common stereotype of the cowboy – that of a drunken ne'er-do-well. Later professional cowboy organizations would denounce such events as injurious to the reputation of cowboys and the sport of rodeo.[162] The Indian warbonnet and Indian campfire races combined ethnographic performance with horse racing. The rules stipulated that Aboriginal men who rode in the warbonnet race must wear beaded and feathered headdresses. Couples competed in the campfire race. Here Aboriginal men and women raced their wagons down the track to the finish line and set up camp. The first couple with a smoking fire won.[163] Later the event was renamed the squaw race and run with Aboriginal women at the reins.[164] Boys' and girls' steer riding, cowboy and Indian races, all these events marked out difference even as they reserved places for men and women, settlers and Aboriginal people. Through

Nakoda and other First Nations contestants in an archery contest, Morley Reserve, 1930s. *Glenbow Museum Archives, NA-1241-561*

parades, pageants, programs, and the rodeo contests themselves, stampedes built communities by producing shared historical narratives that offered value in the present and in the future.[165]

Given these intents and effects of stampedes, it is hard to imagine why First Nations would take part in them. But as we have seen, they did so and in great numbers. They rode in parades, competed in "best-dressed Indian contests," set up Indian villages, and entered rodeo competitions. As scholars have pointed out, minorities engaging in cultural performance occupy exceedingly unstable ground. Although it may offer them personal empowerment and access to a wider public audience, such "ethnomimesis," to use Robert Cantwell's term, is never free of colonizing impulses toward exoticism and neo-colonial processes of commodification. Nor, as

Cantwell says, are they entirely confined by them.[166] Rather, as Néstor García Canclini argues for hybrid cultures more generally, they are "strategies for entering and getting out of modernity."[167] The very desire of organizers to include Aboriginal people shifted the power dynamics appreciably between First Nations and small towns. Moreover, the tensions between small-town elites and government officials regarding Aboriginal involvement created productive fissures in the edifice of colonial repression. Aboriginal people who came to stampedes found for themselves a fleeting and temporary space beyond the grasp of Indian Agents and Indian policy, which gave access to cash and other resources being withheld by officials. Moreover, their participation provided a chance to evade the binaries of cowboy versus Indian, traditional versus modern. They attained visibility as watchful descendants (not remnants) of those who signed the treaties, and some managed to express how they would navigate a path that selectively embraced and refused modernity, that reshaped tradition, that envisioned a different world in which the small towns of Alberta and BC might be considered home for Aboriginal peoples as well as settlers.

Colonial relations, theorists tell us, are always founded in ambivalence, in which Aboriginal people are the objects of both desire and derision.[168] Although much historical work has made plain the effects of the latter, relatively little has focused on the former. And yet it is clear that small towns across British Columbia and Alberta wanted the presence of Aboriginal people in the very events they would use to define themselves as communities of settler ascendancy. In and of itself, this desire is surprising, for many small towns that seemed to welcome Aboriginal people at stampede time were less than welcoming at other times. For Kainai elder Nora (Gladstone) Baldwin, Cardston in the 1930s was not a particularly welcoming place. Its schools would not take Aboriginal children, and only the Chinese restaurants made Kainai patrons feel comfortable.[169] Writing of the late 1930s, Lucien Hanks noted that when the Siksika he knew went to town, they were expected to defer to whites and to wait to be served until all the white customers had been attended to. Restaurant owners, he found, discouraged Aboriginal patronage, and local whites granted the Siksika only two roles in their communities: consumers and tourist attractions. In Gleichen, Hanks wrote, there was Indian Day and White Day, and on the latter, reserve residents were expected to stay out of town. Mission churches too contributed to the segregation, having separate services for Indians and whites.[170] Towns in the BC Interior worked hard at making Aboriginal people uncomfortable when they visited, seizing their horses, applying vagrancy laws, and fining Aboriginal peddlers for selling produce.[171] Towns such as Vernon, Kamloops, and Fort George (now Prince George) all looked covetously at nearby reserve land as new provisions in the Indian Act encouraged forced leases and forced pre-emptions to increase productivity and facilitate town growth.[172] And yet, for one week of the year, they desired the presence of Aboriginal people; indeed, they claimed to be defined by it. The *Fort George Herald* wrote that the "whole race of frontier folk" who gathered for the 1911 Dominion Day festivities encompassed "mocassined [sic] Indians with hatchet faces, their brightly attired women-folk, bronzed lumber jacks, square and chunky or tall and limber, sturdy pre-emptors, prospectors and surveyors, miners and storekeepers ... the men of the river, the woods, the land."[173] Similarly, Pincher Creek was an "Old-Timers Town" wherein any celebration would find "that Indians will be very much in evidence."[174] Fort Macleod declared in 1921 that it would not "forget the redskins" who had made it a centre for trade and commerce.[175] By the end of the 1930s, stampede organizers were extolling Kainai cowboys alongside their white counterparts, so central were they to southern Alberta rodeos.[176] Cardston encouraged First Nations to join in its jubilee celebration, free of charge, as did the Williams Lake Stampede in the 1930s.[177] First Nations who attended stampedes across BC and Alberta may have enjoyed feeling this slight surge in power when they were welcomed rather than excluded from small-town life.

Aboriginal people also exploited the gap between government policy and the desires of small-town elites. Although Indian Agents could and did prohibit Aboriginal attendance at stampedes, organizers often subverted their prohibitions. In 1908, for example, Indian Agent R.N. Wilson cut the rations of all who attended events at Lethbridge and Fort Macleod. The fair committees countered by butchering eight steers and distributing the meat among attendees.[178] Furthermore, money earned at stampedes went directly to participants and therefore stayed out of Indian Agent hands. Stampedes offered a number of opportunities for cash, including contest prizes, the sale of beadwork, and payment for being photographed by tourists.[179] At the Cardston Stampede of 1921, for instance, the prizes for the Indian events were the same as for the open events, $10.00 for first and $7.50 for second, but Aboriginal riders were not required to pay entry

Tom Three Persons often won the "best-dressed" cowboy contest in clothes
designed and made by his wife, Katie. The medal on his chest may be the one
that Fort Macleod minted for him in honour of his bronc-riding win at the 1912
Calgary Stampede. 1912. *Glenbow Museum Archives, NA-689-1*

fees.[180] Best-dressed Indian contests also awarded prizes — ten dollars at the Lethbridge Stampede in 1921.[181] Such prizes highlighted the work of women in producing beautiful clothing, and along with beadwork sales, they put cash in the hands of women and reinvigorated the craft, offering new economic opportunities to reserve residents.[182] Some Aboriginal families pooled their resources and purchased soft drinks or food to sell in the Indian encampments at stampedes.[183] Others rented stock to rodeos for cash.[184] All these economic opportunities added to the financial independence of reserve residents.

Spending time in town also meant slipping beyond the surveillance of the Indian Agent. This alone was worth the price of admission, as it were, and it deeply troubled the agents, who kept a record of the days in which reserve residents were gone. Blood Indian Agent R.N. Wilson complained that the Kainai were absent from 29 July to 12 August in 1907, prime haying time lost to parades and festivities in Lethbridge and Fort Macleod.[185] Sometimes attendance included buying liquor from local settlers or "half-breeds" and joining in the festivities of stampede week in towns where municipal police were less likely, some Indian Agents thought, to prosecute those selling liquor to reserve residents.[186] When six hundred Tsilhqot'in Dakelh, and Secwepemc people converged on Williams Lake for its 1926 stampede, RCMP Constable Lavender reported that he found drinking but not intoxication despite the fact that many "half-breeds" who held liquor permits were in attendance.[187] Still, agents reported that reserve residents were "unsettled" by their involvement in stampedes, distracted by the preparations before the events, and less willing to take instruction from agency employees when they got home.[188] As Kootenay Indian Agent H.M. Helmsing put it, "War dances and other Indian festivities were put on and the Indians went absolutely mad and required constant watch being kept to prevent trouble."[189] Children refused to go to school or ran away if they were forced to attend it.[190] When, in 1923, the parents of children enrolled at St. Eugene's Residential School in Cranbrook threatened to "storm the school like soldiers" to get their children released for that year's festivities in Invermere, Agent Helmsing attributed their stridency to the effects of the upcoming celebrations.[191] Indeed, Ktunaxa ethnographer Caroline Basil writes that stampedes offered "a way to ventilate hostility over a vastly changing world" and a chance to gain recognition from settlers who as often as not exhibited little more than tolerance for their Aboriginal neighbours.[192] Individuals felt personal pride in their accomplishments. Kainai Guy Wolf Child recalled, "I was a very good dancer. Everyone used to watch me ... I always danced at the Stampede and exhibitions they had in Fort Macleod and in Lethbridge."[193] Others noticed that Aboriginal visitors took pride in their encampments and in the interest shown them by town-dwellers.[194] Stampedes produced contact zones, encouraging interaction between settlers and First Nations, inter-actions that did not always conform to the scripts of conquest.

What troubled Indian Agents most, of course, was the extent to which stampedes encouraged pride in Aboriginal identity. R.N. Wilson said it in 1901: "The principal mischief is done with the young Indians to many of whom 'paint and feathers' would be quite unfamiliar but for these town parades. After the Department's officials have labored for many years to induce Indians to adopt the garb and pursuits of white people we have the spectacle of municipal and other bodies deliberately passing resolu-tions and making grants of money which have the direct effect of undoing the Department's work. Prominently in all of these parades are to be seen the newly graduated school boys, their features covered with uncouth war paint."[195]

Despite stampede committee emphasis on Aboriginal participation as representing the past, the Aboriginal people who attended, of course, did so in the present. In this way, they demonstrated forcefully to government agents, missionaries, and to themselves the possibility that their cultural forms, both material and performative, could reside alongside a "modern" life that included ranching, education, and political involvement. Indian Agents seemed particularly vexed that recent residential school graduates were such avid participants in stampedes but doing so helped ease the transition from school to reserve that so many Indian Agents lamented was difficult.[196] Although some observers might have thought it ironic that the Aboriginal people who rode in stampede parades drove to town in cars to do so, the object lesson was also plain. First Nations could be modern and could retain knowledge and pride in their culture.[197] This was not a trivial matter in an era when residential schools, Indian Agents, and missionaries were all trying, in the words of one missionary, to "make them forget that they are Indians."[198] Moreover, portraying the past did not foreclose the possibility of meeting to discuss present concerns. This too worried officials. The missionary at St. Eugene's in Cranbrook anx-iously recorded what he thought occurred at stampedes:

And what [are] the results of these celebrations and gatherings?

1   The Indians are vividly and forcibly reminded that they are Indians that is a race far different from the white race. That they have their own customs, habits and ideals, and a mode of living, which are different from the white man's and which they love and will give up only when and because forced to do so by the circumstances that is by the advent of the white man.

2   They are reminded of the days when they were the sole inhabitants and sole masters of the country, and therefore

3   They are reminded that, according to the BC Indian theory, the white man is a usurper, who has no right, either to possess the land, or (far less) to make laws for the Indians

4   The war dance, which is not only allowed but expected in those occasions is, according to the Indians themselves, a hymn of hate, not any longer against other Indian tribes but against the white man who, today, is the enemy.[199]

Although there is no evidence that going to stampedes encouraged "hymns of hate," it very clearly provided an opportunity for Aboriginal people to speak directly to visiting dignitaries and to local non-Native audiences, sidestepping the official spokespeople for First Nations, the Department of Indian Affairs and missionaries. In 1925 Kainai writer Mike Mountain Horse organized a massive convention in Fort Macleod to raise public awareness about problems with leasing reserve land and unfulfilled promises from Treaty 7. He scheduled the conference for the Dominion Day holiday and called it the Dominion Indian Celebration. Kainai cowboy Tom Three Persons organized a rodeo for the event, and Joseph Mountain Horse set up an encampment with 196 tipis and a pageant designed to show "the different stages of Indian progress in North America," visually represented by modes of conveyance from the travois to the automobile.[200] Although every major Aboriginal leader attended, not all of them participated in the conference organized to speak to their concerns. Prominent chiefs such as Shot on Both Sides disagreed with Mike Mountain Horse's assessment of their situation and with his tactics. Government officials refused to attend the conference, and little was accomplished. But press coverage was strong, conveying the message that government tutelage was failing.[201] During the 1935 Lethbridge Golden Jubilee Stampede, Mike Mountain Horse again sought to reach

Mike Mountain Horse, 1959. *Glenbow Museum Archives, NB-44-92*

a wide settler audience by publishing a series of newspaper articles that ran alongside reports on the stampede. In "The Blood Indians: Our First Citizens," Mountain Horse offered his own rendition of Kainai history leading up to the current progressive age of farms and schools. In closing,

he invited stampede-goers to "meet these first inhabitants of this continent. It may be your last chance to see them."[202] Subsequent articles taught
readers about Kainai spirituality and the symbolism of tipi painting and
rock art, and a radio broadcast on CJOC revealed "the Red Man's view of
the White Man."[203] Although Aboriginal people could not always control
what was said about them at stampedes, they nonetheless used the events
to try, as much as possible, to speak directly to a settler audience.

Finally, Aboriginal people subtly subverted the scripts of conquest that
were implicit in many stampedes. From the start, they blurred the line
between "Indian" and "cowboy" by entering rodeo contests and excelling
at them. As fair organizers struggled to put on self-sustaining events in
the 1910s, Aboriginal cowboys were making names for themselves on
the fledgling rodeo circuits. The charismatic Kainai cowboy Tom Three
Persons gained notoriety riding broncs at the early stampedes in Lethbridge, Raymond, Fort Macleod, and Medicine Hat. By 1910 he needed
no introduction to the small-town audiences of southern Alberta.[204] Within
the decade, other Aboriginal cowboys joined Three Persons in events that
ranged from calf or colt roping to bronc and steer riding. At the Lethbridge Stampede of 1918, Aboriginal riders, mainly from the Blood reserve, accounted for 20 percent of all local contestants.[205] A Kainai named
Holy White Man thrilled Lethbridge crowds in 1918 when he darted beyond the reach of the charging bull from whose shoulders he had just
been thrown.[206] White Feather and Day Chief were among a handful of
cowboys successful in the roping events at Lethbridge that year.[207] Over
the course of the 1920s, increasing numbers of Aboriginal cowboys entered events, including Emil Smallface, Joe Fox, Pete Weaslehead, Willie
Eagleplume, Jim Littleleaf, Jacob Twoyoungmen, Wolf Child, Joe Young
Pine, John Lefthand, and Pete Bruisehead among others.[208] Nor were these
men marginal participants. At the 1928 High River Stampede, Tom
Twoyoungmen, Joe Fox, and Isaiah Powderface shut out all other competitors in bareback riding, taking first, second, and third place respectively.
Similarly, in colt roping, Ken and John Bearspaw took first and second,
whereas Sykes Robinson "upheld the honour of the white man with
third."[209] In British Columbia, Aboriginal men competed because, of
course, they were cowboys too. Tsilhquot'in Joe Elkins was a champion
bronc-rider known for riding in beautiful beaded moccasins.[210] The Bowe
brothers and Harry Shuttleworth, mixed-heritage cowboys, took honours
in calf roping and bareback riding. Joe and Matthew Dick (Secwepemc)

of Alkali Lake were among the best Roman riders. Indeed, entries in every event at the Williams Lake Stampede showed that it was a place where white cowboys rubbed shoulders with their Aboriginal and mixed-heritage counterparts. Repeatedly, Secwepemc men such as Nels Chelsea of Dog Creek and Pierro Squinahan and Patrick Chelsea of Alkali Lake dominated the mountain race.[211] And though the Williams Lake programs tended to stress the Cariboo as a land of opportunity for white men, one in which they had no competitors, program writers nonetheless included Charley Mouse of the Sugar Cane Reserve in the cowboy fraternity, re-marking that "he rides hard and well and gives some of the white boys all they can handle to outride him."[212]

Even in the most explicit stagings of conquest, Aboriginal people could disrupt the narrative, mainly by declining to play their parts. One year at the Williams Lake Stampede, Aboriginal women simply did not enter the squaw race. This, in itself, is surprising since they were excellent riders and keen competitors. Clayton Mack thought his Ulgatcho sister-in-law Josephine Capoose was the best rider he had ever seen. Some of filmmaker Arthur D. Kean's early footage of stampedes in the southern BC Interior shows a fiercely competitive "klootchmans' race," as Aboriginal women were called in the Chinook jargon. But here at the Williams Lake Stampede in the late 1920s, Aboriginal women refused to enter. Instead, two local settler women, a schoolteacher and a bank clerk, donned horsehair wigs and rode in the race themselves in an apparent act of cultural transves-tism. Aware of the ruse, the audience cheered them on with "go darky, go."[213] Similarly, no Secwepemc, Tsilhquot'in, or Dakelh people were willing to participate in the staged "Chilcotin Massacre" in 1928, so white settlers played the Indians who attacked Ollie Curtis in her stagecoach and burned the makeshift Fort Chilcotin to the ground. Such refusals by Aboriginal people to be complicit in the staging of conquest turned the intended "historical reproduction" into a farce laden with irony. Aboriginal actors were also absent from the pageant at the 1935 Lethbridge Golden Jubilee Stampede.[214] Enthusiastic as they were to participate in stampedes and rodeos, there remained limits to what they would do.

Stampedes in southern Alberta and the BC Interior established rodeo as their signature sporting event in the early decades of the twentieth century. Gradually and inadvertently, rodeo became a lucrative paying participant in the community events that materially and imaginatively built kinship among settlers – and with that, identity. As Aritha Van Herk

writes in her Alberta history *Mavericks,* "the cowboy code of neighborli-
ness, loyalty, independence and uncomplaining persistence became part
of the West's code, unspoken but writ larger than the looming mountains."[215] Rodeos played out these values and performed community. Those
who took part, cowboys, Aboriginal people, shopkeepers, and boosters,
all became part of that community. They were not equal players; the power
dynamics of settlement in Western Canada did not permit that. But for
one week each year, the contact zone was centre stage. The old relationships of early settlement were extolled, and Aboriginal people and settlers
came together in celebration of a shared past, bringing about, for a brief
period, a common present and envisioning a collective future. This sense
of optimism must have prompted Kainai Nora Gladstone to pen the following poem in 1945. Though in later life she would remember Cardston
for its discrimination, as a young woman she seemed to have higher hopes
for the world that a stampede could make:

The Cardston Stampede
When the flags are all a-flutter, an' the microphone's a-stutter,
And the buckaroos come whoop-in' round the track;
And the heavens split asunder, as the crowd-cheer bursts like thunder,
And the cowboy clown falls flat upon his back;
When the announcer's voice rings clear – "Prairie folks, you listen here!
Of all the rodeos this little one's the best!"
And the boys cut loose an' shoots, you can bet your high-heel boots it's the
Stampede out at Cardston in the west!
How I'm wishing I was there, cheering, choking – dust in air –
As the buckin' outlaws thump the sunbaked ground;
Hearin' dogie calves a-bawlin, watchin' steer-riders go sprawlin' while the lariat
    loops are spinnin' all around;
Just to think about these things tugs a Westerner's heart-strings,
Yeah! I guess I'm goin' back, no more to roam;
Where Alberta meets Montana, I'll hang out my little banner –
"This is where I'm happy folks, BECAUSE I'M HOME."[216]

2

Truly Western in Its Character

Identities, Affinities, and Intimacies
at Western Canadian Rodeo

*The point is that contact zones are where the action is, and current
interactions change interactions to follow ... Contact zones change
the subject – all the subjects – in surprising ways.*
— *Donna Haraway,* When Species Meet

On Wednesday, 24 September 1930, while his wife and friends looked on
in horror, a truck heading south from Calgary struck Leo Watrin as he
knelt by his car changing a tire. The impact threw him several metres,
and he died two days later in hospital. Watrin was at the peak of his rodeo
career. In 1928 he was Canadian bucking horse champion and had slipped
only slightly to second place the following year. The Watrins were descendants of French fur traders from Minnesota and, like many other Americans,
had come to southern Alberta just after the turn of the century. Leo and
his brothers, Clarence "Slim," Eddie, and Lawrence, were among the first
generation of local rodeo heroes of the region, a fraternity that included
Herman Linder, Pete Knight, Tom Three Persons, and Pete Bruisehead.
Much to the delight of fair committees across the Canadian West, rodeo
was not a mere novelty whose shine eventually dimmed. By 1930 it was
establishing itself as a popular spectator sport; indeed, cowboys were
becoming a favourite cultural icon across the continent. Small-town rodeos
did not simply reflect their popularity. They also gave the men of southern
Alberta and the BC Interior, men like Leo Watrin, the chance to *be* cowboys – to develop and inhabit an identity that drew on the Hollywood
western and other forms of popular culture but more importantly had
salience within local networks of recognition and affection. Watrin's funeral attracted hundreds of local rodeo fans. It was here, at small-town
rodeos, that the reputations of rodeo cowboys were made.[1]

Thinking about the creative potential in encounters, Donna Haraway
writes that "meetings make us who we are in the avid contact zones that

Leo Watrin at the Montreal Stampede, 1926. *Glenbow Museum Archives, PA-3457-14*

are the world. Once 'we' meet we can never be 'the same.'"[2] Rodeo was one such contact zone, and it changed people. It not only created communities, but also identities, affinities, and intimacies. Like the communities brought together and remade by rodeos, those identities were gendered and raced. Masculinities, principally that of the cowboy and the promoter, materialized in and around rodeo. Rodeo masculinities embedded slightly different constellations of meaning for Aboriginal and white men, but certain similarities existed as well. Opportunities for producing femininities were more constrained, but settler and Aboriginal women made spaces for themselves in small-town Western Canadian rodeo. As we saw in the previous chapter, rodeo was about bringing people together and building communities. People, as individuals, converged as well; friendships and more intimate relationships developed. By the end of the 1940s, multiple identities and relationships existed within the contact zones that were inherent in the small-town rodeos of the Canadian West.

Small towns in British Columbia and Alberta loved their homegrown cowboys. Cowboys and cowgirls from home or nearby communities, reserves included, were the stars of these shows. They were not performers but neighbours, the teenaged sons and daughters of family friends, people who might be met on the street throughout the year. Often, siblings shared in the fame. High River had its Watrin brothers; Cardston, the Lunds;

and Williams Lake, the Curtis kids, including daughter Ollie Curtis. Fans avidly followed cowboy fortunes, cheering for them in their successes and groaning with them in defeat. Kamloops audiences grimaced when Skeetchesin cowboy Buckskin Louie from the Deadman's Creek Reserve broke his arm at the 1929 stampede and cheered when he returned to ride the following year. Fans in BC watched the careers of Harry Shuttleworth from the Similkameen, Rolly Hays from Armstrong, Mike Carlin from Chase, Frank Hall from Lac La Hache, Doc Watson from Vernon, Johnny Robins of the Kamloops Reserve, and Cyclone Smith from Williams Lake.[3] This intense interest kept small-town stampedes afloat even in the darkest days of the Depression.[4] In 1932, for example, nearly five thousand spectators cheered on local heroes Herman Linder, Clark Lund, and Pete Bruisehead at the Raymond Stampede.[5] Two thousand fans descended on the tiny Alberta town of Black Diamond in 1936 to see Eddie Watrin win the bronc riding and Don Thompson take the bareback-riding contest. Rodeo stars came to symbolize hope for the West in desperate days. The *High River Times* expressed such sentiments well: "The crowd that follows the thrilling stampede sensations from year to year has come to look for all kinds of nerve and dash from these boys and their appearance is greeted with tumultuous cheers reserved for old friends. They do their full share of upholding the supremacy of the old original cow country, and through their riding, the name of High River is known up and down the continent."[6] These cowboys were so well loved that one might almost think they had always existed. But they hadn't. They had been created only recently.

Rodeo cowboys emerged at a time when gender, both masculinity and femininity, underwent profound and, for some, disquieting shifts. Recently, scholars have demonstrated that a growing array of experts, from churches and labour organizations to men's clubs and the medical profession, debated the effects of modernity on masculinity. Rough and respectable were the dominant categories of masculinity, but male self-expression on the shop floor, in bars, on the street, and in sport was not confined by these dichotomies. Clearly, this era did not craft a unified masculinity: rather, it was always inflected with racialization and sexuality, the interests of class, and the contingencies of place. The rodeo cowboy was one of those forms, and it was itself contested and modulated.[7]

From small towns and reserves across southern Alberta and the BC Interior, a new kind of man materialized – the rodeo cowboy. His was an

Vulcan cowboys, 1915. *Glenbow Museum Archives, NA-217-55*

identity that embodied change, for both settler and Aboriginal men. In the popular imaginings of the time, the West was a space for transformation.[8] From the famous, such as Theodore Roosevelt, to the obscure, such as Martin Frank Dunham and Cliff Kopas, writers extolled the West as a recuperative zone, beyond modernity, where manhood and health could be recovered.[9] This notion that the West transformed lives was not solely figurative. Men and women who came to the Canadian West found that they had to adjust, learn new skills, become, to a degree, new people; they transitioned from "tenderfoot to rider," to use Simon Evans's phrase.[10] Whereas environmental adaptation was a struggle of trial and error, sometimes of devastating proportions, becoming a cowboy offered something magical, especially for the children of immigrants. Herman Linder recalled waking up on his first morning in Cardston, after having moved from Wisconsin: "All you could hear outside the hotel was the rattle of wagons and the sound of horses' hooves. It was like music to us! Warner and I would rush to the window and gape at the cowboys coming in with their fancy boots and wooly chaps, and big hats. What a thrill that was! We vowed someday we'd get ourselves outfits just like that!"[11] His brother Warner confirmed that, for them, fascination led to transformation: "Why Herman and I got so enthused about this cowboy stuff, I don't know. I don't see how you can say we had it in us. Our parents weren't ranch people when they came out here. And we sure never dreamt [that] our Sunday fun could ever turn into a business."[12] The Linders were not alone. The West, it seemed to contemporaries, had that effect on people; it changed them, and becoming a rodeo cowboy was one manifestation of that change.[13]

First Nations also experienced transformations, often of a more un-settling kind. The reserve era, with its stultifying surveillance by the Indian Agent, and the constant pressure to give up land, to become ranchers and then farmers, to go to school only to discover that what was taught there had little use on reserves – all this had its effects on Aboriginal men.[14] Being a cowboy was at once an adaptation to these changed circumstances and a continuation of older identity and community formation. In Alberta, where the reserves were large, young men worked for more established Aboriginal ranchers as well as local settlers. In British Columbia, Aboriginal cowboys hired on at the big settler-run ranches that dominated the Interior and that occupied unceded land claimed by First Nations. It was not sur-prising to the anthropologist John Ewers, for example, to find Blackfeet youngsters imitating calf roping and bull dogging at an early twentieth-century sun dance encampment in Montana. Because it mimicked rodeo, their play seemed to be "of recent origin," and yet it was also akin to the horseplay of young men in the days of the buffalo.[15] The rodeo cowboy emerged as a hybridized indigenous masculinity, embodying rebellious-ness and respectability. Changed themselves, rodeo cowboys, both Aboriginal and settler, worked together throughout the 1920s and 1930s to alter their image, to increase the status and respectability of the sport and its contestants.

As the local cowboy community grew, a range of masculinities associ-ated with rodeo came to the surface. Most contestants remained at the amateur level, and for them rodeoing was just a stage of life, characterized by youthful daring and male camaraderie.[16] During the late nineteenth century and the early twentieth century, rodeo cowboys gained a reputa-tion for being hard drinkers, indefatigable carousers, and shiftless scrap-pers, prone to skipping town without paying their bills.[17] The drunken ride, one of the novelty events at the Williams Lake Stampede, played on the public perception that cowboys were drunkards, but there was some truth to it as well. One year, the Williams Lake Stampede arena manager reported that no pick-up riders were available to work the afternoon's events, because they were all too inebriated to ride. Organizers arranged to have the government liquor store closed between 2:00 p.m. and 5:00 p.m., the hours when most events were run, for the duration of the stampede.[18] In small towns across the region, some cowboys found themselves in jail cells when the rodeo was over, but most authorities turned a blind eye to drunkenness.[19] Busting up hotel rooms occurred often enough that fledgling cowboy organizations addressed it in their rules.[20] Fighting added to the cowboys' sense of toughness. One woman remembered that her uncle, a bronc-rider, fought "at the drop of a hat, and it didn't matter whose hat it was."[21] Gambling and paying for rounds of drinks stripped cowboys of their earnings and gave them a reputation for impecuniousness. Harry Knight, the well-known and well-loved Alberta cowboy, had a "knack for making money and an even more remarkable knack for getting rid of it fast."[22] Living large was part of the early rodeo cowboy identity. For more than one of them, a life of wild rides and good times ended a few short years later on a lonely street corner, dead of drinking or fighting or both.[23]

But there was another version of the cowboy, one grounded less in rough masculinity. These men cultivated an image of rodeo as a family event that emphasized "good, clean sportsmanship."[24] First and foremost, the family of rodeo was the cowboy fraternity itself. Helping out the novice, taking care of the less fortunate, and standing up for each other, these too, as cowboys asserted with their actions, were features of rodeo masculinity. Seasoned men aided new ones. Bronc-rider Joe Fisher helped Herman Linder, early in his career, loaning him a good saddle and a halter, and instructing him to cut down his chaps and shorten his spurs.[25] Cowboys came to depend on the generosity of those who were doing well, even if only at the moment. Cyra McFadden, daughter of rodeo announcer Cy Taillon, remembered her father as living "rodeo to rodeo, making just enough money to keep us in gas and hamburgers," but "if he had extra money, everybody drank, and when we rented a room in a motor court, a luxury, cowboys bunked down on the floor with their saddles for pillows."[26] Cowboys shared their earnings with injured friends and stood alongside them when rivals challenged. Métis cowboy Paddy Laframboise and BC mixed-heritage cowboy Harry Shuttleworth travelled together in the late 1920s. When a bucking horse kicked out Laframboise's front teeth at a rodeo in Twist, Washington, Shuttleworth offered to share the mount money (paid for attempting to ride an animal) he expected to receive in steer riding the next day. But Laframboise entered steer riding anyway and won. There were no hard feelings between them, and together they stood up to the angry jeering of American cowboys who questioned the right of Canadians to enter their hometown rodeo.[27]

Rough and respectable masculinity overlapped in rodeo cowboys. First, they were united by an extraordinary physical toughness. Men often rode while injured. In the summer of 1930, when Leo Watrin was a contender for the championship position in bronc riding, his mount rolled over on top of him, badly injuring his shoulder. Instead of forfeiting, Watrin took a re-ride and put in a "star performance," according to the *High River Times*.[28] In 1936 Warner Linder tore his back muscles and smashed his collarbone during an event but defied doctor's orders by competing in steer decorating next day.[29] Acute injuries were a routine part of the Williams Lake mountain race. Dave Twan skinned his chest and arms in a fall during the 1929 mountain race, but months later when he was still unwell, doctors in Kamloops discovered that one of his kidneys had been punctured in the fall.[30] Indeed, risking death was part of the cowboy mystique, however he conceived of himself. The deaths of Cyclone Smith at Williams Lake and Pete Knight in competition at Hayward, California, were memorialized countless times at rodeos and in later publicity.

If rodeo cowboys did not evade death, they did escape domesticity. A keen impulse toward life on the road also united them. Though some, such as Pete Knight and Herman Linder, brought their wives with them, rodeo was still a world away from home. Travelling the circuit where they made names for themselves, rodeo cowboys drove in loose caravans and lived in motel rooms and bars. Drinking and fighting, as well as fleeting sexual relationships and stormy romantic ones, were part of life on the road. The life strongly appealed to Cy Taillon, who announced rodeos and drank and fought across much of the transborder West in his Packard during the 1930s and 1940s. His daughter Cyra had logged 150,000 miles by her third birthday.[31] Most men didn't travel with their families, mainly because they were young and not yet married. Others simply left their families behind for the season, as Herman Linder had to do once his children were born. As Agnes Linder put it, "It was no fun traveling with a family, especially in the heat of the summer."[32] Sometimes going on the road was a way of dealing with tragic situations, or an opportunity when there were few others. When Walt Knight lost his two infant sons in the summer of 1925, he bought a Model T and joined his brother Pete on the circuit. In the 1930s, Slim Dorin rode the rails from Wetaskiwin,

Alberta, to British Columbia, lured, he once said, by the love of rodeo and thirty-five dollars won in steer wrestling. Following the rodeo road to Merritt, he got a job at the Douglas Lake Ranch. But before he settled down as cowboss, he competed in calf roping, saddle bronc, steer wrestling, and team roping.[33] The sense that the cowboys carried with them – that they were an "undomesticated," independent breed – sometimes boiled over into a kind of casual misogyny in the early years. Rodeo wives or girlfriends felt themselves pitted against groupies called "buckle bunnies," competing for a prize that consisted of a man who was unlikely to settle down for a while in any case.[34] Stock contractors gave their rankest animals names like Cranky Ann and My Darling. The press seldom resisted the obvious comparisons. Describing Herman Linder's ride on the bronc My Darling, the *High River Times* wrote, "the way he treated his darling wasn't so good. She didn't like him either."[35] Perhaps, as some said, no true cowboy ever hit a woman, but much in rodeo portrayed the genders in adversarial terms.[36]

As rodeo became a paying sport, cowboys recognized the need to ensure that it had a good name. Some consciously eschewed the flamboyance associated with rough masculinity and focused on riding to make a living.[37] Clarence "Slim" Watrin of High River was well known on the circuit of the 1920s and 1930s, taking the world championship for bucking horse in 1928 and winning the Prince of Wales Trophy in 1931. But the next year, when he broke his leg in two places at the Sundre, Alberta, rodeo, he chose to retire at the age of thirty. As he remembered years later, "If you can't make any money, you've got to quit."[38] Respectable cowboys, such as Pete Knight, who neither drank nor smoked, and Herman Linder, who travelled the circuit with his wife, consciously sought to improve the image of the sport, at least in part to enhance its popularity with small-town organizing committees. If a town feared the arrival of circuit cowboys for the damage they would do to its reputation (by drinking, fighting, or trashing hotel rooms), it would stop staging rodeos. Men such as Knight and Linder were soon earning a living at rodeo and needed to ensure that the sport would sustain itself.[39] Linder earned as much as $8,000 during the 1930s, and Knight was making $7,000 at the time of his death in 1937. Although some cowboys, such as Harry Knight, remained larger-than-life figures, increasingly there was a place in rodeo for more serious men.

At the rodeo, not all cowboys were contestants – promoters crafted their own masculinities. In the early days of Canadian rodeo, veterans of the

Professional cowboys on the road, 1930. Pete Knight, far right. *Glenbow Museum Archives, NB(H)-16-230*

American Wild West Show circuit put on many of the first stampedes. Of these, Guy Weadick was the best known. He first visited Western Canada as part of the Miller Brothers' 101 Ranch Wild West Show in 1908 and soon returned to Calgary to stage that city's first stampede in 1912. From the start, Weadick was a controversial figure, denounced by some as a shameless American huckster and praised by others as a premier show-man. The 1912 Calgary Stampede was largely a success, but not until 1923 was Weadick, working with Calgary Exhibition manager Ernie L. Richardson, able to make it an annual event. In many ways, Weadick exemplified the transformative potential of the West. Born in Rochester, New York, he learned his cowboy craft on the Miller Brothers' ranch, the training ground for their Wild West showmen. Though Weadick was not ranch raised, he nonetheless absorbed being a cowboy to his very core. In 1920 he and his wife, Flores LaDue, bought a working ranch in Eden Valley, renamed it Stampede Ranch, and operated it as a dude ranch and sometime movie set for the next twenty years.

Guy Weadick and Flores LaDue. No date. *Glenbow Museum Archives, NA-3164-70*

Weadick was always a larger-than-life figure.[40] He loved public attention, demanded the limelight wherever he was, and proved time and again that he was the greatest talker in southern Alberta. He popularized the modern stampede, with stopwatches, scorecards, and elaborate rules for each event. He fought hard to make rodeo a paying proposition, to promote it as a sporting activity worthy of the public investment that he demanded from Calgarians and, later, other Albertans, founding the Canadian Cowboy Contest Managers' Association in 1924.[41] He was a tremendous drinker who crashed automobiles with alarming frequency. By the 1930s, as more conservative expressions of masculinity came to the surface in Western Canada, Weadick found himself out of step with the Calgary Exhibition and Stampede Board. As the board cut prize money in an effort to economize, Weadick predicted disaster. Although the 1932 stampede went off without a hitch, he was nonetheless disheartened. At the awards banquet that closed the stampede, he showed up drunk, where he reportedly said that he had opened the first stampede and that he had just closed the last one. The board responded by eliminating his position, putting Weadick out of a job. A later court decision affirmed that he had been wrongfully dismissed and awarded him a modest settlement. Weadick, however, remained bitter toward the Calgary Stampede for many years.

Nevertheless, he turned his attention to promoting rodeo elsewhere in southern Alberta and the northern Plains states. To these stampedes, he brought his slogan – "A square deal to all, no color, residence or nationality barred. It's open to the world, come and get it" – and particularly encouraged First Nations to enter events such as the Lethbridge Stampede of 1935. He promoted the celebration of the "old-timer," early settlers to southern Alberta, first with a roping contest at the 1935 Lethbridge Stampede and then later with parades and dinners, special events to capture memories and honour pioneers.[42] Weadick was genuinely fascinated by the history of settlement in southern Alberta. As he maintained a presence in Western Canadian rodeo until his death in 1953, he also kept his particular brand of rodeo masculinity alive. He continued to drink hard. Shortly after his dismissal from the Calgary Stampede, he wrote to a friend that he was going "to try and keep right on eating, taking a drink when we feel we need one and in general try and conduct ourselves as we have in the past."[43] Although few criticized Weadick's drinking, it nonetheless contributed to his short-lived and exceedingly stormy relationship with former cowgirl Dolly Mott following Flores LaDue's death in 1951. He continued to be opinionated, writing long-winded letters to the executive of the new Canadian Professional Rodeo Association, in which he denounced post-war rodeos as inauthentic, losing their connection to the ranch life that spawned them and the small towns who supported them.[44]

Until his sudden death in 1953, he continued to represent that dramatic transformation that the West could work in a person, for he had embraced the life of a cowboy like few others. On his tombstone, the ranchers and townsfolk of High River described him as the "loyal son of his adopted west."[45] To his contemporaries, he would always be the "Dean of Rodeo Producers."[46]

When it was announced that Guy Weadick was putting on the 1935 Lethbridge Stampede, Herman Linder informed reporters that he would certainly enter since Weadick was "a good showman and a great favorite with the boys and has always been fair and a good sport."[47] By 1935 Linder was already a well-known rodeo cowboy, and his endorsement of the Lethbridge contest was at least as important as Weadick's reputation as a seasoned promoter. Linder would soon represent another type of promoter, one that would come to dominate the post-war era in particular. He rose through the ranks from championship rider to arena manager, staging his first stampede at Lethbridge in 1939. Promotional material for his stampedes all mentioned his career as a contestant.[48] Indeed, Linder initially competed in the events he organized, but soon he concentrated his efforts on promotion, earning a reputation for putting on good, profitable shows.[49]

Linder's career as a promoter took off during the 1940s after he retired from competing. He typified the new masculinities of the professional cowboys. Unlike Weadick, who earned the loyalty of rodeo cowboys but was never one of them, Linder was involved in the formation of the Canadian Professional Rodeo Association, which put him squarely in the ranks of pro cowboys. He supported their demands to choose judges from among themselves, but he also stood up to unruly cowboys whose behaviour put rodeo as a sport in a bad light. During a head-to-head confrontation with the Vancouver SPCA in 1949, Linder portrayed himself, as did many pro cowboys, as a true animal advocate. Whereas Weadick courted the limelight, Linder never sought attention. His clean, business-like, respectable image linked him to other elite cowboys of his era, including Pete Knight and Clem Gardner, and earned him wide respect. The 1937 Cardston Golden Jubilee Rodeo program described him as "quiet and unassuming, and always a gentlemen," even as he emerged as "Alberta's top-ranking cowboy."[50] Linder's version of masculinity was very different from Weadick's more flamboyant iteration, but both contributed to the

Herman Linder with mementos from his rodeo career, 1950s. *Glenbow Museum Archives, NA-3252-3*

articulations of manhood performed by rodeo promoters. Writing just a few years later, after the Second World War, Clifford Westermeier, rodeo's first historian, described what he saw as the "man in rodeo":

> In conclusion, one might say that the man in rodeo is a hard-working individual who has chosen an unusual profession. This is a work that demands a strong body and heart, a keen eye and mind, no fear, no recklessness, a love for man and beast, a love for competition and fair play. He has raised his profession to one of dignity and usefulness; he has made it a form of entertainment for hundreds of thousands; a successful business for himself; and has given it an honesty of sportsmanship that should be indicative of the first and true American sport.[51]

Westermeier also commented on what he thought was a particularly Canadian phenomenon – the presence of many Aboriginal riders and ropers in rodeo north of the border. Since his day, the work of Peter Iverson, Ben Chavis, and Allison Mellis has revealed that Crow, Sioux, Navajo, Apache, and other Aboriginal people in the United States also embraced the sport. But it was certainly the case that by the 1930s, a great many very good Aboriginal cowboys lived in Canada: in Alberta, Tom Three Persons, Pete Bruisehead, Jim Starlight, and Johnny Lefthand; in British Columbia, Gus Gottfriedson, Harry Shuttleworth, Joe Elkins, Nels Chelsea, and Dave Twan. Among these, by far the most famous was the Kainai cowboy Tom Three Persons, who exemplified another expression of rodeo masculinity.

Like his settler counterparts, Tom Three Persons was the product of change. The transition to reserves, the domineering influence of the Indian Agent, and the impact of residential schooling all affected the bases of Aboriginal masculinity on the Plains. Deprived of bison hunting and horse raids, confined on plots of land, and forced to raise cattle and then to farm, Aboriginal men on Treaty 7 and surrounding reserves found little in any of the new realities to support traditional ideas about masculinity. Older men chided younger ones for not earning the rights of manhood through horse raids and war parties. Still, these early reserve-period generations pursued new modes of gender formation or adapted old ones to new circumstances. According to the anthropologist Lucien Hanks, an explosion of dance and ceremonial societies was partly a response to the decline of hunting and raiding as male rites of passage. Keeping horse herds and later breeding superior racehorses were other ways of adapting the old modes of masculinity to the new conditions. In sparse economic circumstances, leading men still shared what little they had and supported younger men in keeping with long-held standards of Aboriginal masculinity on the Plains.[52]

Generational divisions emerged. During the early decades of the twentieth century, Indian Agents and anthropologists both commented that the younger men seemed more prone to discontent or, in the words of one Indian Agent, to "prove their bravery by defiance of authority."[53] Lucien Hanks noted a similar difficulty in the early reservation period, as young men chafed at the constraints of reserve life, putting their lives at risk by crossing the border to steal horses, defying police, drinking whiskey, and generally disputing all who would exert power over them.[54] Tom Three Persons was of this generation. Born in 1886, of mixed heritage, he was raised on the Blood reserve and attended St. Paul's Residential School. Inheriting wealth in cattle and horses from his stepfather, he married and established a reputation for being a hard worker and a very good rider. Over time, he joined the ranks of the wealthiest men on the reserve, all of whom were transitional or hybrid figures combining economic success in non-Native terms with elements of Kainai masculine privilege and responsibility.[55]

Three Persons earned early notoriety as the Canadian champion in bronc riding at the first Calgary Stampede in 1912. Fort Macleod minted a medal for him, and the governor general, Prince Arthur, Duke of Connaught, sent a congratulatory telegram. Calgary newspapers, however, gleefully and erroneously reported that Three Persons had to be bailed out of the drunk tank in order to compete and that the horse he rode to victory had been tired out by another rider. Neither story was ever proven to be true. The Fort Macleod Board of Trade demanded and received a retraction. At home and across the border on the Blackfeet reservations of Montana, Three Persons received accolades. Older men praised him for defeating his enemies and bringing honour to his people. To the younger generation who had taken on cowboy work, dress, and culture, he demonstrated that success in the white world was possible for a Kainai man. Shortly after his return to the reserve, the All Brave Dogs Society

Tom Three Persons. No date. *Glenbow Museum Archives, NA-778-7*

gave him a new name, Apo'suk, or Weasel Backfat, the name of one of Three Persons' well-respected uncles. By the mid-1910s, he took a second wife, an act that demonstrated material success as well as prestige. It was also an act of defiance as Canadian Indian administration worked to suppress polygamy.[56] By the end of the decade, Tom Three Persons' reputation was growing and with it the place of rodeo in supporting and producing Aboriginal masculinities.

Aboriginal people throughout the Great Plains were drawn to rodeo in this period as small towns across the transborder West put on fairs and sports days, bucking contests and stampedes, incorporating the schedule of stampedes into a seasonal ritual cycle.[57] In this way, then, Aboriginal rodeo cowboys constituted alternative articulations of masculinity, and Three Persons became a role model for other southern Alberta Aboriginal youth. As Indian Agent W.J. Dilworth wrote in 1917, "The fact that Tom Three Persons, a Blood Indian, won the belt and championship at the Calgary Stampede in 1912, has been responsible for the condition, that every boy on the Blood reserve between the ages 17 and 23 wished to be a second Tom Three Persons, and all they think about is saddles, chaps, silver spurs, Race and bucking horses, etc., a full equipment of the above accoutrements makes him a hero in his own eyes, and in the eyes of the admiring young women on the reserve."[58]

Three Persons certainly relished his new status, and he worked to increase his wealth and his distance from the deadening effects of Indian administration. Indian Agent Dilworth underestimated Three Persons' independence when he appointed him and three of his friends to the band council, which was supposed to vote in favour of a major land cession. When Three Persons voted against the surrender in 1917, Dilworth forced him off-reserve. When he returned, following Dilworth's departure in 1919, he was determined to claim as much independence as possible from the Indian Agent, by becoming rich and by keeping his money separate from agency mismanagement. In this he was successful, and by the mid-1920s, he was among a group of wealthy on-reserve men who were known as the "Upper Ten."

Three Persons represented economic self-sufficiency and personal independence, markers of masculinity that were recognizable to Kainai people, government, and settlers. He used his wealth to support other men in ways that replicated the resource-sharing responsibilities of traditional Kainai leadership. He employed young men on his ranch at

Tom Three Persons and a young admirer, 1912. *Glenbow Museum Archives, NA-3164-170*

Bullhorn Coulee and was a generous host to those who came to stay with him. Beyond that, he also trained several young Kainai men in rodeo events. Eddie Heavy Shield, Wilton Frank, Jim Plaited Hair, and Fred Gladstone all enjoyed his tutelage, and they looked up to him. He shared his experiences of biased judging at small-town rodeos and encouraged these men to train for the timed events rather than the roughstock competitions. Soon Aboriginal cowboys dominated the sport of calf roping. Three Persons organized reserve rodeos, including the popular Blood Indian Stampedes of 1922 and 1923, and later drew a crowd of twenty-five hundred people to the Peigan reserve's rodeo in 1926.[59] Replicating the norms of Kainai masculinity, this interest in and support of younger men also fit the model of rodeo masculinity among settler men. In this regard, as in others, rodeo and Kainai values coincided, and the masculinities expressed in the sport had meaning in both settler and Aboriginal circles.

Over the course of the 1920s and 1930s, increasing numbers of Aboriginal men entered rodeos across the region.[60] The names of Pete Bruisehead, Pat Weaslehead, Emil Smallface, Joe Young Pine, and Dick Soup dominated coverage of events at southern Alberta rodeos.[61] Stampedes became a proving ground for the courage, luck, and skill of young men and a popular place for fleeting encounters with young women. They were opportunities for boys and girls from distant reserves to meet and for more formal courtships to be initiated.[62] More and more men joined Three Persons at the various southern Alberta stampedes, so that being a rodeo cowboy and an "Indian" became increasingly fused.

But there was a dark side as well. As among non-Native cowboys, the masculinities associated with rodeo could be infused with drinking and violence, particularly sexualized violence. Three Persons' drinking and recklessness were notorious. One Siksika elder recalled Three Persons simply: "He drank all the time."[63] He made no effort to keep his drinking a secret. In an interview with Fred Kennedy, a reporter for the *Albertan,* he joked that, drunk or sober, he could calf-rope equally well, saying "Well, sir, I saw three calves running ahead of me and I roped the middle one."[64] His inebriated mishaps in newly purchased motor vehicles made southern Alberta papers. In a sense, his public drunkenness was another way in which he asserted his ability to evade the rules under which other Aboriginal people had to live. Indeed, for other Aboriginal men who attended stampedes at Gleichen and Calgary, drinking was part of the freedom of a brief sojourn in the city where it was possible to elude the gaze of the Indian Agent.[65]

Violence sometimes ensued. Three Persons routinely and savagely beat his wives. At the 1912 Calgary Stampede, for example, he beat his first wife, Eliza, for having ruined the dress he bought her to wear when he celebrated his victory ride. In conversation with Esther Goldfrank, the women on the Blood reserve implicated him in a number of sexual assaults on women and girls. As some of Goldfrank's informants put it, stampedes were "overly exciting," and though they might bring wealth, they also brought violence.[66] Indeed, by the late 1930s, when Lucien Hanks and Jane Richardson did their fieldwork in southern Alberta, they noted that the young men who went to stampedes "absorb[ed] the cowboy-poolroom atmosphere" and spent their time in "low-life restaurants" and whorehouses, which, Hanks thought, represented to them the "glamour of white culture." Hanks agreed with Kainai elders who worried that the stampede was a bad influence on Aboriginal men.[67] Further south, David Rodnick thought that some of the Blackfeet he knew were being negatively influenced, both in dress and behaviour, by the "roving ranch hand and the types found at rodeos."[68]

But not all Aboriginal cowboys were attracted to the so-called glamour of white life, and not all of Three Persons' Aboriginal admirers emulated his lifestyle. Pete Bruisehead, for one, was drawn to the stampede by Three Persons' example but cultivated a clean and respectable image for himself.[69] Others used the recognition they garnered in rodeo to enhance their self-esteem, gain independence from Indian administration, increase their status among their own people, and attract an audience in settler society.[70] Rodeo cowboys ascended to positions of leadership, both through election and, as Tom Three Persons experienced, by being named by one of the secret societies. Joe Crowfoot, who became a minor chief in the 1930s, worked with Indian Agents and stampede officials to choose the eight Aboriginal men who travelled to Sydney, Australia, for the Royal Australian Fair in 1939. He went on to positions of leadership both within his own Siksika community and with the Indian Association of Alberta. Others, such as Jim Starlight, Frank Many Fingers, Eddie One Spot, Rufus Goodstriker, and Fred Gladstone, became chiefs or ascended to other positions of leadership.[71] As more prominent Aboriginal men entered and succeeded in rodeo, younger generations took to playing at it, as in earlier days they had played at war or hunting.[72]

Conditions on the Chilcotin Plateau brought out slightly different versions of the indigenous rodeo cowboy. Here hybridity was foregrounded more clearly than on the Plains. In British Columbia, reserves were much smaller than those of Treaty 7, for example, and government did not expect them to be self-sufficient – quite the opposite. Most Interior reserves

Pete Bruisehead with his fellow Calgary Stampede champions, 1927. *Glenbow Museum Archives, NA-1451-29*

were laid out after non-Native ranchers had claimed huge swaths of land. Government's object was to create a wage labour force, and though many Aboriginal people kept cattle and horses, sometimes large herds of them, they also worked on the settlement ranches, folding this work into a seasonal cycle that included both subsistence and waged labour in other sectors. By the early twentieth century, some bands were working hard to run cattle-ranching operations even as they maintained large horse herds, principally for their prestige value. In 1910, for example, First Nations in the Kamloops-Okanagan Agency had 164 stallions, 5,964 geldings and mares, 1,853 foals, 72 bulls, 344 steers, 1,453 milk cows, and 2,230 young stock as well as an assortment of other livestock to a value of $332,551.[73] The status associated with horses, moreover, encouraged some leading men to breed for better racing or working potential. The horses of Terry and Narcisse Jack of the Okanagan and of Andy Manuel of Kamloops dominated racing during the 1910s and 1920s, and the Callious introduced imported Clydesdales to improve the bloodlines of workhorses in the Peace River District.[74] Despite these opportunities, the small size of reserves, the complicated arrangements with which many Interior bands had to contend in order to get water for their lands, and the difficulty of acquiring capital discouraged large-scale operations. Labour was what many Aboriginal men had to offer the emerging provincial economy, and in the Interior, this was cowboy labour.[75] Writing about the Tsilhquot'in at Anahim Lake, the Indian Agent commented in 1905 that "they are also employed by white settlers as cowboys ... being expert riders. They are excellent workers."[76] As more non-Native settlers moved to the region, ranches themselves became contact zones where Aboriginal and white cowboys worked alongside Chinese irrigators and cooks.[77] Harry Marriott described the scene at the Gang Ranch in 1919:

> The ranch always had an entirely Indian crew, with a Chinese cook and two Chinese irrigators. The Indian boys mostly belonged to the Indian village or rancherie, which was only about three quarters of a mile from the main ranch house at Canoe Creek. I got along very well with these Indian boys, they were a real capable bunch as far as ranch work goes, and most of them quiet and slow-spoken. All of them could speak English after a fashion, but their native tongue was Shuswap, which is their tribal form of Indian language ... Like every class of human beings on earth, some were far ahead of others, however, I can certainly say from my own experience that they were a pretty good bunch to lead and to get along with in a ranch operation.[78]

At all levels, then, ranching in British Columbia was a place of convergence in which the skills and values of Aboriginal people met with those of local settlers.

Ranching and rodeo offered something more than a job: they provided a release for some and a place to belong for others. Kamloops Indian Agent John Smith observed that "the cowboys' life" appealed to young men leaving residential schools. In 1913 he wrote,

> The characteristics of the young Indian after leaving school are very general. It appears that in order to make sure, as it were, that they have regained their liberty to do as they like, they take readily to horseback riding, and the excitement attendant upon the cowboys' life seems the best calculated to give full force to their pent up wild nature, hence it is usually the first job they look

for, and which is always easily got. I find, however, that this excitement gradually wears down in the course of a couple of years, and possibly if taken in hand about that time they are likely to get off the horse and settle down on the land.[79]

Relationships beyond those associated with wage labour also characterized the ranching districts of the BC Interior. Ranching scions such as Charles Houghton, Charles Vernon, and Cornelius O'Keefe of the Okanagan, John Allison of the Similkameen, Herman Bowie of Alkali Lake in the Chilcotin, and Louis Minnabarriet of the Basque Ranch near Ashcroft all took Aboriginal partners and produced mixed-heritage families, a pattern followed by lesser-known settlers and one that persisted into the twentieth century.[80] In the earliest years of ranching, building alliances with local First Nations granted access to pasturage needed for open-range ranching while ranchers waited for the provincial government to grant formal pre-emptions.[81] By the 1880s, it became fashionable for elite ranchers to put aside their Aboriginal wives and bring new white ones into the region from Victoria, Central Canada, or Great Britain. Charles Houghton, who already had a family with a North Okanagan woman, married the daughter of coal baron Robert Dunsmuir.[82] In 1877 O'Keefe married the Canadian Mary Ann McKenna, who lived for a time with his Okanagan wife, Rosie, and her two children until Rosie returned to her family at the head of Okanagan Lake.[83] William Pinchbeck, an early rancher near Williams Lake, travelled to England and married a young woman for whom he built a large new ranch house, relocating his pre-existing Aboriginal partner and their children in a little cabin nearby. This pattern of simply taking a new socially acceptable white wife while maintaining an Aboriginal family was not uncommon, though some, such as John Allison's white family, disavowed all knowledge of their father's other progeny for generations.[84] Others resisted the social pressures: Henry Bigby Shuttleworth, a son of English gentry, and Edward Tronson, proprietor of the Vernon Hotel, both remained with their indigenous wives. Doing so, however, made them the objects of ridicule of other settlers who referred to them as "squaw-men," though admittedly, as one observer put it, "rich squaw-men."[85]

In part because of such affinal ties, connections between Aboriginal, mixed-heritage, and white ranchers persisted.[86] The sons of Francis Richter and his Similkameen partner, Lucy, worked on the Richter ranch, were educated in the local school, and went on to own their own ranches as well as prize race- and rodeo horses.[87] Joe Coutlee, the son of Alexander Coutlee, a Hudson's Bay Company employee from Trois-Rivières, and a Nicola Valley woman, was the cowboss at the Douglas Lake Ranch for nearly fifty years until his death in 1944.[88] He too married into the local Shulus community. Antoine Allen, the son of an American miner and a Willamette Valley Aboriginal woman, was among those who drove cattle into the Interior in the 1860s and remained on the Gang Ranch as its cowboss.[89] Mixed-heritage children married among themselves as well as within Aboriginal communities. The eldest Tronson son married Louisa Vernon, daughter of Charles Vernon and his Okanagan partner, Catherine Kalamalka. The Twan family, descendants of steersman Charles Touin and his Tsilhquot'in partner, Mary Cletses, similarly married among other mixed-heritage people as they gained reputations as experienced cattlemen managing the Alkali Lake Ranch and successfully competing at the Williams Lake Stampede.[90] Hybridity resided at the heart of rodeo and ranching society in British Columbia throughout the nineteenth and twentieth centuries, more so than in Alberta where intermarriage between ranchers and local Aboriginal women was more limited and where Métis land grants were situated outside southern Alberta's ranching districts. Only in the Peace River country did Métis families have access to land suitable for agriculture and ranching.

For mixed-heritage men in BC, cowboying offered a way of life. In the 1890s, Indian Agents began to ponder the question of what to do with the mixed-heritage young people who either lived on their mothers' reserves or moved freely between reserves and the white world of their fathers – young people who, in the eyes of some, belonged nowhere. On the one hand, their situation was awkward because of their enduring connections with First Nations. Could they occupy land on the reserve? Could they vote in band elections? Were they entitled to a share in any grant money awarded the band?[91] Though Indian Agents tried to encourage mixed-heritage men to find homes for themselves off-reserve, their marriages to high-ranking Aboriginal women made such a suggestion untenable. Writing about Harry Shuttleworth and his brother George, the Indian Agent of the Penticton Band described the problem:

> These two men are married to the chief's daughter and the other to his niece. They have been warned to leave the Reserve but the chief encouraged them to return to it. They have been dissolute characters; Harry is reforming, but George

is likely to require severe treatment. The removal of these two men from the Reserve is a delicate matter as it must result in the dismemberment of the two principal families in the community. The chief is fond of his daughter and so is his brother; they are both old men and are loathe to part with their progeny.[92]

Louis Bordais, another mixed-heritage son of a Quesnel-area settler, found himself in the same situation, though he worked hard and was considered a good interpreter by the Indian Agent.[93] On the other hand, Indian Agents feared these mixed-heritage men precisely because their indeterminate status gave them flexibility, liminal positions in a social structure that was designed to spatially fix Aboriginal and white in distinct ways. Mixed-heritage men who bore the names of local ranchers such as Coutlee, Sterling, and Minnabarriet vexed Indian Agents precisely because they moved freely from reserve to reserve and because, as legally "white," they were able to purchase alcohol and supply it to those on reserve whose status barred them from buying it themselves.[94] For such men, rodeo was a natural extension of both the "cowboy life" of ranch labour and their "in-between" position in an official settlement world of binaries. It is not surprising, then, that when small BC towns organized rodeos, they turned to these men both as organizers and as contestants. In the Okanagan, the mixed-heritage Richter sons provided stock for the early rodeos there.[95] At Williams Lake, Antoine Boitano was among early stampede organizers. He was born on the Springhouse Ranch, which was operated by his father, and was the son of an Aboriginal woman who later lived on-reserve at Dog Creek. Other "Stampede Notables," as Williams Lake Stampede programs called them, such as Alex Paxton and Isaac Ogden, were also well-known mixed-heritage cowboys and horse-breeders.[96] Mixed-heritage men such as Minnabarriet, the Shuttleworths, the Twans, and the Richters found in rodeo a competitive sport and a social world in which they were rewarded for their skills, where their ability to move in the two worlds of settlement, white and Aboriginal, was not considered a detriment. Although rodeo announcers may have been confused regarding their identity, as when Métis rider Paddy Laframboise was announced as an "Indian" at small-town stampedes, rodeo was at least a place where settler audiences accepted that aboriginality and excellence could converge.[97]

Men tended to dominate the action at small-town rodeos in Western Canada. In Alberta, women appeared mainly at events staged by rodeo

Isaac Ogden, "stampede notable," at Lac La Hache, 1925. *Courtesy of Royal BC Museum, BC Archives, A-02377*

promoters who operated along the lines of the Wild West Show. Addison Day brought Americans Maud Livingston, Kate Canutt, "Prairie Lily" Allen, and Eloise Fox Hastings to the Medicine Hat and Lethbridge Stampedes of 1918.[98] Female riders and ropers were common in Wild West Shows, and many had made the move to rodeo by the 1920s, where they became, as Mary Lou LeCompte argues, among the first women professional athletes.[99] Across North America, nearly five hundred women rode in Wild West Shows, big-name rodeos such as those staged in Madison Square Garden during the 1920s and 1930s, and, following the circuit, at smaller rodeos throughout the transborder West. But as Clifford Westermeier suggests, they were "never particularly welcome" by the rodeo fraternity.[100]

They were certainly uncommon, especially in Alberta where women seldom competed, despite being excellent riders.[101] Those who did enter received press coverage that underscored how unexpected their participation was. In 1926 Dorothy Ion from Jenner made headlines by riding a steer in the Medicine Hat Stampede, but the reporting of her event was coupled with an account of a local doctor who tried his hand at calf roping, attempts that "caused plenty of amusement."[102] Later the same summer, at the Pincher Creek Stampede, "Toots" Davis won the ladies' horse race, but, in her "flashy red uniform," she disrupted the steer riding in the racetrack infield; the crowd gasped as the steer charged her while she walked her horse off the track.[103] When Gladys Qually started to race in small-town southern Alberta stampedes during the mid-1930s, her participation warranted special mention.[104] Though, as Nancy Young points out, there is plenty of evidence to suggest that ranch cowboys respected women's equestrian skills and accepted them as fellow workers on roundup, the rodeo arena was characterized by much more ambivalence.[105] In 1935, for example, the *Lethbridge Daily Herald* printed Herman Linder's opinion on the subject, which was that "girls should not ride in stampedes ... His chief objection is that it is too dangerous for women. 'They might so easily get hurt,' he says. He didn't think it at all likely that they could ride satisfactorily in the same manner as the cowboys with loose stirrup. The girl riders have their stirrups fastened under the belly of the horse and this, Linder claims, does not give them a chance if they are thrown."[106] Linder's views echoed the majority opinion within rodeo by the 1930s as managers gradually eliminated women's roughstock events from their programs.[107] The femininity that women contestants brought to the arena, one that combined a flair for performance with equestrian ability, was something that southern Alberta rodeos largely rejected.

Women's events were more popular in British Columbia, where they were an expected part of any stampede. The Kamloops 1930 rodeo, for example, opened with an exhibition of girls' trick roping, and the Kamloops organizing committee continued to hold girls' steer riding on at least one day of its stampede into the 1930s.[108] At stampedes across the BC Interior, women distinguished themselves in races and rodeo contests.

Ollie Curtis, steer riding, Williams Lake Stampede, 1925. *Courtesy of Royal BC Museum, BC Archives, E-01436*

Clayton Mack first laid eyes on his Ulgatcho sister-in-law Josephine Capoose at the Anahim Lake Stampede in the 1930s, where she won first place in women's bucking horse riding.[109] At Williams Lake, women became headliners, with Ollie Curtis claiming the BC All-Round Champion Cowgirl title in 1927 and the BC Girl Steer-Riding Champion title for three consecutive years.[110] She also participated in the drunken ride, the fun-filled riding exhibition event, and in the daring mountain race.[111] At Williams Lake, promoters boasted about local women's riding ability:

> The girls must not be forgotten either and we don't mind telling you that they lack neither beauty nor the ability to top off a bronk like the best of the punchers. First there's Ollie Curtis, sister to the famous Curtis boys and just as famous herself. Ollie is a home town kid, and says there's no place like the Cariboo. She isn't afraid to tackle anything and has the honour to be the first and only woman to ride in the Mountain Race. Ollie has had hard luck sometimes, but she always takes her losses with a smile and gets ready for next year. One of the most famous lady jockeys in this country is Rita Cunningham. She was the

winner of last year's famous Cowgirls Pony Express Race. The amount of first prizes connected with Rita's name show us what good horsewomanship will do. Mrs. H.H. Spencer is another Cariboo girl who takes part in the big doings. Hazel Smith, now Mrs. Exshaw, a sister to Lloyd, shows him she knows a little about horses too and another sister, Flossie Buchholz, is equally good. Mrs. T. Carolan, Mrs. K.B. Moore, and Miss Church are always ready with the goods when it comes to steer riding and are keen contestants every year for the Pony Express. Little Ollie Lock and Queenie her black mare, show us the beginning of a crack rider and believe us she'll do it.[112]

Speaking to hometown audiences, the Williams Lake Stampede clearly had an interest in appealing to the pride of the district families who were its audience. It is quite clear that in the BC Interior, much was expected of ranch children, and girls as well as boys started working hard at a young age. They were required to be courageous and skilled. Since most grew up in the saddle, it is not surprising that they were skilled riders or that they would participate in stampede events that offered prize money as well as local recognition and good fun.[113] In the process, they offered up other distinctive expressions of rodeo femininity.

That such iterations might serve the interests of boosting the region, interests that promoters keenly shared, becomes clear when we examine the stampede queen contests that began at Williams Lake in 1933. The candidate who received the most votes won the title, a system that relied on businesses to sponsor them, add raffle prizes, and collect the votes.[114] In this way, women were again deployed to signify the development potential of the region, this time by emphasizing their connections to community and by directing attention to participating businesses. Though queens did not win their crowns on the basis of their appearance, stampede promoters nonetheless referred to their physical attributes and described the winner as a "beauty queen."[115] In subsequent years, the promotional aspect of the queen competition extended to the region as a whole as contestants represented various Cariboo districts, encouraging them and the press to extol the virtues and economic potential of their home settlements. So, the 1934 contestant from Wells, a Miss M. Hughes, claimed support from the gold mines there, whereas candidates from the southern Cariboo and the Chilcotin advertised the vast ranching opportunities in their regions.[116]

It is tempting to conclude with Elizabeth Furniss that the queen contest simply transformed the place of women from "active participants to passive, demure foils to the hyper-masculinized cowboys of professional rodeo."[117] Indeed, the 1933 coverage situated women not only in feminine contrast to cowboys but as thoroughbreds "jockeying for position."[118] That year, the *Williams Lake Tribune* declared the Cariboo to be the "last best west, where men were men — and the women were glad of it."[119] As candidates worked the country dances in order to win votes, the press subsumed their competitive efforts into an appropriately feminine support for community.[120] Speaking of the backing received by Rita Hamilton, a mixed-heritage contestant from Lac La Hache who hosted a dance to sustain her run for queen, the *Tribune* wrote,

> Rita's dance at Lac La Hache last Saturday night proved to be very successful. A big crowd was looked for, but the crowd that actually turned out was beyond all expectations, there being well over a hundred people, which speaks to the little lady who, very much against her will, was forced to act as candidate for this district in the Stampede Queen Contest, and while realizing her chances were almost hopeless owing to her sparsely settled district, she has gone ahead and done all she could, not for herself, but for the good of the cause, which should greatly benefit the Stampede.[121]

However, to see the Williams Lake queen contests solely in terms of the desire to portray women as ornaments is to miss certain subtleties. Although the initial contests rejected earlier expressions of Cariboo femininity – of women as tough and able to do men's work (signifying the openness of the early settlement period) – press coverage nonetheless depicted the contestants themselves as both beautiful and capable. In 1938, when each contestant received her own write-up in the *Tribune,* the Riske Creek district candidate, Mary Jasper, was described as having "all the accomplishment that can be acquired locally. Needless to say, she is an artist in the kitchen, a lively cowgirl or teamster as well as being at ease at social functions or in the ballroom."[122] Of Margaret Kennedy of Soda Creek, *Tribune* readers were told that "like many of our popular Cariboo girls, she can turn her hand at anything conceivable, in either men's or women's duties."[123] Similarly, Joy Youngren played on the expectations of femininity when the *Tribune* asked her whether she could cook, clean house, and wash clothes: "Yes," she said, "I love washing ... [hesitation] gold and cleaning up father's sluiceboxes."[124] The place of Aboriginal women in these early contests also disrupts the view that the competitors were mere symbols of settler hegemony. When Rita Hamilton lost her 1934 bid for the title, the committee urged her to run again, and she won the following year. Although many of the official photos of Hamilton as stampede queen show her in classic 1930s ball gowns, she also made her own beaded dress that she wore when she was crowned in 1935 and again at a queens' reunion in 1978.[125] Hamilton went on to open the first beauty salon in the Cariboo.[126] Women at the Williams Lake Stampede troubled many of the binaries of rodeo culture.

The stampedes of the 1930s created other spaces for women. Whereas participation in rodeos had opened worlds of economic independence, mobility, and status to Aboriginal men, it offered few of the same benefits to Aboriginal women. At Alberta stampedes, where best-dressed contests and Indian villages were common, women's work was on display but often in ways that separated it from the women who produced it, at least to set-tler audiences. Although some might know that Katie Three Persons made the clothes for her husband, it was Tom Three Persons who was declared the "best-dressed" cowboy. Changes in Indian policy with regard to the production of more "traditional" handicrafts created new opportunities for Aboriginal women to make money and to participate in the cross-cultural interactions afforded by stampedes. In 1930 Inspector of Indian Agencies George Pragnell began encouraging Indian Agents and fair committees to set up prizes for and displays of basketwork and beadwork. The Department of Indian Affairs had long supported exhibition entries by Aboriginal people that would demonstrate the success of assimilative programs on reserves and residential schools, but now a subtle shift oc-curred. For example, though the 1930 program for "Indian displays" at the Kamloops Fair was titled "From Forest to Farm," the emphasis was increasingly on Aboriginal women's handicraft goods directed toward the tourist market. As Pragnell put it, "You will notice that I have stressed the agricultural and handicraft point of view. In other words, whatever the Indians can make a living at."[127] Pragnell even went so far as to encourage Indian Agents to highlight individual producers in competition with one another rather than promoting productivity, which had been the emphasis in the past.[128] At the Kamloops Fairs of the 1930s, agencies competed against each other, accumulating points for farm produce as well as handicrafts, but individual women set the price on the latter and "gained a little cash for their hard work." Visitors to Kamloops, moreover, praised the quality of work on display and for sale.[129] Spurred on by such successes, Pragnell encouraged Indian Agents to send people and goods all the way to the Vancouver Exhibition where, with a larger market for their merchandise, they might make even more money. In particular, he wanted Aboriginal women from the Cariboo, Chilcotin, and the central Interior to find new markets for their goods because they "depend[ed] very largely on revenue from the sale of basket work and buckskin work."[130] In the 1934-35 Department of Indian Affairs budget, $1,500 was set aside for the Kamloops Exhibition to offer prizes for exhibitors of Native handicraft. Other fall fairs in British Columbia were granted lesser sums for the same purpose.[131] By 1935 Pragnell assured Indian Affairs officials that a ready supply of women manufacturers and their goods was available to travel with departmental support.[132]

The reason for such departmental interest in women's manufacturing on-reserve was obvious. Aboriginal incomes dropped precipitously from $9.75 million in 1929 to $6.75 million in 1938, while relief costs for non-Aboriginal Canadians skyrocketed; Indian Affairs officials were, more than ever, intent on cutting payments to Aboriginal people.[133] At a conference at the University of Toronto in 1939, R.A. Hoey, director of Indian Affairs, noted that at the highest point of relief expenditures for on-reserve populations in 1937-38, the per capita rate for BC Natives was $4.33 and that this could not be reduced any further. Only basic needs were being met, with 75 percent of all relief going toward food and clothing.[134] The solution, according to the Department of Indian Affairs, was in promoting handicraft manufacture for the wholesale and retail trade, which would be run, it argued, through a central warehouse in Ottawa.[135] In 1937 the Welfare and Training Division of Indian Affairs began its efforts to promote the commercial production of handicrafts. When Indian Agents and members of various craft and guild organizations went onto reserves, they most often visited the women whose skills turned moosehide into moccasins and whose beaded work provided an emblematic "Indian artifact" for the tourist and collectors' market. Placing value on women's work and encouraging the exhibition of that work at fairs created new space for Aboriginal women at community stampedes across the Canadian West.[136]

In this process, Aboriginal femininities shifted. Beadwork had long been a feminine mode of expression for Plains and Plateau women. Women prided themselves on and were appreciated for their ability to produce beautiful clothing, some of which also carried significant ceremonial value.[137] Their own appearance and that of their husbands visually testified to their capabilities.[138] The skills associated with this work were closely guarded, transmitted through female kinship networks and, in some cases, included in the crucial training in femininity that occurred during a woman's first puberty seclusion.[139] Creating goods for display and sale at stampedes moved this form of production from the private to the public sphere, encouraged commodification, and offered women direct access to cash. Female producers skilfully navigated the process of moving ceremonial goods into the world of commodities by altering designs, shielding their most sacred symbols from public gaze while carefully assessing the changing interests of the tourist market.[140] Stampede parades provided an opportunity to display their work.[141] Beadwork became an important locus of exchange between Aboriginal women and settlers, exchange that often occurred in the Aboriginal encampments at small-town stampedes and entered negotiations for credit as well.[142] Many of the women whom Esther Goldfrank interviewed in southern Alberta during the 1930s made beadwork to sell at stampedes, which gave them their own source of cash income.[143] Engaging in these forms of production shifted the bounds of femininity, especially in Plains societies but also on the Plateau, by moving women into direct exchange relations with settlers (as opposed to producing furs or pemmican, which men exchanged, as in the fur trade), by putting women in control of the commodification process, and by opening up lines of economic independence. Moreover, as Louise Lincoln argues, beadwork represented cultural and social resilience, and it offered both an economic and communicative strategy by which First Nations engaged with settlers in the contact zone.[144]

More than anything else, small-town rodeo presented an opportunity to socialize. In even the tiniest towns, groups of men and women, sometimes even an individual rancher, erected a small corral, set aside a day, invited their neighbours, and established a rodeo.[145] Especially in isolated regions, rodeos drew excited crowds, and as one woman recalled, "your tongue would just be wore out after the day because you visited people you didn't see since the year before."[146] Sometimes rodeos were also marketing opportunities, which provided a chance to earn cash or exchange surplus goods for needed ones. New settlers brought what goods they could to sell at stampedes; one family sold milk to the Doig River and Métis people who attended the Dawson Creek Stampede in the 1930s.[147] Small-town stampedes brought together Aboriginal people and local settlers who had some things in common with each other. In the BC Interior and southern Alberta, this included the rudimentary conditions of settlement. Most people were relatively poor, settlers and First Nations alike.[148] Young people on ranches and reserves craved entertainment. Writing of the Cariboo in the 1920s, Harry Marriott captured the feeling of pent-up energy:

> There was not a great deal of social life in the Big Bar country for the young folks growing up and in the early 1920s an effort was made by the settlers and a log building was put up with the object of having some sort of Community Hall. In the hall, there were dances ... The dances were more or less always colorful affairs, lively and full of ginger and snap amongst the young folks. Many of the Big Bar boys were natural-born fiddlers, and the girls were all darn good dancers. The sight of these good-looking half-breed gals all tucked out in smart Timothy Eaton dresses with their hair all decorated up with bright colored ribbons, just looked like water in the desert to an active snoozer of a half-lonesome cowboy. Many romances were started and some finished, around the community hall.[149]

Small-town stampedes from the Chilcotin Plateau to southern Alberta constituted a chance to enjoy life, often in an environment that presented cross-cultural opportunities as well. Williams Lake Stampede promoters reported on the event they had created: "A colorful spectacle and unique in various ways, would perhaps aptly describe the twelfth annual stampede held at Williams Lake ... The Indian women, with their multicolored dresses, and the Indian cowboy with his distinctive headgear, mingling [with] the town and country residents, the scene presented was truly western in its character and such possibly as only the Cariboo could produce."[150]

But the Williams Lake Stampede was not alone in encapsulating and reproducing the contact zone. At rodeos across the northern Plains and the Plateau, heroes were created, friendships formed, and rivalries boiled to the surface as the racialized categories that stampedes performed were blurred or hardened. Aboriginal and settler men crafted a common culture, with its own language, dress code, and bodily comportment, when they rodeoed together.[151] For both Aboriginal people and settlers, rodeos became sites of cultural articulation, and in the process they discovered shared values.[152]

What stampedes did was bring Aboriginal and non-Native people together in a sport at which both excelled. Spectators, particularly children, found heroes in the men and women who rode so spectacularly well. Quesnel-area resident Jimmy Webster remembered Henry Duchamps, an Aboriginal rodeo rider whom Webster had hero-worshipped in his youth: "It doesn't matter if he was an Indian or a White. He was a great man who you could only look at in awe."[153] John K. Thompson recalled the skill of the Aboriginal riders he saw at the early Dawson Creek Stampedes, especially Alec Calahazen, who could "dismount from a skittish horse [so fast that] one moment he was in the saddle – the next moment he was standing at the horse's head, trying to quiet it."[154] Ollie Curtis remembered slipping away at night to visit the Aboriginal encampment at the early Williams Lake Stampedes to watch the people play *lahal* (a stick game) around their campfires.[155] One Mormon woman from Cardston recalled that she had little to do with her Kainai neighbours except at stampede time when they sat down together at community dinners.[156] Others were more affected by their encounters. Contemporary First Nations leaders tell stories of early settlers who had devoted little thought to Aboriginal people until they encountered them in a large encampment at a stampede or other celebration – where such an experience changed their thinking about First Nations, encouraging admiration and friendship.[157] That the possibility of such a change in feeling alarmed Kootenay Indian Agent H.M. Helmsing is clear in his description of the 1922 celebration at Windermere: "White men of supposed good standing and white women of similar class were to be seen arm in arm with Indians of the opposite sexes at the dance in the evening and dancing was continued until away late in the morning so you can picture for yourself the effect these conditions have on the natives." He went on to decry "the extent of the freedom granted the Indians putting them on the level of white men among white men."[158] Rodeos contributed to producing alternative affective relationships that had the potential, contemporaries feared, to undo the government's assimilative agenda.

They also enabled old friendships to be renewed. As Lorene Harris Rome, whose family farmed south of Quesnel, recalled, "the Twans, who are a Native family, mingled with the Websters [who were non-Native] quite a lot. If you ever got three or four Twans and Websters laughing you weren't soon to forget it. Both of these families had similar laughs: loud and happy. They were people who liked fun times, horses and stampedes."[159] Indeed, the Webster spread on the west side of the Fraser River was a stopping place for those going to the Quesnel Stampede. As Jimmy Webster recalled in 1998, "Now when the Stampede was on in Quesnel, the road in front of the ranch was full of wagon after wagon taking Chilcotins up to the races. Those Chilcotins, they were great riders and great sportsmen. They'd stop in at the house to get this and get that and shoe their horses, because they knew we had tons of shoes lying around. Dad would give them stuff and sometimes he would trade with them. This happened every year."[160]

Just as Aboriginal riders travelled to the rodeos in settlements, so too did settler cowboys bring their best horses to reserve rodeos where they competed, got into fights with the men, and flirted with the women.[161] In some cases, more organized reunions were attempted at stampedes, as when Benny Franklin, an early settler in the Chilcotin, put on a massive barbecue for the entire Indian encampment at the Williams Lake Stampede to honour his long-standing friendships with many Tsilhquot'in and Dakelh families. In an event that was literally larger than life, Franklin cooked a whole steer in a barbecue pit dug ten feet long, eight feet wide, and three feet deep. Franklin's friend Sam Marwick made him a colossal carving knife by attaching a scythe to a long stick. When the beef was ready, Franklin climbed atop a rock and, brandishing his gigantic weapon, his hair flying, and his weather-beaten face beaming, called his friends to come and get it.[162]

Kainai cowboys, from Tom Three Persons in the 1910s and 1920s to Fred Gladstone in the 1930s, forged enduring relationships with settler cowboys. Three Persons' friendships ensured that he always had work at southern Alberta stampedes.[163] Fred Gladstone had many friends among the early professional cowboys on both sides of the border and viewed his rodeo career, which began in the 1930s, as an essential part of his education.[164] Friendships he made there lasted a lifetime and enabled him to circumvent some of the strictures imposed on reserve residents. For example, one friend co-signed a loan, a process made necessary by the fact that reserve residents could not use reserve land as collateral. At rodeos throughout the northern Plains, anthropologists observed the fellowship between settler and Aboriginal cowboys, though, like some elders, they worried that it exposed Aboriginal cowboys to a life of cheap motels, poolrooms, and beer parlours.[165] More recent anthropological work, however, suggests that new hybrid cultural forms, such as the powwow, arose from combining elements of traditional dancing with structures of the stampede.[166] Aspects of traditional culture such as gambling and horse racing were reinforced by rodeos, and the enthusiasm that settlers shared with First Nations for these events strengthened the events' presence in Aboriginal cultures.[167] As in many sporting cultures, Philip Deloria suggests, shared values reinforced both Aboriginal and settler cultures.[168]

It is more difficult to grasp what being among friends at a stampede must have felt like. Sentiment by its very nature can be transitory. It is tempting to theorize that sentiments that stray from the scripts of colonization or other forms of dominance are especially ephemeral precisely because they are so transgressive. And yet, they remain in the archival record. Photographs, reminiscences, fictionalized autobiographies, and oral histories all give voice to the feelings associated with rodeo. Among the most compelling evidence, because of their visual acuity, are the photographs of Chow Dong Hoy, a Chinese photographer who lived and worked in the BC central Interior from 1905 to his death in 1973. Quesnel's first professional photographer, Hoy took more than fifteen hundred portraits during the course of his career – of Aboriginal people, mainly Tsilhquot'in and Dakelh, Chinese friends, family, and neighbours, and white folks too. By documenting Aboriginal people and Chinese and white settlers as they wished to be represented, Hoy's work decentres the province's history of photography from the dominant images employed by boosters and ethnographers. He was, quite literally, taking pictures of the people he knew and who knew him.[169]

Hoy's remarkable photographs intersect with the world of rodeo because his services were most in demand during the annual Quesnel Dominion Day Stampede. This drew Tsilhquot'in, Dakelh, mixed-heritage, and non-Native ranch families to town for a few days of celebrating, shopping, competing, and visiting. The event facilitated portraiture because people came to town in their finest cowboy clothes. In the more formal portraits, such as the one of Redstone chief William Charleyboy and his wife, Elaine, the Tsilhquot'in couple look calmly at the camera, their faces relaxed. William's eyes smile as he sits comfortably, wearing a suit jacket, vest, tie, and white shirt, with woolly chaps covering his trousers. Elaine Charleyboy

Chief William and Elaine Charleyboy, Redstone, c. 1915 (photo by Chow Dong Hoy). *C.D. Hoy Collection, Barkerville Historic Town Archives, P1583*

is stately in her beautifully embroidered blouse, holding one perfect red apple in her lap. In other photos, Hoy captured the carnival feel of stampede days, as in the shot of a young Henry Rocky of Alexandria, who poses smiling with a bottle of whiskey in his beaded-gauntlet-covered hands, or in the images of an unnamed white woman who stands laughing with a pistol slung on a sash around her waist, her dress and gauntlets fringed in buckskin. Hoy also portrayed something of the contact zone that was inherent in events such as the Quesnel Stampede. Camaraderie pervades the photo of a group of cowboys that includes Quesnel's blacksmith, John Lazzarin, and his Chinese and Aboriginal contemporaries Jerry (or Harry) Boyd, Captain Marc Mack, Chief Michel, Moffat Harris, and Morris Molize, who grin broadly at the camera, their gauntlet-bedecked hands placed jauntily on their hips. Just as their clothing mingled Aboriginal with Western styles, so too did the white, Chinese, and Aboriginal people who gathered at the Quesnel Dominion Day Stampede offer images of mutual enjoyment, playful pleasure, friendship, and more intimate relations.

Along with friendships, rivalries too could be kindled at stampedes. Sometimes the racialized and gendered segmentation placed contestants in uncomfortable or untenable circumstances. Syilx writer Mourning Dove's (Christine Quintasket) semi-autobiographical novel *Cogewea, the Half-Blood* depicted the promise and the perils of a day at the stampede. Like many stampede-goers of the era, its protagonist, Cogewea, is of mixed heritage. The racially segregated nature of many early twentieth-century rodeos poses difficulties for the young girl, as the white competitors in the "Ladies Race" angrily ask, "Why is this *squaw* permitted to ride? This is a *ladies* race," and the Ktunaxa and Pend d'Oreille women who ride against her in the squaw race similarly subject her to "glances of hatred." Cogewea wins both races, but, refused her prize money for the ladies' race and rejecting her winnings for the squaw race, she denounces both prizes as "tainted money." The novel reveals the tensions associated with the "in-between" position of many mixed-heritage people in the transborder West, but it also shows the joys of the stampede, for Cogewea's romance with Jim, the other mixed-heritage character in the story, begins there. Thus, it depicts sensations that, as a mixed-heritage woman of the Plateau, the author undoubtedly experienced and witnessed herself.[170]

As was the case for Cogewea, rodeos were the setting for fledgling romances. With mixed nostalgia and disdain, Treaty 7 elders recalled the relationships that formed at southern Alberta rodeos. For some, their own

Young man standing is Henry Rocky, c. 1915 (photo by Chow Dong Hoy). *C.D. Hoy Collection, Barkerville Historic Town Archives, P1651*

White woman (possibly Jessie Foster) with a gun, c. 1915 (photo by Chow Dong Hoy). *C.D. Hoy Collection, Barkerville Historic Town Archives, P1944*

Cowboys at the Quesnel Dominion Day Stampede. *Left to right:* Jerry (or Harry)
Boyd (Kluskus), Captain Marc Mack (Nazko), John Lazzarin, Chief Michel (Nazko),
unknown Chinese man, Moffat Harris (Nazko), Chief Morris Molize (Kluskus).
Quesnel, c. 1915 (photo by Chow Dong Hoy). *C.D. Hoy Collection, Barkerville Historic
Town Archives, P1887*

courtships began there.[171] For others, the local stampede was the site of
an ill-chosen liaison. One woman recalled hearing of a girl who "went
into the bushes" with some boys at the Cardston Jubilee Stampede and
lost all chances of making an appropriate marriage. Others remembered
that handsome Kainai and Pikuni cowboys "ran around with white girls"
at the stampede.[172] But communities in southern Alberta generally disapproved of mixed relationships. In British Columbia, relationships formed
at stampedes were more enduring. Despite the fact that Hilary Place's
grandmother would not allow anyone with Aboriginal blood into her
home, his mother eagerly reported on the beauty of Rita Hamilton, the
1935 Williams Lake Stampede queen. Attending the queen's ball later
that evening, Place first laid eyes on Hamilton, whose "big dark eyes [were]
flashing as she smiled ... Her gorgeous white dress set off her dark skin
and her beautiful smile." When Place's mother asked him what he thought
of the stampede queen, he said that she was beautiful and that someday

she would be his wife. Four years later, at his twenty-first birthday party, Place met Hamilton again, and this time they began a relationship. They were married on the Easter weekend of 1942. By his own account, Place had a handful of musical instruments and slightly less than fifty dollars to his name. By contrast, partly due to her time as stampede queen, Hamilton owned her own business, a beauty parlour, and her own home, with her business partner, Vi Zirnhelt. Years later, Hilary and Rita Place would provide guidance to another young Aboriginal woman who became the Williams Lake Stampede queen, Joan Palmantier.[173] Palmantier's father, Leonard, had helped found the Williams Lake Stampede. He came to the Cariboo in 1914 with his wife, Hazel, an accomplished rodeo cowgirl, and together they worked the ranches in the area. But this marriage did not last, and in 1935, Palmantier married Josephine Gambush from the Tsilhquot'in First Nation, and they took up land near Riske Creek. As the Places and the Palmantiers indicate, rodeos did not simply re-enact the relations of the contact zone – they created them as well.

Early twentieth-century stampedes offered particular identities, affinities, and intimacies to settlers and Aboriginal people in the transborder West. Troubled by and constrained within the racially segmenting discourses of settlement, shaped by local circumstances that either permitted or prohibited relationships, rodeos nonetheless remained a contact zone that contributed to changing the character of its participants. New Aboriginal and settler masculinities emerged, both rough and respectable. Small towns and reserves cheered on the hometown kid, in some cases either boy or girl. Women, demonstrating both settler opportunities and Aboriginal adaptations to change, participated as well, crafting their own versions of femininity particular to the Canadian West. For some, it was a halcyon period in which small-town rodeos, largely unaffected by the professionalization that was to come, and at least partly separated from the larger social, economic, and political contexts of settler-Aboriginal relations, presented opportunities to earn money, socialize, fall in love, and build self-esteem. Not everyone included here would find places in the rodeos of subsequent years – women and some Aboriginal men in particular would be excluded. Not all felt safe, even in this earlier period, and not all were safe: rodeos could be places where rivalries became vicious, where drinking and violence were not unknown. Whether salubrious or not, they were productive spaces of encounter for individuals as well as communities. This was perhaps their most intriguing contribution to the world of the twentieth-century transborder West.

The nature of that contribution changed continually as the century wore on. Just as Leo Watrin's death in 1930 had made it evident to all that local rodeo cowboys had become celebrities, another death, in 1949, marked a transitional moment in the history of rodeo. In April of that year, after being badly kicked by a young horse he was trying to corral, Tom Three Persons died of his injuries at Holy Cross Hospital in Calgary. He was sixty-three. In the course of his life, he had accomplished a great deal. He was a wealthy rancher with a large herd of Hereford cattle, several fine racehorses of his own breeding, and holdings worth $100,000 at the time of his death. He was a residential school graduate and a member of the All Brave Dogs Society. Settlers called him "progressive," and the *Lethbridge Daily Herald* commented that he was "well-liked by all." He had done a lot of things and been a lot of things. He was, in the words of George Gooderham, "the most colourful, best-known Blood Indian of his time."[174] But his principal identity was inextricably linked to rodeo. Three Persons never stopped being the champion bronc-rider of the 1912 Calgary Stampede. His identity as rodeo cowboy opened doors for him and allowed him to be, in some respects, the epitome of Kainai masculinity – generous, wealthy, handsome, skilled. In other respects, his notoriety enabled him to get away with brutal and selfish behaviour. He made it possible for other Aboriginal cowboys to enter the sport and acted as an object lesson of the pitfalls of its lifestyle. In keeping with the norms of Kainai masculinity, he mentored younger cowboys whose talent he recognized. In this, Kainai values converged with those of rodeo more broadly. He staged rodeos on reserves to offer Aboriginal competitors a chance to ride without fear of prejudice. Like many other rodeo cowboys of the day, Three Persons crafted new identities in conjunction with rodeo itself. Although he was very much a part of the first generation of local cowboys, he did not move with them as they transformed rodeo from a performance to a sport. He did not join the cowboy associations that formed in the 1930s and 1940s. He remained a local hero. Rodeo and Three Persons gave each other notoriety, skills, identities, and relationships, which he would pass on to subsequent Aboriginal cowboys who would take their place in an expanding world of rodeo.

3

A Sport, Not a Carnival Act
Transforming Rodeo from Performance to Sport

*Sports are an alternative to and, simultaneously, a reflection
of the modern age. They have their roots in the dark soil of our
instinctive lives, but the form they take is that dictated by modern
society ... They are the rationalization of the Romantic.*
— *Allen Guttmann*, From Ritual to Record

In many ways, Pete Knight typified the transborder world of rodeo in the
1920s and 1930s. Born in Philadelphia in 1903, Knight was the youngest
of six children who travelled west with their parents to farm in Oklahoma.
Drawn north by the Canadian government's promotion of southern
Alberta as the "last best west," the Knights rented ranchland on the Deep
Dale Ranch, near Crossfield, Alberta. Deep Dale's manager, Dave Togstead,
hosted weekly rodeos on the property, and there Knight learned to ride
bucking horses. He was fifteen when he first entered the Crossfield Rodeo,
coming in second. For the next four years, he made his name on the
southern Alberta circuit, competing in small-town rodeos, earning a
reputation as a fine rider. In 1924 he competed in the Calgary Stampede,
coming in second to another great southern Alberta cowboy, Pete
Legrandeur of Pincher Creek. That same year, Knight contracted with
the Alberta Stampede Company to tour North America. Travelling across
the continent and performing at big-city rodeos, the Alberta Stampede
Company offered Knight steady employment, paying mount money for
each animal he rode. He also continued to compete in Alberta rodeos,
including the Calgary Stampede where, in 1927, he won both the North
American open and Canadian bucking championships. On the road again,
he rode at the Chicago World's Fair in 1933, and in 1934 he contracted
with Tex Austin to ride in Austin's ill-fated attempt to bring rodeo to
English audiences, and he went to Melbourne, Australia, to ride in the
Stewart McCall pageant. Like other elite rodeo cowboys of his era, Knight

Pete Knight riding at Black Diamond, 1924. *Glenbow Museum Archives, NA-462-18*

participated in ventures such as Austin's extravaganza that were more like Wild West Shows than competitive rodeos, but he was dedicated to improving the sport and the lot of competitors. He protested poor judging at the Calgary Stampede. He joined with other cowboys when, in 1936, they banded together to form their first professional association, the Cowboys' Turtle Association. Born an American, Knight retained Crossfield, Alberta, as his home throughout his years on the road. Western Canadians claimed him as their own. Canadian country music legend Wilf Carter concluded his 1934 hit "Pete Knight: The King of the Cowboys" with the words

Canada's proud of her cowboy, who has won great honor and fame,
Let's take off our hats to the "King" of them all,
Pete Knight, from the Alberta plain.

But the transborder world of rodeo was really Knight's domain, and it was here that he earned the title "the Cowboy King." Rodeo certainly changed Pete Knight's life, and he, along with other cowboys, changed rodeo.[1]

The transformational potential of rodeo was not confined to the communities it celebrated, the identities it formed, or the relationships it built: rodeo was itself altered as its popularity grew in the early decades of the twentieth century. Originally included in community events for exhibition only, by the end of the Second World War, it was becoming a sport. In that process and with a sense of some irony, it took on the accoutrements of modernity even as its contestants continued to signify primitivism. The process of turning performance or play into sport has intrigued cultural theorists, and for the most part, it is seen as attendant to modernity. According to Allen Guttmann, play becomes sport when it acquires several distinctive characteristics, including equality of opportunity, rational organization, role specialization, rule making and record keeping, quantification, and bureaucratic organization.[2] Scholarship in the history of sport has recognized the contested and uneven nature of this process – that which moved rodeo from performance to sport was no exception.[3] Promoters and contestants shared a commitment to rationalization, bureaucratization, rule making, and quantification. However, they differed quite fundamentally on other matters: the appointment of judges, how cowboys should be paid, and indeed, whether cowboys were employees of rodeo promoters or independent athletes deserving enough prize money to constitute a living wage. On these issues, cowboys ultimately won the day, indicating as Colin Howell has suggested that the organization of sport emerged, at least in some cases, in conversation between organizers and competitors.[4] The combined efforts of promoters and cowboys toward professionalization, moreover, had an impact on rodeo as a contact zone, as we will see in subsequent chapters. The seeds for this change, however, were sown in the 1930s and 1940s as increasing numbers of cowboys left other employment and took to the road to follow the rodeo circuit. Aboriginal cowboys, with less access to capital and, in Alberta particularly, constrained at times by the control of Indian Agents over mobility, were not among those who banded together to form rodeo cowboy organizations. Women were present, but the limiting views of femininity held by promoters and cowboys cast their participation as performance rather than as competition. As rodeo became increasingly rationalized, it diminished the number of acceptable events, and those associated with female competitors were the first to go. When rodeos re-emerged in the Canadian West from the limitations imposed by the Second World War, they were, in many cases, profoundly different contests, bearing within them different gendered and racialized social relations.

Rodeo became a popular sport in small towns across the West in the 1920s and 1930s. Transborder circuits radiated out from local ones, and the most competitive cowboys travelled thousands of miles, from southern Alberta and British Columbia to California in the spring, home to the northern Plains and the Plateau in the summer months, and then east to the big shows in New York and Boston during the fall. As more and more rodeos dotted the landscape of the northern Plains and the Plateau, cowboys, both Aboriginal and settler, started scheduling their time so as to compete in as many as possible. When Kamloops put on a fine rodeo in 1934, one rider declared that if it became an annual event, he would return each year.[5] The following year, Alberta cowboys Eddie Watrin and Casey Patterson included Kamloops in their schedule, and American cowboys incorporated it into their circuit between the Pendleton Roundup and the Omak Stampede.[6] Herman Linder's itinerary included Fort Macleod, Lethbridge, Medicine Hat, Raymond, High River, Browning (Montana), Calgary, Cheyenne (Wyoming), and Great Falls and Butte, Montana.[7] In the 1920s and 1930s, Harry Shuttleworth, the mixed-heritage cowboy from Oliver, BC, went to southern Alberta to ride at Lethbridge and Cardston, whereas others such as Syilx cowboys Johnny Robins and Jimmy Baptiste went south of the border to Omak.[8] Aboriginal people incorporated stampedes into their own ceremonial and economic cycles, linking rodeos to treaty days and sun dances as well as to waged labour off-reserve and the pattern of farming life on-reserve. Anthropologist Lucien Hanks found that annual sun dance gatherings drew the Kainai off-reserve, and the succession of stampedes kept them away for weeks afterward. Syilx cowboys moved south of the border to rodeo between haying and fruit picking.[9] Settler cowboys, such as Herman Linder, found that they could fit a number of rodeos into their schedule by following the circuit when they were not needed at home on their ranches. From the perspective of organizing committees, being listed on the circuit guaranteed financial success, as visiting cowboys swelled revenues from entry fees and helped boost gate receipts while spending money in town for food and lodging.

So, the first move toward rationalization in rodeo involved instigating a schedule. The growth of rodeo in the 1920s revealed the need for cooperation. Every town wanted its sports day to fall on one of the big summer holidays: Victoria Day or Dominion Day or Labour Day. But a committee that picked a too popular day for its rodeo could find its audiences, and hence its gate receipts, diminished by competition. Cardston's stampede suffered during the late 1920s in just this way.[10] The Alberta government tried to solve the problem by linking provincial funding to a fair committee's willingness to cooperate with others in setting its date; this helped enforce the schedule and kept rivalry for audiences and exhibitors to a minimum among Alberta's fairs.[11] In 1924 the Canadian Cowboy Contest Managers' Association formed with the intent of bettering the sport, diminishing the competition between rodeos, developing a uniform set of rules, and doing "everything in [its] power to place cowboy sport upon the same basis as every other recognized competitive sport in Canada."[12] Individual rodeo committees could become members for ten dollars. By the mid-1930s, the Alberta Stampede Managers Association advertised the dates of the twenty-five stampedes planned for the season, which began at Hussar on 24 May and ended in Kamloops on 12 September.[13] The establishment of such organizations began the bureaucratization process within rodeo.

The organizations also began creating regulations. Over the course of the 1920s, southern Alberta stampedes developed detailed and complex rules for each event, which they communicated to contestants through rule books and scoresheets. Spectators learned the rules through condensed versions published in their rodeo programs. In 1927 the ten-second rule was applied, for the first time, to bucking events at the Calgary Stampede. Under it, a ride was considered successful if the contestant stayed on for ten seconds rather than, as was previously the case, riding a horse to a standstill. This moved events along much more quickly and added the science of precision timekeeping to quell the chaos of the roughstock events. Stampede programs explained the rules regarding reining and spurring, trying to show how judges determined scores for bucking events. Calf roping, wild cow milking, and steer wrestling (formerly called bull

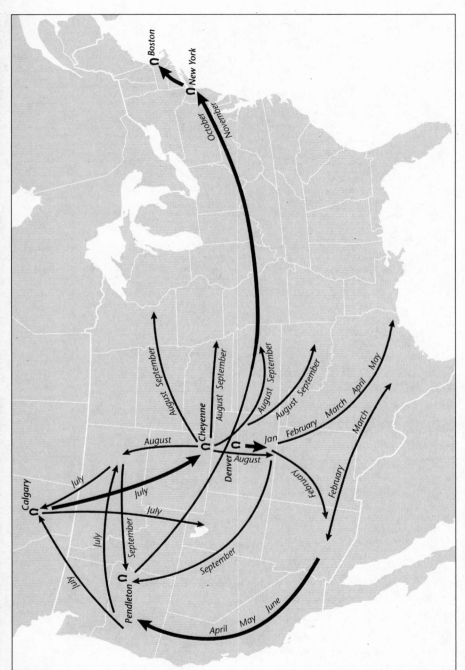

MAP 4 The rodeo circuits that emerged in the 1920s and 1930s.

**CANADIAN COWBOY CONTEST
MANAGERS' ASSOCIATION**

JUDGE'S CHART

Bucker with Saddle

Date _April 30 1930_

26　Name of Rider _Pete Knight_

Number of Horse _61_

Chute Number _7_　Saddled on Infield

RIDER	Per cent.	ANIMAL	Per cent.
Perfect	100	Perfect	100
Excellent	95 ✗	Excellent	95
Very Good	90	Very Good	90
Good	85	Good	85
Fair	80	Fair	80 ✗
Poor	75	Poor	75
Thrown		Animal Fell	

Did not Scratch

Pulled Leather _R Ride_

Lost Stirrup

Rode on Spur

Changed Hands on Rein

Position of Judge—

　　Left Side　　Right Side　　Rear ✗

Name of Judge _Chas Brownfield_

GENERAL REMARKS

Scoresheet used by judges at rodeos sanctioned by the
Canadian Cowboy Contest Managers' Association, 1930.
Stockmen's Library, Cochrane, Alberta

dogging) also became subject to the timer's stopwatch and barrier judges
who called for loss of points or disqualification if the horse and rider left
the gate ahead of time. For each event, rules developed, times were kept,
scoresheets filled in, points accumulated, records tallied. Guy Weadick
initiated many of these changes at the Calgary Stampede, but they soon
spread until, by the 1930s, they were the norm.[14] Rodeo organizers began
attempting to regulate the behaviour of contestants as well. The 1937
program of the Medicine Hat Stampede and Race Meet informed spectators that "all events shall be subject to the Rules and Regulations of the

Canadian Stampede Association. The Stampede Manager will be in full charge of all events, draws and matters pertaining to same. The Management reserves the right to withdraw any contestant's name and entry for any of the following reasons: Rowdyism, Abusing Stock, Attempting to take unfair advantage of rules, Quarrelling with judges or officials, being under the influence of liquor or any unbecoming conduct whatsoever."[15] On the local level, greater standardization meant increased rule making, a move away from rodeo as a rough contest among cowboys and toward its establishment as a respectable sport.

In 1929 the biggest organization of rodeo management, the Rodeo Association of America (RAA), was established "in order to insure harmony among [the rodeos] and to perpetuate traditions connected with the livestock industry and the cowboy sports incident thereto; to standardize the same and adopt rules looking forward towards the holding of contests upon a uniform basis; to minimize so far as practicable conflict of dates of contests; and to place such sports so nearly as may be possible on a par with amateur athletic events."[16] The RAA regularized certain aspects of rodeo. It demanded that committees post their prizes in advance of the competition along with the entry fees for each event. Aiming for standardization, it established a list of recognized events that included bronc riding (with saddle), bull or steer riding, calf roping, steer roping, steer decorating, steer wrestling, team roping, and wild cow milking. To be an RAA contest, rodeos had to stage at least four of these. Not included in this list were the various performance or exhibition events commonly offered by committees, such as Roman racing, relay races, trick roping, and trick riding, in which women often participated. The RAA also instituted a uniform points system that awarded a point to every dollar earned in a recognized event excepting money from entry fees that was added to prize money. The cowboy who held the most points at the end of the year was named "champion," a measure that was intended to discourage the propensity of every community rodeo to declare that its winners were "world champions."[17]

The RAA and the Canadian Cowboy Contest Managers' Association encouraged rodeo promoters to rationalize and standardize their programs and offered them a broader organizational structure in which to do this. By the 1930s, stampedes at Cardston, Raymond, and Medicine Hat placed much greater emphasis on the RAA-approved contests such as bareback and bucking horse riding, moving the "trick and fancy riding" to later in the day or the evening or eventually eliminating them entirely.[18] Cowboys in southern Alberta began to earn RAA points, and local papers reported on their standings. Some committees, such as the one at Lethbridge, instituted their own parallel points system for cowboys riding on more local circuits. In so doing, they advertised the new rationalized system by which championships were awarded.[19] Still, the changes were not evenly introduced. The 1937 Cardston Stampede, organized by Herman Linder, interspersed its afternoon rodeo program with band performances, horse races, and trick roping.[20]

The question of whether cowboys were competitive athletes or salaried performers haunted the transition of rodeo from a show to a sport. For the most part, cowboys argued that, as athletes, they deserved to be judged competently by predictable standards and awarded prize money if they won. Meanwhile, promoters and organizing committees often viewed cowboys as their employees whose job was to provide a crowd-pleasing show. These issues became particularly apparent on the emerging rodeo circuit in the transborder West. Here the limits of the putative equality of opportunity, the advertised "open-to-all" nature of small-town rodeos, could be found. Cowboys who travelled beyond their hometowns where they were known and respected often encountered problems with judging. Judges were often businessmen, politicians, or visiting dignitaries, and they favoured local riders, since doing so tended to please the paying hometown audience.[21] Writing about the Williams Lake Stampede in a 1931 letter to Guy Weadick, Harry Shuttleworth commented that "the cowboys and myself who live in southern BC would like to know if the Stampede held at Williams Lake BC is a member of the Canadian Cowboy Contest Managers Association because if it is there certainly needs to be some changes made. They don't abide by the rules at all and they won't even send us the dates of their show. Their one idea seems to be to give their local riders all the prize money whether they win it or not. So if you will enlighten us any on this show we will sure be pleased."[22]

Nationality and racialization played a role, to be sure. Canadians Paddy Laframboise and Harry Shuttleworth attracted ire at a Twist, Washington, rodeo because the local crowd thought they had no business competing, let alone winning prizes there.[23] Riding in Cheyenne, Wyoming, Herman Linder knew that he had no chance of winning against better-known American cowboys and that they knew it too. After Arizonan Earl Thode won the saddle bronc competition at the Cheyenne Rodeo, he remarked

The events listed in this Raymond Stampede program from 1942 are fully rationalized. *Stockmen's Library, Cochrane, Alberta, box 2743*

to Linder, "See this saddle I won. Look at all the fancy silver on it ... If they had known you as well as they know me, you would've probably had it."[24] Tom Three Persons encountered a judge in Montana who offered him money to be bucked off so that local white riders could win. Later, Three Persons discouraged the Kainai men he trained from entering the rough-stock events in order to avoid such discrimination.[25] Riding the rodeo circuit brought these troubles to the surface.

Charges of corrupt judging, of course, damaged rodeo's reputation as, to use Weadick's 1930s slogan, "a square deal to all, no color, residence or nationality barred. It's open to the world, come and get it." Thus, "desirous of procuring the most competent officials possible from the ranchers of the province," some committees and promoters began to publicize their judges' names in advance, hoping to reassure visiting cowboys that they would be assessed by experienced men who would be fair.[26] Because rodeos attracted both Aboriginal and settler cowboys, off-reserve stampedes appointed Aboriginal people as judges, and on-reserve rodeos found local settlers to do the job. Thus, Chief Peter Squiness of Anahim Lake and the Haida leader Reverend Peter Kelly judged at the Stuie Stampede in 1932, and the Kainai invited rancher Jimmy McNab to act as tie judge as well as the mayors of Lethbridge, Cardston, Pincher Creek, and Fort Macleod to be timers at their stampede in 1938.[27] Nevertheless, very public protests over judging raised awareness. In 1928 the legendarily even-tempered and gentlemanly Pete Knight took a Calgary Stampede judge by the collar and dragged him halfway out of the judging booth before friends broke up the fight. Later that evening, Knight presented all three of the judges with pairs of drugstore spectacles, in a public shaming that won him a reprimand from the stampede board but nonetheless publicized cowboy complaints about the quality of judging, even at Canada's largest rodeo.[28] The process of choosing judges would remain a point of conflict between contestants and promoters for the remainder of the 1930s, although some organizations did attempt to reach agreement with local cowboys. For example, the Canadian Stampede Managers' Association instituted a system in which the competitors them-selves selected one of three judges at the opening of a rodeo. Nonetheless, stampede managers retained the right to choose all other officials and to impose their own choice should the cowboys fail to reach consensus.[29]

Committees and contestants also differed regarding how much the lat-ter should be paid. As cowboys took to the road, some left jobs and working ranches. In the 1930s, when unemployment soared and farms and ranches across the West faced bankruptcy and foreclosure, rodeo no doubt provided young men with otherwise unattainable incomes. And certainly, some cowboys riding these circuits made money. *Time* magazine calculated that in 1935 a rodeo cowboy could make as much as $2,000 a year competing.[30] Alberta cowboy Herman Linder reported that he earned a gross income of between $5,000 and $8,000 during the 1930s.[31] Pete Knight reputedly made $7,000 a year in the early 1930s, when the average managerial income was closer to $1,500. For the top-ranked cowboys of the 1930s, which included Canadians Pete Knight, Herman Linder, Harry Knight, and Lee Ferris the "Canada Kid," life on the road could be handled in style. Pete Knight and his wife, Babe, stayed in the best hotels, drove the latest automobiles, and wore the finest clothes. Successful cowboys like Knight sometimes bankrolled those who were moving up the ranks, helping them buy food, giving them lifts from rodeo to rodeo, and even, in one case, renting a residence in Arkansas to house some injured cowboys while they recuperated from the season's injuries.[32] Travelling the circuit forced cowboys to come to grips with the economics of rodeo, and it provided them with a sense of community upon which collective action could be built.[33]

The pay structures of rodeos varied widely. By the 1920s and 1930s, most small-town rodeos operated as competitions rather than as contracted performances. As we have seen, the days in which promoters, such as Addison Day, came to town with a troupe of cowboys and cowgirls ready to ride had largely ended. Small-town committees found it much more profitable to charge contestants relatively small entry fees for events and then pay out prizes that, depending on the size of the rodeo, might range from sacks of flour to beautifully crafted cowboy hats or other donated merchandise to cash prizes from five to fifty dollars. The profits came from gate receipts, but ensuring a good entry from cowboys was also important. Keeping prizes low enhanced profits and ensured that the show would go on another year. Though this trend was dominant among small-town rodeos, hybrid arrangements persisted. Some small-town rodeos continued to pay mount money: this meant that cowboys paid no entry fees and won no prize money but were simply remunerated for riding an animal.[34] The most complicated and least transparent pay structures, however, were used at the large shows that dominated the end of the circuit year and were held in big cities in Central Canada and on the eastern seaboard of the United States. These shows attracted massive audiences and were advertised as family entertainment; hence, they provided superb ground upon which cowboys could launch collective action to engage the wider public in their attempts to improve their lot.

Cowboys and rodeo were extremely popular during the 1930s. Increasingly, cowboys on both sides of the border represented not only values associated with the "Old West," such as determination, physical toughness, and independence, but also new expressions of masculinity that featured a willingness to cooperate, to stand up for community against powerful outside forces such as banks, and to include women and even children in their vision of a modernizing West.[35] In part, this had to do with the place of film and radio in producing new images of the cowboy and the fact that women and children were the principal audiences of both mediums. Gene Autry once described himself as a "New Deal Cowboy," likening his goals to those of Franklin Delano Roosevelt, saying that he "never hesitated to tackle many of the same problems: the dust bowl, unemployment, or the harnessing of power. This may have contributed to my popularity with 1930s audiences."[36] At the same time, Canadians eagerly consumed cowboy stories from their own West. During the 1930s, BC filmmaker, homesteader, and entertainer Arthur D. Kean told his stories of the new Canadian West on his Canadian Broadcasting Corporation (CBC) show *Sails and Saddles,* and in a *Toronto Star Weekly* column. Kean was inundated with letters from young people and their parents who eagerly awaited his stories about cowboys, horses, and the "wilds" of British Columbia and Alberta. Sixteen-year-old Tom Dunsmore of Leaside, Ontario, anxiously asked Kean about the type of rope needed for a good lasso, concerned that the curtain rope his father had bought for him was not the right sort. A Quebec father asked Kean for guidance in making leather chaps for his daughter, who had gone "completely loco on Cowboy clothing, action and speech." He urged Kean to respond quickly because he "would have no rest at all until these chaps make their appearance."[37] In 1937 Kean spoke at the Toronto Children's Aid Society annual foster father and son banquet. Cowboy stories were so popular that the training school for boys at Bowmanville, Ontario, asked Kean to make an appearance there, saying, "They are still talking about the talk you gave them at Camp last Summer. The romance and the spirit of adventure which prevails in your stories has a strong appeal to our youngsters and I might add to the members of our staff too."[38] In Canada and the United States, cowboys and cowboy culture were enormously popular.

Promoters and cowboys both capitalized on this trend. Rodeos across the continent attracted large audiences, and so a transborder circuit developed that included Toronto, Montreal, New York, and Boston. With the help of the RAA, event organizers ensured that their dates did not conflict with each other, and the RAA-initiated points system meant that cowboys who aspired to championships had a reason to compete in rodeos where the dollars they won translated into points earned.[39] Fans on both sides of the border followed their local cowboys as they made names for themselves in Salinas, Chicago, Detroit, and New York.[40] These big rodeos paid their riders in a complicated and not always transparent manner. Some promoters paid travel costs and per diem rates for selected contestants. For example, Enochson's rodeo in Philadelphia paid Paddy Ryan, winner of the Roosevelt Trophy at the Pendleton Roundup, $100 a day plus expenses to compete in its two-day event, and Colonel John Kilpatrick, president of Madison Square Garden in New York, contracted with Herman Linder to ride the circuit in 1939.[41] Other promoters advertised prize money but then refused to pay. In June 1932, when a Toronto-area stampede committee paid out prizes only to winning cowboys from south of the border, the Canadian cowboys absconded with sixty-five broncs, holding them until the committee paid up, and three others went to civil court.[42] Some promoters developed a two-tiered pay structure, in which cowboys competed for prize money and cowgirls were hired as salaried performers. Whereas the latter was almost always certain to be paid, the former had to bear the expenses of extended travel without any guarantee of being remunerated.

Soon, collective action among cowboys was in the air. In January 1932, riders participating in the National Western Rodeo in Denver discussed forming a "protective association of cowboys designed to raise the standards of rodeo personnel all over the country and place rodeo performance on an equal plane with other competitive sports." About ninety-five cowboys signed up to what was called the Cowboys Association of America. The group's self-definition and even its demands ("to compell [sic] certain annual rodeos to pay more money to its performers") reveal how invested cowboys were in changing rodeo from a performance to a sport and yet how uncertain and incomplete that process was.[43] We can see this transformative moment in the words of purpose above: to "place rodeo *performance* on an equal plane with *other competitive sports.*" Initially, cowboys focused on ensuring that organizing committees treated them as competitors whose livelihood was dependent on being paid the prize money that was their due, on making those prizes large enough that they could make a living on the circuit, and on raising the status of rodeo to that of a competitive sport. The Cowboys Association of America concentrated its effort on increasing payouts, collecting funds for those injured in the sport, offering its own cowboy-centred points system that valued all-round contestants who could compete in a number of events from steer wrestling to bronc riding, and, through committee work, improving the standards of each event. The transborder nature of high-end rodeo meant that Canadians as well as Americans were present from the start, with Kimberley, BC's Smokey Snyder heading up one committee.[44] Despite its orderly beginning, however, little was ever heard from this early organization.

But the push toward collective action continued. In 1936, when Canadian and American cowboys amassed at Boston Gardens, a major confrontation with management launched a new association. Although the RAA had forced its member organizations to post, in advance, the money they intended to pay out at a rodeo, it did not stipulate a minimum purse per event. Big shows advertised big purses, but they also ran multiple performances. For example, the 1936 Madison Square Garden contest (7-25 October) posted a purse of $45,000, but it ran twenty-six shows, with the result that the average payout for any single event was less than $500. At Boston, the circumstances were much worse – the total purse for the eleven-day competition was a mere $6,400. Divided up, the purse per event was so low that even winning contestants would have difficulty recouping travel and accommodation expenses. But the Boston Gardens Rodeo was the last event of the year at which cowboys could earn money and hence points toward the championships. When they arrived in Boston in October and realized the situation, they put forward a petition demanding an immediate increase in prize money and the addition of their own entry fees to this total. Sixty-one cowboys signed the petition and promised not to compete unless their demands were met. They backed up their point by booking train tickets for themselves and shipping for their horses to return home if the organizer of the event, the venerable Colonel W.J. Johnson, did not accede to their demands. In response, Johnson invited cowboys at a Chicago rodeo to replace the ones in Boston, but when they arrived, they sided with the striking contestants. When the show opened, the protesting cowboys booed from the stands as stable grooms, chute men, and contract performers tried to fill in for them. The next day, they told the press that they were leaving the city, and then Johnson stepped in. Increasing the total purse to $14,000, which now included the cowboys' entry fees and a donation from Boston Gardens manager George V. Brown, he demanded, in return, that all collective action would cease. But it was too late for that. On 6 November 1936, the Cowboys' Turtle Association (CTA) was formed.[45] It was the first lasting association of its kind, and it sought to change both the sport and the cowboy himself.

The mandate of the Cowboys' Turtle Association was "to raise the standard of rodeos as a whole and to give them undisputed place in the foremost rank of American sports. This is to be done by classing as 'unfair' those shows which use rules unfair to the contestants and those which offer purses so small as to make it impossible for contestants to make expenses. The Association asks a fair deal for contestants as well as rodeo organizations and hopes to work harmoniously with them."[46] Over the next years, weathering lockouts, strikes, and internal dissension, the CTA fought for its place as rodeo cowboy representative, but these struggles only increased the public's awareness of the cowboys as contestants who deserved the level of sportsmanship and fair play accorded other athletes.[47] By the end of the 1930s, both the CTA and the RAA publicly announced that they were working for the betterment of the sport. As Guy Weadick reported in the RAA's official publication, *Hoofs and Horns,* the demands of each were as follows:

Contestants' demands:

1 Fair and reasonable purses offered and distributed so that it will offer best chance to make money
2 Fair entry fee and added to the purse
3 Competent arena help, judges etc.
4 "Official" RAA events open only to proven contestants
5 Separate classes for "amateur" and "beginners" and the fact advertised.

Management's demands:

1 Contestants to enter far enough in advance of opening date to allow scheduling

2   Proper dress, proper equipment on first day through final performance

3   Contestants must pay entry fee.[48]

Gradually, the RAA accepted that "proven contestants" were CTA members, and the CTA claimed for its membership the title of "professional" while allowing amateur contests to run alongside its events. Working out the place of organized rodeo was not an easy process, but by the end of the Second World War, when the CTA changed its name to the Professional Rodeo Cowboys Association, and the Cowboys' Protective Association was established (1944), professional rodeo cowboys were recognized as athletes and rodeo as a sport. As popular announcer Cy Taillon liked to make plain, rodeo was a "sport, not a carnival act," its contestants were athletes, not "cowpokes," and newspaper coverage of it should appear in the sports pages, not the entertainment section.[49]

Professionalization influenced and was influenced by changing definitions of the cowboy, which veered away from national categorizations even while they encoded gendered ones. Canadians Herman Linder, Pete Knight, and Harry Knight were present at the early CTA actions and soon held positions on the organization's executive. At their 1937 meeting in Fort Worth, Texas, CTA members elected Linder as their first vice-president and Harry Knight to represent the saddle bronc riders.[50] Canadian press reaction to the events of 1936 was generally positive though slightly tinged with sarcasm. The *Calgary Herald* asked if "rodeo [was] going revolutionary" but generally took the line that the cowboys needed a "fair shake" because "these men, traveling distances from place to place, have heavy expenses, and take chances on returns."[51] The presence of respected men such as Herman Linder meant that the new organization would include Canadians. It did not include women, however. Female riders and ropers were at the Boston show, but because they were contract performers, and hence paid a fee for appearing, they were not included in the CTA's actions.[52] Eventually, the CTA did make provisions to include contract performers, but until then, the fact that points were not awarded to their events meant that, effectively, contract cowgirls had little reason to join the CTA. Moreover, as we have seen, professional cowboys-turned-promoters in Canada, men such as Herman Linder, shared the opinion of the RAA and the CTA that women's events, particularly saddle bronc, in which the stirrups were fastened under the belly of the horse, did not contribute to rodeo's image as a risky but not unduly dangerous sport.

Colonel W.J. Johnson's world championship rodeo, Boston, 4-12 November 1932. *Glenbow Museum Archives, NA-462-30*

Linder told reporters in 1935 that "girls should not ride in stampedes," and indeed, when the CTA spoke of the new professional rodeo cowboy, it was really referring to cow*boys*.[53] Transforming rodeo from performance to sport was truly, as sports scholars say more generally, a gendered process from which women were excluded.[54]

At first, presenting rodeo as a sport promised to make it even more open to Aboriginal cowboys. Weadick's slogan – that a rodeo should be "open to all, no race or nationality barred" – followed him to Lethbridge and High River, where he organized rodeos in the 1930s. No doubt, making judging more transparent and ensuring that judges were not just local businessmen who were determined to see local riders win also improved their chances of success, though Aboriginal observers still feared that rodeo was a "white man's game."[55] About 15 percent of contestants in Lethbridge rodeos during the 1930s came from reserves.[56] At Raymond, seventeen Aboriginal competitors entered the stampede and race meet, which drew a total of ninety-two men to its events.[57] At Cardston in 1946,

Aboriginal athletes took prizes in calf roping (Frank Many Fingers, first place), steer decorating (Rufus Goodstriker, first, and Frank Many Fingers, a tie for third with Pat Wolf), bareback bronc riding (Jim Owns Different Horses, fourth), and wild cow milking (Ken Feathers, first, and Frank Many Fingers, second); they dominated the finals in calf roping.[58] Competing near their home communities, before judges and audiences who knew them, seems to have encouraged Aboriginal cowboys to restrict their participation to small-town stampedes, as we have seen in earlier chapters.

They were less likely to join the larger circuit, a decision grounded in a number of reasons. First, lack of access to capital closed doors for many would-be circuit riders of Aboriginal heritage. Wallace Mountain Horse, for example, told Pauline Dempsey that when he was a young man he could not afford to travel to rodeo: "I was really good at roping and riding but to go around and follow the rodeos at the time I was that age, I didn't have no transportation. It was later on that we had transportation. People like ... James Gladstone, Cecil Tallow and Joe Bullshields who were well-to-do, well, they were the ones who had transportation but [for] the rest, [it was] very difficult for them to get around with no cars. So I never joined [the] rodeo [circuit] though I was really good at it."[59] Second, partaking in local small-town rodeos during the 1920s and 1930s did not necessarily afford local cowboys opportunities to advance beyond those circuits. Small-town stampedes frequently rewarded winners with sacks of flour, sugar, or potatoes, prizes that could not be applied to the championship point system of the RAA and other organizations, which was based solely on cash winnings. Similarly, the biased judging encountered by many cowboys when they competed far from their home turf may have been worse for Aboriginal cowboys, who would not have accumulated the points necessary to make attending the big eastern rodeos worthwhile.[60] Finally, in Alberta in particular, the interventionist role of the Indian Agent also limited Aboriginal cowboys' access to the transborder circuit. Whereas BC Indian Agents expected Aboriginal people to leave their reserves to earn a living, Indian Agents in Alberta tried to make them stay on-reserve to look after crops and livestock. While settler cowboys were making names for themselves in the 1910s and 1920s by contracting with the promoters of travelling rodeo shows, Indian Agents frequently refused the requests of these same entrepreneurs to include Aboriginal riders. Later, the agents could and did refuse passes to Aboriginal cowboys whose participation in rodeos would interfere with their agricultural labour on reserves. Even in the 1930s, when opportunities for earning cash incomes were greatly reduced, Indian Agents capriciously turned down requests from Aboriginal cowboys for passes to leave the reserve and ride for money.[61] By way of contrast, mixed-heritage cowboy Harry Shuttleworth and Métis cowboy Paddy Laframboise, neither of whom were under the control of Indian Agents, followed local circuits that crossed provincial boundaries, and Aboriginal cowboys from British Columbia joined in rodeos wherever they were available in the locations of their itinerant labour. So, though Aboriginal participation was central to community rodeos in Western Canada during the 1930s and 1940s, it simply did not appear at the big eastern rodeos where cowboy collective organizing got its start. For the 1930s, then, Aboriginal cowboys were not part of the process of professionalization.

Reinventing rodeo as a sport also offered professional cowboys an opportunity to reform their image. Recognizing that the old stereotype of the drunken, carousing, belligerent man was hurting the sport, the RAA and the CTA agreed to form rules to deal with it. If a cowboy skipped town without paying his bills, the CTA picked up his tab, fined him, and banned him from competing. Reinstatement was at the discretion of the CTA Board of Directors. The CTA also fined cowboys for brawling, rowdyism, and drunkenness, and with the intent of encouraging better grooming. Looking back on the work of pro cowboys, Herman Linder concluded that "they have made Rodeo today what it is ... There used to be a lot of cowboys ... who weren't the best kind of guys ... [With organizations in place] if he doesn't behave himself in a mannerly way he's put on the carpet and fined and maybe expelled from rodeos for a certain period of time."[62] The CTA also sought to educate the public on the nature of the rodeo cowboy. He was not, for example, an amateur looking for fun. He was not engaged in play. Rather, he was an athlete who deserved a living wage. Clifford Westermeier linked the makeover of the rodeo cowboy with the work of the CTA:

The Cowboys' Turtle Association has not only increased the benefits of the cowboy, but it has also brought about a remarkable change in his character and appearance. This is not to be taken as a sign that the cowboy-contestant has grown soft, because he is organized and relies on the backing of an Association for his protection; on the contrary, his protection has given him greater strength, but in a less belligerent manner. He has lost much of his former attitude of "going-out-and-getting" what he wants, regardless of the cost. The cowboy with the backing of the Association has someone interested in his welfare, and thus he takes a greater interest in himself and others – he has a feeling of being wanted. No longer must he go to the contests with fear and worry concerning unfair judges, timers and flagmen. If he wins, he collects the money he has honestly won, because he has met the best men in the sport in fair competition.[63]

By the 1940s, rodeo had fully reworked its identity from performance to sport. Those most involved in that shift sought the transformation of the cowboy as well.

The war intervened to encourage Canadian cowboys to form their own professional organization. Many of them still farmed or ranched (Herman Linder, for example, did not attend some American rodeos, because their timing interfered with work on his farm) and were exempted from conscription by agricultural deferments. If they crossed the border to compete, they would be considered professional rodeo cowboys and consequently lose these deferments. But if they stayed home, they could not accumulate enough points to maintain their standing within the sport as a whole. Canadian cowboys also wanted the benefits that CTA members received, even if they did not participate in American rodeos.[64] And so, in 1944, a group of them banded together to form what they eventually named the Cowboys' Protective Association (CPA). Each contributed a dollar to a mutual insurance fund and adopted the CPA mandate "to organize professional rodeo contestants in Canada for their mutual benefit and protection; to raise the standard of cowboy contestants; to co-operate, in so far as possible, with rodeo management; to bring about honest advertising by the rodeo associations."[65] Ken Thomson of Turner Valley, Alberta, became the CPA's first president.[66]

In some ways, the Canadian organization was much like its American counterpart, the CTA. The CPA's rules focused on distinguishing the pro cowboy from the amateur and on discouraging behaviour that damaged the reputation of contestants. It demanded that committees offer adequate prizes and that they guarantee they had the funds to cover them. It demanded that cowboys be given control over who would be allowed to judge, insisting that judges be appointed by a committee of competitors and that the judges themselves had competed in the past.[67] The stipulations that committees guarantee prize money up front and that entry fees be included in prizes helped ensure that winning men could recoup the

Rules of the Cowboys' Protective Association, 3 September 1944

1. All the rodeos must be approved by the Rodeo Association and billed as such
2. Any rodeo that can't meet the Association rules and regulations must be billed as an amateur contest
3. Any cowboy who has never won any money in an Association show will be classed as an amateur rider
4. Any rodeo manager must be approved by the Association
5. All prize money must be guaranteed and placed in the bank before the show starts
6. All rodeos must state on their bills that they are covering the cowboy's insurance
7. The cowboys must be allowed to appoint their own judges, two in number, and each judge must be or has been an all round rider to be eligible for a judge
8. All entry fees must be added to the contest as Final Money
9. Any contestant who is hurt must be allowed to take his stock the following day for the day previous
10. Any contestant willfully damaging hotel rooms or fixtures will be subject to a fine to the Association $50.00 and expenses
11. Any professional rider contesting in a non-association show will be subject to a fine by the Association
12. Association rules and regulations:

    a. Contest prizes must meet the following rules:
    b. Saddle riding: $10.00 entry fee; day money: 1st $50, 2nd $30, 3rd $20, 4th $10. Finals consisting of total entry fees and split 40%, 30%, 20% and 10% added to the purse
    c. Decorating: $10.00 entry fee; prize money the same as saddle riding
    d. Calf Roping: $10.00 entry fee; prize money the same as above
    e. Bareback riding: $5.00 entry fee; day money: 1st $30, 2nd $20, 3rd $10, 4th $5; entry fees added to final prize money split 40%, 30%, 20% and 10% added to purse
    f. Steer riding: $5.00 entry fee; prize money same as bareback
    g. Wild cow milking and wild horse race will be optional for committees.

expenses they incurred while participating in rodeos across the Canadian West.

Although the CPA had much in common with its American equivalent, it did differ in one respect: it recognized the place of Aboriginal competitors in the sport. At the first CPA annual meeting, in 1945, Padgett Barry and Jack Martin moved that "the Indian cowboys of each province should have a representative on the CPA Board."[68] As a result, the members elected an executive that included two representatives for "Indian cowboys" (see page 130). Fred Gladstone represented Aboriginal cowboys of Alberta, and Gus Gottfriedson did the same for those of BC.[69] These positions gave elite cowboys from Canadian reserves a voice in reformulating both rodeo as a sport and competitors as athletes.

The 1930s and 1940s were a time of transition for rodeo and rodeo cowboys. New organizations such as the Rodeo Association of America, the Cowboys' Turtle Association, and the Cowboys' Protective Association bureaucratized the sport, introducing standardized rules, scoring, and point systems. On many of these issues, cowboys and managers agreed. Both wanted an events schedule that would be free of timing conflicts. Constructing programs so that rodeo events were separated from performances of trick roping and riding also served the pragmatic needs of competitors travelling the circuit and their desires to be seen as athletes, not performers. Articulating the rules also served both committees and contestants, as audience expectations of the sport were crafted in the process. However, they heartily disagreed about judge selection and the processes used for calculating, guaranteeing, and paying prizes. Capitalizing on the popularity of the cowboy in the 1930s, cowboy organizations chose to launch collective action at large rodeos that drew huge audiences and hence attention to their plight. That these organizations, particularly the Cowboys' Turtle Association, were successful challenges the view of some sports historians that sports organizations always perpetuate the power structures within society. Lest we conclude, as the *Calgary Herald* hinted, that cowboy organizations were "revolutionary," it is worth

FACING PAGE

TOP: Gus Gottfriedson, CPRA Indian representative for British Columbia. *BC Cowboy Heritage Society*

BOTTOM: Fred Gladstone, CPRA Indian representative for Alberta, 1950. *Glenbow Museum Archives, NA-564-3*

CALGARY STAMPEDE
FRED GLADSTONE CALF ROPING

The First CPA Executive

President: Ken Thomson
Vice-President: Johnny Glasier
Secretary-Treasurer: Blair Holland
Chairman, Board of Directors: Fred Galarneau

Directors
Saddle Bronc Riding: Carl Olsen
Steer Decorating: Dick Andrews
Calf Roping: Albert Galarneau
Bareback Bronc Riding: Frank Duce
Steer Riding: Frank Vorce

District Representatives
Southern Alberta: Jack Martin
Central Alberta: Urban Doan
Northern Alberta: Bob Fisher
Saskatchewan: Don Dewar, Jerry Myers
British Columbia: Dave Abrahams, Hap Leary

Indian Cowboys
Alberta: Fred Gladstone
British Columbia: Gus Gottfriedson

All-Round Cowboy Activities
Wally Lindstrom

noting that some power differentials were widened. Women, for example, were largely excluded from rodeo as organizations of managers and cowboys deleted women's events from the emerging sport. Aboriginal cowboys stood to gain from the sport's repeated declarations of equal opportunity, but larger social, economic, and political structures constrained their participation in the organizational work of rodeo. However, their importance to small-town rodeos encouraged the Cowboys' Protective Association to set aside executive positions for Indian representatives, thus opening

Pete Knight, Salinas, California, 18 May 1937. *Glenbow Museum Archives, NA-462-21*

a space for their involvement in the ongoing process of producing rodeo, its forms, functions, and communities. In this, the practices of small-town, rural, and reserve rodeos shaped the transborder world of professional rodeo in uniquely Western Canadian ways. Understanding rodeo necessitates balancing local histories with transnational ones.

Late in the day on 23 May 1937, Pete Knight mounted the bronc Duster at the Hayward, California, rodeo. Knight rode for eight seconds before Duster suddenly dropped his head and threw him over his shoulders. As the great horse came down, he landed both front hooves on Knight's chest. Knight survived long enough to make it to hospital, speak a few words to his wife, Babe, and die with his cowboy boots still on. Rodeo cowboys and fans from across the continent travelled to Hayward for his funeral. The town's businesses shut down for the day, and flags hung at half-mast. Farther north, on British Columbia's Douglas Lake Ranch, the foreman quietly told the cowboys of Knight's demise. No one spoke. They worked in silence that morning. Wilf Carter wrote another song in Knight's honour, called "Pete Knight's Last Ride," though it was never as popular as his 1934 hit "Pete Knight: The King of the Cowboys." Years later, in 1981, Knight would be the first inductee in the Canadian Professional Rodeo Association's Hall of Fame, having been inducted first into the Hall of Fame at the National Cowboy and Western Heritage Museum in Oklahoma City and the Pro-Rodeo Hall of Fame of the Museum of the American Cowboy. In 1977 tiny, struggling Crossfield honoured him by naming its arena after him, and again competitors, fans, and townsfolk gathered to remember Knight, the American who learned to rodeo in Alberta and took his talents to the world. Pete Knight typified the trans-border and local affiliations that characterized rodeo cowboys as rodeo transformed from a community performance to an international sport.[70]

4

Heavens No! Let's Keep It Rodeo!
Pro Rodeo and the Making of the Modern Cowboy

Identities and memories are not things we think about, but things we think with.

– *John Gillis,* Commemorations:
The Politics of National Identity

In the opening scenes of the 1972 National Film Board production *Hard Rider,* the narrator introduced Syilx (Okanagan) rodeo cowboy Kenny McLean as a true Canadian: "part Scottish, part Indian – a Canadian cowboy going down the road."[1] The film presented McLean as doubly inscribed – Indian and cowboy – an authentic hybrid, a hyphenated Canadian of Trudeau-era multiculturalism. It followed McLean's itinerant life as a pro rodeo cowboy and included a meeting between the Canadian Professional Rodeo Association (CPRA) executive board (to which McLean belonged) and Calgary Stampede general manager William Pratt. The meeting quickly turned to a discussion of how best to deploy the rodeo cowboy. Pratt declared,

> What we really need to create is a new image for the cowboy ... He's regarded as a quiet, taciturn man who shows no emotion, who chews tobacco, who is really stupid, probably has a few teeth missing and we've got to create a new image for him ... We don't have any coloured men and we need them. And if we had a long-haired kid, with long yellow hair to his shoulders dressed in old-fashioned [clothes] that is what this sport needs ... And if I had Kenny McLean, I'd put him in an Indian headdress everywhere he went.[2]

While McLean chuckled and shook his head, the CPRA executive jumped to his defence, all talking at once, one saying, "If you put Kenny in a headdress, well, Lord, for one thing, you'd hinder his riding." Another asked, "Do you think a cowboy ought to come out of the bush like a jackpine

Kenny McLean. *Photograph by Jack Stocks, courtesy Okanagan Archive Trust Society, www. oldphotos.ca.*

savage?" and another answered, "Heavens no! Let's keep it rodeo!"[3] A fundamental struggle for rodeo cowboys lay at the core of the exchange. What identities, whose values, and what gendered and racialized categories would be performed at pro rodeos across the country? Like the CPRA, professional rodeo cowboy associations in the second half of the twentieth century were determined that they, not stampede managers, humane societies, or the media, would craft and enforce these definitions. CPRA members came to embrace a set of norms that were grounded in the respectable masculinities of the pre-war rodeo cowboy, adding precepts drawn from Cold War–era imperatives of manliness. The rodeo cowboy, as the CPRA envisioned him, was a sober provider for his family, a humane steward of stock, and a good representative of the sport. He managed risk rationally without sacrificing physical toughness. He supported novices, not necessarily through personal mentorship as in the pre-war era, but through institutionalized insurance schemes. The casual misogyny of the past remained but was limited by the emphasis on family, which opened up spaces for female participation. Women formed their own organizations and gradually stretched the definitions of modern rodeo to include female contestants and the forms of femininity that they brought to the sport. Elite Aboriginal cowboys, such as Kenny McLean, contributed to these definitional activities, which were worked out at meetings and at rodeos in the middle decades of the twentieth century.

Writing about social memory, James Fentress and Chris Wickham argue that as communities develop, they craft shared narratives. Through these narratives, identities and social cohesion grow. Frameworks of meaning, particular to the community and important to its surviving sense of self, shape those stories and how their tellers see the world. They in turn transmit meaning over generations, between members and to outsiders.[4] Professional cowboys, both through their self-defining activities within the CPRA and in their reminiscences, expressed values and beliefs, memories and narratives that articulated belonging to a particular and special world – the on-the-road realm of the pro cowboy. On the road, families, both Aboriginal and settler, travelled together, so that the world of rodeo became a liminal contact zone, a place of shared values that emphasized respectability over racialization, that privileged family over gender-based restrictions, and that saw itself as caring for animals in a way that few others understood. These values were the foundation upon which a distinctive subculture materialized over time.

This era, from the late 1940s to the early 1970s, was the golden age of rodeo when cowboys in film, on television, on stage, and in the arena dominated the North American cultural scene. The desired return to normalcy, and the resultant nostalgia for a social order thought to be natural, enhanced the cowboy's iconic status in both Canada and the United States. Hollywood and television westerns brought the myth of the frontier to big and small screens as gun-toting men took decisive action in a world characterized by ambivalence and contradiction.[5] By the mid-1950s, one-third of evening television viewing time was devoted to westerns, and a generation of youngsters grew up playing cowboys and Indians, Davy Crockett, and the Lone Ranger.[6] Rodeo seemed to perform the myth of the frontier in real time. Its apparently simple narrative, of man's domination over the natural world through knowledge and skill, as in calf roping, or through determination and brute force, as in bull riding, seemed to promise reassurance in the Cold War era. In the 1940s and 1950s, national magazines such as *Time, Maclean's, Newsweek, Life,* the *Saturday Evening Post,* and even *Better Homes and Gardens* and the *Ladies' Home Journal,* published articles about rodeo and its athletes.[7] Midcentury Hollywood films *The Lusty Men* (1952) and *The Misfits* (1961) included actual rodeo footage and used rodeo cowboy characters to explore themes of modernization and masculinity in the no-longer-frontier West. Rodeo cowboys in Hollywood's imagination were reckless and violent, loyal yet unpredictable, inexplicably attached to a destructive way of life, living out fantasies of the "Old West" in a New West that was dominated by agribusiness and interstates. Even Canada had its own rodeo cowboys immortalized in made-for-TV movies such as *Goldenrod* (1977) and the CBC television series *Cariboo Country* (1960, 1964-67).[8]

Against this backdrop, professional rodeo cowboys on both sides of the border sought to define their sport and themselves. In Canada, organized by the Cowboys' Protective Association (CPA) (renamed the Canadian Professional Cowboy Association in 1965), they actively intervened to promote their vision of the sport when communities staged rodeos in the post–Second World War period.[9] Rejecting the prevailing image of the day, which depicted "cowboys and Indians" as fundamentally opposite polarities (whether the Indian symbolized nobility or savagery), Canadian pro rodeo cowboys sought common cause with their Aboriginal counterparts and encouraged them to join their organization. From 1945, the CPRA established two Indian representative positions, and at no point

Future Canadian prime minister Joe Clark in his cowboy outfit, High River, 1945. Cowboy clothes and toy guns were tremendously popular among children from the 1930s through the 1950s.
Glenbow Museum Archives, PA-3520-546

during its first twenty-five years did its executive lack an Aboriginal member. Top-notch cowboys Kenny McLean, Fred Gladstone, and Gus Gottfriedson added their voices and their views to decision making at the highest level of Canada's pro rodeo organization.

From its earliest meetings, the CPRA set the terms upon which the pro community would both imagine itself and present itself to outsiders, or as one cowboy put it, "to protect the cowboys and also make rodeo more attractive to the general public."[10] First, it defined the sport, by identifying as "professional" only those rodeos whose prize lists, entry fees, and judges it approved.[11] Rodeos that received CPRA sanction were required to include four main events: bronc riding with saddle, Brahma steer riding, steer decorating, and calf roping, which had to be run according to CPRA rules.[12] Contestants in these events earned points according to the money they won, and like the RAA, the CPRA awarded championships on the basis of points earned. Other events, such as bareback bronc riding and native (i.e., not Brahma) steer riding, were classified as semi-major, but this category was eliminated in 1946, with the result that only the four main events were defined as "professional"; all others were considered amateur and did not have points ascribed to them. Pro cowboys had little interest in competing in amateur events since doing so would not contribute to their standings, but for a while committees continued to stage them for local contestants.

The CPRA then proceeded to describe the pro cowboy. The basic definition was tautological – a professional cowboy competed in professional rodeos. Once he became a CPRA member, he could enter only CPRA-approved rodeos or risk being penalized. Non-members were free to enter any rodeo, but as soon as they won enough prize money ($100 in 1946, $500 in 1956, and $2,000 in 1966), they were compelled to join the CPRA ("go pro") or risk being fined, blacklisted, and barred from all CPRA events. Even young riders, under the age of twenty-one and still requiring a parent's consent to compete, had to adhere to this rule.[13] The only exceptions were Aboriginal cowboys, who were permitted to enter rodeos on their own reserves or adjacent ones without penalty. However, they could not claim against the CPRA's insurance should they be injured at such an event.[14] Although the goal was to make rodeo a paying proposition, it did not became a primary source of income until the late 1960s, even for its most elite athletes in Canada.[15] Professionalism, at this stage, promised financial independence in exchange for obedience to a set of rules, but in the 1950s, the CPRA was still not fully able to guarantee that the rodeo life would pay for itself.

The CPRA insurance plan was the main draw for membership, especially in the years before Canada established socialized medicine. Originally, for every event they entered, cowboys contributed a dollar toward insurance; the plan covered medical costs for those who were injured, and in the event of death, it contributed to funeral expenses. Management matched the funds collected from cowboys, so that by the end of 1944, its first year of operation, the insurance scheme paid out $1,200, with a tidy sum left over to seed itself the following year. The CPRA never considered this scheme a true insurance plan but rather stipulated that it was a "gentlemen's mutual agreement among cowboys," covering expenses to a maximum of $200.[16] Nonetheless, during its first twenty-five years, the CPRA paid thousands of dollars in medical expenses, often exceeding the set limits for payout.[17]

When cowboys asked for more than the $200 limit, CPRA executive meetings considered their cases individually. Board members often approved these requests, and their reasons for doing so reveal some of the larger motivations of the CPRA, which were shared by many rodeo cowboys. Being able to pay doctors and hospitals assured the cowboys of their respectability as financially contributing members of society, and it countered their residual reputation for leaving town without paying their bills. Repeatedly, cowboys who were making their case for payment, and board members who agreed with them, argued that a CPRA member had a right to carry on without "a heavy debt weighing over his head." Furthermore, the pecuniary reputation of all rodeo cowboys was enhanced when local doctors and hospitals were paid.[18]

Through its insurance scheme, the CPRA managed risk in a way that did not diminish the excitement of rodeo or the reputation of competitors for physical toughness. At no point in its first twenty years did the CPRA offer any procedural change that would have increased the safety of contestants.[19] Physical risk was part of the rodeo cowboy's persona. But it did not have to extend to his financial life and his respectability. That rodeo could inflict damage on a man was a given; the CPRA insurance scheme was designed to help him pay his bills should this occur. Other post-war modes of risk management, such as workers' compensation, contributed to modern masculinity; the CPRA insurance plan did the same for the rodeo cowboy, promoting an image of manliness that was rational and responsible but physically tough and demanding.[20]

CPRA interests extended beyond the rules of the sport. They were also about crafting the rodeo cowboy. First, the association sought to contain rowdyness, the rough masculinities of cowboy culture. The executive introduced fines for drunk and disorderly behaviour, investigated complaints, and called members to appear before it to answer charges of using profanity, appearing drunk in public, or damaging hotel rooms. Particularly impatient with drunkenness, it banned liquor from its meetings in 1947.[21] The following year, it received complaints from a Falkland, BC, rodeo committee that a CPRA member had been drunk while judging a rodeo there. On behalf of the Falkland committee, H.E. Churchill wrote, "I believe when a man is judging and getting good pay for it the best he could do is to stay sober." The CPRA executive agreed to investigate, writing that it had heard that this particular cowboy had recently "sworn off liquor."[22] In 1952 three award-winning cowboys were fined for having passed out under their table during the awards ceremony in Calgary's Palliser Hotel.[23] This annual banquet for Canadian rodeo cowboys was also the scene of a fight between two chuckwagon-racers in 1955; the CPRA fined each of them $100.[24] In 1962, after a CPRA member created a disturbance at the annual banquet for the second time, he was fined $500.

Behaviour generically described as "unsavoury" also came in for scrutiny and discipline as when one member was banned from all future banquets for "unsavory behavior at same," in 1963.[25] The CPRA fined three chuckwagon-racers in 1964 for "disorderly conduct and profanity" at the Hand Hills Rodeo.[26] Even rodeo clowns could be fined if they used "profane" language in their acts.[27] The CPRA was particularly intolerant of cowboys who destroyed property: when one cowboy smashed a challenge trophy, he was suspended and told to reimburse the Nicola Valley Rodeo Committee for its cost.[28] Similarly, when the Kingsway and Haney Hotels in British Columbia reported that visiting professional cowboys had wrecked their rooms, the CPRA intervened as it did with similar incidents at Ponoka in 1968.[29] No one was immune from scrutiny, and even some of the leading figures in Canadian rodeo were called to account for their behaviour. Both Herman Linder and Reg Kessler received CPRA censure for infractions such as using "abusive language," impatience, and yelling at new contestants as well as "swearing in the arena."[30] Even as popular culture, from Jack Kerouac's Neal Cassady to Montgomery Clift's Perce Howland in *The Misfits,* emphasized the anti-social, rebellious, and flawed characteristics of the drifting man of the West, of whom the rodeo cowboy was an easily identifiable example, pro contestants in Canada tried hard to counter this stereotype.[31] Still, there was a certain irony here: that the epitome of freedom-loving manhood – the cowboy – should have his behaviour constrained by his own association. No doubt, more than one rodeo cowboy and more than one CPRA executive member understood that sometimes the rules were meant to be broken. On a broader scale, the fact that the CPRA needed to impose rules, fines, and other disciplinary action demonstrates that its view of the respectable cowboy was not undisputed and underscores how the 1950s and 1960s, no less than other decades, saw a multiplicity of masculinities lived and articulated.

Canadian cowboys more readily agreed on other matters. The CPRA generally supported those who wished to be considered self-directed athletes rather than attractions for commodification by stampede organizers. Rodeo cowboys had to address the expectation that they would dress flamboyantly and obediently participate in parades and best-dressed competitions. They chafed at rules that permitted managers to "insert some sort of compulsion to force cowboys to enter the Grand Entry if requested to do so."[32] During meetings with stampede managers in 1968, the CPRA executive explained that best-dressed cowboy contests were "not too popular" with the contestants themselves and suggested that if they were to continue, the cowboys should be judged in both their street and work clothes. Organizers knew that forcing cowboys to appear in the parade would not make them popular. As one such organizer put it, "they hated taking part in the grand entry. Well I think it wasn't what they were there for, but as an association person, like someone who's trying to promote it ... I put out more than one of these letters, you know, these rules will be followed or you won't get your start, so you take part in the grand entry or you don't get to ride."[33] But CPRA members also recognized the desirability of presenting themselves in identifiable dress and so passed a motion in 1961 that "every rodeo contestant must appear in the arena in complete cowboy attire including long sleeve shirt and large cowboy hat," and threatening a ten-dollar fine for non-compliance.[34] And in 1967, Kenny McLean suggested that the awards banquet should become a semi-formal affair so as to eliminate the wearing of blue jeans, which, he thought, created a "bad image in the public eye." The board of directors readily agreed.[35] The CPRA rules for attire were meant to visibly mark out the respectability of the professional rodeo cowboy in keeping with modes of masculinity that increasingly saw clothing as a manly form of self-expression.

During the early years of professionalization, the CPRA spent considerable time creating, debating, and enforcing rules designed to protect stock. From the first days of the sport, urban audiences had expressed shock and horror at the treatment of animals in rodeo. At the first Calgary Stampede, in 1912, women, in particular, condemned steer wrestling as cruel.[36] When Tex Austin, an American promoter, took rodeo to London's Wembley Stadium in 1924 and 1934, the Royal Society for the Prevention of Cruelty to Animals denounced it. Austin lost over $20,000 in 1924, and his return in 1934 prompted the British parliament to pass the Protection of Animals Act (1934), under which roping an untrained animal or riding a bucking horse or bull became an offence, a move that effectively made rodeo illegal in Britain.[37] Rodeos in rural areas seldom met with protests over their treatment of animals, though if blood were drawn or an animal injured, cowboys and organizers were called to account. Guy Weadick cautioned CPRA secretary Jim Maxwell in 1950 that rodeo would not always be free of controversy and that the public particularly objected to the use of the flank strap to stimulate bucking:

> They are not for the rough stuff any more. That's out. People are watching for cruelty this season. The rules will just have to be enforced and lived up to. Flanking has been crude and is dynamite unless done properly. I saw that coming for quite awhile back. Punks around chutes, and flanking and picking up stock are one reason the kicks are in. Only experienced men should be use[d] for such work. I make mention of some of these things based on letters received. From now on the boys with savy [sic] will have to look after things and the inexperienced hands put to one side. They are harmful.[38]

Moreover, as rodeo's popularity grew, it expanded its geographic reach and encountered people who were much more sensitive to its treatment of animals. Cruelty charges were laid against the Cowichan Exhibition Committee regarding its 1954 rodeo in Duncan on Vancouver Island. Three local people, referred to as an "anti-rodeo committee," alleged that the calf roping was unnecessarily abusive and that the horses "were coming out tired from the chute and were 'making noises.'" The charges were eventually dropped, but the CPRA lawyers advised the executive to refuse to defend the event's organizers, the Vancouver Island Kinsmen Club.[39] In 1967 a lower Fraser Valley stampede manager asked if spurs could be covered ("perhaps with a tip similar to the bottom of a hospital crutch") because the spurs of bareback riders had drawn blood more than once. He continued, "The last time was a fairly large cut that drew blood rapidly.

I rode alongside and covered up as much as I could, however I don't like to see this happen and especially not in front of 8000 to 10000 people."[40] Rodeo promoters and the CPRA were justifiably sensitive. The 1950s saw increased mobilization on behalf of animal rights. In 1951 Christine Stevens formed the Animal Welfare Institute, and three years later, the Humane Society of the United States broke away from the more conservative American Humane Association. The Humane Society's principal focus was on scientific research using animals and, to a lesser extent, factory farming, but the notion that animals had the right to be free of pain and discomfort, even the momentary discomfort (as many saw it) of being roped, had firmly entered public consciousness by midcentury.[41]

The CPRA tried to diminish animal rights criticism of rodeo by creating elaborate rules governing animal treatment in its events. The first particular matter for debate was the acceptable method of calf roping. Early calf roping had favoured the dally method, in which the rope is tied in a half hitch around the saddle horn, after the calf has been caught, with the loose end held by the roper, who can take up or allow slack in the rope as necessary. By the mid-1950s, the American tied-down method (in which the knot was tied more firmly to the saddle horn) was preferred, partly because the training of calf-roping horses had been improved and the possibility of an untrained horse dragging a calf consequently diminished. Several attempts were required before the CPRA agreed to allow tied roping in its events, partly because it feared that audiences might still be exposed to calf dragging, and partly because it feared that the change would favour American calf-ropers, who were more accustomed to tied roping.[42] Rules penalizing a roper whose horse dragged a calf more than three feet were revised in 1961 so that a field judge could stop any amount of dragging, a modification that some thought would penalize American ropers.[43] Similarly, the CPRA executive created rules to eliminate the "jerking down" of a calf by either horse or roper, further clarifying the regulations in 1964 to state that the "roper will be penalized ten (10) seconds if calf is jerked down by the horse with the first jerk of the rope, which is used when the calf is tied. A jerk down means that a calf is jerked straight over backwards, landing on its back."[44] Good calf-ropers could have times as low as seven or eight seconds, which made a ten-second penalty substantial.

The treatment of chuckwagon horses was another focus of CPRA concern. It banned the practice of whipping horses with the chuckwagon's

Chuckwagon racing, Camrose, Alberta, 1957. *Glenbow Museum Archives, NA-4266-5*

lines in 1949.[45] In 1956 it ruled that chuckwagon-racing venues must provide box stalls for horses crippled in a race to keep them "out of the sight of the public."[46] In 1962 the manner in which chuckwagon outfits treated their horses – the "cruelty exercised by some chuck wagon men to their horses in the barns" – was the subject of a special CPRA meeting. The executive determined that such behaviour was intolerable and drafted a letter to all chuckwagon outfits, threatening fines and suspensions to those who persisted in it.[47] Here too concerns regarding drunkenness surfaced because it prompted neglect and cruelty. In 1964 the SPCA sparked a minor controversy when the *Calgary Herald* relayed its suggestion that liquor be banned from the chuckwagon barns. The SPCA immediately apologized, saying that it had not meant to deny a chuckwagon-racer a drink but was worried solely about "cruelty to animals due to drunkenness."[48] Nonetheless, it did wonder if drinking and betting encouraged "rough treatment," resulting in "considerable discomfort to the horses."[49] Taking the high ground, the CPRA accepted the apology, perhaps because the executive already knew that drinking was causing problems among

some chuckwagon-racers. In 1960 Ralph Loosmore of Twining, Alberta, filed an official protest against a prominent chuckwagon-racer for consistent drunkenness at the reins of his wagon. During a pre-race warm-up session, the cowboy was so intoxicated that he "simply fell out of the wagon," with the result that his horses ran loose on the track until they hit a truck. One horse cut its hip. Despite this, he insisted on participating in the race. When it was over, getting him off the track proved difficult. He finally climbed out of the chuckwagon and went directly to the bar, leaving his horses tied to the wagon until midnight. Loosmore claimed that this man had been very drunk at three different races. Jim Maxwell responded for the CPRA executive by writing a stern letter to the racer, describing the executive's response to reports of his behaviour: "They took a very dim view of it. A number of them were all for barring you outright but after some discussion and realizing that you practically live for these races, they agreed to give you another chance and told me to advise you that if any report comes in that you have been drinking so you are affected in your driving a chuck wagon, you will be barred from racing at any further [CPRA] approved wagon races."[50] When similar reports were made about other chuckwagon-racers, the CPRA executive summoned them to appear before it, fining those whose public mistreatment of horses had damaged the association's image.[51] Increasingly, it met with the SPCA, heard its concerns about the abuse of chuckwagon horses, and conveyed these to meetings of stampede managers, securing infrastructure that would improve the race conditions for horses.[52]

Karen Merrill writes that cattle ranchers transformed their image of manliness to encompass the care and control of domestic spaces and their occupants, including stock, after the collapse of open-range ranching in the final decades of the nineteenth century.[53] North of the border, Canadian ranchers learned by tragic experience of the need to be more active in the care of their cattle, helping in births, feeding calves, providing food in winter, and studying animal husbandry.[54] By the time rodeo became popular in the 1930s, the image of the manly stockman was of a kindly rancher caring for his cattle. Whatever their background, rodeo promoters emphasized their roots in this tradition, and during the middle decades of the twentieth century, it found its way into many venues. In the BC tourist film *Land of the Overlanders* (1965), a segment on cattle ranching described a cowboy's work on a cow-calf operation: "When it becomes a question of putting mother and young together again [after branding], to do this, an otherwise tough cowboy becomes a tender-hearted human being."[55] From the 1930s, rodeo organizations had advanced the view that because rodeo cowboys were often ranchers themselves, they knew best how to care for animals.[56] In the post-war period, the organizations sought to cooperate with humane societies, eventually drafting a mutually-agreed-upon set of sixteen rules for the appropriate treatment of rodeo stock.[57]

The CPRA sought its own rapprochement with animal advocates. After the SPCA's controversial recommendation that drinking be banned in the chuckwagon barns, Harold Mandeville wrote an editorial in the *Canadian Rodeo News,* the official CPRA publication, declaring the mutual respect between professional rodeo cowboys and the SPCA: "There may be a few cowboys that disapprove of these SPCA men around rodeos, but the contestants as a whole and our association are very pleased that they are on hand."[58] He went on to voice what would become a common argument among rodeo cowboys – that "rodeo stock are cared for more than any form of animal except for the eight or ten seconds they are in action.

The rodeo stock are also long-lived animals. Just to name one horse in many, a saddle bronc ... Sleepy Sam is 32 years old and is still performing."[59] Repeatedly, throughout the middle decades of the twentieth century, the CPRA and its American counterpart the Rodeo Cowboys of America (RCA) claimed the humane treatment of stock as part of the ethic of the pro cowboy. A 1970 *United Farmer* article, drawn largely from a CPRA press release of the same year, stated that "professional bucking horses of rodeo work less, live as good and last longer than any other working horse in the world. Even more than slick thoroughbreds of the race tracks, the ill-tempered renegade bronc is the pampered prince of the equine kingdom. Rodeo broncs buck in either 8 or 10 second stretches. Even the busiest bucking horses are rarely out of the chute more than twice a week, or more than 30 times a year. Their 'working year' is less than five minutes."[60] In avoiding accusations of animal cruelty, associations such as the CPRA defined the rodeo cowboy as a humane guardian of stock, part of a manly image that included responsible caretaking.

Having worked hard to make professional cowboys conform to a more respectable image, the CPRA also informed the press of its official definition of the cowboy. A 1962 CPRA press release outlined the association's history and claimed that it had cleaned up both rodeo and contestants. In judging, in awarding championships, and in ensuring adequate prize money and standardized entry fees, the CPRA told the press, it had transformed rodeo into a sport. Moreover, inviting a few hundred competitors to town was no longer a risky venture: "There was a time when it was almost impossible for a cowboy to obtain a hotel room, as a few irresponsible cowboys took delight in either demolishing their rooms or skipping out without paying for them. A few stiff fines and suspensions imposed by the association soon convinced everyone concerned that the CPRA would not tolerate this kind of behaviour from its members."[61] The press release explicitly defined "the rodeo cowboy." Rejecting notions of authenticity that sought to discredit contestants because they were not "working cowboys," the CPRA emphasized that they could come from any walk of life, "from stump ranches ... [to] large cities, ... and other places where you would least expect a rodeo cowboy to come from." And yet, the CPRA argued, they differed from the professional athlete in that they were not governed by coaches and other bosses who told them "what time to go to bed, what they should eat, or what month to go in training." They were "self-made men," and though there was no substitute for learning to "take the hard knocks," the rodeo community provided its own training as older more experienced men took promising novices under their wing. However, this did not produce a relationship of dependency, for, "when the kid starts to win a little he buys a car of his own and takes off, but its no surprise, and there is no hard feeling." The CPRA went on to explain the taciturn, slightly superior air of many rodeo cowboys, particularly in their relations with reporters: they had learned to focus their "mind on just one thing," the upcoming ride in which they might win big or be badly injured. The possibility of injury or death was ever-present to the cowboy, a prospect he faced bravely, knowing that the rodeo community would take care of his family. The press release included a story of the benefit rodeo held at Alsask, Saskatchewan, to help the widow and family of Dick Nash, killed at the Hardisty Rodeo in 1961. Stock contractors had donated animals and contestants had travelled from miles around, some coming by plane, to compete without any advantage to themselves, so that the people of Alsask would come, pay their admission, and enjoy a good show while all the proceeds went to Nash's family. The cowboy, then, was generous. Finally, the press release noted that even the professional rodeo cowboy probably had a life outside the arena, going on to be successful in business, ranching, and other careers because of the lessons learned through rodeo.

The CPRA made a clear distinction between its members and amateurs and those not within its network. It did admit that some of the younger cowboys "over play their role in the old west" but added that this was "just harmless fun that they soon out grow." They differed from the "would-be cowboy," the "undesirables ... who have created an untrue picture of the real cowboy who is rodeoing for a living or perhaps just for a hobby." Because rodeo was open to all, the CPRA recognized that it attracted some who should be weeded out, and so it cautioned the press to "remember that everyone who wears a big hat is not necessarily a cowboy." It concluded its lesson by admonishing reporters to alter their views: "The next time you see a rodeo try to think of the cowboy as an individual, many with families to provide for, competing for prize money, which to many of them is their entire living, not as a group of irresponsible wild men just coming to town for a spree."[62] Masculine providers, responsible yet independent – this was the image the CPRA sought to promote.

Press releases of the later 1960s also highlighted masculinity, describing rodeo cowboys as "men who answer a challenge" and likening them to the "pioneers who answered the challenge of the wilderness. The businessmen [who] answer the challenge of new markets." Moreover, the cowboy was brave, choosing rodeo "because he's willing to ride against the odds as long as he can ride in freedom." Finally, whereas other athletes depended on codes of sportsmanship to bolster their integrity, the cowboy relied on nothing more than "a quality of honesty so taken for granted that it doesn't have a name. It's simply part of being a man." Ultimately, whereas ranch cowboys might ride the range in pickups and watch television, the rodeo cowboy was the only true cowboy left, "a sound horse under him, a stout rope in his hand, riding the last frontier." Individual stampedes, such as the one at Williams Lake, reprinted or adapted these CPRA press releases and included them in their programs.[63] In this way, cowboy associations worked to convince audiences of their point of view.

This emphasis on freedom, on connecting risk in rodeo with that in business and on the manliness of honesty and generosity, is a hallmark of Cold War–era masculinity, as the work of Christopher Dummitt and K.A. Cuordileone has revealed. There were ironies and contradictions in the image, however. First, the stress on the rodeo cowboy as a self-made man had much more to do with the historical construction of rancher masculinity than with that of working cowboys, who were itinerant wage-labourers. Jacqueline Moore's work nicely underscores the distinction between cowboys who worked and lived outside the norms of "civilization" and ranchers who perpetuated those norms.[64] The distinction was class-based, and, like race, class was something that the CPRA did not recognize. In its definition, all rodeo cowboys were entrepreneurs. Second, the cowboys epitomized the rejection of modernity, yet they embraced it as well. Their masculinity was linked to pastoralism and the escape from the effeminizing influences of modernity, with its diminished requirement for physical stamina and its cloying domesticity. But they were also modern, calculating risks both financial and physical, and contributing to a community that mitigated those risks through sharing information (about bucking broncs) and resources (through the CPRA's own insurance plan).[65] But whatever they did to moderate risks, their world was one of unquestioned toughness, a characteristic that was irrevocably linked to freedom in the Cold War era, when decisiveness and robustness were thought necessary to national security.[66]

As advanced by the CPRA, the definition of the rodeo cowboy was ex-plicitly masculine. As we saw in previous chapters, female contestants were edged out during the early years of professionalization.[67] Some rodeo fans were unhappy with this development. One anonymous woman writer lodged her complaint with Bert Shepperd, rancher and keeper of Alberta's cowboy record, writing that "it's time Guy Weadick moved over and made room for his wife and partner, Flores LaDue." She proceeded to list the women who had wowed the crowds at the 1912 Calgary Stampede, names she feared were being forgotten in the new world of professional rodeo.[68] Even where women's historical involvement was not forgotten, stampede organizers depicted it as a quaint aspect of the past, as in Lethbridge's sixtieth anniversary stampede program, which included a note on "Cowgirls' Bronc Riding," saying only that "there are very few rodeos of today that stage cowgirls' bronc riding as a contest ... but there was a time when it was as hotly contested as any event of the rodeo."[69] Times had changed, and by the immediate post-war era, women were often portrayed as antithetical to the rodeo cowboy. Individual cowboys sometimes described their wives as barriers to freedom. Writing to CPRA secretary Blair Holland in 1945, rodeo cowboy Larry Beany regretted his wife's presence on a recent trip, blaming her for inhibiting his plans: "I figured on stopping in Lethbridge and seeing you on my way down but brought an old married bag down to Regina and she wanted to come right through. Never again will any Damn woman ever tag on my trail."[70] Will Senger, a cowboy who founded Cloverdale's pro rodeo, told reporters that dedicating his life to the sport cost him two marriages. Commenting on the demise of the first one, Senger joked that "the first wife said, 'Either the horse goes or I go.' I said, 'Honey, I've had this horse longer than I've had you.'"[71] Whereas wives might slow men down, single women encountered on the circuit, sometimes called "buckle bunnies," offered other dangers. A 1962 article on Canadian saddle bronc champion Marty Wood contained this exchange between the respectable Wood and a woman troublemaker in a bar:

Freddie [Greer] and Marty were having one last drink in the bar and a woman walked in.

"Say, cowboy," she called to Marty.

"Yes'm."

"Do me a favor, willya? Be standing here talkin' to me when my boy friend comes in – I wanta make him jealous."

"Ma'am," said Marty. "I'm a happily married man, thank you. I don't hardly need trouble like that. Sorry."

"Shucks," said Freddie, "She coulda asked me, ah'm a bachelor."[72]

Rodeo cowboys' ambivalence toward women was legendary.[73] Conducting fieldwork in the late 1970s, Elizabeth Atwood Lawrence found widespread misogyny among US rodeo cowboys, who dismissed women's participation in rodeo. The men with whom she spoke thought that women trick riders and ropers were useless. They looked down on barrel racing and goat tying in professional rodeos, two events to which women were restricted at that time. The men were adamantly opposed to female participation in roughstock events, often claiming that it would damage their reproductive organs, or "end their family-making days." Even if they survived intact, their femininity and their desirability would be lost. As one contestant and editor of a rodeo magazine offered, "I wouldn't ask a woman bull rider out for a date," whereas another imagined that a female roughstock rider would be "a different breed of girl, rougher more masculine."[74] Lawrence's informants displayed marked ambivalence regarding marriage as the mechanism by which they themselves were domesticated – a view that found its way into 1950s and 1960s novels and films about rodeo. William Crawford's *Bronc Rider*, published in 1965, characterized a bronc-rider's wife as a "dirty bitch" and depicted sex as the enervating source of mistakes and injury.[75] Casual misogyny pulsed through much of the cultural production attendant to rodeo.

However ubiquitous such attitudes were, they were also very much contested, though perhaps with less volume than they were asserted. Attending a rodeo in 2004, I saw a T-shirt that read "Cowboys' Motto: Party til she's pretty." Following my gaze, the organizer turned to me and said, "Not all men who come to rodeos are cowboys."[76] Here again is that differentiation between cowboys and those who simply appear to be cowboys. Indeed, pro rodeo cowboys, in keeping with the respectable image cultivated by their organization, made their own distinctions. When I asked one veteran competitor to tell me about the contestants of the mid-1960s, he chuckled, naming each one as either a "hellion" or "a family man." When I asked what differentiated the two, he chuckled again and said that the hellion was the family man who left his wife at home. Then he glanced over his shoulder to check whether his wife, who was working in the concession booth behind us, had heard him.[77] For this individual, rough and respectable masculinities surfaced intermittently throughout a single life, emerging not essentially but as the situation warranted.

His distinction signalled another expression of masculinity, one that represents both the longevity of the sport in Western Canada and the success of professionalization in making it a paying proposition – rodeo cowboy as family man. Many Canadian pro cowboys, both settler and indigenous, *were* family men, and their personal histories are redolent with pride in rodeo lineages. Bull-rider Kelly Armstrong represents the third rodeo generation in his family; his grandfather entered every event at the first Calgary Stampede, and Kelly's father, Larry, rode in all three rough-stock competitions.[78] Bull-rider Duane Daines's father, Jack, won the Canadian Novice Bronc Riding Championship in 1956 and 1957, and his uncle, Ivan, was National Finals Rodeo Champion (for bronc riding) in 1970. During the 1960s, the Daines brothers built the original rodeo grounds in Innisfail, Alberta, running its "little britches rodeo" for young competitors in the 1970s.[79] Barrel-racing mothers encouraged their daughters to enter the sport, and team roping is often done by mixed-gender family teams, particularly at smaller rodeos. Like her pioneer barrel-racing mother, Isabella Miller, Bobbi-June Miller barrel-raced and goat-tied, and her daughter, Skylar, began competing in junior barrel racing in the late 1990s.[80] Nakoda steer-wrestler Jess Beaver followed his father into rodeo.[81] As Hugh Dempsey put it in the film *Gift of the Grand-fathers,* rodeo dynasties are not uncommon on reserves. Fred Gladstone's son Jim (Kainai) won the 1977 world championship calf-roping contest in Oklahoma, and Fred's daughter Caen (Gladstone) Bly was a champion barrel-racer in the Indian Rodeo Cowboy Association in 1968, 1969, and 1970.[82] Families such as the Gottfriedsons (Secwepemc) in Kamloops and the Bruiseheads (Kainai) in southern Alberta share histories of rodeoing and stock contracting that span as many as four generations.[83] Joan (Perry) Gottfriedson's daughter is a barrel-racer, and her sons are bulldoggers and calf-ropers.[84] Rodeo promotion too was often a family enterprise. When Deb Fleet moved from riding broncs to providing stock and announcing rodeos, his wife kept the books and did the paperwork. His sons then took to riding bulls.[85] Gwen Johansson followed in her father's footsteps by organizing rodeos in the Peace River District.[86] Peigan Pat Provost built on his family's long-standing success as ranchers to begin a stock-contracting business in the 1970s.[87] For Pete "Duke" LeBourdais

(Secwepemc), rodeo was a family sport, and his photo albums were filled with images of his children roping and riding.[88] Rodeo's interest in lineages is shared by settler and indigenous cowboys.

For some, travelling the rodeo circuit was an extended family vacation. As such, it built its own definitions of femininity and domesticity. When the wives or daughters of pro cowboys wanted to do more than just travel along, as one rodeo cowboy told me, "who were we to say no?"[89] From his perspective, women's events were the natural outgrowth of rodeo as a family sport, which was itself a result of reconfiguring the rodeo cowboy as a family man. Not all pro cowboys shared his view, however, and the women who carved out a space for themselves in pro rodeo did so through a skilled deployment of concepts such as femininity and family.

The Canadian Barrel Racing Association was formed in 1957. At first, it focused on promoting the relatively new sport of barrel racing but soon began to support women's participation in cow riding, goat tying, calf roping, steer undecorating, and team roping. In 1962 it changed its name to the Canadian Girls Rodeo Association (CGRA).[90] During its early years, it worked hard to ensure that women's events were included in rodeos throughout the Canadian West. It was especially successful with barrel racing. Cardston's rodeo included ladies' barrel racing in 1955.[91] In 1958, in a meeting with the Canadian Barrel Racing Association, the Foothills Cowboys Association agreed to allot time and money to ladies' barrel racing in its contests, including the final show at Didsbury that fall, so long as the CBRA could guarantee at least six contestants.[92] By 1962 the event was a recognized feature of the southern Alberta circuit, being run at Cardston, Medicine Hat, Lethbridge, Raymond, Fort Macleod, Taber, Foremost, Bassano, and Brooks.[93] Rodeos in the Peace River country included barrel racing (for both men and women), and in 1966, the Dawson Creek Rodeo also offered ladies' steer undecorating, adding goat tying three years later.[94] Other towns, such as High River, Lethbridge, Lloyd-minster, and Drumheller, responded eagerly to invitations to host all-women contests; High River was the first to do so, in 1962.[95] But by 1970, ladies' barrel racing was still "entirely optional" to professional rodeo organizers.[96] Even some committees that offered it had little sense that barrel-racers were as dedicated as rodeo cowboys to their sport. The Lethbridge Rodeo program of 1964 reported that they were an exception to the general rule that "the feminine gender may not make it a practice to enter many rodeo events, [nonetheless] most of the entrants have been training at home for weeks prior entering barrel racing events."[97] The Calgary Stampede initially resisted the pressure to include barrel racing, saying in 1965 that its afternoon program was already too full.[98] It offered barrel racing in 1969 but scheduled it on "kiddies day."[99] Barrel racing remains the only women's event at the Calgary Stampede.

Mary Lou LeCompte argues that the women who participated in girls' rodeo in the United States were mostly unmarried, with little knowledge of the role that women had played in rodeo during earlier times.[100] This was not the case for the women who formed the CGRA: they were experienced equestrians with ties to pro rodeo through husbands, fathers, or brothers. Committed to rodeo and to promoting women's place within it, the CGRA added its own gendered dimension to the professional rodeo community and to the definition of the cowboy. As individuals, CGRA members demonstrated a toughness not unlike that of their male counterparts. But in their life histories, toughness was tempered by references to family, not unlike those made by pro cowboys. CGRA founder Isabella Miller is a good example of this. In the late 1950s, when she became involved in organizing on behalf of women in rodeo, she was just a teenager, but she already had years of experience in riding and competing at rodeos. Her parents recalled putting her on horseback before she was out of diapers. At fifteen, she was travelling across Alberta to compete. Two years later, she stormed a Calgary Stampede organizers meeting, demanding that they offer barrel racing. By 1969 she was earning over $1,700 in prize money as a champion barrel-racer.[101] Her tremendous horse skills also opened other doors, and by the 1970s, she was working as a wrangler and stunt rider for Hollywood, coaching Charles Bronson's riding in one film, tending to Paul Newman's horses in another, and staging spectacular wagon crashes.[102] Though her first marriage to mechanic Mel Miller, also begun in her teen years, did not last, she was devoted to her three daughters, Billie-Ruth, Bobbi-June, and Tyler. For the Millers, as for other pro competitors, rodeo was a family event. Bobbi-June followed Isabella into rodeo, earning her junior all-round championship and her junior goat-tying championship as well as being awarded senior barrel-racing champion three times. As she put it, "When you are raised around it [rodeo], you kind of know no better." Bobbi-June's daughter Skylar was barrel racing by the late 1990s, so three generations of women in the Miller family were competing at the same time.[103] In her sixties, Isabella met former all-round cowboy champion Arnold Haraga (of southern Alberta)

Isabella Miller. *Courtesy of Bobbi June Radford*

and married him. They had four years together before he died of cancer. Less than six months later, in early 2007, Isabella's horse stumbled and threw her to the ground. She died two days afterward, of a massive aneurism caused by the fall, just short of her sixty-sixth birthday.[104] Her family's memories of her merge toughness with physical beauty, love of life, and devotion to family.

Joan Perry is another example of the kind of femininity that women brought to rodeo. Born on the Douglas Lake Reserve in southern BC, Joan worked on her parents' ranch until she was sent, at twelve, to the Kamloops Indian Residential School. Four unhappy years later, she returned to the ranch where she again went to work, hauling hay and caring for stock. From her grandfather, she says, she learned considerable horse savvy, and as a teenager, riding the family workhorse, King, she entered local gymkhanas, winning prizes and ribbons. In 1956 she met and married Dave Perry, a Secwepemc rodeo cowboy and stock contractor with a ranch at Cache Creek. Their names regularly appear together in the CPRA newspaper, *Canadian Rodeo News.* Joan worked alongside Dave and other cowboys, training horses, riding pick up, and competing as a barrel-racer. In 1964 the regular BC column in *Canadian Rodeo News* reported that she was training Dave's calf-roping horse since "as we all know there is nothing like good barrel training to improve a rope horse."[105] The same year, she was runner-up in ladies' barrel racing at the Kamloops Rodeo.[106] Throughout the 1960s, Joan and Dave Perry maintained a successful partnership in rodeo, ranch life, and raising six children.

Dave Perry died suddenly of a heart attack in 1970. Joan did not falter. During the week, the children did their chores and went to school, while Joan ran the ranch with the help of her daughter Joyce, who handled the administrative details of the business. On weekends the family rodeoed together. Joan taught them all to ride and, with the assistance of neighbour Archie Williams, honed their competitive spirit. Meanwhile, the rodeo community rallied around to help with the travelling. Echoing Joan's view of the rodeo world, one writer concluded, "It's the cowboy way for people to help each other out, and rodeo cowboys are all one big family."[107] For Joan Perry, rodeo has always been about family and skill. In the 1970s, she was a pioneer of barrel racing in British Columbia, one of the first to ride at the Williams Lake Stampede, and in 1976, she won the "best all-round" in the Interior Rodeo Association circuit.

Joan's strong leadership skills also made her a sensitive and intelligent horse trainer. When her barrel-racing horse Bucko lost one eye, she taught him to run the course in a reverse pattern so he could see the barrels as he approached them. He was Joan's "once in a lifetime horse," and she rode him to further championships in barrel racing and team roping, as well as in cutting horse competitions.[108] Throughout the 1970s and 1980s, she conducted horse-handling and barrel-racing workshops, continuing

Joan Perry. *BC Cowboy Heritage Society*

to support her family and contribute to rodeo, particularly to women's involvement in the sport. Joan's biographies always stress both her grit and her dedication to family, and she has often attributed the success of her children to rodeo, stating that it helped them remain self-confident and well adjusted despite their father's untimely death.[109] As she put it in a 2004 interview, with rodeo, "You keep your kids together, you keep them out of trouble, and once they finish school, you hope they can go on from there."[110] Her second husband, rodeo luminary Ron Gottfriedson, concurred that rodeo builds families and teaches children respect, determination, the value of hard work, and self-confidence.[111]

Barrel-racers and women competitors, then, combined the hardiness of the rodeo cowboy with a dedication to family that did not soften their image. Although the CGRA worked to place women in rodeo, it did not take an adversarial position vis-à-vis male contestants or seek to alter the overall feminine image of rodeo women. Nonetheless, it stressed the cooperation and support they received and were willing to give their male counterparts. Indeed, the motto "We Salute the Cowboys" was emblazoned on the program of the first All-Girl Championship Rodeo and Race Meet, which was held at High River in 1962.[112] Three years later, anticipating the next all-girls' rodeo, which would be at Didsbury, the CGRA asked stock contractor Harry Vold to be the arena director, certain that "he [would be] a drawing card, and things would run smoothly under his supervision."[113] Vold declined the offer. The CGRA minutes record little condemnation of men who were not supportive, though members must have been frustrated when, for example, Jeanne Twa tried to set up a pony chariot race for a women's rodeo at Calgary in the fall of 1975 and reported that "any pony chuckwagon men whom I talked to said they would not be interested in having a girl drive their horses in case something happened to one of the animals. They just did not seem to think that it was a good idea and did not seem to be too interested."[114] Thirty years later, women chuckwagon drivers still reported hearing the occasional "The driver is a girl?" but contemporary chuckwagon driver Tracy Stott of Olds, Alberta, concluded a 1994 interview by saying, "When you're out on the track, it's not men against women, it's team against team, and the best team wins."[115] The fact that many CGRA members and others who competed in barrel racing or other women's events belonged to rodeo families must have muted their criticism of cowboys and accounts for their emphasis on support. Indeed, in its official discussions of barrel racing, the CGRA said that it began when "women traveling the rodeo circuit with their husbands wanted an event of their own."[116] As barrel-racer Monica Wilson explained, her rodeo debut came about precisely because she was "bored with going to rodeos just to watch" as her husband, Bob, rode bulls and wrestled steers.[117] Many early stars of women's rodeo were the daughters and wives of prominent professional cowboys. Rose Marie Linder, Connie Gladstone, Pearl Mandeville, and the Duce sisters all claimed genealogies in pro rodeo.[118] Here again family was the ground upon which women in the 1990s continued to stand. Tracy Stott's father, Jack, raced chuckwagons, and Tracy grew up at the track, warming up her father's horses by the time she was ten years old. As she put it, "I've been around the track, stepped on and snorted on by horses. It would be unnatural for me not to be around horses. This is just who I am."[119] Linda Shippett-Huble followed not just her father, William, but also her mother, Jean, into chuckwagon racing. Her mother started off in barrel racing and moved into pony chariot and then to chuckwagon races.[120] The depth of family connection helped diminish the disruption in having women compete in what, until recently, had been men's events.

The CGRA was successful in its efforts to set aside certain women's events, to promote them, and to create a space for women in the increasingly masculinized world of professional rodeo. Other women have used that space to leverage further participation. Tsilhquot'in education worker Joan (Palmantier) Gentles comes from a large rodeo family. Her father was Leonard Palmantier, a founder of the Williams Lake Stampede, and her family was steeped in the rodeo history of the BC Interior. She was rodeo queen at the Williams Lake Stampede before she moved on to barrel racing. When all-girls' rodeo came to the region, she competed in bronc riding as well. Then she broke her leg. Rather than being sidelined, she tried timekeeping but disliked it because "you're looking at the stopwatch, you're not watching what's going on out there." So she tried her hand as a flag judge, and when her performance generated many compliments, she considered becoming a full-fledged rodeo judge. She felt well situated to do so: her three brothers had competed for many years, she knew a lot about roughstock, and she had been around these animals all her life. So she studied the rules and, finally deciding to take the plunge, enrolled in the CPRA judging school at Calgary. As she recalled,

I faced a lot of discrimination by the old men there. The first day was really hectic, but I just let them be. And by the third day they were shaking my hand and appreciating and respecting the knowledge that I had ... It was tough to sit there and kind of be mellow because I am an advocate for females. I am an advocate for women and I am an advocate for Aboriginal people. I am an advocate for the underdogs. But you know when you need to stand up and you know when to just let them learn. And y'know, by the third day and writing the exam I did very well on the exam. And they told us our scores that day and I

Joan (Palmantier) Gentles. *The Museum of the Cariboo Chilcotin (home of the BC Cowboy Hall of Fame)*

was among the top. So from there I started judging and then I started assisting in putting on the judging clinics and at first they'd only allow me to do the female stuff, the female events at the rodeo. And finally they allowed me to be a participant in teaching the whole thing. So it was kind of being mellow, but making the point that yes we are capable, yes we are very observant, and yes we can do it. So I did quite a bit of judging.[121]

Goat tying at the all-girls' rodeo, Tsuu T'ina reserve, 1967. *Glenbow Museum Archives, NA-2557-65*

The work of women such as Joan Gentles, her persistence and skilled engagement with those "old men" of rodeo, opened doors for even greater female involvement. Increasingly, women have re-entered the roughstock events. Sto:lo Kaila Mussell is the first woman to ride broncs in PRCA (Professional Rodeo Cowboys Association, the American equivalent of the CPRA) rodeos.[122] Though she remains the only woman to do so, young women are rising in the ranks through the regional associations. At the 2009 Nemiah Valley Rodeo, for example, ranchers in the stands asked interestedly whether the "girl" – Terris Billyboy – would be competing that year. They seemed genuinely pleased when she appeared in junior steer riding.[123] With just a dash of pink on her helmet, Billyboy continued the tradition in which femininity and toughness sit comfortably together for some women in the world of rodeo.

Finally, like the professional cowboys of the CPRA, women of the CGRA were concerned with appearances. CGRA rules stipulate that contestants

Marie Crowchild and Patricia Simon, all-girls' rodeo on the Tsuu T'ina reserve, 1965. *Glenbow Museum Archives, NA-2557-59*

must "appear in the arena in complete neat and clean western attire, including long-sleeved shirts and cowboy hats, [which] must not fall off during a race."[124] Members who argued with officials were disciplined, as were those who abused their horses, particularly, as the minutes recorded in 1970, "at shows where the SPCA is strong."[125] But the CGRA also wished to counter or co-opt the growing importance of queen contests. Members were pleased when legendary bronc-rider Dick Cosgrove supported their bid to "escort" the 1964 Calgary Stampede queen in that event's parade, thus adding the presence of skilled competitive horsewomen to the section

Calf roping at the all-girls' rodeo on the Tsuu T'ina reserve, 1966. *Glenbow Museum Archives, NA-2557-60*

of the parade that might otherwise have focused mainly on female beauty.[126] They also staged their own queen contest at their "all-girl rodeo" in 1964; its judging criteria were weighted 60 percent on "horsemanship and ability, 20% on appearance and personality and 20% on knowledge."[127] Careful not to criticize other queen contests, they nonetheless approved heartily when prominent queens, particularly those at Calgary, revealed an interest in improving the position of women in the sport. Such was the case when former Calgary Stampede queen Julie Thoreson qualified as a CGRA judge for the ladies' cutting horse competition, an event that the "Out of the Barrel" column in the *Canadian Rodeo News* called "another big stride in further developing women's horsemanship."[128] When the

Calgary Stampede queen of 1964, Sharon Patterson, also won the rodeo queen for the Canadian Barrel Racing and Rodeo Association, she was declared a "true rodeo queen."[129] During an era in which the queen was the most prominent female presence at community rodeos and the Calgary Stampede, female competitors were eager to present another face to the crowd.

Although the pro cowboy was overtly gendered, processes of racialization within professional rodeo were much more muted, even downplayed. The pro community sought to set itself apart from the small towns that staged rodeos and, to a degree, saw both "cowboys and Indians" and the history they represented as commodities deployed to promote local business and attract tourists. In part, the CPRA's job was to protect rodeo cowboys from simply being performers in a local game of representation, and, as we saw with Kenny McLean earlier in this chapter, that included Aboriginal cowboys. All cowboys, whatever their heritage, were part of the nomadic world of rodeo, the community that, in the language of the sport, formed by "going down the road." Pro cowboys and their families were often away from home for months at a time, so they created their own community. Their gruelling travel schedules separated them from the towns that staged the rodeos they attended. As it moved across the landscape, their community became a liminal contact zone, one where Aboriginal and settler cowboys worked together, travelled together, and raised families together.

Contestant lists clearly reveal that Aboriginal people maintained their presence in professional rodeos. Though their numbers declined as a result of professionalization (see Chapter 5), a significant minority of Aboriginal people competed at various rodeos across British Columbia and Alberta. At the 1964 Fort Macleod pro rodeo, for example, 30 of the 129 contestants listed reserve communities as their homes. Across the Canadian West, at rodeos big and small, at least one big-name Aboriginal cowboy always competed, from Fred Gladstone in the 1950s, to Kenny McLean in the 1960s, to Jim Gladstone in the 1970s; an Aboriginal child with an interest in rodeo could always find a hero to admire. Of course, all sports claim to be open to everyone, but unlike baseball, for example, rodeo never operated with a colour bar.[130] So, though rodeo as a settler event may have been about Aboriginal dispossession, as scholars Joan Burbick and Elizabeth Furniss assert, professional rodeo eschewed small-town imperatives, rejecting at least in part the staging and restaging of conquest that lay at the heart of some rodeos. The fact that it did so rankled at settler rodeos, but adopting this stance removed the pro community from the larger social drama in which it played a part. It created, articulated, and adhered to its own standards, which both Aboriginal and settler rodeo folk claimed as their own.

Several themes emerge in biographies of and interviews with Canadian professional rodeo families: family, cooperation, mobility, and freedom are greatly valued. Add to that an appreciation for animals and a sense of separation from the towns and cities through which they pass, and the conceptual framework for the pro community comes into focus. Historians and anthropologists who have studied Aboriginal rodeo describe these values as particularly Native. In *Riders of the West: Portraits from Indian Rodeo*, Peter Iverson argues that "the world of Native rodeo is built on a foundation of family, constructed, generation by generation, on time-honored values. Knowledge. Hard work. Practice. Patience. Determination. Courage. Competition. Achievement."[131] The documentary film *The Gift of the Grandfathers* declares that horsemanship is a "vibrant part of Western First Nations culture."[132] And Morgan Baillargeon and Leslie Tepper introduce their beautiful volume *Legends of Our Times* by writing that, "for Native cowboys throughout the Americas, their traditional beliefs, practices, and especially their history impart an additional dimension to cowboy culture. For many there exists a special relationship with the animals with which they work."[133] But settler rodeo families also subscribe to these values. Interestingly, whereas pro rodeo cultivated these principles through the rules and public discourses of its organizations, most rodeo families situate them within their own histories, often in ranching, rural, or reserve life. This suggests that both Aboriginal and settler rodeo folk shared the ideals that drew them to the sport and were reaffirmed by it.

The professional rodeo community was forged on the road. During the post-war era, serious competitors travelled at least every weekend, from the first rodeos of the spring season on the Victoria Day weekend to the last ones in September. For elite athletes, the season extended throughout the winter at indoor rodeos and in the southern United States. Whatever their level of commitment or skill, contestants covered thousands of miles in a season, following a punishing schedule in which they often drove through the night or left a rodeo before it ended so as to reach the next one on time. As one popular book on rodeo suggested, "It's said that if the rodeo doesn't kill you, the commute will."[134] For others, travelling was an opportunity to experience the freedom of life on the road and the "high" of moving on to the next competition.[135] Being accompanied by family made the road a little easier. Some made families of the people with whom they journeyed.

The professional rodeo circuit made homes on the road and family of the people encountered there, whether their heritage was Aboriginal or settler. The NFB production *Hard Rider* followed all-round cowboy champion Kenny McLean as he toured the 1967 circuit. It opened with an early morning driving scene with McLean at the wheel of his pickup truck and camper, his young son, Guy, nestled on his lap. For viewers, McLean personified the rodeo cowboy as family man. Early in the film, McLean's wife, Joyce, explained that they shared the responsibilities of life on the road ("we take turns driving and taking care of Guy") and tried to mitigate the less pleasant aspects ("living out of suitcases and cafés"). McLean portrayed himself as a devoted father and husband: "I like to have Joyce and Guy around all the time. I believe if they had to stay home I wouldn't rodeo."[136]

The Gladstone family had a similar experience. Roping on the pro circuit in the 1940s, Fred and Edith Gladstone hauled five horses and three children, covering tens of thousands of miles on the Plains, though they were heavily involved in Kainai political life as well as running the family ranch. Gladstone hoped that bringing his son Jim on the circuit would improve their relationship. In a letter to his parents, he wrote that he had "been away rodeoing with Jimmy. I thought we may be able to get along better if we got to know one another a little better, we seem to [have] got along OK on the road, but as soon as we get home, I just can't seem to get him out of bed and that's when I blow my top. I guess all boys his age like to sleep in the AM."[137] Despite Gladstone's frustrations during his son's teen years, father and son developed mutual respect. Jim went on to championship-level calf roping. Asked if he could take credit for this, Fred told interviewer Charles Ursenbach in 1975, "I guess I helped him a little bit. He did most of the training himself, he had the desire to rope, and I didn't discourage him or anything like that."[138] Two years later, when Jim Gladstone won the world championship for calf roping at the national finals in Oklahoma City, he credited his father for pioneering the sport and supporting his pursuit of it.[139]

Rufus Goodstriker and his son grease a chuckwagon wheel, Goodstriker farm, Blood reserve, 1959. *Glenbow Museum Archives, PA-3820-1-3*

In rodeo, family extended beyond blood relatives. Friends became family as older cowboys and their families followed the pattern of assisting younger competitors. Country singer Ron West recalled his youth as a time when families such as the Gottfriedsons and the Palmantiers took him in and treated him like one of their own.[140] Pete "Duke" LeBourdais fondly remembered the training he received from Dave Perry in roping and in life as he travelled with Dave, his wife, Joan, and their children to local rodeos throughout British Columbia.[141] The genealogies cited by successful contestants go beyond blood ties and often move between Aboriginal and settler communities. For example, Chilcotin rancher Mike Isnardy transported Joan Palmantier's barrel-racing horse when she could not afford the necessary truck and trailer. And Hilary and Rita Place guided her when she was rodeo queen for the Williams Lake Stampede. Rancher and rodeo cowboy Bill Evans remembered Secwepemc Alex Dick as a rider who influenced him. Mutual support, a strongly held value among professional cowboys, reached beyond lines of racialization as when Canadian champion Mel Hyland said of Jim Gladstone's 1977 win at the national finals in Oklahoma City, "I feel as good as if I'd just won another championship." Like Tom Three Persons before him, Gladstone received praise from both settler and Aboriginal communities. Two hundred people awaited his triumphant return home at Calgary's airport and again in Cardston. The Calgary Stampede Board commissioned a plaque in his honour, and the Kainai Magpie Society gave him the name Many Guns.[142]

Travelling companions became family as well. Barrel-racer Monica Wilson referred to the women she toured with as sisters, saying, "there's a closeness there, a bond that people feel for each other when they go so many miles together." They looked after each other's health and their morale.[143] An Aboriginal rodeo queen who followed the circuit to promote professional rodeo in the 1950s made friends with the other queens and was accorded respect by the cowboys and trick riders who worked with her.[144] The film *Hard Rider* is replete with scenes of rodeo cowboys, some Aboriginal, some not, hanging out together, playing cards. When one Aboriginal cowboy loses at poker, he jokingly remarks that the "white men were screwing the Indians again." Fred Gladstone also spoke in a light-hearted way about the people with whom he travelled: "Years ago we used to go down the road and you travel with a group of people just like a gypsy camp or circus, going from town to town and you get to know a lot of people."[145] Moving together as a group, especially when families were involved, promoted a sense of kinship among professional rodeo athletes. Joan (Perry) Gottfriedson described it this way: "And the rodeo itself, the non-Native and Native got along really well. You camped out and all your kids played with each other, and you weren't afraid that someone was gonna run off with your kids, or, you know, what's happening nowadays. It was good. You brought your kids up, you worked with them, and you were with them all the time."[146] Her husband and his brothers agree. Ron

Gottfriedson, whose father, Gus, was one of the first Indian representatives on the CPRA executive, remembered that, during his early days of competition, there was discrimination against non-whites participating in rodeo, especially in the southern United States. As he said, "You could count the Natives in pro rodeo on one hand." But in Canada, the Gottfriedson name was well known, and he travelled with rodeo cowboys who became his best friends. Pooling their financial resources, Gottfriedson said, they could journey for weeks, with each one putting his earnings in the glovebox. Remembering his days of touring the circuit with a carload of buddies, Gottfriedson concluded that "in the pro ... rodeo circuits, you helped everybody and everybody helped you. And that's the way it was ... It didn't matter the colour of your skin or what. That was the rodeo life, that was rule number one, and it wasn't anything to do with Indian rodeos or pro rodeos or amateur rodeos or anything; everybody just got along and helped each other and that's the way it was." His brother Garry, a university-trained poet, rancher, and horse-breeder, agreed: "The guys I started out with [at high school rodeo] became lifelong friends ... There weren't any other Indians that year in high school rodeo, so I was the only Indian with all these cowboys, so that was a mixed crowd that I hung out with and we're still friends today."[147] Barrel-racer and rodeo queen Joan (Palmantier) Gentles said the same thing: "Inside the rodeo arena, I feel very comfortable. And I feel like I'm a part of the family, and I watch other people and ... we're all cheering one another on. I don't feel like an outsider ... I don't think we see colour inside that arena."[148] Rodeo cowboys expressed a kinship that went beyond social and cultural distinctions. During an interview just before his death in 2004, Bill Evans reported that he travelled the circuit with Aboriginal friends. His wife, Lil, of the Colville First Nation, agreed that "they respected each other and helped each other out." Al Byer, a Merritt organizer of high school rodeo, recalled,

> The local Native kids travelled with anybody. I mean, there was no such thing, any concerns of if you're Native or if you're white, or whatever. It was just strictly there to help each other. And that's one big thing about rodeo that I've always found. And you'll even see it today, even in your pro circuits. Cowboys get down and help their fellows competing against them. They'll help them set them up and tell them if they've had that animal out bucking at that event, they'll explain to the guy just exactly what that horse or bull is gonna do, and it's just a great comradeship as far as I'm concerned with rodeoing.[149]

Indeed, camaraderie is valued by Native and non-Native rodeo people alike. When the Linnell family travelled throughout British Columbia, taking their daughters to barrel-racing, pole-bending, and queen contests, they often looked to other rodeo families for aid. While en route to the rodeo at the Mt. Currie Reserve, their vehicle broke down by the side of the road, their trailer loaded with horses and tack. Within minutes, other rodeo families had stopped to help, and they were soon on their way. As the elder Linnell said, "If you are having a problem, the guys chip in and help out ... [They're] a different kind of people."[150]

This sense of being a "different kind of people" is common among professional cowboys. Commenting on differences within the rodeo community, Bill Evans argued that if trouble occurred, it was between the cross-cultural rodeo community and the towns it visited. There local men seemed to want to "mix it up" with the rodeo cowboys. The scheduling of rodeos often meant that pro cowboys could not stay to take part in dances or other community events, further distancing them from the towns in which they competed. Tensions between rodeo and the larger society also affected and were played out in the sport of rodeo. Lil Evans recalled that the biggest fight she ever saw was at a 1960s Kispiox Rodeo in northwestern BC where the "hippies" and the cowboys went at it.[151] Studying rodeos in the BC Interior during the late 1960s, anthropologist Roger Haugen noted that the pro cowboys, including Aboriginal cowboys, kept their own company, whereas the spectators paid varying degrees of attention to the rodeo itself and seemed more intent on partying, visiting, gambling, and fighting. As a result, the experiences of the professionals who competed at places such as Anahim Lake differed greatly from those of the locals.[152]

Increasing differences regarding the treatment of animals have also somewhat distanced the pro community from small-town folks as well as urban people. But the relationships between contestants and animals have changed over time. A team of anthropologists who interviewed Aboriginal rodeo cowboys in the 1990s asked them specifically if their relationship with animals differed from that of their settler counterparts. Some answered that it did, but many stated that rodeo people generally had a better understanding of and appreciation for animals than most non-rodeo people did, both for roughstock and the horses used in timed events. This view clearly agrees with the stance taken by pro rodeo associations in Canada and the United States since the 1940s. Yet through the

1970s, there remained considerable evidence that ideas of conquest and domination retained salience in pro rodeo circles, especially with reference to the roughstock. In *Hard Rider,* a scene designed to demonstrate the ongoing linkages between contestants and ranching shows Kenny McLean working with other cowboys to brand a herd of recently captured wild horses as they screamed and struggled, their eyes wild with terror. Elizabeth Lawrence, likewise, found that pro cowboys differentiated between the wild and the tame, expressing the need to dominate or eradicate the former and praising the latter.[153] Some old BC ranching families see rodeo as an expression of the skills required to control animals in order to care for them.[154] Others disagree, saying that rodeo is a throwback to older, harsher times when stock, particularly young stock and especially colts, was accidentally killed through the violence of older methods. They assert that current ranching methods are much more humane.[155] And yet, as we have seen, rodeo has set its own standards of animal care and has punished those whose abuse of animals threatens the respectability of the sport. Sometimes it has worked in concert with animal protection advocates.

Many contestants express nothing but respect for the animals they encounter, and certainly in the timed events, horses are their partners. Joan (Perry) Gottfriedson recalled her one-eyed barrel-racing horse, who challenged her training skills in so many ways and with whom she overcame tremendous obstacles, as her "once in a lifetime horse."[156] Joan (Palmantier) Gentles similarly looked back on the important role of horse training in her childhood on the Chilcotin Plateau. Barrel-racer Monica Wilson reminisced about impressive partnerships between rider and horse, which sometimes led her to tears, including the team of Kristie Peterson and Bozo. In Wilson's opinion, the animals attracted both competitors and fans to the sport of rodeo. Like Joan Gottfriedson, she most valued the horse with whom she faced the greatest challenges. Strong bonds between horses and riders, moreover, are not confined to women. As Wilson recalled, "I've seen rough, tough cowboys break down over the loss of a horse."[157] Certainly, this was the case for champion calf-roper Percy Minnabarriet: due to the carelessness of someone who left a gate open, his prized calf-roping horse wandered onto a nearby highway where it was struck by a passing car. A fifty-year career on the BC rodeo circuits ended on that darkened highway because Minnabarriet could not conceive of continuing without the horse.[158]

Increasingly, articulate contestants express love even for the rough-stock. Monica Wilson described roughstock riders who "tip their hat" to a horse that has thrown them. Bull-rider and stock contractor Kelly Armstrong told Dave Poulsen that "my bulls are like my kids to me." He went on to describe their intelligence, their talent for assessing a rider and how best to throw him, and their canny ability to find the out-gate in an unfamiliar arena.[159] Similarly, Duane Daines viewed the broncs he drew in his career as individual personalities, remembering their names and their particular proclivities.[160] Some roughstock cowboys purchased their favourite broncs so that they could live out their days on their spread. As Daines put it, "I guess it isn't surprising that some guys like to be able to look out the window and see a horse out in a pasture that they rode ten years ago at Calgary or Red Deer or Hanna. It's a nice memory for the cowboy and a good home for an old horse in his retirement years."[161] Gradually expanding acceptance of gentler training methods has spread to rodeo as well, though some would say that they had already existed there for a long time. Mike LeBourdais credited his father, Pete "Duke" LeBourdais, for using horse-whisperer methods long before Tom Dorrance and Monty Roberts popularized them.[162] Similarly, Blanche, a rodeo queen of the 1940s whom Joan Burbick interviewed, described her own methods, which were based on those of Dorrance and Roberts, as grounded in a deep respect between horses and riders.[163] Within rodeo circles, the rhet-oric of respect is deeply held. When a young woman attending the 2009 Nemiah Valley Rodeo became alarmed by a bronc struggling in the chute, a rancher sitting next to her patiently, if a little condescendingly, explained that a bucking horse's life is one of short bursts of work surrounded by months, even years, of pampering. Moreover, he added, after machinery replaced workhorses, some horses avoided slaughter only because rodeo gave them a new purpose. The shift from the emphasis on domination to one of collaboration between human and animal is neatly signalled by the changing language of the prayers used in rodeo circles. In *Hard Rider,* a Christian minister opens a late 1960s rodeo in Texas with a prayer invok-ing men's God-given right to dominate animals. Such is not the trope of more contemporary prayers, however. More recently, the "Cowboy Prayer" has become popular in cowboy circles, particularly at funerals. Its words – "We don't ask for special favors; we don't ask to draw around a chute fightin' horse or to never break a barrier: Nor do we ask for all daylight runs or not to draw a steer that won't lay" – resonate with those who see rodeo as the expression of an ethic that accepts animals as they are.[164]

Through the Canadian Professional Rodeo Association, Western Canada's pro community worked collectively to promote its sport and to reinvent the identity of the rodeo cowboy in the late twentieth century. Through its insurance plan and the guidelines that regulated not just the sport but also the behaviour of competitors, the CPRA sought to increase their respectability in line with dominant expressions of masculinity during the Cold War era. The emphasis on rodeo as a family sport, which was part of the drive to ensure its propriety, created avenues for female participation. Women contestants drew upon and built feminine identities that mingled physical and mental toughness with devotion to family and to animals – attributes that also underscored respectability. Whereas pro rodeo grappled explicitly with gender, it tended to downplay racialization while consciously including Aboriginal cowboys and their families. Its values – attention to family and community, care for animals, and a desire for freedom as defined by mobility – are claimed equally by cowboys and Aboriginal peoples. Self-consciously produced by and institutionalized in pro rodeo, they have made the pro circuit a contact zone. Never a well-defined space of contact, the pro community moves across landscapes and through towns, setting up camps, meeting in hotels, and creating spaces for itself that stand somewhat apart from the dominant social forces of contemporary Western Canada. Over the course of the late twentieth century, professional rodeo has produced new identities, new communities, and its own ways of thinking about the West and the people, whether Aboriginal or settler, who live there.

5

Going Pro

Community Rodeo in the Era of Professionalization

*All popular culture is a process of struggle, of struggle over
meanings of social experience, of one's personhood and its relations
to the social order and of the texts and commodities of that order.*
— *John Fiske*, Understanding Popular Culture

In Paul St. Pierre's *Breaking Smith's Quarterhorse,* the protagonist Smith
goes to Williams Lake to retrieve his Tsilhqot'in friend Antoine, who has
ended up in jail in a case of mistaken identity. Smith goes to town, freshly
shaved, wearing his "hand tooled riding boots that were normally reserved
for Stampede time," and bails Antoine out. But when his friend wishes
to attend to further business, Smith urges him to leave, saying, "This is
not a town for people like you and me anymore Ol' Antoine. It is not a
place for cowboys and Indians now. It is a businessman's town now. You
come back to Namko with me."[1] The sense that Williams Lake had ceased
to be a "place for cowboys and Indians" emerged mainly because of
the changing economics of mid-twentieth-century British Columbia. No
longer the edge of settlement, increasingly focused on modern modes of
industrial resource extraction, especially forestry and the manufacturing
of pulp and paper, the Cariboo-central Interior held few places for small-
scale ranching and the mixed economies in which Aboriginal people had
engaged.[2] In particular, the extension of forestry, with its network of logging roads, massive machinery, and clear-cutting techniques, put First
Nations, settlers, and companies in direct competition for land as cut-
blocks consumed hunting and gathering sites. Mechanization in ranching
reduced the need for extra labour at haying time, and the ranches employed fewer and fewer cowboys.[3] Williams Lake was the administrative
and commercial hub in a new set of relations that characterized a mod-
ernized Canadian West. It was, indeed, as St. Pierre described it, a businessman's town.

The professional rodeo staged at Williams Lake, like those at many other towns in Western Canada after the Second World War, was also a modern affair. The influence of the Canadian Professional Rodeo Association (CPRA) on the organization of rodeos increased during these decades, and some community rodeos welcomed the new standards it brought to the sport. Pro rodeo cowboys and barrel-racers conferred a certain skill level and prestige on local events. Being on the pro circuit meant a guaranteed entry for small-scale rodeos, which often survived on a shoestring budget. The pro contestants who came to town were governed by CPRA codes of behaviour, which, inasmuch as they followed these rules, lessened some of the tensions generated by their presence. CPRA-approved judges and scheduling removed much of the conflict from organizing, ensuring an easy and profitable affair. The advantages of holding a professional rodeo prompted many towns to stage them, opening their doors to the peripatetic community of contestants that included Aboriginal and settler cowboys, barrel-racers, and their families.

Professionalization, however, brought struggles of a different sort, and not all communities welcomed the change. For one thing, raising and guaranteeing prize money challenged many organizing committees. Some worried that local men and women, including nearby First Nations, would be excluded from events in which professional athletes dominated. Rodeo remained popular, and communities found it a compelling way to express the cultures of small-town Western Canada, for tourists and for themselves, so they had no wish to surrender it to professional organizers and cowboys. Some staged amateur events alongside professional ones, and some added or played up local features such as queen contests and mountain races to provide venues for local women and men. Some joined with pro cowboys to promote "little britches rodeo" for junior competitors or "girls' rodeo" for women, thus extending the lines of interaction between rodeo and communities.

Some webs of interaction, however, were stretched to the breaking point. In many cases, the professionalization of small-town rodeo excluded local Aboriginal contestants. As in the 1930s, in the post-war era many Aboriginal competitors found the costs of travelling the pro circuits to be prohibitive. New, higher entry fees required by the CPRA closed off local rodeos to them as well. Although parades still featured so-called Indian sections, few small-town rodeos maintained a formal Indian village after the war, so Aboriginal women lost this opportunity to market their goods.

As contact zones, rodeos became increasingly fragmented. Pro cowboys minimized racialization, and the small towns that hosted them either did not know or did not care that some of them, such as Kenny McLean, were Aboriginal or of mixed heritage. Meanwhile, local riders known by small-town crowds to be Aboriginal were often unable to enter the professional events and thus found themselves relegated to amateur contests with lower entry fees and lower-valued prizes. Finally, as small towns used rodeos to articulate their own version of the past, one that historicized whiteness and justified a status quo in which Aboriginal people were increasingly disadvantaged and marginalized, Aboriginal people and their supporters challenged the place that they held in small-town rodeos. They expressed their own world views at rodeo, and in some cases, these were not welcomed by organizers. Nevertheless, some Aboriginal participants continued to provide alternative versions of Western Canada's history from within the arena. Others chose to withdraw entirely, as we will see in the next chapter.

The end of the Second World War promised new economic prosperity to towns in British Columbia and Alberta. Global demand for natural resources, from wood products to minerals to oil, offered a chance at the "good life" for residents of both provinces. Tourists travelled new and improved road systems and spent disposable income of unprecedented levels in small towns across the Canadian West. And just as a continent-wide fascination with the cowboy drew attention to professional rodeos, so too did small towns seek to capitalize on the post-war fervour for the western. As Paul Voisey observes of post-war High River, the attraction of an aristocratic English ranching past faded in favour of one that lauded cowboys, cattle drives, and the elements of the Hollywood western.[4] Williams Lake resumed the rodeos it had held before the war and advertised that they offered visitors "three wild nights in the Cariboo."[5] Even Bassano, Alberta, whose pre-war board of trade motto had been "There will always be an England," advertised its post-war stampede with the line "the best in the west, by a dam site," playing on its location at the Bassano dam.[6] Organizing committees from Cremona, Alberta, to Kamloops, BC, initiated, resumed, or expanded rodeos in the years immediately following the war. The success of one often prompted the establishment of another. After attending the Kamloops Rodeo in 1944, Jack Shannon and Clarke Greenaway brought the idea back to the Cloverdale Kinsmen, who staged the first Cloverdale Rodeo in 1945 with the slogan "the West Goes Wilder."[7] From the fall of 1946 to the spring of 1947, organizing committees in Kelowna, Kamloops, Hardisty, Vernon, Merritt, Oliver, and Cloverdale all wrote to the CPRA asking what was required to set up professional rodeos in their towns.[8] Jake Twoyoungmen organized the Morley Stampede in 1946 and asked the CPRA to approve the prize list for bronc riding, calf roping, bareback riding with surcingle, men's steer riding, wild cow milking, a wild horse race, a maverick race, and a stake race.[9] In the 1950s and 1960s, at least eighty small towns, rural communities, and reserves in southern Alberta and the BC Interior staged professional rodeos.[10]

For tourists, however, the attraction of pro rodeo did not lie in its modernity: rather, the drawing card was the escape from modernity that rodeo's celebration of the past seemed to offer. As historians of post-war tourism have shown, Americans and Canadian sought connection with history as tourists, whether with fisher folk in Nova Scotia or in the "wilds" of the Canadian Shield.[11] BC tourism promoters identified the province's past, represented in part by Aboriginal culture and Aboriginal people themselves, as a key feature to be commodified for the tourist market.[12] Cowboys too offered an anti-modern image to sell to tourists seeking relief from the conformity of modern life. In a 1961 article titled "Williams Lake: Heart of the Cariboo," BC's tourism magazine *Beautiful British Columbia* advertised the province as a land of cowboys and pioneers. Visitors were promised a "land rich in history," with "sturdy log cabins, a few stage coaches and a diminishing coterie of men who recall the lusty days of their youth when the cowboy was king."[13] At the centre of the region was Williams Lake, and here, the article asserted, tourists would experience the region's past and feel the "dynamic undertone which is always close to the surface in this country," through the Williams Lake Stampede. *Beautiful British Columbia*'s writers wanted to impress readers with the stampede's superior genuineness by claiming that cowboys from over five hundred ranches in the region competed there for fun, not money, giving the stampede "a more authentic western flavor than any other Stampede in North America."[14] In photo spreads that included panoramic views of the Thompson River, herds of wild horses, cattle grazing on rolling hills, abandoned log cabins, and action shots from the stampede numerically dominated the article. Clearly, tourism promoters felt that rodeo offered visitors a chance to experience the past in a dramatic spectacle and to rub shoulders with living examples of pioneer independence in a rapidly modernizing province.[15]

Local entrepreneurs in both Alberta and BC shared this view of the promotional potential of cowboy history and of rodeo as its expression. The Lethbridge and District Exhibition and Rodeo Committee and the Lethbridge Diamond Jubilee Committee welcomed visitors to their rodeo in 1951 with the promise that they would enjoy a "return to the 'GOOD OLD DAYS' of not so long ago" and "remember those pioneers who laid the foundation of this progressive city of ours in Sunny Southern Alberta."[16] Amid photos and text celebrating the town's history from its origins as Fort Whoop-Up were glossaries of "Cowboy Lingo" designed to clarify rodeo vocabulary for visitors and hence to grant them admission to the closed world of the rodeo cowboy as well as a fleeting sense of being an "insider."[17] The High River Agricultural Society asserted that its town was "rich in history," embracing rodeo as an expression of its past and identity. Furthermore, it claimed greater authenticity for its event on the grounds that it was "much closer to the real west" than its competitors in other centres.[18] Indeed, Guy Weadick, by 1946 a booster for the High River region, explained the success of the town's rodeo: "They are fortunate of course in being located in the real ranching country where many of the Canadian contestants have come from during the years and the local folks not only like cowboy sports, but understand the technical points that govern riding roping etc. ... For that reason they enjoy a fine moral support of the entire district which is absolutely necessary in any locality indulging in the presentation of such entertainment."[19]

Embracing a version of history and an identity linked to that of the cowboy offered small towns both a marketable commodity and a positive self-representation that emphasized the values of hard work, entrepreneurialism, hospitality, trust, and community. More than one small town invoked such visions of itself in calling upon residents to contribute to staging or promoting rodeo events.[20] As one Alberta headline read, "Rodeo Promotes Volunteer Service for Advance Work." But this was not just any volunteer work: as the press asserted, it required iron will, physical strength, and aptitudes akin to those of the first generation of pioneers that rodeo had come to celebrate.[21] Values of hospitality, also thought to be rooted in the pioneer experience, offered other opportunities for local residents to show their support. Kamloops organizers called on the hospitality of town residents to help accommodate the tourists who were expected to attend its 1950 rodeo.[22] Folks recalled the Williams Lake Stampede of the 1950s and 1960s as a time when the whole town caught stampede fever, stayed up late preparing floats for the parade, and welcomed ranchers and reserve residents from the outlying districts into an expansive and generous community.[23] Though rodeo feted only a short period in the West's history and ignored all subsequent economic developments from grain to oil production, the drama of rodeo, along with the values it purported to represent, provided a shared sense of history and community to participants.[24] For towns such as High River and Williams Lake, the stampede was a community ritual that performed their own versions of the past, a bloodless, benign, and benevolent history in which settler ascendancy was a foregone conclusion.[25] As the Williams Lake Stampede Association secretary Bev Powell explained in 1958, "the Stampede ... holds a deeper significance ... It is the symbol of history – the history of the peopling of the West. It sums up for us the battle of the pioneer who forced his way through the prairies, over the mountains, blazing the way for the populations which followed and the conquering of the wilderness. And today, our Stampede, especially, our Williams Lake Stampede, symbolizes their success by bringing back to us a touch of the 'old days.'"[26] Rodeos presented opportunities for many small towns to remember their frontier past, praising the sacrifices made by settlers in a sanitized official narrative that omitted the dispossession of Aboriginal people.[27]

On a more material level, they contributed to communities by providing fundraising opportunities for local charities and a focus for volunteer labour in building new infrastructure for outdoor activities. A rodeo proposed for Kamloops in 1945 promised that proceeds would go to the hospital fund and the Canadian Legion.[28] The 1946 High River Rodeo donated its earnings to a fund designated for the construction of a memorial centre.[29] A 1945 stampede organized at Taylor Flats in the Peace River country left as its legacy a dance hall with electric lights, a grandstand, and the first public address system in the region.[30] As in the pre-war period, rodeo offered certain compensations to the communities that hosted them. A 1950 editorial in a southern Alberta paper reminded readers that "some mighty fine projects have been aided and built by Stampede profits."[31] Not a few community centres, swimming pools, arenas, and grandstands in small-town BC and Alberta owed their existence to rodeo organizers.

Pro rodeo offered extra benefits. Organizers boasted of the quality of its contestants. When Kamloops decided to get CPRA approval and offer a pro rodeo in 1950, it told its prospective audience that it had transformed the event from a "local 'wild and wooly' cowboy show to a large and smooth running professional rodeo, that only the best contestants and performers can afford to participate in."[32] Similarly, the Williams Lake Stampede Association promised that affiliating with the CPRA would draw riders from greater distances and "offer keen competition in all events."[33] When a group of international pro cowboys descended upon Coleman, Alberta's one-day event in July 1960, the resultant "keen competition" was, in the eyes of some, "one of the best rodeos in years."[34] Small-town committees hoped that local contestants would meet the challenge of competing against professional cowboys and praised them in the highest terms when they did.[35]

Putting on a pro rodeo also guaranteed entries. Pro cowboys, as we have seen, travelled constantly to amass points and prize money so as to qualify for championships and make a living at the sport. When rodeo committees approached the CPRA for approval, they had to acquiesce to its scheduling priorities so that the pro cowboys had a steady string of rodeos at which to compete. Although this irritated some committees, most acknowledged that changing the date of their event was a small price to pay for ensuring that the maximum number of professional cowboys were able to attend. The example of a rodeo at Cremona is instructive here. In 1949 a committee of local cowboys and businessmen in this central Alberta town decided to stage an amateur rodeo on Dominion Day. Committee members began to meet in April and did so every Monday, working out financial and infrastructural arrangements. They gathered a group of local men to build chutes, corrals, and a small grandstand. Town merchants advanced them supplies against the rodeo's projected earnings. Individuals from Cremona made cash donations, some as low as ten dollars, but all heartily appreciated by the committee. The modest prizes prompted a reasonable entry from local cowboys, particularly those from the Nakoda reserve at Morley. Indeed, Morley residents placed in all the contests, including a first in bareback won by Howard Ear, a first in men's steer riding won by Al Soldier, and a first and second in steer decorating won by Don Dixon and George Labelle respectively.

Although the rodeo provided an exciting spectacle, entries were few, with the result that, in most events, the total entry fees paid by contestants were disappointingly small. In wild steer decorating, the wild horse race, wild cow milking, saddle bronc, boys' steer riding, and bareback, the amount netted in entry fees was not enough to cover the amount owing in prize money. Indeed, at the end of the rodeo, the committee owed prize winners a total of $108.00. In addition, the cost of renting horses and paying for pick-up riders and timekeepers (at a modest daily wage of ten and five dollars respectively) left the committee in a further debt of $228.50, not including the supplies advanced by local merchants. By the end of 1949, the committee members were paying the outstanding bills from their own pockets.

The following year, the CPRA vetted Cremona's rodeo as a pro event, meaning that it agreed with the date set and approved both the prizes offered and the judges selected. Professional cowboys swelled the ranks of contestants, especially in calf roping, steer riding, and steer decorating, where entries were between two and three times higher than for amateur events such as boys' steer riding and wild cow milking. In the pro events, pro cowboys took the lead: Reg Kessler won the bareback riding, and Wilf Gerlitz won steer riding. Aboriginal contestants still won in the amateur events, and Paul Dixon took first in calf roping. This time, the Cremona Rodeo was a financial success, owing largely to the greater number of entries and a gate receipt that topped $500. Though only a modest surplus of $7.75 was realized in 1951, the rodeo was producing a surplus of over $200.00 by 1952 and was well on its way to becoming a lucrative venture.[36]

As well as increasing revenue, professionalization offered certain guarantees to organizing committees. Local businessmen and especially hotel keepers were not always enthusiastic about the prospect of a group of rodeo cowboys descending on their town. Their wild and reckless reputation, which still lingered in the immediate post-war period, prompted some hoteliers to refuse to rent rooms to them. Organizing committees could use the CPRA's attitude toward cowboys who trashed their rooms and, more importantly, its practice of paying for damages or bills unpaid by its members, to encourage hoteliers and other businesses to welcome visiting cowboys. Indeed, as the CPRA explained to small-town committees, it helped make rodeo a success by "providing rules for ... the orderly conduct of contestants."[37] These rules did encourage local hotel keepers to take a chance on professional cowboys. As the former secretary of the Hudson's Hope organizing committee explained,

I remember there were a lot of motels where they wouldn't let you in, like, if you went in with your hat on, because they had too many rooms trashed. And now I talked to the fellow at the Sportsman [motel] here, and he certainly didn't wanna [let cowboys stay] ... And that made it difficult for rodeos when they were going around trying to get sponsorships, because you used to go and ask for a donation for people to sponsor events ... You couldn't go to the hotels and say look what kind of business you're gonna get, because they didn't want that kind of business. Basically, it was a problem. That was one of the things the association was instrumental in dealing with because we had a blacklist, and if you didn't pay your hotel bill, which was one of the things which used to happen ... or you trashed the room, which was another thing that used to happen, you were blacklisted until you had straightened it out.[38]

Similarly, when CPRA members failed to pay their entry fees, the association did so for them, recouping the fees and imposing a fine on recalcitrant cowboys, and it made sure that organizing committees were not out the money. In contrast, when non-CPRA members bounced cheques or left town without paying their fees, organizing committees could do little about it.[39] Affiliating with a larger regulatory body in promoting professional rodeo calmed the fears of some local people and offered recourse to those who doubted the respectability of the pro cowboy.[40]

Professionalization, however, was also a point of conflict and anxiety. During the 1940s and 1950s, letters from rodeo committees to the CPRA office voiced fears that the financial commitment required by the CPRA was too high, that local and novice riders would be excluded, particularly Aboriginal riders, and that many small-town rodeos would fold if forced to go professional. Some argued that guaranteeing prize money up front, before entry fees had been paid, and adding a portion of the fees to the prize money was financially unviable in many communities.[41] For committees faced with upgrading facilities after the war, the added costs of staging a pro rodeo seemed excessive.[42] The Taber Rodeo Committee informed the CPRA that it could not meet the association's financial requirements, particularly the minimum limits set on prize money. Though it agreed to try a professional rodeo in 1945, it nonetheless opined, "the object of your association is to further rodeo. Yet your rules are designed to kill small and one day shows from which novices, your future champions, gain their experience."[43] Other committees shared this opinion and added that local competitors could not afford the entry fees set by the CPRA:

"The contestants at this show are practically all local boys who are trying to learn to contest and this is likely the only show they ride at each year, however, there are a few who eventually go on to other rodeos and eventually become good competitors. This show, however, feels that these boys should not be asked to pay the $10 entry fee for the privilege of competing against experienced riders and in fact, [we] know that these boys would not do so."[44]

In 1948 similar concerns were aired at Williams Lake, where a group of local cowboys expressed the view that the CPRA rules were actually designed to boost the income of professional cowboys at the expense of local competitors and their communities.[45] Interprovincial rivalries sometimes flared. Saskatchewan rodeo organizers complained that the predominance of Albertans in the CPRA meant that too few Saskatchewan men were appointed as judges at events such as the one at Swift Current in 1945.[46] For some, such as British Columbian Henry Carson, the CPRA restrictions meant that "a person is foolish to try and run a show."[47] And indeed, as long-time competitor and CPRA supporter Harry Shuttleworth pointed out, putting the money up front simply made the July 1947 Princeton show financially prohibitive.[48] In 1959, fifteen years into the life of the CPRA, small-town committees were still finding that paying the prize money demanded by the CPRA produced financial hardship. That year, W.A. Palmer of Heffley Creek clarified the BC situation for the CPRA: "Regarding the rodeos here in BC, most of them are very small and cannot afford very big prize money. Most of the entry fees are high so the cowboys have some prize money. Last year was one of our better years, some of these rodeos had to take money from their dances to make their rodeos pay expenses. If the prize money was raised at these rodeos, instead of helping rodeo it would cause some of them to fold."[49]

Some organizing committees were particularly anxious about the effect of higher entry fees on Aboriginal competitors. Writing to the CPRA in 1945, the Fort Macleod Rodeo Association requested that the saddle bronc entry fee be reduced from $10.00 to $7.50 "in view of the fact [that] the Fort Macleod show depends to a great extent upon the cowboys of the Indian Reservation to fill out their list of contestants." Though CPRA secretary Blair Holland approved the request, the new CPRA secretary refused it the following year, saying that Holland's generosity had been in error.[50] As we have seen, the CPRA allowed reserve rodeos more flexibility in order to promote rodeo in Aboriginal communities. Its allowance of a reduced entry fee for the Morley Stampede, organized by Jake Twoyoungmen in 1946, suggests that the ten-dollar entry was too high for Aboriginal competitors, just as small-town organizers feared.[51] Association rules prohibiting non-members from competing at pro rodeos where prize winnings exceeded a certain threshold and rules that blacklisted members who rode in amateur events put Aboriginal cowboys in conflict with the CPRA, despite its dispensations to reserve rodeos.[52] For some, the elimination of "Indian" events, as professional contests came to dominate rodeo programs, meant that Aboriginal contestants were being edged out. Joe Young Pine suggested that some chuckwagon races be designated for Indians only since very few Kainai racers had the thoroughbreds that were becoming standard in the sport as its status and prize winnings increased.[53] Over time, organizers and contestants blamed professionalization for declining Aboriginal participation in rodeo after the Second World War. As Willard Martin, organizer and publicist for the Williams Lake Indian Stampede Association, suggested, "Perhaps with the change in status of the rodeo to that of a very sophisticated affair, we see very little Indian participation and it is fast diminishing. If one could determine the reason and eliminate it, it is quite probable that minor contributing factors could become of no consequence and participation could increase. It has been said that complete withdrawal by the Indians from the Stampede would certainly decrease the very western feeling that does make the celebration a success."[54] Although elite Aboriginal cowboys held important places in pro rodeo, the increased costs associated with professionalization shut out a great many Aboriginal contestants, who had neither the money nor the inclination to go on the circuit, from their own local rodeos.

Despite these issues, many small-town and reserve rodeos went professional, particularly in the immediate post-war years. High River did so almost right away. Its first post-war rodeo, in 1946, was a professional event offering large prizes in the $400 range for the pro competitions, higher than the prizes at many other small-town rodeos of the era. Organizers added entry fees to the prize money, and money won was calculated as points earned for pro cowboys as they sought CPRA championships. Offering both professional and amateur events meant that local people could still compete in separate contests, but the difference between the pro competitor and the amateur was not lost on viewers, who were impressed by the skills of the former.[55] Spectators packed the High River grandstand for the professional events – as many as seven thousand did

Stoney (Nakoda) Indian Rodeo, 1946. *Glenbow Museum Archives, NA-5679-6*

so in 1947.[56] Louis Bradley, proprietor of the local clothing store, was the show secretary, and Guy Weadick was its chief publicist.[57] In 1948, Slim Pickens, who had not yet embarked on his Hollywood career, was its clown and bullfighter.[58] In its early years, High River's pro rodeo boasted about the number and quality of its professional cowboys, but observers also thought that local riders and ropers improved over time. Though competitors from Albuquerque and Los Angeles won the big pro events, local men such as Floyd West of High River and Albert Fox of Nanton took prizes in amateur bronc riding and amateur calf roping.[59] In 1952, however, High River did away with the parallel amateur competitions, which meant that its events featured pro cowboys only.[60] The locals seldom won these contests, and within a few years, the press seemed to lose interest in them, allocating considerably more column space to the evening entertainers and the events in which locals competed, all the while acknowledging the quality of the contests staged for pro cowboys and high-end stock.[61]

The professional rodeo attracted tourist interest, goodwill, and dollars to High River. By 1951 over thirteen thousand spectators were crowding its grandstands.[62] Tourists from Calgary and Lethbridge attended the High

River Rodeo, and visitors from as far away as Toronto used new movie cameras to capture the action.[63] When it was televised in 1951, friends in England watched with interest.[64] High River's rodeo also attracted the attention of the Hamilton Wright Organization of New York, producers of newsreel images, who were travelling Alberta shooting footage for tourist publications and for sale to American newsreel companies.[65] When local hotels and motor courts filled up, accommodating the overflow gave families a chance to earn some money and demonstrate their hospitality. Organizers urged women, in particular, to open up their spare rooms and demonstrate their Western "impromptu hospitality" while earning a little unexpected "pin money."[66] High River's pro rodeo turned a significant profit in 1953, with $3,000 in income exceeding expenses. The rodeo association's businessmen kept half of the sum as a financial cushion for subsequent years and invested an additional $500 in the rodeo grounds but distributed the rest to local causes including the fund for a memorial centre and a teen town, and to help the local ball club improve its grounds.[67] By the late 1950s, the various organizations staging the annual rodeo were taking between $190,000 and $230,000 each year. Though high expenses kept net profits low, the rodeo paid for itself and generated business for the merchants of High River and income for its citizens.[68]

High River organizers worked hard to sustain local interest. The evening program included Indian races, which drew competitors from the nearby Nakoda reserve at Eden Valley/Longview, and a calf-branding contest that pitted High River's rodeo committee representatives against those of nearby Stavely.[69] Stock-cutting contests and chuckwagon racing rounded out the competitive portion of the evening, which also included the distribution of prizes for the best-dressed cowboy, cowgirl, and Indian man and woman. By 1952, when the amateur events were discontinued, local commentators started to distinguish between rodeo and competitions such as stock cutting, writing that the latter had "an authentic touch far surpassing most of the traditional rodeo features." By the mid-1950s, High River's organizers were advertising that their evening program was all locally produced.[70]

The emphasis on the local included First Nations. In 1947 visiting Nakoda from Morley set up a tipi encampment on the rodeo grounds, and tourists flocked to take their pictures as they camped or rode in the parade.[71] Within three years, over a hundred Nakoda in forty tipis were camping there, under the direction of Nakoda Paul Dixon of Pekisko.[72]

Steer riding at the Morley Rodeo, Nakoda reserve, 1960. *Glenbow Museum Archives, NA-2557-51*

The 1949 parade float for the South Fork Trading Post featured Nakoda leader Mark Left Hand riding on the grille of a car festooned with beadwork, fur and buckskin clothes, and trailing a travois.[73] In 1957, when poor entries prompted criticism, only the Nakoda riders in the parade earned congratulations.[74] Indian dancing became an important feature of the evening entertainment during the mid-1950s, and retailer and Rotarian Jack Pickersgill visited the Eden Valley Reserve in search of drummers, dancers, and singers. Pickersgill and his entertainment committee advertised that all Aboriginal participants were local.[75] Nakoda organizer Peter Dixon staged the evening show, which featured some sixty dancers, and Ezra Left Hand acted as master of ceremonies, giving the Nakoda control over their presentation.[76] As the 1950s progressed, the contemporary concerns of the Nakoda people penetrated the consciousness of High River organizers and fans. When the rodeo committee offered a medal as a new prize for the best-dressed Indian man in the 1954 parade, Nakoda women protested that a separate women's section of the best-dressed contest should be established and that a medal should be offered to them too. Though a *High River Times* editorial made humorous reference to the more militant actions of white feminists, it nonetheless concluded that the successful protest of the Aboriginal women indicated that "the women may be more influential in the tribe councils than is supposed. They may conceivably become the best avenues through which necessary improvements in health, education and occupational interests may be realized."[77] As High River welcomed its Nakoda neighbours to its rodeo, it increasingly recognized the complexity of Aboriginal lives in a modernizing West.[78]

Another significant feature of the post-war pro rodeos at High River was the focus on old-timers. Prompted in part by High River resident Guy Weadick's fascination with the mythic West, organizers invited first-generation settlers to ride in their parade, which was led in the first year by Senator Dan Riley, known to some as "the Cowboy Senator." When the rodeo committee presented Riley with a Roland Gissing painting, he took the opportunity to express the view of these old-timers that nostalgia for the past was best balanced with an appreciation for modern efficiency: "As I look at this picture, I see the country as I first saw it, a primeval one. And today, a country that is providing food for the starving millions. It is a most appropriate picture for any old-timer in the west."[79] In subsequent years, the *High River Times* ran stories celebrating the work of pioneer men in establishing the ranches of the district.[80] Such stories made clear what the old-timer represented in terms of community identity. As Charles Clark, the *High River Times* editor, put it in 1947, "the Old Timer is a man to follow. He knows neither uncertainty nor doubt."[81] The following year, High River's rodeo became the official meeting point for the Old Timers' Association, and, organizers hoped, commemorating the region's fiftieth anniversary of settlement offered particular attractions to visiting tourists.[82] Guy Weadick's success at establishing George Lane Memorial Park in 1951, named for a pioneer rancher and co-founder of the Calgary Stampede, provided focus for the usual praise of the settler era.[83] The old-timers honoured by the High River Rodeo of the 1950s and 1960s were not from the generation that had lived in the region when First Nations had predominated demographically or that intermarried with Aboriginal people.

Rather, they were descendants of the later settlement generation, which arrived after the Treaty 7 reserves were laid out and the Indian Act restrictions on Aboriginal ceremonial and mobility were in force. By the mid-1950s, High River's honoured old-timers were second-generation Albertans such as Ruth Hanson, whose credentials as an old-timer, as the *High River Times* explained, were "through her father ... her husband ... and in her own right." Hanson's life, it seemed, was dominated by her brothers' fame as polo players and her husband's business dealings with Senator Riley, but her hospitality at her Chinook Ranch home earned her guest of honour at the 1954 High River Rodeo.[84] Gender was never far beneath the surface as contemporary writers tried to grasp the meaning of the history presented by the old-timers. Female old-timers who gathered at the 1948 festivities, it was reported, "toss[ed] off the hazards and discomforts as mere incidentals and recall[ed] instead the fact that they were young, tremendously important as women, and had the rich feeling that their lives were worth while." In contrast, a "bitter old bachelor" described the end of the "good old days" as coinciding with the arrival of "three white women ... [who] immediately set up three distinct social circles."[85] Such a contrasting set of images was embedded in the gendered discourses associated with settlement in the West. Indeed, it was part of larger imperialist thinking whereby women, as civilizers, were both builders and destroyers – building a new way of life and destroying an older one, in which frontier masculinities were ascendant.[86] As the decade progressed, the definition of "old-timer" evolved further. By 1958, Guy Weadick, who had been instrumental in encouraging the recognition of old-timers, had come to represent the category himself. That year the rodeo committee renamed Frontier Days as Weadick Days and sponsored an "I rode with Guy Weadick" contest to draw out early rodeo performers for some "interesting reminiscing," now making the master commemorator the subject of commemoration.[87] Through it all, histories of whiteness were being expressed; whether they were settler or senator, male or female, old-timers represented white ascendancy on the Canadian Plains. Honouring them replaced the historical re-enactments of the Wild West Show but retained the storyline of the conquering pioneer heroes who displaced both the wilderness and Aboriginal inhabitants to claim the Canadian West as home.

Nonetheless, cowboys remained central to rodeo, and despite its success, the High River Rodeo Committee shared one concern with professional cowboys – training the next generation of competitors. As pro rodeos became more numerous throughout the Canadian West, some cowboys worried that young men, with little capital, were finding it difficult to get a start in the main events close to home. As early as 1947, roping clubs formed in High River and Nanton to enable amateurs to gain weekly practice in calf roping, bronc riding, and steer decorating.[88] Black Diamond cowboys did the same the following year.[89] In 1952, when the High River Rodeo dispensed with its amateur contests, a new venue was required so that young people, both boys and girls, could hone their skills and become a part of the rodeo community. Little britches rodeo arose from this need. In May 1959, High River held Canada's first rodeo of this type. Designed for contestants under age sixteen, it offered steer riding, bareback bronc riding, a wild colt race, barrel racing, and a wild colt scramble. The rodeo committee promoted the event, and stock contractor Harry Vold provided the animals. The Legion handled the gate and promised to put the proceeds toward sports equipment for local youth. The rodeo received over one hundred entries from thirty-five Alberta youngsters, and nearly fifteen hundred people attended it despite inclement weather.[90] As in pro rodeo, the children of professional rodeo families dominated among the winners, with Wayne Vold, son of Harry Vold, taking the prize belt buckle for the all-round best cowboy.[91] Attendance grew the following year, with over four thousand people coming out for the little britches rodeo. Here, as in the early years of rodeo, contestants in riding events included local Aboriginal cowboys, male and female. Floyd Bearspaw of Longview won the steer-riding event, beating fifty-eight boys and girls including Lucille Green and Dianne Kewley of Pincher Creek and Phyllis Peel of Midnapore. Girls and boys competed in barrel racing and in the wild colt scramble.[92] If its intent were to replicate the pre-war rodeos that claimed to be "open to all," at least in their early years, little britches rodeo delivered. Moreover, it proved lucrative. In 1964 it netted nearly $1,500 in profit, whereas the pro rodeo showed a slight loss that year.[93] The following year, organizers estimated that more than thirty-six thousand spectators visited High River to watch the youngsters compete. Moreover, many of the original contestants had gone on to the pro circuits.[94] In 1966, when the little britches rodeo was held on the new rodeo grounds, even the appearance of a dust storm did not deter High River

Men relaxing after cutting logs for construction of the High River Rodeo grounds, 1946. *Glenbow Museum Archives, NA-5499-1*

fans. As the *Times* editor opined, "if the public is offered something it wants, no small degree of discomfort is going to discourage spectators."[95] Indeed, over $4,500 in gate receipts proved his point.[96]

A perceived need to maintain and strengthen community support prompted organizers to invite the Canadian Barrel Racing Association to stage Canada's first all-girls' rodeo at High River in 1962. The nineteen women organizers amassed nearly $4,000 for prize money, offering a $1,200 purse to the contest's signature event, barrel racing. The rodeo also included cow riding, calf roping, cow cutting, goat tying, a ladies' saddle horse race, quarter horse races, thoroughbred races, a "kids' ketch and keep," and an animal scramble.[97] Held on 28 June, it was attended by the minister of citizenship and immigration, Ellen Fairclough, providing a chance to see "real Western life" at her first rodeo. Intent on claiming the all-girls' rodeo as a community venture, the *High River Times* remarked that "although the show is featuring women only the men are behind the scenes in arranging for its success." Furthermore, it pointed out that the women were locals, not professional riders from elsewhere.[98] The event was a tremendous success as five thousand people crowded the rodeo grounds and taxed the town's services to provide meals and accommodation.[99] Professional rodeo remained popular in High River, but organizers worked hard to keep local competitors in the game and local audiences interested by experimenting with rodeo for young people and for women.

In the post-war period, the Williams Lake Stampede too tried to balance local priorities with the exigencies of staging a professional rodeo. For the first ten years after the war, it struggled simply to survive. The stampede had been suspended during the war and was not revived for nearly seven years. During that time, the stampede grounds, its chutes, corrals, and grandstands, had all fallen into disrepair. Then the Elks Hall, used for the stampede dance, burned to the ground in 1947. The committee that organized the post-war stampedes was new to staging such large events, though not to rodeo.[100] It cautiously approached the possibility of affiliating with the CPRA. Although it looked forward to the top-notch competitors that professionalization would bring, it did not wish to exclude local contestants. At a 1948 meeting, local cowboys voiced suspicions of the CPRA and told the stampede committee that its insurance coverage was not worth the membership fee. In March 1948, the committee narrowly decided to adopt CPRA rules, though it pledged to keep the purses to a minimum due to the building costs it was facing. Nonetheless, its secretary, Mrs. Ollie Norberg, warned CPRA secretary Jim Maxwell that "should we have any trouble with the co-operation of the [CPRA] riders contesting at our show I am afraid our membership will be withdrawn next year and as I was instrumental in adopting the rules I would not like to see this happen."[101] The press announced in 1948 that the Williams Lake Stampede had gone professional, a decision it suggested would end the stampede's reputation as offering "three wild nights in the Cariboo." In fact, the organizing committee dropped that slogan in favour of "Three Days of Fun."[102] Flooding elsewhere in BC that year prompted the committee to cancel the rodeo. In 1949, however, it withdrew from the CPRA and made the stampede amateur again, though it retained the pro format.[103] Williams Lake rejoined the CPRA in 1956, and in 1957, it added CPRA-approved chuckwagon racing to a program that included saddle bronc, bareback, calf roping, steer decorating, wild cow milking, and steer or cow riding.[104]

Williams Lake Stampede Contestant List, 1956

Bareback Riding
Joe Adams, Spences Bridge
Leslie Curnow, Spences Bridge
Dave Perry, Cache Creek
Bob Gottfriedson, Kamloops
Joe Bob, Sugar Cane
Gilbert Bowe, Springhouse
Don Haddrell, Ashcroft
Pat Williams, Cache Creek
Adam Elkins, Alexis Creek
Ray George, Cache Creek
Marvin Elkins, Alexis Creek
George Keener, Williams Lake
Freddie Palmantier, Riske Creek
Walter Salomon, Riske Creek
Joe Alex, Pavilion
Herman Seller, Soda Creek
Ken Glenville, Cloverdale
Dale Lightfoot, Cloverdale
Bob Evans, Bellaview, Alberta
Jim Hook, Kamloops
Garry Hook, Kamloops
Bob Hill, Kamloops
Henry Bowe, Springhouse

Calf Roping
Percy Minnabarriet, Cache Creek
Dave Perry, Cache Creek
Philip Lulua, Upper Hat Creek
Wilf Lulua, Upper Hat Creek
Willard Antoine, Cache Creek
Gilbert Bowe, Springhouse
Peter Barker, Dog Creek
Bruce Watt, Big Creek
Jim Hook, Kamloops
Garry Hook, Kamloops
Bill Twan, Alkali Lake
Ivan Bowe, Springhouse
Antoine Harry, Dog Creek
Jimmy MacDonald, Cache Creek
Tom Desmond, Dog Creek
Tony Bellow, Kamloops
Louis Bates, Williams Lake

Saddle Bronc Riding
Percy Minnabarriet, Cache Creek
Gilbert Bowe, Springhouse
Pat William, Creekside
Leo Nelson, Creekside
Jimmy Johnson, Alkali Lake
Tommy Elkins, Alkali Lake
Alvin McLeod, Meldrum Creek
Stanley Ned, Sugar Cane
Freddie Palmantier, Riske Creek
Joe Alex, Pavilion
Richard Dick, Alkali Lake
Len DeRose, Alkali Lake
George White, Cloverdale
Bob Copeland, Keremeos
Charlie Baptiste, Castle Rock
Jack Elkins, Alexis Creek
Van Nadon, Vancouver
Emery Lewis, Vernon
Louis Bates, Williams Lake
Pee Wee English, Clinton
Alfred Garrigan, Clinton

Steer Decorating
Percy Minnabarriet, Cache Creek
Dave Perry, Cache Creek
Gilbert Bowe, Springhouse
Don MacDonald, Williams Lake
Bob Johnson, Keremeos
Pascal Bates, Williams Lake
Boyd Sherman, Kamloops
Slim Dorin, Williams Lake
Red Allen, Tonasket, Washington

Brahma Bull Riding
Garry Hook, Kamloops
Joe Adams, Spences Bridge
Leslie Curnow, Spences Bridge
Dave Perry, Cache Creek
Bob Gottfriedson, Kamloops
Gilbert Bowe, Springhouse
Henry Bowe, Springhouse
Don Haddrell, Ashcroft
Pat Williams, Creekside
Leo Nelson, Creekside

The 1956 entry list included pro cowboys such as Dave Perry and Garry Hook as well as competitors from as far away as Cloverdale and Tonasket, Washington, but local and Aboriginal contestants predominated.[105]

By 1958 the stampede had reinvented itself as a professional rodeo geared for the tourist market. In part, it was aided by the BC centennial of that year: Princess Margaret toured the province in its honour, and a committee of Williams Lake merchants staged a special two-hour rodeo for her visit. The event lost money (over $1,000), and the provincial centennial committee was ultimately forced to pay the local committee's amusement taxes. Nonetheless, the Williams Lake Rodeo was publicized in *Princess in Wonderland,* a provincial Department of Recreation and Conservation film commemorating the royal visit.[106]

Williams Lake organizers were ready for an influx of tourists for their annual rodeo two weeks later. Its program included four pages of introductory remarks, welcoming tourists to the Cariboo and featuring a one-page panegyric of the "Colorful Cariboo" written by rancher-turned-author Rich Hobson, whose 1951 *Grass beyond the Mountains* was enjoying continued success. A "Dude Dictionary" explained the rules and regulations of the pro events, and an exceedingly odd ethnography of local First Nations declared that the lahal (stick) game that visitors could watch at the Indian encampment had "prehistorically covered the world." The program promised tourists something truly unique and authentic at the Williams Lake Stampede. Not only would they see "real cowboys ride real outlaw wild bucking broncs," but they would experience genuine hospitality that was like a "friendly family circle where the only password is an open countenance and a friendly smile."[107] Clearly, the stampede committee expected its audience to consist largely of tourists and thus tailored its program with them in mind.

By the 1960s, the stampede was reliably attracting top-quality contestants from across the transborder West to compete before tourist audiences who would spend money eating and sleeping in town. Nonetheless, Williams Lake residents started to wonder if the stampede truly were a local affair.[108] In an era when many small towns staged professional rodeos, Williams Lake sought to mark its event as special. One strategy was the continuing assertion that the Cariboo was home to the last real cowboys. Therefore, organizers stressed that, at their event, local people (and local animals) demonstrated the traditional skills of the ranching frontier. Despite this, the visiting cowboys dominated the scene, as was the case at

Cowboy Country: The West for tourist consumption. *Courtesy of Royal BC Museum, BC Archives, I-16971.*

pro rodeos generally. So, other events, including the stampede queen contest, dances at a venue known as Squaw Hall, and the revival of the mountain race during the 1990s, were intended to imbue the stampede with local flavour. This entwined with the overall strategy employed to set it apart from other stampedes – the emphasis on Aboriginal participation. During the 1950s, there were two queen contests – one for white competitors and one for First Nations. This was later discontinued, and through the 1960s and 1970s, Aboriginal women were sometimes selected as stampede queen. In the 1960s, Squaw Hall, a dance hall run for Aboriginal people, gave organizers an opportunity to speak about the distinctiveness that Aboriginal attendance bestowed on the stampede. Finally, the 1990s revival of the famed mountain race offered a further

occasion to demonstrate the uniqueness of the Cariboo and the importance of Aboriginal people to the stampede. But the stampede was also a
site of struggle for Aboriginal people and for settlers, who saw the past
and the present of the Cariboo in markedly different ways.

The appearance of several popular histories of the Cariboo, including
Rich Hobson's *Grass beyond the Mountains* and the CBC series based on
Paul St. Pierre's Cariboo-Chilcotin stories, which aired in 1960 and 1964-
66 as *Cariboo Country,* presented the Williams Lake area and its stampede
as the last real frontier.[109] Williams Lake organizers were quick to capitalize
on this publicity, claiming in 1960 that their stampede was the region's
own special event and dedicating that year's program to the "Cariboo
Cowboy," who was "very real and when he is just a memory in many places,
he will still be here in all his resourcefulness, his vigor, his Spartan sim-
plicity, his good heart and his bad language, ridin' the range, rollin' his
own, defying wind, weather, hardship, and going broke ... in his own
sunny serene way."

Just to drive the point home, the program declared that

> these boys are not here to exhibit vaudeville acts but the thrilling feats of skill,
> daring and endurance learned on the wide plateaus and among the wild cattle
> of the Cariboo; thrilling feats of rope, rein and saddle, feats that are "all in a
> day's work." Without these boys, the Williams Lake Stampede could not boast
> 34 years of spectator interest and a growth making it the second largest Stampede
> in Canada, nor could we boast a genuine wild west show. And so we dedicate
> the program to the most colorful and most necessary participant – the Cariboo
> Cowboy.[110]

Stampede secretary Bev Powell's history of rodeo, in which she presented
the stampede as a "symbol of history," was reprinted from the 1958 centennial stampede program, as was a piece of doggerel titled the "Old
Cow-Puncher," which eulogized a ne'er-do-well cowboy said to be "the
type of Vanished Cowboy ('cept in Cariboo, of course)." But facing the
poem was a page listing the high point holders in pro rodeo, none of
whom were from the Cariboo – indeed, most were Albertans.[111] Nonetheless, stampede president Darwin Collins continued to stress that local
cowboys and even local stock took "great pride in putting on a good show
for the audience."[112] In 1970 programs began reprinting sections from
those of the 1920s, favouring the ones that lauded local riders, both men

and women.[113] Lengthy listings of top CPRA money winners were balanced with a rodeo biography of Kenny McLean, who was identified as a British Columbian but not as Syilx.[114] If the 1970 program elided McLean's Aboriginal identity, subsequent programs emphasized the presence of Aboriginal people. In 1971 Chief Dan George of the Burrard Reserve in North Vancouver was the guest of honour at that year's centennial stampede. For many, he was forever linked to the Cariboo-Chilcotin by his portrayal of Ol' Antoine in both the CBC series *Cariboo Country* and the feature film *How to Break a Quarterhorse,* which was also based on St. Pierre's books. His celebrity status as an Academy Award nominee for his role in *Little Big Man* simply increased his prominence. Local organizer Bernice Prior later said that escorting Chief George during his visit to Williams Lake was the high point of her career with the stampede.[115]

The Williams Lake Stampede also used rodeo queen contests to enhance local content. Before the Second World War, women who wished to become stampede queen had to collect votes in a massive popularity contest. In 1950 the queen contest was reinstated and the voting system was retained, this time with two categories: white queen and Indian queen. In the first year, Norma MacDonald reigned as white queen. Enthroned on her own float in the parade, she was accompanied by an entourage that included her princesses and the 1939 queen, and was flanked by RCMP officers. Katherine Wycotte of the nearby Sugar Cane Reserve, who was crowned Indian queen, rode on horseback, dressed in buckskin and accompanied by her own retinue of Aboriginal princesses, directly behind the white queen's float.[116] Wycotte was Indian queen again the following year, and she thanked the people of the Sugar Cane Reserve for all their support. Indian Agent William Christie thanked the stampede association for the "nice gesture of crowning an Indian Queen" and offered the opinion that "the Indians' contribution to the Stampede assured its success." Chief David Johnson of the Alkali Lake Reserve took the opportunity to welcome both Aboriginal and non-Aboriginal people to the stampede.[117]

But the voting procedure was controversial, so the contest went into abeyance until 1958 when a panel of judges was assigned to choose an Indian and a white queen on the basis of their riding ability, beauty, poise, personality, voice, and dress.[118] Good riding was important to the judges, who assessed the contestants' skill at an annual event called the trail riders playday.[119] That year, Lorraine Squinahan of the Alkali Lake Reserve was Indian queen, and Jean Stevenson of Williams Lake was white queen.[120]

In the early decades of the contest, the queens were expected to be horsewomen first and beauty queens second. In 1957 the rules governing the contests emphasized horse skills, stating that contestants "must be able to saddle a horse and ride at walk, trot and gallop. They must have a horse to use during the Stampede." But every year, the more traditional beauty contest held during the aquatic show just before the stampede upstaged the stampede queen competition. In 1964 Hilary Place began to organize the queen contest; he changed the judging system, abolished the parallel Indian and white crowns, and pledged to lay more emphasis on "beauty of figure and face." Fifty percent of the judging criteria now related to beauty, 25 percent to personality, and 25 percent to special skills, which need not include riding.

The women of Williams Lake and environs protested vigorously. One wrote the *Tribune* that "according to the Judge, the girls won't know one end of the horse from the other ... This is not fair to the girls who can ride ... and take pride in their horsemanship."[121] Another objected that the stampede "had forgotten that it was a western event, mainly concerned with horses, steers, cowboys and western music."[122] Moreover, both Aboriginal and settler women argued that the new criteria especially disadvantaged Aboriginal women. Clearly, the women of the Cariboo had their own definitions of what was authentic, which did not include a beauty contest. That stampede management still wished to be seen as authentic by both locals and tourists was made clear when it instigated a new judging system, which awarded twenty points for riding ability, thirty for personality, thirty for beauty, and twenty for other talents and merits. No one had opposed abolishing the racially segmented white and Indian queen contests.

Most queen contenders in these years were white, though at least one Aboriginal woman entered each time.[123] In 1966, while Joan Palmantier was attending business college in Kamloops, Hilary and Rita (Hamilton) Place asked her to enter the Williams Lake Stampede queen contest. She was shy, more comfortable with elders than with people of her own age, and feeling vulnerable after the death of her father, Leonard Palmantier, just two years before. Nonetheless, she won the title that year. In 1967, with the support of the Williams Lake Indian Band Homemakers' Club, she participated in the National Indian Princess Pageant in Winnipeg. Palmantier benefited from her time as rodeo royalty, making many appearances and developing poise and ease at public speaking. Williams Lake embraced her as its own, making her its "sentimental favourite" in the national competitions and praising her representation of the town at events such as the Calgary Stampede. For her part, Palmantier spoke frankly about the issues that faced the Secwepemc and Tsilhquot'in people whom she represented. In a speech before the National Indian Princess Pageant judges, far away in Central Canada, she described Williams Lake as "a little cowtown in Northern BC," where, in high school, she had learned to "stand up for herself and meet people half-way." Decrying racial discrimination as "on a par with saying a 'white horse is better than a black one,'" she pledged to work on behalf of her people by collecting their graphic designs, songs, and dances in order to preserve their cultures and to work to open an Indian friendship centre. Indeed, Palmantier had a long career in advocacy, becoming one of the first Native court workers in BC before attending UBC to get a bachelor of education in 1980.[124] Aboriginal women who entered the Williams Lake Stampede queen contest almost always listed knowledge of Aboriginal history and culture as among their "hobbies." Pearl Myers, the 1973 queen contestant from Stone, said she "intend[ed] to make her career working for her people," a hope voiced by many entrants.[125] Cultural awareness, even advocacy, seems to have been perfectly acceptable among Williams Lake Stampede queen contestants.

However, this level of acceptance was more apparent than real. Within the Williams Lake queen contest itself, all competitors were expected to confine themselves to their role as stampede ambassador, beautiful and respectable. With her impeccable rodeo lineage, Palmantier could speak about racial discrimination in faraway Winnipeg, but the people of Williams Lake expected something more lightweight at home. For the public speaking contests, contestants were given relatively safe topics such as "why hippies don't ride horses" and "how the stampede could be more family-oriented." In 1975, however, one woman deviated from her appointed topic, and the ensuing uproar revealed much about the deployment of aboriginality and femininity at the Williams Lake Stampede.

When Madelaine David, the Indian Friendship Centre candidate, approached the podium for the 1975 stampede queen speech contest, she was slated to speak on the subject of "rodeo." But, in what appeared to be an impromptu revision of her prepared, rehearsed, and vetted speech, David began to talk about the struggle of First Nations to maintain their culture. Tears rose in her eyes as she asked the all-white audience, "Do you believe that if white society were asked and forced to believe that all

their ancestors throughout all time had been living in the wrong way ...
how long, if [they] were proud of [their] people, would it take [them] to
change, willingly?" The audience exploded. One woman strode from the
hall, exclaiming, "She didn't write that speech." Another confronted
David, saying that she had changed her speech at the last minute to address an "illegal topic." When a reporter asked for clarification, one woman
explained, "They're not allowed to speak on racial, religious or political
issues." Asked if, in essence, this meant that candidates were not permitted
to speak on serious topics, the woman said yes.

Contest organizer Marie Plante reported that no contest rule barred
women from addressing serious matters. But she added that no one ever
had; apparently, it was common sense that the queens would not raise
vexed issues. Madelaine David challenged assumptions about appropriate
behaviour for contestants. Asked why she had changed her topic, she said
that her speech had not been coming together, but when she started to
write about her own people and their struggle for cultural integrity, the
words just flowed. Asked if she regretted her decision because of the reaction it sparked, she said, "No not really. Not even if it might have lowered
my chances. I was really proud of my speech." Madelaine David was not
stampede queen that year.[126]

Why was Joan Palmantier permitted to speak on racial discrimination,
whereas Madelaine David was not? Perhaps the explanation lies in
Palmantier's stampede lineage or the fact that she addressed audiences
in Winnipeg rather than directly confronting the people of Williams
Lake. Perhaps it was due to changing times. In 1967, when Palmantier
appeared before the Winnipeg judges, Aboriginal people were just beginning to speak out at a number of public venues. Chief Dan George delivered his "Lament for Confederation" speech to thirty thousand people
in Vancouver's Empire Stadium that year. The increasing conflict over
land and resources was not yet fully under way in 1967, and the intensity
of protest occasioned by the 1969 assimilationist revisions to the Indian
Act remained in the future. Perhaps it was simply that, by 1975, when
David took the stage, the tensions between First Nations and non-Natives
in British Columbia had reached the point where her speech could be
greeted only with anger, where audiences had begun to retreat into the
comfort of a rigidly defined femininity, one that permitted no contention
or advocacy. But the fact is, David did speak. As Colleen Ballerino Cohen,

Richard Wilk, and Beverly Stoeltje note, beauty contests can be points of rupture, when disagreements surface regarding both community values and issues far beyond the specific matters of the contest.[127] The stampede queen contest at Williams Lake had long provided a way for town elites to speak about the region, but they could not monopolize the visual representation of the queen or her performance of femininity. The women of Williams Lake, and the queens themselves, insisted that they were more than pretty faces. The desire of promoters to highlight aboriginality as a particular feature of the stampede, combined with the specification that the queens demonstrate "intellect and personality," provided a space in which Aboriginal women could express themselves. When they did, their words and the subsequent reaction gave voice to the larger social forces circulating around the stampede more generally.[128]

These forces included a deepening antipathy between townsfolk of the BC Interior and Aboriginal people living on nearby reserves. Anthropologist Michael Ames observed in the 1950s that Xaxli'p people, living on the Fountain Reserve just north of Lillooet, felt excluded by the "better class" of settlers, including merchants and landowners, though the Xaxli'p mixed fairly freely with the cowboys with whom they worked on local ranches. Beyond their networks of kin and friendship, they felt discrimination at every turn, especially from police and employers.[129] Aboriginal people's reports of racism were confirmed by high-profile murder cases, such as that of Rose Marie Roper from Alkali Lake in 1967, and the 1971 beating death of Fred Quilt (from the Tsilhquot'in reserve at Stone), which brought to national attention the fractured relations between settlers in the Cariboo-Chilcotin and the Tsilhquot'in, Secwepemc, and Dakelh peoples. Further north, outside of Vanderhoof, the hit-and-run deaths of Sai'k'uz residents Larry Thomas (1974) and Coreen Thomas (1975) deepened the mistrust between the Dakelh community at Stoney Creek and the RCMP, who seemed unwilling to investigate the deaths.[130] Fear and prejudice infected these relations on many levels: from the courtroom and police cells, to hospitals and clinics, to everyday encounters in the streets and in hotels.[131] The Williams Lake Stampede captured these associations in all of their complexity. It was true that for many the attendance of Aboriginal people at the stampede signified commonality, mutual enjoyment, and respect.[132] For others, Aboriginal people and imagery were commodities that could be exploited to popularize the stampede.

Through the 1950s, 1960s, and 1970s, the Williams Lake Stampede displayed other images of aboriginality and femininity that were not nearly as liable to disruption as the queen contest. The Indian Open-Air Dance Hall, dubbed the Squaw Hall, became a stampede icon in the 1960s and 1970s, and its history was grounded in the complicated relations between First Nations and settlers in the contact zone that was the Williams Lake Stampede before the Second World War. Although Aboriginal people had long attended the stampede, they were excluded from its uptown dances. When the stampede emerged from its wartime exile, two directors decided to remedy this situation, so they built a forty-by-sixty-foot dance floor at the stampede grounds whose four walls were open to the sky, all made from donated materials. By the mid-1960s, the Indian Open-Air Dance Hall had become the place for stampede-goers to end their Saturday night party. In 1964, while the queen's ball was held at the Elks Hall, a western dance took place in the Open-Air Dance Hall, with music by Hilary Place and the Saddle-ites.[133] Though the sky opened and rain drenched the dancers, the all-night event earned over $1,800, saving the stampede from near bankruptcy that year.[134] In 1970 the new slogan for the stampede – "the Wildest in the West" – suggested that the local colour supplied by the "world famous Squaw Hall" and combined with the presence of internationally renowned cowboys made it particularly "wild."[135] The following year, stampede officials stated that over eight thousand people danced until dawn at Squaw Hall, an experience "never to be forgotten."[136] The sense that the experience at Squaw Hall was more salacious than that to be had at the queen's ball was made clear in the 1971 stampede program, which declared that Squaw Hall was "a place to let your hair down, drink your refreshments and do almost anything that your morals will permit you to do."[137] This conflation of immorality with Aboriginal femininity had a long history in the transborder West, and as Jean Barman argues, it had particular salience in BC where it inflicted suffering on Aboriginal women in domestic service, in residential schools, and in the courts.[138] Over the next decade, increasingly wild behaviour at the Squaw Hall and the growing awareness of the derogatory associations it brought to the fore prompted the stampede committee to close it down.[139]

Wildness was not to be entirely abandoned, however. Today the iconic event of the Williams Lake Stampede is the mountain race. Throughout the 1960s and 1970s, programs that chronicled the history of the stampede always mentioned the mountain race and the courageous men and women who rode in it. In the original version, contestants rode down the side of Fox Mountain and into the stampede grounds. Due to the construction of the Cariboo Highway, this was no longer possible, because a line of hard asphalt now separated the stampede grounds from the mountain.[140] In 1992, however, the stampede board decided to reinstate the mountain race as one of four events designed to encourage local participation (the other three were a pony express race, wild cow milking, and team cattle penning).[141] The new race began at the top of the stampede bowl, a natural amphitheatre in which the stampede grounds sit, and sent riders down the embankment, ending with a round-the-track lap on the flat.[142] Unlike the race of the past, in which horses were killed and riders seriously injured, the new version reflected the changed image of the rodeo cowboy. The rules required that veterinaries approve the horses as fit before they could be ridden. The first and most treacherous half of the race was to be run cautiously to prevent injuries to the horses. Riders were to wear western clothing, just like professional rodeo cowboys: cowboy boots, blue jeans, a western-style long shirt, chaps, and a "traditional cowboy hat." No special safety gear was suggested, but stampede programs playfully told audiences that "socks and underwear were optional." Still, like the suicide race at the Omak Stampede in Washington State, the mountain race promoted an image of recklessness and daring. Like Squaw Hall, it was intended to put the wild back in the professionalized Williams Lake Stampede.

Immediately, it became a contest in which Aboriginal men and women excelled. From its reinstatement, Alkali Lake chief Bill Chelsea was its most consistent winner on his horse Mr. Little. Chelsea was born on the Gang Ranch in 1945, the son of Anastasia and Patrick Chelsea. He and his fourteen siblings worked on the Alkali Lake Ranch until they went to St. Joseph's Residential School. Becoming chief at Alkali Lake in 1990, Chelsea then focused on an Alkali Lake–run logging operation, Ecolink Forest Service.[143] He continued an Alkali Lake tradition for successful mountain racing as his father, Patrick, was a well-known rodeo cowboy. Chelsea later organized the mountain race on the Stone Reserve in the Chilcotin. In the mid-1990s, another Aboriginal name became associated with the Williams Lake mountain race – Kathleen Gottfriedson. A member of the Colville First Nation in Washington and the daughter of Abe Dick, Gottfriedson won the 1996 mountain race on a gelding called Red.[144] Though perhaps unintentionally, the resurrection of the mountain race has provided another opportunity for Aboriginal people to participate in the Williams Lake Stampede in a venue that is not constrained by the costs and regulations associated with pro rodeo.

Yet segmentation and racialization appear in all the places where Aboriginal people find themselves. As Williams Lake organizers sought to make their stampede special, they relied, at least in part, on the turnout of Aboriginal people. Although this encouraged some Aboriginal people to participate, it raised a host of questions. What was the cost of that involvement? How could they countenance the presentation of aboriginality as immoral (as at Squaw Hall), or as beautiful but silenced (as in the case of Madelaine David), or even as daring (as in the mountain race)? For some, as we will see in the next chapter, the price was simply too high.

Ultimately, professionalization fragmented the contact zone that was small-town rodeo in Western Canada. As many organizers feared, the increasing costs of competition excluded Aboriginal people from many small-town rodeos. Indeed, committees worried that the predominance of professional cowboys would lessen the appeal of the event to local audiences. Committees in smaller centres, such as High River and Williams Lake, tried to put their own signature on events. For High River, the old-timer as well as little britches and girls' rodeos promised to bring audiences to its Frontier Days and to provide a particular feel that would set it apart from its competitors. Williams Lake turned to aboriginality as the feature that made its stampede unique. In the process, spaces remained for Aboriginal participation, but, especially at Williams Lake, these were set off from the mainstream pro events. Fragmentation, antipathy, and increasing mutual distrust were not, however, solely the result of professionalization. By the 1960s and 1970s, relations between First Nations and settlers across Western Canada had shifted dramatically. Although *Cariboo Country* depicted the easy relations between Smith and Ol' Antoine, Paul St. Pierre expressed other ethics when he wrote about life in the Chilcotin. In *Breaking Smith's Quarterhorse*, the central character, Chilcotin rancher Smith, opines that "the best organized of all worlds was one in which Indians helped Indians and whites helped whites and both sides minded their own business." Though Smith seldom followed this maxim, the author was not incorrect in describing the mid-twentieth-century Canadian West as a place where racial segmentation was rapidly becoming the norm.[145]

6

Where the Cowboys Are Indians

Indian and Reserve Rodeo in the Canadian West

*Belonging to an intimate public is therefore a condition of
feeling general within a set of porous constraints, and of feeling
held or sustained by an evolving sense of experience that confirms
some homogeneity and elaborates social distinctions.*
— *Lauren Berlant,* The Female Complaint

It was mid-afternoon when the drizzle finally quit. As the clouds slowly lifted, a high ridge appeared beyond the Nemiah Stampede rodeo grounds. People pointed to barely visible figures moving about on the ridge, but it was impossible to tell what they were doing. Snatches of overheard conversation revealed that the much-anticipated mountain race was about to begin, officials having made their way to the summit startline. Work crews had already spent hours clearing rocks and other debris from the path of the racers who, in one of the last true mountain races in Canadian rodeo, would soon be hurtling downslope at dizzying speed.

The announcer began to warm up the audience preparatory to welcoming the contestants, who would be introduced before they ascended the ridge to begin the race. Pointing to the ridge, where a large crowd had now gathered, he explained the race, its distance and course, including the final leg when riders traverse a narrow but fast-running creek before they cross the finish line and enter the open-air arena. The race, he said, was the pride of the Xeni Gwet'in First Nation. As part of the Nemiah Valley Stampede, it was sponsored by the Xeni Gwet'in government. That year, 2002, filmmakers were recording the race as part of a larger public relations project intent on raising awareness of the Xeni Gwet'in's upcoming legal battle to retain sovereignty over their beloved Nemiah Valley, a sovereignty never ceded but nonetheless claimed by the provincial government.[1]

Advertising the Nemiah Valley Stampede, 2009. *Author photo*

As riders assembled outside the arena, the time for their introduction arrived. "You've heard of the great Tsilhquot'in warriors," the announcer began, "the men who defended our territory and our people in the Chilcotin War? They were great men, brave men. Well, today, here are our great Tsilhquot'in warriors again, in our mountain-racers, who ride today." And then, as the competitors rode great flourishing circles around the arena, focused but smiling, he introduced each rider and horse, indicating where they were from and how many times they had competed. One rider stood out, dressed all in black, his mount groomed to satiny perfection, tack glittering with silver. This race was more than a race. The announcer's introduction made it clear that it was also an expression of deep-running Tsilhquot'in identity, a connection to the past, a performance of Tsilhquot'in masculinity, and a vivid display of skill, athleticism, discipline, and grit. His words wove strands of history around each racer, and with those strands, filaments of feeling – pride, outrage, anguish, resilience – curled across generations and between community members, drawing them tighter into what Lauren Berlant describes as an intimate public.

Berlant writes that the "concept of the 'intimate public' thus carries forward a common sense or a vernacular sense of belonging to a community ... A public is intimate when it foregrounds affective and emotional attachments located in fantasies of the common, the everyday, and a sense of ordinariness, a space where the social world is rich with anonymity and local recognitions, and where challenging and banal conditions of life take place in proximity to the attentions of power but also squarely in the radar of a recognition that can be provided by other humans." Berlant describes intimate publics as *juxtapolitical;* they flourish alongside the public sphere but include feelings, identities, and attachments. The "aesthetic and spiritual scene" created by people who have suffered historical and ongoing injustice and marginalization may provide "relief from the political," as Berlant writes, but as the Nemiah Valley Stampede demonstrated, the political is never far from hand. The world of reserve rodeo and the professional circuit of the Indian Rodeo Cowboy Association (IRCA) were not explicitly political, were not explicitly about dealing with the continuing struggle of Aboriginal peoples in the Canadian West, but the sense that being an Indian rodeo cowboy entailed having experienced those struggles in a personal way was what bound the community together.[2]

Indian and reserve rodeos did not represent a complete retreat from the contact zone.[3] For one thing, though Indian rodeo officially limited participation to those who could demonstrate "Indian status" under Canada's Indian Act, the lack of treaties in BC forced more flexibility in determining who had status than was ever allowed by the imposed definitions of the Canadian government.[4] The experience of rancher and rodeo cowboy Bill Evans and his son Bill Jr. illustrates the problems that Indian status could pose. While travelling with Gil Bowe, the two men decided to enter an Indian rodeo on the Soda Creek Reserve. At first, the rodeo committee would not accept Bill Jr. because his father was white. But Bill Sr., who had followed the BC circuit for years, approached one of the directors and asked if he was familiar with a well-known Aboriginal rodeo cowboy named Earl Marchand. "Earl's my son's uncle," he declared, and with that, the committee decided that Bill Jr. was "enough Native" to compete. He would rodeo for many more years on the Indian and pro circuits, which he said were more accepting of him as a mixed-heritage contestant than other all-Native sports tournaments.[5] Moreover, some reserve rodeos welcomed participants and audiences from all communities. The Nakoda reserve at Eden Valley invited local townsfolk to its stampede in 1950, and settler cowboys competed at Morley's Stoney (Nakoda) Indian Rodeo in 1951 and 1953.[6] What constituted an "Indian rodeo" was not the exclusion of settler participants but the authority of committees staffed entirely by Aboriginal people to make the rules. Indian and reserve rodeos remained contact zones but with the power shifted toward Aboriginal rather than settler people.

These rodeos retained another characteristic of the contact zone: they continued to be creative sites of social and cultural formation. Indian rodeo was grounded in, but not held hostage to, a discourse of discrimination. Like other community rodeos, reserve rodeos struggled with the effects of professionalization, and some Aboriginal cowboys endeavoured to enter the expensive and demanding world of the modern pro cowboy. The lingering sense that these obstacles were different for Aboriginal cowboys prompted established figures, such as Fred Gladstone, to start organizations that would encourage young men from their own communities to enter the sport. During the late twentieth century, at least six Indian rodeo associations formed, extending from the Prairies through southern Alberta to the Chilcotin Plateau.

These groups disrupted the bland dichotomies of racialization. Residential schools and popular culture both reaffirmed that the central struggle of the Western story was between cowboys and Indians, with the latter decidedly in the losing role. But as each generation of Aboriginal cowboys came forward to claim a place in the arena, and as those individuals gained a louder and more coherent voice through Indian rodeo cowboy associations, the idea that Aboriginal peoples had lost their place in the contemporary West was proven false. Nor were Aboriginal cowboys constrained by the dominant images generated in Hollywood. Instead, they and their families expressed identities that emphasized family, community, and a special connection to animals. Finally, though rodeo remained mostly juxtapolitical, it nonetheless contributed to the political careers of many First Nations leaders, and the discursive disruption of Indian rodeo was itself political, decolonizing work. Rather than moving out of the contact zone, Indian rodeo brought the zone into a world of Aboriginal design.

Reserve rodeos had a long history, as we have seen, dating back to the 1920s, when rodeo began in Western Canada. In the 1940s, they expanded, became more formally organized, and in some cases, tried to affiliate with

Vehicles and people assembled for rodeo on the Nakoda reserve, Morley, 1949-50. *Glenbow Museum Archives, NA-5719-2*

the emerging pro rodeo associations. Alberta reserves at Morley, Eden Valley, Brocket, and Gleichen ran rodeos independent of Indian agency officials.[7] E. Cousineau, Indian Agent at Morley, informed Jim Maxwell, the Canadian Professional Rodeo Association (CPRA) secretary, that he (Cousineau) had nothing to do with organizing the stampede there. Instead, the Stoney Indian Agency Stampede Committee – with Eddie Hunter as secretary – ran events.[8] Johnny Lefthand put on rodeos at Eden Valley, and the Blood Indian Reserve Association staged rodeos on that reserve in the 1950s, drawing competitors from across southern Alberta and northern Montana.[9] In British Columbia, the Kamloops, Mt. Currie, Deadman's Creek, and Inkameep Reserves each held rodeos, and the Allison family ran one on its Chopaka Ranch in the south Okanagan as did the Palmantiers at Riske Creek.[10]

The CPRA allowed pro cowboys to compete in non-CPRA reserve rodeos, but only if they were "treaty Indians." This obviously put Métis, BC First Nations, and people of mixed heritage in an uncertain position. Sometimes

riders were fined and blacklisted just for participating in their own community rodeos. When reserve rodeos sought to affiliate with the CPRA or
other bodies such as the Foothills Cowboys Association of southern
Alberta, they met further obstacles. For them and reserve cowboys alike,
adhering to association rules was difficult. The associations demanded
hefty prizes that must be guaranteed in advance as well as infrastructure
that met their standards, and they reserved the right to inspect arrangements beforehand in order to grant their imprimatur.[11] For some, too
much authority rested in settler hands.

By the second half of the twentieth century, the place of Aboriginal
people in community events, such as stampedes, was coming under intense
criticism.[12] Nakoda chiefs and councillors, such as John Snow, demanded
greater decision-making roles at Banff's Indian Days. Katie Anderson,
editor of the Banff School of Fine Arts newspaper, dismissed the event as
a "Vaudevillian side-show" and reported on the "racist and sexist jokes"
told by an Indian Days announcer who appeared to have no connection
to the Aboriginal people featured there.[13] Disputes erupted at the Calgary
Stampede regarding the old rules that gave management total control
over who could be in the Indian village.[14] At Williams Lake, management's
decision to charge Aboriginal people for camping on stampede grounds
was greeted with consternation, for the right to camp for free had long
been perceived as recognition of their importance to the event.[15] Moreover, it was widely believed that discrimination against Aboriginal cowboys
was a fact of life in rodeo. Tom Three Persons encouraged a whole generation of Kainai competitors to take up calf roping because the judging
of roughstock events was, as he put it, too open to "human error." Those
involved in mid-twentieth-century amateur and high school rodeo continued to perceive discrimination when Aboriginal contestants went up
against local favourites.[16] As the Hobbema cowboy Todd Buffalo put it,
"You've always got the downfall of being an Indian cowboy, when I went
to amateur rodeos, I'd get the shaft."[17] Like sport more generally, rodeo
did not always smooth over the cleavages so embedded in twentieth-
century life; speaking about small-town rodeo in BC, one former bronc-
rider said simply, "Some white guys are always gonna be white guys."[18]
Professionalization was supposed to put a stop to capricious judging, but
it introduced another set of problems.[19] The Williams Lake Indian
Stampede Association (formed in 1965) wondered if pro rodeo would
leave Aboriginal cowboys behind.[20] Administering complex sets of rules

and regulations produced confusion and suspicion, and committees could be dismissive when Aboriginal competitors asked for clarification. When fifteen-year-old Chantelle Daychief began barrel racing in the late 1980s, she was excluded from the novice category because she had competed once before. When her father asked why she was being forced to compete with much older and more experienced professional barrel-racers, the manager of a southern Alberta rodeo told him, in Daychief's words, that "it was his jackpot and that I had no room to talk. From that statement I took it personal."[21] In some ways, the increasing cash prizes and rising stakes of rodeo simply added to the tensions that inflamed emotions.

As we have seen, the growing costs of the sport also eliminated many Aboriginal people from small-town competition. The mandatory equipment was expensive. In the 1970s, the gear required for the roughstock events, which were the cheapest ones, ran upwards of $400. Due to the expenses incurred by its four years of training, a good calf-roping horse could cost between $3,000 and $10,000.[22] Travelling the circuit required cash outlay and was more expensive for calf-ropers, steer-wrestlers, and barrel-racers, who transported their horses.[23] Not long after the pro organizations had reshaped the sport, Aboriginal cowboys who had joined the pro circuit looked around and saw few others coming up the ranks.[24] The feeling developed that "Native riders were getting jobbed," as Fred Gladstone put it.[25]

One way of encouraging young competitors was to offer them the best aspects of professionalism without the troubling interventions of non-Native committees, organizations, and officials – by forming all-Indian pro rodeo associations. The first of these in Western Canada was the Lazy-B 70 Rodeo Club, which was established on the Blood reserve in 1954. Fred and Horace Gladstone, Rufus Goodstriker, Floyd and Frank Many Fingers, Ken and Tuffy Tailfeathers, all veteran rodeo cowboys, founded the club to encourage young men to train for the sport and to provide them with competitive venues where racialized discrimination would be minimized.[26] Older cowboys were pleased with the talent they saw emerging in the next generation.[27] Other reserves started their own clubs, and it soon became clear that enough support existed for a broader association. In 1964 the All-Indian Rodeo Association (AIRA) was formed. In 1970 it changed its name to the Indian Rodeo Cowboy Association (IRCA) to acknowledge that though only Indians could compete, all spectators were welcome to attend.[28]

FIRST ANNUAL
ALL INDIAN
RODEO

A Youngman Brothers
(Located 5 Miles Southwest of Gleichen)
═══ ON ═══
SATURDAY, JUNE 6

Entries Close 10 a.m., Saturday, June 6th

50% OF ENTRY FEE ADDED TO PURSE		
ENTRY	**PURSE**	**Entry Fee**
SADDLE BRONC	$100.00	$10
BAREBACK RIDING	$100.00	$15
STEER DECORATING	$100.00	$15
CALF ROPING	$100.00	$15
COW RIDING	$ 50.00	$15
ALL ENTRY FEES ADDED—		
Ladies' Barrel Race	$35.00	$ 5
Girls' Barrel Race	$20.00	$ 5
Boys' Steer Riding	$20.00	$ 3

Grand Entry 1:00 p.m.

President	Arthur A Youngman
Vice-President	Harry A Youngman
Arena Director	Arthur A Youngman
Secretary-Treasurer	Mathew A Youngman
Announcer	Randy A Youngman
	Adolphus Weaselchild
Livestock Supplied By	Arthur, Harry & Roy

This Rodeo Is Approved by the All Indian Rodeo Association

Refreshments Served on the Grounds

Admission to Grounds - - $1.25
Children Under 12 Years Free

Management Not Responsible For Any Loss Or Accident

PRINTED BY THE STRATHMORE STANDARD.

NOTICE DON'T HAVE TO BE MEMBER OF ASSOCIATION TO ENTER RODEO

All-Indian rodeo, Gleichen, 1964. *Glenbow Museum Archives, NA-1713-18*

The IRCA primarily brought together rodeo cowboys from southern Alberta, stringing together a circuit at Hobbema, Siksika, and on the Blood reserve.[29] Soon other regions created their own organizations, beginning with the Northern Indian Rodeo Cowboy Association in 1973.[30] In the late 1970s, a loose organization of BC cowboys became known as the British Columbia Indian Rodeo Association, and they went on to form the Western Indian Rodeo and Exhibition Association (WIREA) in 1981.[31] Despite the proliferation of other Indian rodeo organizations, groups cooperated, for the most part, respecting each other's suspended lists and reporting on each other's rodeos. In 1974 Indian rodeo groups from across Canada and the United States came together to establish the Indian National Finals Rodeo (INFR), which ran its first championship in 1976, when it was recognized as an official American Revolution bicentennial event. The INFR soon established itself as a transborder venue in which the best Aboriginal cowboys competed for world championship titles. In 1981 it paid approximately $80,000 in prizes and awards.[32] Locally, Indian rodeos expanded both their payouts and their circuits in the 1980s. The Sarcee Annual Rodeo of 1980 offered nearly $17,000 in prize money, and in BC, the nineteen WIREA rodeos of 1983 paid out over $175,000. By the end of the century, Indian rodeo had become a well-organized and lucrative sport.

Indian rodeo embraced professionalization. Nothing suggests that the Indian cowboy associations wished to turn back the clock to the days when rodeos were largely amateur affairs. Rather, the founding members of the IRCA, WIREA, and other organizations were drawn largely from the ranks of pro cowboys: for example, Bud Connoly of Browning, Montana, Jim and Fred Gladstone, Gordon Crowchild, and Bob Gottfriedson served on the AIRA executive. Moreover, the IRCA and WIREA mainly adapted the rules and by-laws of the CPRA when they registered as societies (the IRCA in 1970 and WIREA in 1981).[33] Like the CPRA, the IRCA set minimum thresholds on prize payouts and entry fees as well as maximum limits on prizes won by non-members riding on special permit. It determined which events would be constitutive of an approved rodeo, promised financial assistance for injuries incurred there, established and explained the point system that produced champions, and listed the various offences that could result in suspensions; these included quarrelling, fighting, using abusive

WIREA rodeos, 1983

Rodeo	Entries	Total payout ($)
Ashcroft	230	12,255
Head of the Lakes (Vernon)	266	10,850
Anahim	201	9,425
Lillooet Lake (Mt. Currie)	228	11,990
Double G (Kamloops)	298	11,140
Similkameen (Cawston)	228	9,290
Alkali Lake	265	13,240
Lillooet Lake (Mt. Currie)	190	10,730
Adams Lake	237	9,305
Oliver	153	5,600
Canim Lake	150	6,550
Pavilion	217	11,220
Sugar Cane	212	8,175
Cheam	133	6,250
Quilchena	266	10,030
Tobacco Plains	92	3,990
Lillooet Lake (Mt. Currie)	144	8,515
Chase	151	6,020
Year End	174	9,565
Total	3,835	174,140

Note: Lillooet Lake (Mt. Currie) held three rodeos in 1983.
Source: Ethnology files, Legends of Our Times, Western Indian Rodeo Association files, E99.5, box 665, file 5, CMC.

language, intoxication, attempting to influence officials, and passing bad cheques.[34] Some early members took pride in these strict guidelines, which included publishing the names of suspended members in the *Kainai News,* the Blood reserve's own newspaper. This encompassed not just members in their own organization but those in the CPRA, the Foothills Cowboys Association, the North Central Montana Association, and the Chinook Rodeo Association, among others.[35] Given this, it seems clear that many Aboriginal cowboys had no quarrel with the rules and regulations of pro rodeo. Rather, the problem lay in their sense that, in non-Native rodeo, these were not always applied evenly to all contestants.

The impetus for forming Indian rodeo associations was the feeling that Aboriginal riders "weren't given a fair shake."[36] In this sense, the world of Aboriginal rodeo was a felt world, an affective community, where common interests and shared experiences produced a social unit that was not

Bareback riding, Morley All-Indian Rodeo, 1964. *Glenbow Museum Archives,
NA 2557-54*

limited by national configurations, though many cowboys and cowgirls
retained alliances to being Kainai, Siksika, Secwepemc, Tsilhquot'in, or
Canadian or American. The 1970s and 1980s were an era of growing
politicization, whether of a pan-Indian variety, as expressed in the
American Indian Movement of the United States or the Native Indian
Brotherhood in Canada, or of more local alliances such as the Indian
Association of Alberta and the Union of BC Indian Chiefs. While these
overtly political organizations took centre stage in negotiating with government, Indian rodeo offered another kind of community for Aboriginal
people in the rural Canadian West. It acknowledged the feelings of racialization at the personal, familial, and organizational level and turned those
feelings into a unifying force. Grounded in a discourse of discrimination,
these were the emotional networks through which all-Indian rodeo grew.[37]

What sustained it was something else, however – another constellation of feelings. The expansion of all-Indian rodeo was founded in a much more hopeful set of propositions: that rodeo and the identities associated with being an Indian cowboy (or cowgirl) could be deployed to sustain Aboriginal cultures – indeed, that rodeo was itself Aboriginal.

This hope overturned one of the major dichotomies of North American culture – cowboys versus Indians – the central antagonism of the Hollywood western. Its pervasiveness led to ironic chuckling even among Aboriginal cowboys who, gathered at an early All-Indian Rodeo Association meeting, heard themselves being called to order with "welcome cowboys and Indians."[38] When children in residential schools watched Hollywood westerns, it could lead to darker feelings, even for those whose fathers, uncles, or brothers were themselves Indian cowboys. These children recognized the irony but found it hard to identify with the Indians of western fare, for they were always losing. Remembering the experience years later, Siksika elder Ruth Scalplock remarked, "We had movies at the school and I used to find it funny when they showed cowboy and Indian films. We all sided with the cowboys [laugh]. I was ashamed to be an Indian girl or woman for the longest time. I felt if I sided with the cowboys I wouldn't get scolded or get into trouble."[39] Such stories have prompted some scholars to question the wisdom of adopting the cowboy identity at all. As Jan Penrose explains, "Indian cowboys rely on racialization ... The capacity for dominant groups to construct the terms of reference that structure the world means that even though new categories and associated identities may be produced, they remain embedded in and consequently vulnerable to dominant conceptual frameworks."[40] According to this view, to be a cowboy is to perform the myth of the frontier, the narrative line that displays and reiterates white ascendancy, a metanarrative that determines what can be known about the past and that places limits on what can be envisioned for the present and future. On some level, rejecting rodeo altogether might have been easier for Aboriginal people.

Instead, they indigenized it. Gerry Attachie of the Doig River First Nation put it unequivocally: "It's part of our tradition: horses and rodeo."[41] Refusing the binary of cowboy versus Indian is subversive. Marilyn Burgess contends that Aboriginal cowboys trouble the standard histories of the Canadian West, a view that fits more easily with the ways in which Aboriginal cowboys talk themselves.[42] As Ed Calf Robe, a former saddle bronc rider and proud participant in the Calgary Stampede's Indian village, told a *Geist* magazine reporter, "We are trying to educate you guys about Indians [after] all that bad publicity we got from Hollywood. Cowboys and Indians really got along; it's only in Hollywood they fight ... All Indians are cowboys at one time or another."[43] For many contemporary Aboriginal cowboys, there is no need to choose between identities. One can be a championship grass dancer and a champion bronc-rider, even if the necessary costume changes can seem daunting, as one of Morgan Baillargeon's informants explained: "I'm a child of leaders, of chiefs. I grew up traditional dancing, fancy dancing. I'm ... a champion grass dancer. I consider myself the only world champion bronc rider in the rodeo arena and in the powwow movement ... We'll go out to the fair at Pine Ridge, I make the grand entry, undress, go over to the rodeo, put my cowboy outfit on, ride my bronc, got my saddle, went back over to my tipi, put my dancing outfit on and got right back into contesting – also took first that time too."[44] The interchangeability of "cowboy" and "Indian" underlines flexibilities unimaginable in the metanarratives of conquest.

On the margins perhaps of popular culture, Aboriginal cowboys occupy a space where the fixed categories of cowboy and Indian, culture and nature, and modernity and tradition are destabilized.[45] Indeed, cultural critics remind us that fusing "traditional" and "modern" can produce subversive mimicries that perform the complicated entanglements between people that are characteristic of the contact zone. Perceiving Indian rodeo as an invented tradition goes only partway toward understanding its significance to processes of decolonization. Rather, as Colleen O'Neill suggests, "tradition and modernity are expressions of 'difference' rather than historical benchmarks that distinguish a particular community's place in time. Aboriginal peoples have developed new traditions in modernizing contexts and in the process have contested the terms of modernity itself."[46] In this sense, we can see Indian rodeo as a "new tradition" that serves Aboriginal people in particular ways, an imaginative process not unlike that employed by small towns in using the sport to fashion their own images.

Seeing rodeo as a new Aboriginal tradition rests upon a foundation of finding something different, something distinctly Aboriginal, in the sport. Doing so calls for imagining "Aboriginal" as having unifying characteristics that differ from the attributes of others. In the book *The Gift of the Grandfathers,* Tsuu T'ina bullfighter and rodeo clown Richard Bish tried to clarify how Indian rodeo differed from other versions: "In Indian rodeo, there is a bonding and it's natural ... You can talk about traditional things, about family. It is your time to gather, it is traditional and spiritual at the same time."[47] The 1981 program of the Indian National Finals Rodeo similarly laid claim to rodeo as particularly Aboriginal, grounding it in history: "It has been said that the Indian was 'in fact' the first American cowboy. Their horsemanship skills were copied and generated by the very earliest white settlers ... Due to the early Indian tradition of their love for and protection of natural resources in a rugged outdoor environment and, more important, their love for their sacred horses, the last three quarters of a century has directed the Indian toward the ways of the rugged early-days cowboys, because that type of life matches their own livelihood." The program added that the INFR's goal was to "bring people of all cultures together to share in our rich Indian history, culture and view a competitive sporting event on a national basis."[48] Not only did the INFR stage championship rodeo but it also included a powwow, an exhibition of Aboriginal arts and crafts, and a Miss Indian Rodeo pageant in its annual event. Thus, all-Indian rodeo produced its own definitions of Aboriginal that stressed commonalities among diverse First Nations, Métis, and mixed-heritage people, traits that diverged from those of settlers. Aboriginal people were said to share a different relationship with animals, a stronger commitment to family, and a greater emphasis on community. In this last area, rodeo is clearly juxtapolitical, as cowboys and cowgirls apply the lessons learned and connections made there to political careers and community development.

Some Aboriginal people attest to a special, spiritual relationship between themselves and animals, especially horses. Stories about how the horse came to the people, brought by the grandmothers to a young man on a vision quest or subdued for human use by Snk'lip – Coyote, the Okanagan trickster – set otherworldly contexts for contemporary human-horse interactions.[49] Aboriginal cowboys claimed a particular affinity for horses, an almost visceral need to be with them. As one respondent told Baillargeon, "There has been a bonding with Native Americans and horses for generations. Take a Native American away from horses for three or four months, [and he will] feel lost."[50] George Saddleman, a WIREA board member, rodeo organizer, and announcer, agreed in one interview that "animals are just as much a part of us as we are of them."[51] Harry Setah and Roger Williams of the Xeni Gwet'in similarly link their identities to their close bond with horses. Describing their battle to preserve the wild horse herds of the Brittany Triangle, Williams stated, "it's all for the horses, for our tradition; horses are part of our life."[52] From the Peace River country in the north, where Garry Oker described Dunne-za ways of taming a horse, to Whispering Pines in the south, where Mike LeBourdais credited his father, Duke, with developing his own version of "horse whispering," Aboriginal cowboys and cowgirls claimed that a strong empathy with animals was inherently Aboriginal.[53]

Whatever the spiritual origins of this tie, it is also grounded in more mundane and material factors. Past midcentury, horses remained the main mode of transportation for First Nations in the BC Interior; in some instances, this was due to the lack of roads, but it could also reflect the difficulty in obtaining a driver's licence far from urban centres such as Williams Lake.[54] Horses were also readily available. The Xeni Gwet'in captured them from the wild herds that inhabited the Nemiah Valley, careful to take only foals and to leave the fillies to replenish the herds.[55] Duke LeBourdais remembered rounding up wild horses with his aunt and uncle in the 1940s; returning to his parents on the Clinton Reserve, he rode horseback from Williams Lake, a distance of over a hundred miles. He was fifteen.[56] Others described a world in which, as children, they were surrounded by horses and where horses were a part of everyday life.[57] Secwepemc poet Garry Gottfriedson said that, growing up on his father's Kamloops Reserve ranch in the 1960s, his brothers and sisters all rode horses before they rode bikes.[58] Caring for and playing with horses were part of childhood for First Nations in southern Alberta as well. Kainai Fred Gladstone was wrangling horses by the age of nine, rounding them up for use on his father's ranch or to ride to school.[59] Tsuu T'ina Sandra Crowchild also grew up around horses, learning that they were individuals, with personalities and feelings, deserving respect.[60] Joe Medicine Shield told Morgan Baillargeon that his daughter learned important lessons about taking care of another living thing, putting its needs first, when she got her first barrel-racing horse.[61]

The popular culture that has materialized around Indian rodeos in the latter decades of the twentieth century connects First Nations with horses and the land by emphasizing stewardship, not dominance. Kinship with animals is the manifestation of the enduring link between First Nations and the land, the relationship that defines them as a people animated with the spirits of ancestors, both human and animal. This is clearly both strategic and affective. It is strategic because proving such a connection is central to land-claims cases, particularly in BC. Furthermore, it fosters alliances with environmental groups, which, though fraught, have halted resource extraction in areas that are the subject of First Nations court battles. The Xeni Gwet'in connection with the wild horses of the Brittany Triangle was one such example. Portraying Aboriginal rodeo as grounded in non-exploitive spiritual relationships with animals also binds contemporary participants, whether First Nations, Métis, or of mixed heritage, to elders who are remembered through stories about their accomplishments alongside well-loved horses. Aboriginal histories from rodeo country are filled with tales of equestrian skill, bravery, and self-sacrifice for the care of animals.[62] Writing from the Okanagan, Thomas Pierre remembered the accomplished horseman, William Armstrong, and concluded that "what is old is still important today. For I am one of the lucky ones to be able to learn and ride with one of our greatest cowboys ... In the coming years, I am sure there will be a horse and a boy as their ancestors were. The interest never wanes."[63] As the narrator of *The Gift of the Grandfathers* put it, "The spirits of great horsemen and buffalo hunters live within the places of our soul. Our past lives with us."[64] Such connections also produce feelings of pride, identifying Aboriginal peoples as more humane, more savvy, more capable, and more committed to training than their settler counterparts.[65] However, not all Aboriginal cowboys perceive this special relationship as inherently Aboriginal. Kainai Pete Standing Alone, an accomplished artist and activist, told Morgan Baillargeon, "I think that there is no difference between an Indian and non-Indian in their attitudes towards animals in rodeo; at least I've never noticed. If there was any difference it would be coming from people who are not involved [in rodeo] whether it be an Indian or a non-Indian."[66] This assertion constituted a significant moment of rupture during his interview with Baillargeon, which signalled that beneath the increasingly standard narrative of Aboriginal distinctiveness, rodeo continues to be a contact zone where settler and Aboriginal ideas about animals merge.[67] Nonetheless, the sense of being distinctive, being special, remains.

History also animates Indian rodeo in another way, through attention to genealogies and family. It is hard to find an Aboriginal rodeo cowboy who cannot recount a detailed family tree of cowboys and cowgirls. For the Gottfriedsons, the lineage began with Gus Gottfriedson's father-in-law, Andy Manuel, who produced superb racehorses in the early decades of the twentieth century.[68] Gottfriedson himself rode broncs in rodeos and organized them through midcentury, winning the Canadian Wild Horse Race Championship in 1945. With Manuel, he sold a herd of horses to the army in the Second World War and drove them overland to the coast. He supplied rodeo stock until he turned the business over to his sons in 1979.[69] His sons Bob and Ron became championship competitors and carried on the family name in rodeo. Tsuu T'ina bullfighter Richard Bish recognized his uncle Bob Gottfriedson as a significant influence of his career. Ron Gottfriedson married Joan Perry, the widow of famed bronc-rider and stock contractor Dave Perry. As we have seen, she is particularly clear on the value of rodeo in providing wholesome activity for youth. Joan's sons are ropers and bulldoggers, and her daughters barrel race, so it's no wonder that she perceives rodeo as a "family thing." Early rodeos on the Kamloops Reserve and in Kamloops itself relied on Gottfriedson organizational abilities, talent, and roughstock for their success.[70]

The Gladstone family in southern Alberta boasts a similar pedigree. Fred Gladstone learned to rope on his father's ranch under the tutelage of Tom Three Persons. He went on to championship calf roping and to executive positions in all-Indian rodeo and the CPRA. His son, Jim, was the IRCA president during the late 1960s and in 1977 was the world champion calf-roper, winning the Pro Rodeo Cowboy Finals in Oklahoma City that year. Jim Gladstone's sister Caen Bly competed in barrel racing while editing the *Kainai News*. Family names such as Bruisehead, Lindley, Beaver, Provost, Bowie, and Lefthand carry with them histories of rodeo excellence.[71] As Hugh Dempsey remarked, "family dynasties are common in Indian country."[72]

Contemporary cowboys stated that travelling with family was one of the advantages of Indian rodeo. Cecil Louis noted that most men he knew took their families with them, giving the children a chance to see many different communities.[73] Travelling also enhanced kin connections. In the 1970s, most of the off-reserve visitors to the Mt. Currie Rodeo were former residents who came home for the annual event.[74] Though many Aboriginal cowboys understood that family travel was common throughout the circuits, they nonetheless applauded it as particularly important to them. Ron and Robin Johnson, Blackfeet from Browning, Montana, followed the circuit from March through to the fall. Ron bulldogged and team roped, Robin barrel raced, and their daughters competed in barrel racing, pole bending, and goat tying. Even their three-year-old loved to rope. For Robin Johnson, rodeoing was part of being Blackfeet, and travelling with her family was a way of passing on her family and community traditions.[75]

Gender identities, remembered and revised, were embedded within these discourses, as family histories of rodeo tended to reiterate traditional gender divisions. Women talked about travelling with their children, preparing camp, and feeding whoever came by for a meal, but men seldom mentioned the domestic arrangements associated with being on the road. Nonetheless, masculinities and femininities did not remain static for Aboriginal rodeo families. Mid-twentieth-century ethnographies focused on the rough masculinities of the hard-drinking rodeo cowboy, but by the end of the century, Aboriginal cowboys talked more about rebuilding careers in sobriety, a message they carried to young people. As Ken Tailfeathers told Caen Bly in a 1969 interview, "My advice to the young cowboys is to practice and stay away from the whiskey. Rodeoing is a rough, demanding career, especially for an Indian."[76] Fred Gladstone also spoke openly about how he turned his life around through his involvement with Alcoholics Anonymous.[77]

Adherence to a code of tough physicality remained part of Indian rodeo masculinity. Ron and Joan (Perry) Gottfriedson listed Ron's injuries over the years: broken arms, broken ribs, broken collarbone. In their interviews, rodeo cowboys repeatedly mention the ability to compete while injured. When Ron Gottfriedson participated in the special stampede organized for Princess Margaret's 1958 visit, he rode saddle bronc and bareback with a broken foot. He had the cast cut off beforehand, and a doctor injected his damaged limb with local anaesthetic. When he was thrown from his mount during the bareback event, only the skills of the pick-up rider prevented him from falling on the foot.[78] After an eighteen-hundred-pound horse flipped over on him in the chute, Duke LeBourdais spent eighteen months recovering from broken bones. When he returned to bareback riding, he was badly injured again and took up calf roping and bulldogging after that.[79] Indeed, the physicality of the sport leaves its mark on men. Few veteran cowboys move as fluidly on foot as they do on horseback, as old injuries generate arthritis. Though Monty Palmantier has not ridden in rodeos for years, the fused vertebrae in his neck are a painful reminder of those days. Few complain. "That's what you get for being a cowboy" was all that Wallace Mountain Horse had to say on the subject.[80]

Femininities within Aboriginal rodeo also changed over time, as they did in pro rodeo, and family played a role as well. Rodeo families were pleased that events had opened up for women, particularly barrel racing. Here too, injuries were the norm, and cowgirls, such as Indian rodeo finalist Sandra Crowchild, competed with broken bones. Women's injuries in roughstock events, however, garnered a greater range of reactions. When these events returned to reserve rodeos in the late twentieth century, some thought that the men who watched the female competitors "wanted to see them get thrown and stepped on."[81] Others felt pressure from families to stop riding roughstock. Joan (Palmantier) Gentles broke her tailbone in an all-women bareback event. The break was painful and her tailbone remained sensitive for years, but she continued to ride, using a blanket as a cushion. Ultimately, she returned to barrel racing, in part because her husband did not want her to be hurt again.[82] Still, being skilled horsewomen linked Aboriginal cowgirls with family and community histories. Okanagan historian Shirley Louis found many examples of women in her community's past who had superb equestrian skills, which enabled them to provide for their families and maintain their independence or gain the upper hand in conflicts with men. For men and women in Aboriginal rodeo families, the sport demanded toughness, but this did not negate femininity. As Nakoda Cara Currie, barrel-racer and former rodeo queen, stated, rodeo "is not a violent sport, but it isn't easy. You have to be tough, tough-minded, tough-spirited and tough physically."[83] Not only did families hope that the sport would teach important lessons to youth, they also observed that it was a good training ground for other achievements.

Rodeo functioned in the juxtapolitical realm, contributing to community development and building capacity for leadership. Thus, it deserves a place in the history of Aboriginal activism. As early as the 1960s, non-Native observers expressed surprise at the efficiency of Aboriginal people who cooperated to stage stampedes and other celebrations, which were intended solely to build community feeling.[84] Reflecting on the origins of the Mt. Currie Rodeo, Chiefs Baptiste Ritche and Adam James affirmed in the late 1960s that it was primarily a community festival, a particularly "Indian celebration." Though it became more formal in 1962 when an arena, chutes, and corrals were added, both men agreed that, since its inception before the turn of the twentieth century, it had had little other

Horse race at the Mt. Currie Rodeo, 1967. *Courtesy of Royal BC Museum, BC Archives, I-15893*

purpose than to fete the community.[85] Only after the new infrastructure increased the numbers of off-reserve visitors did its second function become clear – as a fundraiser for various organizations, including the reserve's Athletic and Homemakers' Clubs.

The theme of celebrating the community pervaded the Mt. Currie Rodeo, beginning with the parade, which consisted mainly of floats representing local reserve groups and children who rode in horse-drawn wagons or walked. The opening ceremony included several songs described as "traditional festival or celebration songs." Anthropologist Roger Haugen, who attended the Mt. Currie Rodeo in 1970, wrote that it functioned mainly as a social occasion. Events were run, though not very efficiently, as riders and spectators congregated around the chutes, talking and "joshing" throughout. Most of the community and many visitors attended the evening dance. After the rodeo ended, people told Haugen that it was the main money-maker for reserve organizations. Shortly afterward, he attended a rodeo on the Fountain Reserve, which confirmed his view that reserve rodeos were primarily social in nature. As one person told him, "There are usually Indians at rodeos and so I meet new people and old friends too."[86] Indeed, the Fountain Rodeo attracted Aboriginal competitors and their families from across the BC Interior. Though it was more professionally run than its Mt. Currie counterpart, with stock and judging provided by Duke LeBourdais and his brother, its success as a social occasion prompted Fountain chief Pat Alec to anticipate continuing it in the future.[87]

For many Aboriginal people involved in rodeo, social occasions could be venues for community revitalization. Although non-Native experts in community economic development hoped to see collective efforts in logging or manufacturing, rodeos promised community enhancement of a different sort. Many rodeo cowboys of the late twentieth century saw rodeo as a vehicle that could engage youth in a new Aboriginal tradition and keep them clean and sober. Hobbema cowboy Todd Buffalo hoped that it might reach Aboriginal youth raised off-reserve, who had little to connect them to their Aboriginal identity. By honouring Indian cowboy heroes such as Pete Bruisehead or Jim Gladstone, he hoped to teach these young people that they had something to be proud of.[88] Other Hobbema cowboys thought that rodeo would help Cree reserve youth move into the wider world and learn skills that would bring them personal acclaim and engender pride in their Aboriginal identity. They saw themselves as role models, and through the medium of ethnographic video recording, sought to connect with youth who were tempted by drugs and alcohol, to encourage them to get along without substances. Cardly Elmer and Merrill Yellowbird both hoped that rodeo and the horsemanship it entailed would teach Hobbema youth to be responsible and to think of those who supported them as well as of future generations. This, they said, was the value of rodeo to the Cree people of Hobbema.[89] Similarly, Secwepemc George Saddleman saw rodeo as a means of reconciling traditional values with modern times, of creating new traditions that embodied the past in the present: "Through leadership, through community events, through recreation, we are rebuilding our society, as we'd like to see it, not as the history books described it. We are rebuilding it ourselves."[90] For Indian rodeo organizers and cowboys, the hybridity inherent in being an Indian cowboy was productive. For all its contradictions and racializing tendencies, the category seemed to deal effectively with modernity without abandoning values deemed traditional. Families travelled together and moved along lines of kinship both biological and arising from rodeo friendships. They seemed to be fairly egalitarian and encouraged young women to take up the roughstock events in which women had competed in the past. Indian rodeo cowboys evinced a tough masculinity but one that was constrained by responsibilities to family, community, and past and future generations. Repeatedly, they referred to careers lost to drugs and alcohol, and to those regained in sobriety. They spoke of combining traditional values of horsemanship with the discipline of athleticism. They looked forward to accomplishments that would create pride for them in their communities and generate opportunities for them off-reserve. If Indian rodeo had been formed in a discourse of disappointment, it built on feelings of optimism.

Lauren Berlant wrote that twenty-first-century critics find it frustrating that the work of intimate publics did not easily translate into political action. Certainly, Indian and reserve rodeo did not seem to address the many and pressing political concerns of the day. In the *Kainai News* sports pages, rodeo events do appear to be "relief from the political," activities far removed from the relentless struggles of late twentieth-century First Nations politics: the White Paper on Indian Act reform and constitutional crises, from repatriation to the Meech Lake and Charlottetown Accords. If Indian rodeo functioned as a "relief from the political," it was no doubt a welcome one.

Rodeo contestants, however, did not shun politics. For example, well-known cowboys Fred Gladstone and Gus Gottfriedson were also political leaders. A board member of the Indian Association of Alberta and of Kainai Industries, Gladstone was also the Alberta representative to the National Indian Brotherhood (a precursor of the Assembly of First Nations) and the Indian Council of Canada. Gottfriedson worked with the National Indian Brotherhood and was chief of the Kamloops Indian Band.[91] WIREA directors were similarly drawn from the ranks of reserve leadership. Of the ten WIREA board members in 1983, five had already served as chief or councillor in their home communities. Others, such as Bob Pasco, were also involved in development initiatives such as the Western Indian Agricultural Corporation.[92] Indeed, some Aboriginal politicians spoke explicitly of how life on the rodeo circuit prepared them for politics. Roger Williams, the Xeni Gwet'in chief who led his people into their court battle over land, said that the grit he acquired in the arena now defined him as a leader. In Aboriginal government offices, such as the Douglas Lake Band office, past chiefs and councillors smile down from photos on the wall, some wearing the headdresses of traditional regalia but most in cowboy hats.

When the filmmakers of *Wild Horses, Unconquered People* recorded the Nemiah Stampede mountain race, the weather was sunnier than on the day that I attended. As the Xeni Gwet'in and their guests watched, the racers again ascended the ridge above Nemiah's stampede grounds. They spoke candidly to the camera about the dangers of the race and the feelings of honour and pride they brought to it. It bound them together in an act that was both political and affective. They were a long way from the law courts that would eventually hear their arguments regarding what had been their territory for centuries. And yet, they were not so far away. Through the stampede and the mountain race, they demonstrated their connection to the land, to their traditions, and to what they called the "last true horse culture in North America." Just as non-Native spectators were present, so too was a world opening before the Xeni Gwet'in via the camera lens that recorded the race. In their own valley, they were in the contact zone. By drawing the viewer into the excitement of the race, they invited their audience into their world, their own intimate public that was both affirming to them and intensely political.

Across Western Canada, Indian and reserve rodeo drew audiences into events of Aboriginal design. Motivated in part to evade the discriminatory aspects of community stampedes and professional rodeo, Indian and reserve rodeo articulated their own definitions of the Indian cowboy and cowgirl. They found a role for rodeo in family and community development. They established their own circuit and their own heroes. In so doing, they offered Aboriginal images of masculinity and femininity much different from those of social pathology that characterized media coverage of First Nations at the end of the twentieth century. When Xeni Gwet'in chief Roger Williams won the mountain race in 2002, he offered an image of Aboriginal masculinity that combined courage, sobriety, political savvy, a deep connection to tradition – and an identity that embraced both the cowboy and the Indian.

Conclusion

Cultural performances remain one of the principal ways in which North Americans experience Aboriginal people. In her controversial award-winning book *Bones: Discovering the First Americans,* Elaine Dewar wrote that she knew nothing about Aboriginal people before she began her research other than what they displayed through dancing and drumming at fairs and festivals. She was probably not alone. It is tempting to dismiss festival encounters as staged and hopelessly superficial. They may be. Yet they are also thresholds, entry points, "teachable moments," and for some, they are the *only* moments when images of Aboriginal people, other than those in the news or from Hollywood, intrude on their consciousness. Cultural performances are limited in their duration, but they rest on larger processes of planning and orchestration that bring people together, learning something about each other as they go, perhaps rediscovering something of themselves. And as Dewar found, their power to intrigue lingers. They bolster self-esteem, preserve culture, and affect observers – that was what made them so dangerous to those who would have eradicated Aboriginal culture early in the twentieth century. Their persistence as a form of political action makes it necessary for us to understand how such events came to be, what histories they enact, what stories they tell, and what stories they evade. Other scholars have studied Wild West Shows, exhibitions, and spectacles. This book portrays the history of rodeo as a cultural performance that was integral to the growth of communities in Western Canada, both settler and Aboriginal, that brought people together into contact zones of surprising possibilities, of mutual enjoyment, of confrontation, of dismaying discrimination, and of embodied display, in which the tired myth of the frontier scripts encountered players bent on improvisation. A transborder sport of hemispheric reach, rodeo offers a glimpse into the history of the West that is wilder, more complex, and less bounded but not wholly free from the political, social, and economic forces that pressed in on Aboriginal and settler communities in varying ways throughout the twentieth century.[1]

Seeing rodeo as a contact zone has alerted us to other interpretive possibilities. We can move beyond thinking about rodeos and stampedes as simply reifying community values. Rather, they seem to constitute communities, to build them both materially and discursively. Early in the century, town elites used rodeo to attract settlers, investors, and tourists. The bucking contest staged for the benefit of journalists visiting Cardston in 1906 was just one moment in that long history when rodeos helped advertise a town and its region as a place where "the spirit of the Plains" promised growth. As new settlement frontiers moved north, the Williams Lake Stampede of the 1930s advertised the Cariboo region as prime cattle country where the possibilities of economic development were only just opening up. Stampedes in southern Alberta, the BC Interior, and the Peace River District competed for the spending power of visitors who jammed restaurants and auto-courts, campgrounds and grandstands, bringing much-needed cash to support flagging rural economies, especially in the darkest days of the Depression. Celebrations such as Lethbridge's 1935 Golden Jubilee stimulated the economy, employed out-of-work men, offered cash for bucking stock to reserve residents, and redistributed scarce resources. In both new and more established settlements, staging a rodeo offered a chance to raise funds and organize volunteer labour for infrastructure improvements. Stampede committees and their volunteers built new leisure-activity venues including grandstands, racetracks, and arenas. Particularly after the Second World War, rodeos contributed their profits to more elaborate facilities, such as aquatic centres and sports complexes. In the hopes of attracting trade during stampede week, businesses spruced up their storefronts, hired extra staff, and bought advertising space in stampede programs and local newspapers. Rodeo committees contributed to all these community ventures, helping to redistribute wealth in tight regional economies.

In many cases, Aboriginal communities added to this enterprise in various ways. By walking in the parade, by setting up encampments and villages, by entering rodeo contests and races, by leasing stock, and by hiring on as pick-up riders and chute bosses, they participated in rodeos and stampedes across the Canadian West. Without Aboriginal involvement, some early twentieth-century towns discovered, stampedes failed financially. So they distributed food to Aboriginal participants when Indian Agents threatened to withhold rations if they attended the local stampede. Stampedes paid cash to elders and families to walk in parades and for setting up encampments, dropped entry fees for Aboriginal contestants, and offered prizes and markets for the sale of women's designs of clothing and beadwork. The growth of rodeo as a popular sport in the first half of the twentieth century was very much the result of cooperation between Aboriginal people and settlers. After the Second World War, Aboriginal participation gave some small-town rodeos an edge over rivals, adding local talent in an era when professional cowboys dominated the scene. For all those towns that built new arenas or contributed to hospitals or social service organizations out of rodeo profits, Aboriginal people working with townsfolk made that happen.

Rodeo built communities in other ways as well. Here its cultural work is more troubling. For, in regional centres, small towns, and rural communities in the Canadian West, it told stories about struggle and opposition, humans and animals, and cowboys and "Indians." Through parades, programs, grandstand entertainment, and implicitly in the contests themselves, it performed scripts of domination. It displayed the myth of the frontier, what Elizabeth Furniss called the "frontier cultural complex," that justified the dispossession of Aboriginal people, the unfettered extraction of resources, and the ascendancy of white settler societies.[2] As such, it fit into larger patterns of cultural formation including fairs, exhibitions, public celebrations, and commemorations that slotted the world into putatively unchanging binary opposites: "Indians" and cowboys, the wild and the tame, primitivism and modernity, rough and respectable, buckle bunnies and rodeo queens. But these categories were produced at rodeos rather than simply reflected by them. When rodeo committees called for volunteer labour, asking their neighbours to demonstrate that the pioneer spirit of hard work and hospitality was still alive in their town, they were setting up a grid of values that became real when they were enunciated and acted upon.[3] When the committees celebrated old-timers, they created the history of whiteness. When they set up Indian villages or set aside separate events or sections of the parade for Aboriginal participation, they marked out difference in the same register that treaty making and reserve allocation had, both visually and spatially. And sometimes they enacted crude stories of conquest, in images and stereotypes that trouble us still.

The structures of early rodeo, however, could not contain all the stories it had to tell. Town elites and organizing committees could not entirely deny the social, economic, and political forces that brought settlers and Aboriginal people together. Indeed, these connections were necessary to the staging of a small-town rodeo, as organizers found that the presence of Aboriginal people was key to financial success. Small-town elites and Aboriginal leadership, then, stood together to resist Ottawa's attempt to prevent reserve residents from attending stampedes. Aboriginal spokespeople such as Mike Mountain Horse used stampedes and the publicity they generated to reach settler audiences with the issues facing reserve residents. Settlers flocked to on-reserve rodeos, bringing cash that eluded the hands of Indian Agents. Connections of family and friendship resurfaced as well. The presence of Aboriginal and mixed-heritage cowboys at rodeos attested to the economic relationships between ranches and reserves, and to the more intimate relationships between ranchers and Aboriginal women. New associations formed at stampedes: friendships, rivalries, romantic entanglements, and marriages. Rodeos in Western Canada were made possible by, and perpetuated, contact zones that saw settlers and Aboriginal people mixing in ways that did not always follow the scripts of colonization, though they never entirely escaped them. Their stories, their micronarratives – alternative, oppositional, defiant – challenge perspectives that see rodeo as nothing more than a presentation of the myth of the frontier.[4]

Some micronarratives emerge from the edges of the documentary record – as in the illustrative anecdote in which an Indian Agent, attempting to convince his superiors that stampedes threatened the racial order of the West, revealed that townsfolk and Aboriginal people danced the night away in a contact zone created by rodeo. We can hear them in the memories of childhood, when youthful settlers saw Aboriginal men as brilliant riders, and young men fell in love with the stampede queen, a mixed-heritage daughter from a small town down the road. We see them too in the Dominion Day photos of a Chinese Canadian who took portraits of his friends and neighbours, or in the group portrait of the Lethbridge Stampede organizing committee where town fathers and reserve leadership sit side by side. We see them in newsreel footage, where Aboriginal women race down the main street of a southern BC Interior town and in the fictionalized autobiography of a woman who won such a race and found only bitterness in victory. They surface in the social memory of rodeo, the "dynamic negotiation between individual and community, personal experience and wider historical events" that adds nuance and complexity to its history.[5] These are the micronarratives of the contact zone, where binary oppositions are ironically twisted, blurred, or inverted, where for a variety of social, economic, and political reasons, the stories of conquest give way, at least momentarily.

These stories are troubling too, but in a different way. They disrupt the stereotypes held by many Canadians about small towns and remote and rural communities – that they exhibit more racial antipathy, more segregation than urban settings. There is no denying that towns from Cardston in southern Alberta to Williams Lake in the BC Interior have had very troubled relations with their Aboriginal neighbours. Indeed, during the past twenty years, a certain amount of scholarship has explored the topic, and *A Wilder West* offers much on the subject as well.[6] But the stories told by rodeo suggest a more complicated version of the past. Using techniques developed by historians to read colonial texts for subaltern history, my research on rodeo has opened up pathways to finding alternative histories of small-town life where everyday interactions, individual relationships, friendships, and feelings exceed the narrow confines of the twentieth century's racialized politics. This is emphatically not a scholarship of denial, of denying racism or colonialism, but rather one that seeks to disrupt the very stereotypes and categories upon which racism is based. This history of rodeo offers up images and examples where "local knowledge and social action are mediated by dialogue," and where people and communities are changed by the stories they hear and the stories they tell.[7]

Sometimes these stories gather into a history of a new community. Professional rodeo has crafted its own histories, self-consciously making gendered identities and social ideals. Here too we can envision these histories as oppositional, as confronting popular images of rodeo cowboys as reckless, hyper-masculine, and cruel to animals. The Canadian Professional Rodeo Association worked hard to recraft both the image and the behaviour of rodeo cowboys, and its standards show remarkable influence among the cowboys and their families as they recount their own histories of the sport. And yet the stories of pro rodeo are not exactly outside of the dominant culture; indeed, they are a good example of how social memory can merge with prevailing metanarratives in some respects and diverge from them in others.[8] Pro rodeo highlighted gender and downplayed racialization. For its members, it reserved the privileges of masculinity, which included the right to earn a living at the sport and methods of risk management that did not diminish claims to toughness while mitigating the financial hazards associated with injury or even death in the ring. Through a process of rationalization, it defined rodeo as a sport and excluded the events in which women most commonly participated. But embracing respectability in the 1950s meant being a family man, and establishing rodeo as a family sport opened up the pro arena to women and children. Women's and little britches rodeo developed their own storylines within the larger narrative of pro rodeo.

Although it tended to minimize racialization, pro rodeo welcomed Aboriginal cowboys. Indeed, it reserved places for them on the CPRA executive and crafted rules that were meant to facilitate their membership in the organization. Rodeo, therefore, acted as a contact zone in another way. The itinerant world of pro rodeo was populated by Aboriginal and settler cowboys travelling together, raising families together, and building a new and alternative community together. In this way, they broke down the oppositions between whiteness and indigeneity that were so central to the stories of the Canadian West and so often a performative component of community rodeos. If, as John Carlos Rowe says, "any attempt to recognize or comprehend the culture of another is an act of hybridity," the on-the-road pro community offered plenty of chances for that.[9] For one Aboriginal competitor, expressing a central narrative of pro rodeo in Canada, "rodeo brought Native and non-Native communities together because sport is always an even playing ground."[10]

However, the pro community was no better than any other at solidifying its principal narrative, and it too contains multiple stories, not all of which conform to the main message. For a time, the habit of minimizing racialization meant that many Aboriginal pro cowboys remained unrecognized. Sometimes local knowledge filled in the gap. One museum curator in the BC Interior took offence when a scholar criticized her display for not specifying which rodeo stars were Aboriginal. She told me that everyone in the community knew who they were and that explicitly mentioning their identity was unnecessary. In other instances, overflow from the multiculturalism discourse forced the aboriginality of a rodeo cowboy into the limelight, as in the case of the 1970s film *Hard Rider*, which focused on Syilx cowboy Kenny McLean. But looking back, few pro cowboys thought of rodeo in racialized terms, which in the context of late twentieth-century Canada, too often meant eliding the history of Aboriginal people in the sport.

Recapturing that history, Aboriginal cowboys tell their own array of stories. Some of these speak to connections between rodeo and historical cultures, to essential and enduring connections with land and animals. Long histories of rodeos on reserves and of Aboriginal cowboys have prompted First Nations to claim the sport as their own. Others see a history of discrimination that necessitates either complete withdrawal or participation only in rodeos organized by Aboriginal committees. Some scholars have criticized these moves as essentialist, failed recuperations of real power and control over social, economic, political, and cultural resources.[11] Separating culture from material conditions is untenable to be sure, but the histories of reserve and all-Indian rodeo show that rodeo is more than a form of cultural capital: it contributes to community formation in very real ways, by stimulating pride, encouraging physical re-creation and skill, bringing investment dollars onto reserves to build infrastructure, infusing cash to local clubs and organizations, and building a myriad of skills necessary for political life. Stories of exclusion from the wider world of rodeo produce an affective sphere, an "intimate public" that offers alternative engagements with the sport even as they validate Aboriginal perspectives that seek not integration with, but insulation from the gaze of the other.[12] The reaction to Aboriginal rodeo has not been uniform either. Cowboys who had experienced the multi-ethnic world of pro rodeo saw its all-Indian equivalent as exclusionary, whereas some said that it offered a safer place for a mixed-heritage athlete than other all-Native sports. Multiplicity, then, is a feature of the stories of Aboriginal cowboys too.

Cultural history has made us more comfortable with the possibility that many narrative lines may emerge in our sources. It has also made us aware of the contradictory impulses of our age. Oppositional cultures arise and struggle with dominant forms, borrowing from the consciousness and concepts they deploy.[13] Discourses of difference still have their place, but increasingly scholars and activists demand a more complicated narrative.[14] Rodeo cowboys do too, in their own subtle ways. When I interviewed Duke LeBourdais at the Whispering Pines Rodeo, I brought along lists of contestants submitted to the CPRA by local small-town and reserve rodeos. I wanted him to help me distinguish Aboriginal from settler cowboys.

Instead, he told me stories about people, stories that said nothing about the racialized categories I was using, but rather about the abilities, the habits, the behaviour of the men he knew. For him, at that moment, the "us" and "them" of contemporary Aboriginal-settler relations was simply not very important. Rather, in his memory, identities were always contextual and relational. The history of rodeo on reserves and in small towns and rural communities offers stories and images that help us move beyond bland dichotomies, to see "us" and "them" as the very icons of denial in a world that is always already more complicated than that.

Glossary

Rodeo has its own language. Terms that were used by ranchers historically have been supplemented by the definitions of professional rodeo. I draw here on the official event descriptions and rules of the Canadian Professional Rodeo Association as well as glossaries in Michael Allen's *Rodeo Cowboys in the North American Imagination* and Peter Iverson's *Riders of the West: Portraits from Indian Rodeo.*

All-round: The award for best overall performance at a particular rodeo or for the season.

Bareback riding: Instead of a saddle, a double-thick leather pad called a rigging is cinched to the horse's back. The rigging has a hand-hold, which riders use to stay aboard. There are no stirrups and no reins. Riders sit on the horse and must keep their spurs above the break of the shoulders until after the first jump. They will be disqualified if they touch the animal or equipment with their free hand or are bucked off before the eight-second (formerly ten-second) ride is completed. In the earliest days of rodeo, a successful ride saw the horse ridden to a standstill.

Barrel racing: A rider crosses the scoreline and directs her/his horse in a cloverleaf pattern around three barrels and back across the scoreline as quickly as possible to achieve the minimum time. Knocking down a barrel results in a five-second penalty, but the contestant may, from a riding position, hold the barrel from falling. Failing to follow the cloverleaf pattern results in disqualification.

Barrier: A spring-loaded rope that is stretched across the opening of a calf-roping (tie-down roping) or steer-wrestling chute and released to give the calf or steer a head start. If the roper or steer-wrestler crosses the scoreline before the animal leaves the chute, the contestant is penalized for "breaking the barrier."

Breakaway roping: A timed event in which the rider's rope is attached by a string to the saddle horn. The rider throws the rope over a calf's head and lets go of it. Timing ends when the calf pulls the string off the saddle horn.

Bronc: A horse that is willing to buck, used in bareback and saddle events.

Bulldogging: See *steer wrestling.*

Bullfighter: The bullfighter acts to distract the bull after the dismount in order to allow the contestant to exit the arena safely.

Bull riding: Riders hold a braided manila rope, which is tied around the bull and weighted with a cowbell. Brahma bulls are now the norm because their loose hide makes riding them even more challenging. Riders are disqualified for touching any part of the animal or if they are bucked off before the eight-second ride is completed.

Calf roping (now officially called tie-down roping*):* In this event, the rider must successfully rope a calf in as little time as possible. The calf is given a head start and crosses the scoreline before the rider breaks the barrier (a rope across the chute). If the rider breaks the barrier prematurely, a ten-second penalty is added to the time. The cowboy then rides to the calf, ropes it, dismounts, runs down the rope, and throws the animal by hand. If the calf is already down when the cowboy reaches it, more time is added. The cowboy then ties any three legs of the calf with a rope called a piggin' string. The tie must stay on for six seconds or the roper is disqualified. The horse works, too, in this event: it must judge the speed of the calf, stop in a single stride, and hold the rope taut while the roper runs to the calf.

Chute: A narrow fenced lane that connects two or more corrals, the rodeo chute terminates in a small gated pen just large enough to hold the bucking stock and to enable a competitor to mount and to adjust his/her gear.

Chute-fighting horse: A horse that is unsettled in the chute.

Circuit: A series of rodeos to which a contestant travels to compete in a season.

Dally: After an animal is roped, the contestant dallies (wraps) the rope around the saddle horn several times.

Flank strap: A padded (sometimes with sheepskin) strap placed around the bull's or bronc's flanks. When snugged into position, it stimulates the animal's natural instinct to throw off the rider.

Goat tying: In this timed event, a contestant rides into the arena, dismounts, ties any three legs of the goat (as in calf roping) and then ties the goat to a stake with a rope, generally fifteen feet in length.

Hazer: In steer wrestling, the hazer rides alongside the steer to keep it running in a straight line.

Hobbling: In rodeo, this is the method of tying the stirrups together under the bronc's belly. As a practice, it is supposed to help the rider stay on the horse, but it is dangerous to the rider if the horse falls. It is no longer permitted.

Hung up: A rider who is caught on a horse or a bull while dismounting.

No time: This term applies when a cowboy has gone off course, broken the scoreline, or gone over time and will not receive a time in a timed event.

Pick-up man: The cowboy on horseback who assists the bronc-rider or bull-rider in dismounting after the eight-second ride.

Pole bending: In this timed event, a contestant rides a slalom course consisting of six poles set about twenty feet apart and then returns to the starting line. A time penalty is added for each pole that is knocked over.

Re-ride: An opportunity for a second attempt at an event, which is sometimes permitted when a rider draws an animal that will not buck vigorously enough.

Roughstock: Events that involve riding bucking horses, bulls, and in some cases steers.

Saddle bronc riding: The contestant rides a saddled bronc (bucking horse). Saddles must be approved by organizations such as the CPRA. Other equipment includes dull-rowell spurs, leather chaps, and a braided rein. The rider must sit on the horse with his spurs over the break of its shoulders until it completes its first jump out of the chute. Riders are disqualified if they touch any part of the animal or the equipment (except the braided rein), if they lose a stirrup, or if they are bucked off in less than eight seconds. (Formerly, they were required to stay on for ten seconds, whereas in early days they rode the horse to a standstill.)

Stampede: In 1912 Guy Weadick named the festival celebrating Western heritage in Calgary the "Calgary Stampede." Since then, this name has been given to similar events across the west. Stampedes are organized around a rodeo and may also include parades, races, a midway, and evening performances.

Steer decorating: In this timed event, which is a modification of steer wrestling, a rider places a ribbon attached to an elastic band on the steer's horns.

Steer that won't lay: A steer that will withstand having its head twisted and will not go over on its side in steer wrestling.

Steer undecorating: In this timed event, a modification of steer wrestling, a rider removes a ribbon that has been attached to a steer's back.

Steer wrestling (formerly called bulldogging*):* The event in which a mounted contestant rides up to a running steer (which is given a head start), drops down onto it, grasps its right horn, and hits the ground in such a way as to stop it. Then, using the left hand as leverage under the steer's jaw, the contestant throws it off balance and wrestles it to the ground, where it must lie flat before the official time is taken. An additional rider, the hazer, ensures that the steer runs straight. In the 1910s, bulldoggers sometimes bit the steer's lip in order to twist its head.

Stock contractor: The person who provides roughstock.

stock cutting: A competition that tests the skills of rider and horse to work together in order to move stock from one place to another, to divide the herd, or to separate one animal from the group.

Team roping: Two cowboys, a header and a heeler, work together to rope a steer in the shortest possible time. After the steer is given a head start, the header must rope it in one of three acceptable catches: the head and one horn, both horns, or around the neck. Crossing the scoreline early results in a ten-second penalty. Once the header catches the steer, he wraps the rope around the saddle horn (dallies) and turns left with the steer in tow. The heeler must then rope both legs of the steer and then dallies his rope. When the contestants are facing each other and both ropes have been pulled tight, time is called. If the heeler catches only one leg, a five-second penalty is incurred. If he throws his rope before the header has turned the steer left, this is called a crossfire and results in disqualification.

Timed events: Events such as barrel racing, calf roping (now called tie-down roping), steer wrestling, and team roping are timed. Deductions are made for prematurely breaking the start barrier (scoreline) or for inadequately or incorrectly roping the animals.

trick riding and *trick roping:* Performance events that demonstrate riding and roping skills that are not utilitarian, such as riding standing up or roping in a particular pattern.

Wild cow milking: A rodeo event in which a rider ropes a range (or wild) cow, and a second contestant (called the mugger) holds the cow, milks her (often into an empty beer bottle), and then runs with the bottle across the finish line.

Notes

Introduction

1 Following the Canadian Constitution, I am using "Aboriginal" to include First Nations, Métis, and Inuit peoples. I use "Indian" where it is the proper title of an organization, such as the Indian Rodeo Cowboy Association, and in historical references, such as Indian Agent. Wherever possible, I employ the specific First Nations designation for people or places, using terms current for 2011 (Kainai, for example, instead of Blood). See J.R. Miller, *Skyscrapers Hide the Heavens: A History of Indian-White Relations in Canada*, 3rd ed. (Toronto: University of Toronto Press, 2000), 350, for a discussion of the constitutional process that resulted in this inclusive definition. I use "Métis" for people who self-identify as members of the Métis Nation and "mixed-heritage" for those with Aboriginal and non-Aboriginal ancestry who do not identify as Métis. See Jean Barman and Mike Evans, "Reflections on Being, and Becoming, Métis in British Columbia," *BC Studies* 161 (Summer 2009): 59-73, for a detailed treatment of the legal and constitutional issues associated with the designation "Métis." Finally, "settler" applies to individuals or families who came to Western Canada and are of European or Asian heritage, after Taiaiake Alfred's *Wasáse: Indigenous Pathways of Action and Freedom* (Peterborough: Broadview, 2005).

2 In August of 2003, large forest fires swept through the area. The local Louis Creek sawmill, a major employer, burned to the ground. At one point, three thousand people were evacuated. See "Fires Devastate British Columbia," *CNN Sunday Morning*, 23 August 2003, http://transcripts.cnn.com/.

3 Richard White, "Race Relations in the American West," *American Quarterly* 38,3 (1986): 396-416.

4 Stephen Tatum, "The Problem of the 'Popular' in the New Western History," in *The New Western History: The Territory Ahead*, ed. Forrest G. Robinson (Tucson: University of Arizona Press, 1997), 159.

5 In the 1980s and 1990s, a number of studies depicted rodeo as a ritual that confirms settler hegemony over Aboriginal people, the domination of animals by humans, and masculinist and misogynist gender relations. See, for example, Elizabeth Atwood Lawrence, *Rodeo: An Anthropologist Looks at the Wild and the Tame* (Chicago: University of Chicago Press, 1982), and Joan Burbick, *Rodeo Queens and the American Dream* (New York: Public Affairs, 2002). Beverly Stoeltje was less critical of rodeo, but she also argued that it confirmed and validated community mythology in her article "Rodeo: From Custom to Ritual," *Western Folklore* 48 (July 1989): 244-60. Canadian scholars have criticized rodeo, and the stampedes of which they are a part, as performing the myth of the frontier and other "national dreams" that support domination of white settler society over Aboriginal people, workers, and nature. See Elizabeth Furniss, *The Burden of History: Colonialism and the Frontier Myth in a Rural Canadian Community* (Vancouver: UBC Press, 1999); Daniel Francis, *Imaginary Indian: The Image of the Indian in Canadian Culture* (Vancouver: Arsenal Pulp Press, 1993); and Daniel Francis, *National Dreams: Myth, Memory and Canadian History* (Vancouver: Arsenal Pulp Press, 1997). Burbick and Furniss, in particular, were influenced by Richard Slotkin's *Gunfighter Nation* and other writers of the new Western history. Slotkin's own view of myth is much more dialogic than that advanced by those who apply his ideas. See Richard Slotkin, *Gunfighter Nation: The Myth of the Frontier in Twentieth-Century America* (New York: Atheneum, 1992). Richard W. Slatta argues convincingly for the hemispheric similarities between cowboys in North and South America in his *Comparing Cowboys and Frontiers* (Norman and London: University of Oklahoma Press, 1997).

6   In making this point, I draw on the body of work that discusses gender and presents it as the result of normative performance, through, to quote Judith Butler, a "stylized repetition of acts." Scholars of rodeo have described it as a ritual that confirms the social order. In this study, I want to consider the ways in which rodeo constitutes social order and helps to craft the categories that it displays – specifically, cowboys, cowgirls, whiteness, and aboriginality. See Judith Butler, *Gender Trouble* (New York: Routledge Classic, 2006), 191.

7   Mary Ryan, "The American Parade: Representations of the Nineteenth-Century Social Order," in *The New Cultural History*, ed. Lynn Hunt (Berkeley: University of California Press, 1989), 131-53; see also Bonnie Huskins, "The Ceremonial Space of Women: Public Processions in Victorian Saint John and Halifax," in *Separate Spheres: Women's Worlds in the 19th-Century Maritimes*, ed. Janet Guildford and Suzanne Morton (Fredericton: Acadiensis Press, 1994), 145-61.

8   Susan Neylan, "'Here Comes the Band': Cultural Collaboration, Connective Traditions, and Aboriginal Brass Bands on British Columbia's North Coast, 1875-1964," *BC Studies* 152 (Winter 2006): 35-66.

9   Peter Iverson, *Riders of the West: Portraits from Indian Rodeo* (Vancouver: Greystone Books, 1999); Mary Lou LeCompte, *Cowgirls of the Rodeo: Pioneer Professional Athletes* (Urbana and Chicago: University of Illinois Press, 1993); Mary Lou LeCompte, "Cowgirls at the Crossroads: Women in Professional Rodeo, 1885-1922," *Canadian Journal of the History of Sport* 20,2 (1989): 27-48; Burbick, *Rodeo Queens;* Morgan Baillargeon and Leslie Tepper, *Legends of Our Times: Native Cowboy Life* (Vancouver: UBC Press, 1998); Bill Cohen, ed., *Stories and Images about What the Horse Has Done for Us: An Illustrated History of Okanagan Ranching and Rodeo* (Penticton: Theytus Books, 1998); Ian Dyck, "Does Rodeo Have Roots in Ancient Indian Traditions?," *Plains Anthropologist: Journal of the Plains Anthropological Society* 41,157 (August 1996): 205-19; Allison Fuss Mellis, *Riding Buffaloes and Broncs: Rodeo and Native Traditions in the Northern Great Plains* (Norman: University of Oklahoma Press, 2003); Lynda Mannik, *Canadian Indian Cowboys in Australia: Representation, Rodeo and the RCMP at the Royal Easter Show, 1939* (Calgary: University of Calgary Press, 2006).

10   Lawrence, *Rodeo*. The recent interest in producing an animal-centred history of rodeo flows from Lawrence's study of the ways in which the views of particular animals produced a dichotomy of the wild and the tame, which overlapped with certain gendered and racialized perspectives. See Waterloo historian Susan Nance's website for her developing work in this area: "Born to Buck," http://www.susannance.com/.

11   Mary Louise Pratt, *Imperial Eyes: Travel Writing and Transculturation* (London and New York: Routledge, 1992), 6-7.

12   James Clifford, *Routes: Travel and Translation in the Late Twentieth Century* (Cambridge, MA: Harvard University Press, 1997), 7.

13   Elsbeth A. Heaman, *The Inglorious Arts of Peace: Exhibitions in Canadian Society during the Nineteenth Century* (Toronto: University of Toronto Press, 1999); H.V. Nelles, *The Art of Nation-Building: Pageantry and Spectacle at Quebec's Tercentenary* (Toronto: University of Toronto Press, 1999). See also Keith Walden, *Becoming Modern in Toronto: The Industrial Exhibition and the Shaping of a Late Victorian Culture* (Toronto: University of Toronto Press, 1997), and John C. Walsh and Steven High, "Rethinking the Concept of Community," *Histoire sociale/Social History* 32,64 (November 1999): 255-73.

14   David M. Wrobel links small-town boosterism and the celebration of heritage in his study of Western American town promotion in *Promised Lands: Promotion, Memory and the Creation of the American West* (Lawrence: University Press of Kansas, 2002); for work on boosterism and heritage that spans the border, see John W. Bennett and Seena B. Kohl, *Settling the Canadian-American West* (Lincoln: University of Nebraska Press, 1995), 7.

15   Slotkin argues that "the traditions we inherit, for all their seeming coherence, are a registry of old conflicts, rich in internal contradictions and alternative, political visions, to which we ourselves continually make additions." Slotkin, *Gunfighter Nation*, 658-59. Although Western Canadian communities cultivated "wild west" identities through rodeo, they did so with some ambivalence and not without conflict. Moreover, in certain communities, the meaning of this identity shifted over time, as we will see, especially in Chapters 1 and 4.

16   Wade A. Henry, "Imagining the Great White Mother and the Great King: Aboriginal Tradition and Royal Representation at the 'Great Pow-Wow of 1901,'" *Journal of the Canadian Historical*

Association, n.s., 9 (1998): 155-86; Ian Radforth, "Performance, Politics and Representation: Aboriginal People and the 1860 Royal Tour of Canada," *Canadian Historical Review* 84,1 (March 2003): 1-32; Paige Raibmon, "Theatres of Contact: The Kwakwaka'wakw Meet Colonialism in the British Columbia and at the Chicago World's Fair," *Canadian Historical Review* 81,2 (June 2000): 157-90; Susan Roy, "Performing Musqueam Culture and History at British Columbia's 1966 Centennial Celebrations," *BC Studies* 135 (Autumn 2002): 55-100.

17 Author, field notes, Soda Creek, 19 May 2000.

18 Gerald Vizenor calls such performers "warriors of survivance," in his *Manifest Manners: Postindian Warriors of Survivance* (Hanover, NH: Wesleyan University Press/University Press of New England, 1994); see also Dan Moos, *Outside America: Race, Ethnicity and the Role of the American West in National Belonging* (Hanover, NH: Dartmouth University Press/University Press of New England, 2005), 146-207.

19 Clifford, *Routes,* 200. Though most scholarship properly highlights the struggle attendant when an event occurred, other works inform us that even when Aboriginal people could not contest the ways in which they were deployed, their memory of the event and the way they speak about it today have made it a site of struggle retrospectively. See, for example, Frieda Esau Klippenstein, "Myth-Making at Fort St. James," *The Beaver,* August-September 1994, 22-29.

20 Andrea L. Smith, "Heteroglossia, 'Common Sense,' and Social Memory," *American Ethnologist* 1,2 (May 2004): 265. For example, the fairly uniform and triumphalist characterization of Aboriginal engagement with rodeo on the Plains, as presented by Mellis in *Riding Buffaloes and Broncs,* is challenged by two very different versions of the ambivalence that surrounds the cowboy versus Indian binary. See Michael Yellow Bird (Hidatsa), "Cowboys and Indians: Toys of Genocide, Icons of American Colonialism," *Wicazo Sa Review* 19,2 (Fall 2004): 33-48, and Virginia Driving Hawk Sneve (Lakota), *Grandpa Was a Cowboy and an Indian and Other Stories* (Lincoln: University of Nebraska Press, 2000), 45-51.

21 See, for example, "Bloods Win Big Money at Sarcee Rodeo," *Kainai News,* 15 July 1968, 15. See also Iverson, *Riders of the West,* 82.

22 Baillargeon and Tepper, *Legends of Our Times,* 216-17.

23 Julie Cruikshank, *The Social Life of Stories: Narrative and Knowledge in the Yukon Territory* (Lincoln and London: University of Nebraska Press, 1998), xv, 156-57, 159. The idea of "emergent authenticities" comes from Robert Jarvenpa's discussion of Erik Cohen's article "Authenticity and Commoditization in Tourism," *Annals of Tourism Research* 15 (1988): 371-86, in Robert Jarvenpa, "Commoditization versus Cultural Integration: Tourism and Image Building in the Klondike," *Arctic Anthropology* 31,1 (1994): 26-46.

24 Recent interpretations of the Wild West Show confirm the political and material possibilities for Aboriginal performers in the early twentieth century. See Moos, *Outside America;* and Louis S. Warren, *Buffalo Bill's America: William Cody and the Wild West Show* (New York: Alfred A. Knopf, 2005); as well as the now classic L.G. Moses, *Wild West Shows and the Images of American Indians, 1883-1933* (Albuquerque: University of New Mexico Press, 1996). See also Amy M. Ware, "Unexpected Cowboy, Unexpected Indian: The Case of Will Rogers," *Ethnohistory* 56,1 (Winter 2009): 1-34. Studies of Aboriginal participation in Canada's various centennial events similarly report the political implications of that participation.

25 The scholarship in this field is vast. For a sampling of works that link sports culture with masculinities in the twentieth century, see John M. MacKenzie, "The Imperial Pioneer and Hunter and the British Masculine Stereotype in Late Victorian and Edwardian Times," in *Manliness and Morality: Middle-Class Masculinity in Britain and America, 1800-1940,* ed. J.A. Mangan and James Walvin (Manchester: Manchester University Press, 1987), 176-98; Roberta J. Park, "Biological Thought, Athletics and the Formation of a 'Man of Character,' 1830-1900," in Mangan and Walvin, *Manliness and Morality,* 7-34; Clifford Putney, *Muscular Christianity: Manhood and Sports in Protestant America, 1880-1920* (Cambridge, MA: Harvard University Press, 2001); Thomas Winter, *Making Men, Making Class: The YMCA and Workingmen, 1877-1920* (Chicago: University of Chicago Press, 2002); Colin Howell, "A Manly Sport: Baseball and the Social Construction of Masculinity," in *Gender and History in Canada,* ed. Joy Parr and Mark Rosenfeld (Toronto: Copp Clark, 1996), 187-210; Nancy C. Boucher, *For the Love of the Game: Amateur Sport in Small-Town Ontario, 1838-1895* (Montreal and Kingston: McGill-Queen's University Press, 2003); John Fiske, *Understanding Popular Culture*

(London: Routledge, 1990), 98, 99; Axel Bundgaard, *Muscle and Manliness: The Rise of Sport in American Boarding Schools* (Syracuse, NY: Syracuse University Press, 2005), 32; Boria Majumdar, "The Vernacular in Sports History," *International Journal of the History of Sport* 20,1 (March 2003): 107-25; Daniel S. Mason and Gregory H. Duquette, "Newspaper Coverage of Early Professional Ice Hockey: The Discourses of Class and Control," *Media History* 10,3 (2004): 157-73; Stacy L. Lorenz and Geraint B. Osborne, "'Talk about Strenuous Hockey': Violence, Manhood, and the 1907 Ottawa Silver Seven-Montreal Wanderer Rivalry," *Journal of Canadian Studies* 40,1 (Winter 2006): 125-56; for another discussion of violence, masculinity, and sport, see Kevin B. Walmsley and David Whitson, "Celebrating Violent Masculinities: The Boxing Death of Luther McCarty," *Journal of Sports History* 25,3 (Fall 1998): 419-31; Brian Stoddart, "Identity Spin: Imagined Cultures in Australian and Indian Cricket," special issue, *South Asia* 23 (2000): 63-74; Boria Majumdar, "Cricket: The Indian History of a British Sport," *Journal of the History of Sport* 20,1 (March 2003): 162-70; on football in India, see Paul Dimeo, "Colonial Bodies, Colonial Sport: 'Martial' Punjabis, 'Effeminate' Bengalis and the Development of Indian Football," *International Journal of the History of Sport* 19,1 (March 2002): 72-90; Michael A. Robidoux, "Historical Interpretations of First Nations Masculinity and Its Influence on Canada's Sport Heritage," *International Journal of the History of Sport* 23,2 (March 2006): 267-84; Philip J. Deloria, *Indians in Unexpected Places* (Lawrence: University of Kansas Press, 2004), 117-18; Michelle Patterson, "'Real' Indian Songs: The Society of American Indians and the Use of Native American Culture as a Means of Reform," *American Indian Quarterly* 26,1 (Winter 2002): 44-66; and Janice Forsythe and Kevin B. Walmsley, "'Native to Native ... We'll Recapture Our Spirits': The World Aboriginal Nations Games and North American Aboriginal Games as Cultural Resistance," *International Journal of the History of Sport* 23,2 (March 2006): 294-314.

26   Clifford Westermeier, *Man, Beast, Dust: The Story of Rodeo* (1947; repr., Lincoln: University of Nebraska Press, 1987); Kristine Fredriksson, *American Rodeo: From Buffalo Bill to Big Business* (College Station: Texas A & M University Press, 1985); Wayne S. Wooden and Gavin Ehringer, *Rodeo in America: Wranglers, Roughstock and Paydirt* (Lawrence: University Press of Kansas, 1996), which includes a potted history of rodeo and describes the sport as it existed in the late twentieth century; Michael Allen, *Rodeo Cowboys in the North American Imagination* (Reno and Las Vegas: University of Nevada Press, 1998); Max Foran, ed., *Icon, Brand and Myth: The Calgary Stampede* (Edmonton: University of Alberta Press, 2008); John R. Gillis, introduction to *Commemorations: The Politics of National Identity* (Princeton: Princeton University Press, 1996), 10.

27   Adele Perry, "The State of Empire: Reproducing Colonialism in British Columbia, 1849-1871," *Journal of Colonialism and Colonial History* 2,2 (Fall 2001), http://muse.jhu.edu/; Adele Perry, *On the Edge of Empire: Gender, Race, and the Making of British Columbia, 1849-1871* (Toronto: University of Toronto Press, 2001); Adele Perry, "The Autocracy of Love and the Legitimacy of Empire: Intimacy, Power and Scandal in Nineteenth-Century Metlakatlah," *Gender and History* 16,2 (2004): 261-88; Adele Perry, "From 'the Hot-Bed of Vice' to the 'Good and Well-Ordered Christian Home': First Nations Housing and Reform in Nineteenth-Century British Columbia," *Ethnohistory* 50,4 (2003): 587-610.

28   Warren, *Buffalo Bill's America.*

29   Ann Laura Stoler, *Carnal Knowledge and Imperial Power: Race and the Intimate in Colonial Rule* (Berkeley: University of California Press, 2002); Ann Laura Stoler, ed., *Haunted by Empire* (Durham: Duke University Press, 2006), 3; Catherine Hall, "Commentary," in Stoler, *Haunted by Empire*, 455-61; Sylvia Van Kirk, "A Trans-Border Family in the Pacific Northwest," in *One Step over the Line: Toward a History of Women in the North American Wests,* ed. Elizabeth Jamieson and Sheila McManus (Edmonton: Athapaska University Press, 2008), 81-99. The intense pressure put upon the children of fur trade relationships to distance themselves from their Aboriginal mothers and other kin only shows the discomfort that such hybridity brought to the colonial enterprise. As Jean Barman, Adele Perry, Sarah Carter, and others have shown, women, as sexual partners and domestic workers, found themselves under particular scrutiny of rough and respectable colonial men, a scrutiny that too often resulted in violence. Sarah Carter, *Capturing Women: The Manipulation of Cultural Imagery in Canada's Prairie West* (Montreal and Kingston: McGill-Queen's University Press, 1997); Adele Perry, "Metropolitan Knowledge, Colonial Practice and Aboriginal Womanhood: Missions in Nineteenth-Century British Columbia," in *Contact Zones: Aboriginal and Settler Women in Canada's*

Colonial Past, ed. Katie Pickles and Myra Rutherdale (Vancouver: UBC Press, 2005), 109-31; Robin Jarvis Brownlie, "Intimate Surveillance: Indian Affairs, Colonization and the Regulation of Aboriginal Women's Sexuality," in Pickles and Rutherdale, *Contact Zones*, 160-78; Joan Sangster, "Domesticating Girls: The Sexual Regulation of Aboriginal and Working-Class Girls in Twentieth-Century Canada," in Pickles and Rutherdale, *Contact Zones*, 179-204; Jean Barman, "Aboriginal Women on the Streets of Victoria: Rethinking Transgressive Sexuality during the Colonial Encounter," in Pickles and Rutherdale, *Contact Zones*, 205-27; Kim Greenwell, "Picturing 'Civilization': Missionary Narratives and the Margins of Mimicry," *BC Studies* 135 (Autumn 2002): 3-45; Mary-Ellen Kelm, ed., *The Letters of Margaret Butcher: Missionary-Imperialism on the North Pacific Coast* (Calgary: University of Calgary Press, 2006); Brett Christophers, *Positioning the Missionary: John Booth Good and the Confluence of Cultures in Nineteenth-Century British Columbia* (Vancouver: UBC Press, 1998).

30   Greenwell, "Picturing 'Civilization'"; Kelm, *The Letters of Margaret Butcher;* Christophers, *Positioning the Missionary.*

31   Nicholas Thomas, *Colonialism and Culture: Anthropology, Travel and Government* (Princeton: Princeton University Press, 1994), 15.

32   Homi K. Bhabha, *The Location of Culture* (New York and London: Routledge, 1994), 83.

33   For just a few examples, see Jamieson and McManus, *One Step over the Line;* W. Keith Regular, *Neighbours and Networks: The Blood Tribe in the Southern Alberta Economy, 1884-1939* (Calgary: University of Calgary Press, 2009); Jordan Sanger-Ross, "Municipal Colonialism in Vancouver: City Planning and the Conflict over Indian Reserves, 1928-1950s," *Canadian Historical Review* 89,4 (December 2008): 541-80; and Patricia K. Wood, "Pressured from All Sides: The February 1913 Surrender of the Northeast Corner of the Tsuu T'ina Nation," *Journal of Historical Geography* 30 (2004): 112-29.

34   Stoler, *Haunted by Empire,* 7.

35   Richard W. Slatta, *Comparing Cowboys and Frontiers* (Norman: University of Oklahoma Press, 1997).

36   "Pincher Creek Plans Big Fair," *Lethbridge Daily Herald*, 6 June 1918, 8.

Chapter 1: An Old-Timers' Town

1   "In Southern Alberta: Impressions of One of the Party of Lady Journalists," *Lethbridge Daily Herald*, 19 July 1906, 3; "A Good Time: Visit of Lady Journalists to Lethbridge and District," *Lethbridge Daily Herald*, 28 June 1906, 3.

2   For a detailed history of Cardston's history of relations with local Kainai and Pikuni people, see W. Keith Regular, *Neighbours and Networks: The Blood Tribe in the Southern Alberta Economy, 1884-1939* (Calgary: University of Calgary Press, 2009); see also Sarah Carter, *The Importance of Being Monogamous: Marriage and Nation Building in Western Canada to 1915* (Edmonton: University of Alberta Press, 2008), 84-89.

3   John C. Walsh and Steven High, "Rethinking the Concept of Community," *Histoire sociale/Social History* 32,64 (November 1999): 272.

4   Benedict Anderson, *Imagined Communities: Reflections on the Origins and Spread of Nationalism* (London and New York: Verso, 1991), xiv.

5   James Clifford, *Routes: Travel and Translation in the Late Twentieth Century* (Cambridge, MA: Harvard University Press, 1997), 218.

6   Ibid., 213-14; Pauleena MacDougall, *The Penobscot Dance of Resistance: Tradition in the History of the People* (Durham: University of New Hampshire Press, 2004), 7, 188.

7   Sarah Carter, *Capturing Women: The Manipulation of Cultural Imagery in Canada's Prairie West* (Montreal and Kingston: McGill-Queen's University Press, 1997), 173-75; Donald G. Wetherell and Irene R.A. Kmet, *Town Life: Main Street and the Evolution of Small Town Alberta, 1880-1947* (Edmonton: University of Alberta Press, 1995), 259; Faith Moosang, *First Son: Portraits by C.D. Hoy* (Vancouver: Presentation House/Arsenal Pulp Press, 1999); "Dominion Day," *Fort George Herald*, 1 June 1911, 1.

8   Wetherell and Kmet, *Town Life,* 259-60.

9   Tony Rees, *Polo: The Galloping Game: An Illustrated History of Polo in the Canadian West* (Cochrane, AB: Western Heritage Centre Society, 2000); Paul Voisey, *High River and the Times: An Alberta Community and Its Weekly Newspaper* (Edmonton: University of Alberta Press, 2004), 131; Ken Mather, *Buckaroos and Mud Pups: The Early Days of Ranching in British Columbia* (Victoria: Heritage House, 2006), 147.

10   "Blackfoot Fair" poster, 23 March 1914, Blood Agency Fonds, M-1788, file 98, Glenbow Museum
      Archives (GMA), Calgary; Principal of Qu'Appelle School to D.C. Scott, 6 May 1914, Department
      of Indian Affairs (DIA), Black Series, RG 10, vol. 3826, file 60511-4, pt. 1, Library and Archives
      Canada (LAC), Ottawa.
11   Morgan Baillargeon, "Native Cowboys on the Canadian Plains: A Photo Essay," *Agricultural History*
      69,4 (Fall 1995): 556.
12   "First Blackfoot Fair ... To Be Held at the Blackfoot Reserve, Sept. 28, 1898. $125 in Prizes,"
      Horseman's Hall of Fame, M-2111, box 3, file 21, GMA.
13   Hugh Dempsey, *Tom Three Persons: Legend of an Indian Cowboy* (Saskatoon: Purich, 1997), 20-29.
14   "The First Stampede in Canada," The Town of Raymond: Home of the First Stampede, http://
      www.ourfutureourpast.ca; Terry Cooke, interview by author, Dawson Creek, BC, 12 December
      2003.
15   "Sugar City Is Canadian Home of Cowboy's Rodeo," *Lethbridge Daily Herald*, 24 June 1939, 12.
16   "Dominion Day Celebrations," *Lethbridge Daily Herald*, 18 July 1914, 9.
17   Lorain Lounsberry, "Wild West Shows and the Canadian West," in *Cowboys, Ranchers and the Cattle
      Business: Cross-Border Perspectives on Ranching History*, ed. Simon M. Evans, Sarah Carter, and Bill
      Yeo (Calgary: University of Calgary Press, 2000), 139-52. This conclusion replicates that of Elizabeth
      Furniss concerning the Williams Lake Stampede. See Elizabeth Furniss, *The Burden of History:
      Colonialism and the Frontier Myth in a Rural Canadian Community* (Vancouver: UBC Press, 1999). For
      more on Stastia and Jim Carry, see the Jim and Stastia Carry Fonds, M-8468, GMA, and Faye
      Reineberg Holt, *Awed, Amused and Alarmed: Fairs, Rodeos and Regattas in Western Canada* (Calgary:
      Detselig Enterprises, 2003), 97-104.
18   Elsbeth A. Heaman, *The Inglorious Arts of Peace: Exhibitions in Canadian Society during the Nineteenth
      Century* (Toronto: University of Toronto Press, 1999).
19   Wetherell and Kmet, *Town Life*, 261.
20   Editorial, *Kamloops Telegram*, 11 September 1919, 2.
21   Voisey, *High River and the Times*, 43; Donald Wetherell with Irene Kmet, *Useful Pleasures: The Shaping
      of Leisure in Alberta, 1896-1945* (Regina: Canadian Plains Research Center, 1990), 320; Holt, *Awed,
      Amused and Alarmed*, 9.
22   Quoted in Voisey, *High River and the Times*, 43.
23   Wetherell with Kmet, *Useful Pleasures*, 311-12.
24   "Eliminate Racing at Fort Macleod Fair – Agricultural Society Unable to Stand Pressure and Banks
      Won't Come Across," *Lethbridge Daily Herald*, 10 July 1914, 6.
25   "The Lethbridge Stampede and Fair Add for an Amalgamated Fair," *Lethbridge Daily Herald*, 10
      July 1918, 10.
26   Ken Favrholdt, "The Origins of the Kamloops Exhibition Association," 27 August 1981, Kamloops
      Fall Fair files, Kamloops Museum Archives (KMA), Kamloops; Elizabeth Duckworth, "A Tradition
      in Fall Fairs," 14 September 1989, Kamloops Fall Fair files, KMA. The 1918 Armstrong Fair, for
      example, offered an "Agricultural Exhibit that you will find full of interest, education, profit, music
      and mirth"; it also advertised amusements including a midway, "Indian Horse Races, White Men's
      Horse Races [and a] Horse Bucking Contest for championship of British Columbia." The latter
      offered substantial prizes of fifteen and ten dollars. "Come to the Armstrong Fair," *Vernon News*,
      12 September 1918, 5; Doug Cox, "Okanagan Roots," 1987, typescript, Oliver and District Heritage
      Society Archives, Oliver, BC.
27   "Gossip on the Side," *Lethbridge Daily Herald*, 9 July 1907, 3.
28   Minutes, Stampede Committee of the Board of Trade, 14 May 1918, Medicine Hat Agricultural
      Society, 1914-24, M78.34. 2, file 18, Esplanade Archives (EA), Medicine Hat, Alberta.
29   "Prospects Bright for Big Exhibition and Stampede," *Lethbridge Daily Herald*, 3 May 1918, 9;
      "Stampede and Fair Was Satisfactory Considering Adverse Circumstances," *Lethbridge Daily Herald*,
      29 July 1918, 1.
30   Minutes, Stampede Committee of the Board of Trade, 29 May 1918, Medicine Hat Agricultural
      Society, 1914-24, M78.34. 2, file 18, EA.
31   "Tranquille's Race Meeting; Special Train Will Be Run Over C.N.R. from City to the Grounds,"
      Kamloops Sentinel, 8 August 1924, front page; "No Stampede for This City," *Kamloops Sentinel*, 4
      September 1925, 1.

32 "Wintering Band Near Kamloops," *Kamloops Sentinel,* 6 October 1925, 1.

33 "Crowd Gets Thrills of Lifetime at the Big Successful Stampede," *Kamloops Sentinel,* 23 October 1925, 1; "Cyclone Smith of Cariboo Hero of Stampede; Great Event Was Not Sufficiently Patronized," *Kamloops Sentinel,* 27 October 1925, 1.

34 Editorial, *Kamloops Sentinel,* 30 October 1925, 3.

35 "Early Peace River Country Stampedes," undated typescript, acc. 2000.084, series 19-08, item 184A (1920s), South Peace Historical Society Archives, Dawson Creek, BC; "Program of Eighth Annual Stampede and Sports; Friday and Saturday, July 13th and 14th, 1928," Fall Fair and Rodeo Programs, MS 049 2001.041, South Peace Historical Society Archives.

36 Newspaper clipping, undated, Stampede files, box 1, Williams Lake Library (WLL), Williams Lake.

37 Thomas Francis Murray, Indian Agent, to D.C. Scott, 7 July 1925, DIA, Black Series, RG 10, vol. 3827, file 60411-5, LAC; "Stampede at the Blood Indian Reserve," *High River Times,* 23 June 1938, 3; "Blood Indians Win Many Honors at Brocket," *Cardston News,* 1 July 1926, 1.

38 Police Report, 7 July 1926, DIA, Black Series, RG 10, vol. 3827, file 60511-5, LAC.

39 Police Report, 30 June 1928, DIA, Black Series, RG 10, vol. 3827, file 60511-5, LAC.

40 "High River Perspective," *High River Times,* 2 August 1928, 1; "Two High River Boys Won Stampede Championships," *High River Times,* 19 July 1928, 1.

41 "Indian Rider Gravely Hurt," *Kamloops Sentinel,* 7 May 1925, 1.

42 "Local Favorites at Stampede," *Lethbridge Daily Herald,* 26 July 1918, 3.

43 Ibid.

44 "Taber Fair Brings Rain," *Lethbridge Daily Herald,* 27 July 1921, 1.

45 "As Others See Us," *Cardston News,* 24 September 1925, 4.

46 Program, 1931, Stampede files, box 1, WLL.

47 "Roundup and Carnival Successful in Every Way," *High River Times,* 16 August 1928, 1.

48 "Stampede Creates Life in the West as It Once Existed," *Calgary Herald,* 1917, 3.

49 "Cardston Has Five World Champions," *Cardston News,* 19 June 1930, 1.

50 "7000 People Visit Lethbridge during Their Exhibition," *Lethbridge Daily Herald,* 23 August 1906, 1; "Small Stampede Held at Cowley," *Calgary Herald,* 1 June 1923, 3; "5000 Attend Cardston's Stampede," *Cardston News,* 24 September 1925, 4; "Ten Thousand Visited the Stampede Thursday; Big Days Friday and Saturday," *Lethbridge Daily Herald,* 26 July 1918, 1.

51 Wetherell with Kmet, *Useful Pleasures,* 13-16; "Lethbridge Stampede and Fair Advertisement for the Amalgamated Fair," *Lethbridge Daily Herald,* 10 July 1918, 1; "Cardston Stampede Thrills Crowd," *Cardston News,* 26 July 1928, 1.

52 Program, 1931, Stampede files, box 1, WLL.

53 Philip Deloria, *Indians in Unexpected Places* (Lawrence: University Press of Kansas, 2004); L.G. Moses, *Wild West Shows and the Images of American Indians, 1883-1933* (Albuquerque: University of New Mexico Press, 1996); Amy M. Ware, "Unexpected Cowboy, Unexpected Indian: The Case of Will Rogers," *Ethnohistory* 56,1 (Winter 2009): 1-34; Louis S. Warren, *Buffalo Bill's America: William Cody and the Wild West Show* (New York: Alfred A. Knopf, 2005), 397; Joy Kasson, *Buffalo Bill's Wild West: Celebrity, Memory and Popular History* (New York: Hill and Wang, 2000).

54 Donna Livingstone, *The Cowboy Spirit: Guy Weadick and the Calgary Stampede* (Vancouver: Douglas and McIntyre, 1996).

55 R.N. Wilson to J.A. Marckle, Indian Inspector, 3 May 1908, Blood Agency Fonds, M-1788, box 3, file 21, GMA.

56 "Was a Big Success," *Lethbridge Daily Herald,* 23 August 1906, 1.

57 R.N. Wilson to J.A. Marckle, Indian Inspector, 3 May 1908, Blood Agency Fonds, M-1788, box 3, file 21, GMA.

58 "All Records Broken: The Lethbridge Exhibition the Greatest Ever Held – The Horses and Grain Attract Special Attention – Financial Success," *Lethbridge Daily Herald,* 9 August 1907, 1.

59 Tom Laird to R.N. Wilson, Indian Agent, 15 May 1908, Blood Agency Fonds, M-1788, box 3, file 31, GMA.

60 Katherine Pettipas, *Severing the Ties That Bind: Government Repression of Aboriginal Ceremonies on the Prairies* (Winnipeg: University of Manitoba Press, 1994), 149-50.

61 Fort Macleod Board of Trade to W.M. Graham, 8 May 1924, DIA, Black Series, RG 10, vol. 3827, file 60511-5, pt. 1, LAC.

•

62   "Lethbridge and the Lethbridge Fair: An Appreciation by an Old Country Journalist," *Lethbridge Daily Herald,* 14 July 1914, 4.

63   Lucien M. Hanks and Jane Richardson Hanks, *Tribe under Trust: A Study of the Blackfoot Reserve of Alberta* (Toronto: University of Toronto Press, 1950), 57.

64   Quoted in "From Other Sanctums: Indians and Fairs," *Lethbridge Daily Herald,* 25 October 1910, 4.

65   J.W. McNichol, Report on Stampede, 1912, Royal Canadian Mounted Police, RG 18, series A-1, vol. 394, file 465-10, LAC. The controversy also occupied column space in the *Lethbridge Daily Herald:* see "Gleichen Backs Up Methodists," 29 October 1910, 5; "Interview Met with Affidavit," 26 August 1910, 6; and "From Other Sanctums: Indians and Fairs," 25 October 1910, 4.

66   Pettipas, *Severing the Ties,* 149.

67   "Good Program of Sports and Races," *Lethbridge Daily Herald,* 11 July 1921, 6.

68   "Taber Fair Gets Under Way," *Lethbridge Daily Herald,* 25 July 1921, 8.

69   "Taber Proud of Success of Fair," *Lethbridge Daily Herald,* 30 July 1921, 8.

70   "Pincher Creek Fall Fair Opens," *Lethbridge Daily Herald,* 22 August 1921, 8.

71   "PC Veterans Have Big July 1 Program," *Lethbridge Daily Herald,* 13 June 1921, 8.

72   "Fort Macleod Jubilee One Big Stampede, Pageant and Carnival," newspaper clipping, 8 May 1924, RG 10, vol. 3827, file 60511-5, pt. 1, LAC.

73   Advertisement, *High River Times,* 24 July 1924, unpaginated.

74   Full page advertisement, *Cardston News,* 5 August 1926, 8.

75   "Cardston Fair Big Financial Success," *Cardston News,* 19 August 1926, 1.

76   Indian Agent George H. Gooderham to D.C. Scott, 29 April 1923, DIA, Black Series, RG 10, vol. 3827, file 60511-5, pt. 1, LAC; Police Report, 6 September 1923, DIA, Black Series, RG 10, vol. 3827, file 60511-5, pt. 1, LAC.

77   "Cardston Will Stage Big Celebration on Dominion Day," *Cardston News,* 3 June 1926, 1.

78   "Exhibition Board," *Lethbridge Daily Herald,* 27 July 1935, 1.

79   Correspondence between Indian Agents, Inspector of Indian Agencies, and Department of Indian Affairs, Headquarters, September 1925-March 1926, DIA, Black Series, RG 10, vol. 3827, file 60511-5, pt. 1, LAC.

80   James McGuire to Indian Agent H.M. Helmsing, 11 April 1926, DIA, Black Series, RG 10, vol. 4093, file 600,180 pt. 1, reel C10187, LAC; Indian Agent R. Ferguson to Headquarters, 12 July 1934 DIA, Black Series, RG 10, vol. 4093, file 600,180, pt. 1, reel C10187, LAC; Deloria, *Indians in Unexpected Places,* 55, 115.

81   "Come to the Armstrong Fair," *Vernon News,* 12 September 1918, 8.

82   Typescript on the Oliver Riding Club, undated, Oliver and District Heritage Society Archives, Oliver, BC; Doug Cox with the Keremeos Elks Lodge, no. 56, *Rodeo Roots: 50 Years of Rodeo in the Similkameen and Okanagan* (Penticton: Skookum, 1988), 20, 34.

83   Stampede program, 1927, Stampede files, box 1, WLL; "Those Cariboo Stampedes," newspaper clipping, undated, Stampede files, box 1, WLL; Police Report, 25 June 1926, DIA, Black Series, RG 10, vol. 3827, file 60511-4, pt. 1, LAC.

84   Newspaper clipping, undated, Stampede files, box 1, WLL; "Many Hard Riders in City," *Kamloops Sentinel,* 12 September 1930, 9.

85   Wetherell with Kmet, *Useful Pleasures,* 192.

86   "Was a Big Success," *Lethbridge Daily Herald,* 23 August 1906, 3; "Taber Fair Brings Rain; Splendid Livestock One of Outstanding Features," *Lethbridge Daily Herald,* 26 July 1921, 1.

87   Nora (Gladstone) Baldwin, interview by Frances Roback, 15 February 1993, Interviews for Childhood Exhibit, M-9204-11, GMA.

88   "Cyclone Smith of Cariboo – Hero of the Stampede," *Kamloops Sentinel,* 27 October 1925, 1.

89   "Largest Crowds in History of the Grounds," *Lethbridge Daily Herald,* 2 July 1926, 1.

90   "5000 Attend Cardston's Stampede," *Cardston News,* 24 September 1925, 4.

91   Minutes, Agricultural Society, 19 July 1923, Medicine Hat Agricultural Society, 1914-24, M78.34. 2, file 18, EA.

92   Wetherell and Kmet, *Town Life,* 265-66.

93   Cariboo Stampede Association, Receipts, 1929, Stampede files, box 1, WLL.

94   "$15,000 Spent by Board during Three Days of Fair," *Lethbridge Daily Herald,* 27 July 1935, 7.

95   Ibid.

96 Regular, *Neighbours and Networks,* 132; Nora (Gladstone) Baldwin, interview by Frances Roback, 15 February 1993, Interviews for Childhood Exhibit, M-9204-11, GMA; Mrs. Chris (Katherine) Shade, at her home on the Blood reserve, interview by Pauline Dempsey, Interviews for Childhood Exhibit, M-9204-31, GMA.
97 Furniss, *Burden of History,* 166; Moosang, *First Son,* 121.
98 "Leading Exhibition in Southern Alberta," *Lethbridge Daily Herald,* 2 August 1906, 2.
99 Howard Palmer and Tamara Palmer, *Alberta: A New History* (Edmonton: Hurtig, 1990), 222-23.
100 Jean Barman, *The West beyond the West: A History of British Columbia,* rev. ed. (Toronto: University of Toronto Press, 1996), 243.
101 "Sundre to Hold Stampede Again June 13 and 14," *Calgary Herald,* 19 May 1923, 13.
102 "Stampede Help," *High River Times,* 16 July 1931, 8.
103 "About the Fair," *Lethbridge Daily Herald,* 1 August 1907, 9.
104 "Date of Fair Will Not Be Changed: Agricultural Society Buildings Will Be Rushed," *Lethbridge Daily Herald,* 30 May 1910, 1.
105 "Exhibition Board Faces Big Deficit but Optimistic for the Future," *Lethbridge Daily Herald,* 22 August 1918, 6; "Stampede for One Day of Fair, Race Program Now Being Considered," *Lethbridge Daily Herald,* 20 May 1921, 9.
106 "Best Horses in World at Big Stampede," *Kamloops Sentinel,* 20 October 1925, 1.
107 "Magrath Fair," *Lethbridge Daily Herald,* 16 July 1914, 5; "Plan for Fair at Garden City: Committees Appointed to Draft Sports Program," *Lethbridge Daily Herald,* 25 July 1921, 8.
108 Voisey, *High River and the Times,* 48-56.
109 Wetherell and Kmet, *Town Life,* 260; Barman, *The West beyond the West,* 236.
110 "Stampede Recreates the Life of the West as It Once Existed," *Calgary Herald,* 30 July 1917, 3.
111 "Fifth Avenue Stampede, Williams Lake BC, June 30th, July 1st and 2nd, 1923," program, Stampede files, box 1, WLL.
112 "Memo and Articles of Association for Cariboo Stampede Association (1926)," Stampede files, box 1, WLL.
113 Ibid.
114 "Fifth Annual Stampede," 1923, Stampede files, box 1, WLL.
115 Ibid.
116 Wetherell and Kmet, *Town Life,* 24-25.
117 Stuart Hall, "Whose Heritage? Un-Settling 'the Heritage,' Re-Imagining the Post-Nation," in *The Politics of Heritage: The Legacies of "Race,"* ed. J. Littler and R. Naidoo (London: Routledge, 2005), 22.
118 Ullrich Kockel, "Reflexive Traditions and Heritage Production," in *Cultural Heritages as Reflexive Traditions,* ed. Ullrich Kockel and Mairead Nic Craith (New York: Palgrave Macmillan, 2007), 21.
119 Robert Rutherdale, *Hometown Horizons: Local Responses to Canada's Great War* (Vancouver: UBC Press, 2004), 23-34.
120 Palmer and Palmer, *Alberta,* 83.
121 Ibid., 125-26.
122 Ibid., 127.
123 Advertisement, *Lethbridge Daily Herald,* 10 July 1918, 10; "Prospects Bright for Big Exhibition and Stampede," *Lethbridge Daily Herald,* 3 May 1918, 9; "Stampede and Fair Was Satisfactory Considering Adverse Circumstances," *Lethbridge Daily Herald,* 29 July 1918, 1.
124 Palmer and Palmer, *Alberta,* 221-22.
125 Ibid., 230-32; Aritha Van Herk, *Mavericks: An Incorrigible History of Alberta* (Toronto: Viking, 2001), 170.
126 Barman, *The West beyond the West,* 132.
127 Ibid., 179-86.
128 Ibid., 186; Mary-Ellen Kelm, ed., *The Letters of Margaret Butcher: Missionary-Imperialism on the North Pacific Coast* (Calgary: University of Calgary Press, 2006), xi; Jack Boudreau, *Sternwheelers and Canyon Cats: Whitewater Freighting on the Upper Fraser* (Prince George: Caitlin, 2006).
129 Barman, *The West beyond the West,* 236-39; Michael Dawson, *Selling British Columbia: Tourism and Consumer Culture, 1890-1970* (Vancouver: UBC Press, 2004), 14-43.
130 Barman, *The West beyond the West,* 241-42.

131   James Murton, *Making a Modern Countryside: Liberalism and Land Settlement in British Columbia* (Vancouver: UBC Press, 2007), 35-37.
132   Barman, *The West beyond the West,* 242.
133   Murton, *Making a Modern Countryside,* 168-81.
134   Eric Collier, *Three against the Wilderness* (Toronto: General Paperbacks, 1959); Richmond P. Hobson Jr., *Grass beyond the Mountains* (Toronto: McClelland, 1951).
135   Dawson, *Selling British Columbia,* 64-79.
136   Ibid., 78.
137   Cox with the Keremeos Elks Lodge, *Rodeo Roots,* 22; "Rodeo," *Merritt Herald,* 29 August 1979, 8.
138   "Continued Fine Weather Concludes Exhibition," *Kamloops Sentinel,* 13 September 1935, 1.
139   Barman, *The West beyond the West,* 245, 260.
140   Mary Ryan, "The American Parade: Representations of the Nineteenth-Century Social Order," in *The New Cultural History,* ed. Lynn Hunt (Berkeley: University of California Press, 1989), 131-53; see also Bonnie Huskins, "The Ceremonial Space of Women: Public Processions in Victorian Saint John and Halifax," in *Separate Spheres: Women's Worlds in the 19th-Century Maritimes,* ed. Janet Guildford and Suzanne Morton (Fredericton: Acadiensis Press, 1994), 145-61.
141   Reverend John McDougall to R.N. Wilson, Indian Agent (Blood Agency), 23 June 1908, Blood Agency Fonds, M-1788, box 3, file 21, GMA; M. Rautin, Central Committee of the Masonic Fair, to R.N. Wilson, Indian Agent, 10 February 1908, Blood Agency Fonds, M-1788, box 3, file 21, GMA.
142   "A Local Budget," *Lethbridge Daily Herald,* 2 August 1906, 3.
143   "Taber Fair Brings Rain: Thousands of Exhibits – Indian Parade Marks Opening – One of South's Best Exhibits," *Lethbridge Daily Herald,* 26 July 1921, 3.
144   "Lethbridge Fair and Celebration," *Lethbridge Daily Herald,* 26 June 1926, 6.
145   Heaman, *The Inglorious Arts of Peace;* H.V. Nelles, *The Art of Nation-Building: Pageantry and Spectacle at Quebec's Tercentenary* (Toronto: University of Toronto Press, 1999); Frederick Gleach, "Pocahontas at the Fair: Crafting Identities at the 1907 Jamestown Exposition," *Ethnohistory* 50,3 (Summer 2003): 419-55.
146   "From Redman to Buffalo to Joyous Present," *Lethbridge Daily Herald,* 26 June 1926, 6.
147   Newspaper clipping, 1924, A.D. Kean Papers, Add. MSS 2456, box 1, file 5, British Columbia Archives, Victoria.
148   Ibid.
149   "Raymond Stampede Spurs and Stetsons Will Reign," *Lethbridge Daily Herald,* 26 July 1926, 3.
150   "Cariboo Stampede & 8th Annual Gathering Celebrating Canada's Diamond Jubilee June 30th and July 1st & 2nd 1927," program, Stampede files, box 1, WLL.
151   "Ninth Stampede and Annual Gathering of the Cariboo, June 22nd and 23rd 1928, at Williams Lake, BC," program, Stampede files, box 1, WLL.
152   Ollie (Curtis) Matheson, undated interview, newspaper clipping, undated, Stampede files, box 1, WLL.
153   "Eleventh Stampede and Annual Gathering of the Cariboo, 1930," program, Stampede files, box 1, WLL.
154   "Official Program, Golden Jubilee, July 22, 23, 24, 1935," Manuscript Collection, acc. no. (UID) 19811022005, Galt Museum and Archives, Lethbridge.
155   Jenéa Tallentire, "Strategies of Memory: History, Social Memory and the Community," *Histoire sociale/Social History* 34,67 (May 2001): 197-212.
156   "Official Program, Golden Jubilee, July 22, 23, 24, 1935," Manuscript Collection, acc. no. (UID) 19811022005, Galt Museum and Archives.
157   "Cardston Golden Jubilee, Souvenir Program," 1937, Manuscript Collection, acc. no. 1973512300, Galt Museum and Archives.
158   Quoted in "Cariboo Stampede & 8th Annual Gathering Celebrating Canada's Diamond Jubilee June 30th and July 1st & 2nd 1927," program, Stampede files, box 1, WLL.
159   Ibid.
160   "Cariboo Stampede, June 23, 1928," program, Stampede files, box 1, WLL.
161   "Pincher Creek's Fall Fair and Race Meet Starts Tues; Pincher Creek Fall Fair Opens on Aug 23 1921," *Lethbridge Daily Herald,* 22 August 1921, 8.

162 Newspaper clipping related to Colin Curtis, who first competed in the drunken ride at age eleven, undated, Stampede files, box 1, WLL.

163 Ollie (Curtis) Matheson, undated interview, newspaper clipping, undated, Stampede files, box 1, WLL.

164 "Millie Pulver Remembers the Squaw Race," newspaper clipping, undated (c. 1967), Stampede files, box 1, WLL.

165 John W. Bennett and Seena B. Kohl, *Photographs from the Northern Plains Cultural Ecology Project and the Maple Creek Regional Research Project, 1961-1975* (St. Louis: Department of Anthropology, Washington University, in cooperation with the Medicine Hat Museum and Art Gallery, 2002), 168-69, EA.

166 Quoted in Clifford, *Routes*, 200.

167 Néstor García Canclini, *Hybrid Cultures: Strategies for Entering and Leaving Modernity* (Minneapolis: University of Minnesota, 1995), 7.

168 Homi K. Bhabha, *The Location of Culture* (New York and London: Routledge, 1994), 66.

169 Nora (Gladstone) Baldwin, interview by Frances Roback, 15 February 1993, Interviews for Childhood Exhibit, M-9204-11, GMA.

170 Hanks and Hanks, *Tribe under Trust*, 147-49.

171 See John F. Smith to Department of Indian Affairs, 16 November 1916; Harry Priest, City Clerk, City of Merritt, to John F. Smith, 8 September 1916; J.D. McLean, Assistant Deputy and Secretary Indian Affairs, to John F. Smith, 20 September 1916, all in DIA, Black Series, RG 10, vol. 4083, file 493,555, pt. 1, LAC. American towns did the same thing: see David Rodnick, *The Fort Belknap Assiniboine of Montana: A Study in Culture Change* (New Haven: privately printed, 1938; New York: AMS Press, 1978), 89. (This work was originally presented as Ronick's 1936 PhD dissertation in anthropology at the University of Pennsylvania, Philadelphia.)

172 "Cropping of Indian Lands," *Vernon News*, 3 October 1918, 3; Mary Balf, "The Mosquito War of 1939," undated, Local History Collection, KMA; see also Patricia K. Wood, "Pressured from All Sides: The February 1913 Surrender of the Northeast Corner of the Tsuu T'ina Nation," *Journal of Historical Geography* 30 (2004): 112-29.

173 "Dominion Day in South Fort George," *Fort George Herald*, 15 July 1911, 1; "Dominion Day," *Fort George Herald*, 8 July 1911, 2.

174 "Pincher Creek Plans Big Fair," *Lethbridge Daily Herald*, 6 June 1921, 8.

175 "Many Entries for Fort Macleod Fall Fair," *Lethbridge Daily Herald*, 2 August 1921, 8.

176 "Cardston Plans Rodeo," *Lethbridge Daily Herald*, 14 July 1939, 8.

177 "Cardston Golden Jubilee Souvenir Program," 1937, Manuscript Collection, acc. no. 19735123000, Galt Museum and Archives; "Eleventh Stampede and Annual Gathering of the Cariboo, 1930," program, Stampede files, box 1, WLL.

178 Blood Agency to Secretary, Department of Indian Affairs, 3 May 1908, Blood Agency Fonds, M-1837, box 7, file 56, GMA.

179 Hanks and Hanks, *Tribe under Trust*, 79; Esther Goldfrank field notes, 1 July 1939, Esther Goldfrank Fonds, M-243, GMA.

180 "Cardston Is Not Overlooking 1st: South Town Prepares Elaborate Program for Dominion Day Celebration," *Lethbridge Daily Herald*, 21 June 1921, 8.

181 "Good Program of Sports and Races for the Big Fair: Indian Races, Football Match, Dancing, Aerial Stunts All on the Bill," *Lethbridge Daily Herald*, 11 July 1921, 6.

182 Hugh Dempsey, interview by author, 21 August 2003; George Pragnell to W.J. Ditchburn, 9 October 1931, DIA, Black Series, RG 10, vol. 7557, file 1120-1, pt. 1, LAC; D.C. Scott to A. Meighen, 5 May 1919, DIA, Black Series, RG 10, vol. 3827, file 60511-5, pt. 1, LAC.

183 Hanks and Hanks, *Tribe under Trust*, 79.

184 Esther Goldfrank, *Changing Configurations in the Social Organization of a Blackfoot Tribe during the Reserve Period (the Blood of Alberta, Canada)* (Seattle: University of Washington Press, 1966), 69; Newspaper clipping, 7 July 1925, DIA, Black Series, RG 10, vol. 3827, file 60511-5, pt. 1, LAC.

185 R.N. Wilson to Headquarters, 3 May 1908, Blood Agency Fonds, M-1837, box 7, file 56, GMA.

186 J.H. Gooderham, Inspector of Indian Agencies, "Report on Blackfoot Agency, Gleichen, Alberta, 4 April 1911," *Sessional Papers*, 1912, no. 1, 562; "Brocket Indians Fined, Pincher Creek for

Intoxication," *Lethbridge Daily Herald,* 16 August 1930, 5; "William Hay Gets Three Months in Jail," *Lethbridge Daily Herald,* 5 July 1939, 6; "Indians Fined," *Lethbridge Daily Herald,* 6 July 1939, 6.

187   Police Reports, 25 June 1926 and 7 July 1926, DIA, Black Series, RG 10, vol. 3827, file 60511-5, pt. 1, LAC.

188   Indian Agent to Secretary, Department of Indian Affairs, 24 July 1938, DIA, Black Series, RG 10, vol. 410, file 253,430, pt. 1, LAC.

189   Indian Agent to Secretary, 27 December 1922, DIA, Black Series, RG 10, vol. 3827, file 60511-5, pt. 1, LAC.

190   Ibid.

191   Indian Agent to Secretary, 6 July 1923, DIA, Black Series, RG 10, vol. 3827, file 60511-5, pt. 1, LAC.

192   Caroline Basil, "Report on Rodeo, Ranching of the Kutunaxa People," 1995, Legends of Our Times Fonds, E99.4, box 665, file 4, Canadian Museum of Civilization Archives, Gatineau.

193   Quoted in Adolf Hungry Wolf, *The Blood People: A Division of the Blackfoot Confederacy: An Illustrated Interpretation of the Old Ways* (New York: Harper and Row, 1977), 234-35.

194   "Our Point of View," *Lethbridge Daily Herald,* 11 August 1908, unpaginated.

195   Quoted in Pettipas, *Severing the Ties,* 147.

196   Hanks and Hanks, *Tribe under Trust,* 24; John Smith, "Report of the Indian Agent, Kamloops Indian Agency, 1913," *Sessional Papers,* 1914, no. 1, 53.

197   George H. Gooderham and Philip Godsell, *Northern Plains Tribes,* vol. 3, *Piegans* (Calgary: Glenbow Foundation, 1955), 13, George H. Gooderham Fonds, M-4350, GMA.

198   Missionary to Indian Agent H.M. Helmsing, 29 December 1922, DIA, Black Series, RG 10, vol. 3827, file 60511-5, pt. 1, LAC.

199   Ibid.

200   Joseph Mountain Horse to W.L. Mackenzie King, 7 February 1925, DIA, Black Series, RG 10, vol. 4093, file 600,107, pt. 1, LAC.

201   Yale Belanger, "'An All Round Indian Affair': The Native Gatherings at Fort Macleod, 1924, 1925," *Alberta History* 53,3 (Summer 2005): 11-24.

202   "The Blood Indians: Our First Citizens," *Lethbridge Daily Herald,* 11 July 1935, 104-5, 107; Mike Mountain Horse, *My People, the Bloods* (Calgary and Standoff: Glenbow-Alberta Institute and Blood Tribal Council, 1979).

203   "Mountain Horse to Speak 'over Air,'" *Lethbridge Daily Herald,* 17 July 1935, 6; "Strange, Symbolic Signs on Indian Teepees Explained," *Lethbridge Daily Herald,* 24 July 1935, 7.

204   Dempsey, *Tom Three Persons,* 28-29, 58-59, 64, 88-89.

205   "Official Programme of the Southern Alberta Amalgamated Fair and Stampede, 1918," Manuscript Collection, acc. no. 20081041000, Galt Museum and Archives.

206   "News of Big Stampede and Fair," *Lethbridge Daily Herald,* 24 July 1918, 7.

207   "10,000 Visited the Stampede on Thursday," *Lethbridge Daily Herald,* 26 July 1918, 1.

208   "Ray Knight, Canadian Roping Ace Defeats Galbraith at Cardston," *Lethbridge Daily Herald,* 16 August 1926, 5; "Wildest Bucking Cardston Has Ever Seen," *Lethbridge Daily Herald,* 7 July 1921, 6; "Noll and Bruisehead Divide Riding Honors at Pincher Creek," *Lethbridge Daily Herald,* 11 August 1926, 5; "Cecil Henry Wins Riding Honors at Raymond Stampede," *Lethbridge Daily Herald,* 29 July 1926, 3; "Racing and Stampede Results," *Lethbridge Daily Herald,* 26 August 1921, 4; "Cardston Fair Big Financial Success," *Cardston News,* 5 August 1926, 19; "Celebrations on July 2 & 3 Well-Attended," *Cardston News,* 8 July 1926, 1; Dempsey, *Tom Three Persons,* 88.

209   "Rodeo Results," *High River Times,* 16 August 1928, 3. .

210   British Columbia Cowboy Heritage Society, Inductees, "Joe Elkins," BC Cowboy Hall of Fame Archives, http://www.bcchs.com/.

211   "Williams Lake Stampede Attended by a Large Crowd in Spite of Bad Weather," *Kamloops Sentinel,* 4 July 1930, 4; Newspaper clipping regarding Dave Twan and mountain race in 1929, undated, Stampede files, box 1, WLL; Police Report, 25 June 1926, DIA, Black Series, RG 10, vol. 3827, file 60511-5, pt. 2, LAC.

212   "5th Annual Stampede," 1924 program, Stampede files, box 1, WLL.

213   "Those Cariboo Stampedes," newspaper clipping, undated, Stampede files, box 1, WLL.

214   "Historical Pageant Will Depict City's Rise and Growth," *Lethbridge Daily Herald*, 13 July 1935, 7; "Local Pageant Will Have Cast of 200," *Lethbridge Daily Herald*, 18 July 1935, 11; "Old Timers Will Hold Picnic July 21 on Site of Fort Kipp," *Lethbridge Daily Herald*, 24 June 1935, 7.
215   Van Herk, *Mavericks*, 174.
216   Nora Gladstone, "The Cardston Stampede," *Cardston News*, 12 July 1945, 1.

Chapter 2: Truly Western in Its Character

1   "Leo Watrin Dead," *High River Times*, 2 October 1930, 1. Scholars frequently distinguish between "real" cowboys and those who compete in rodeos. In the Canadian West of the early twentieth century, this is both a less important and a more complicated distinction. Although some, such as the Linders, were not ranching people, most rodeo cowboys came from a ranching background and therefore had "cowboyed" on their own ranches. Jacqueline Moore makes the important distinction between those young men who worked on their own family ranches and cowboys who were in fact wage labourers, highlighting the class dynamics of cowboying. In Canada, both waged cowboys and family-ranch working cowboys rodeoed. The image of rodeo cowboys as completely divorced from ranch life is simply inaccurate for Western Canada before 1950. Nonetheless, rodeo cowboys, such as Leo Watrin, came to stand for a masculinity that was based in popular culture and in local expressions of ranching culture. Michael Allen, *Rodeo Cowboys in the North American Imagination* (Reno and Las Vegas: University of Nevada Press, 1998), 12, 27-30; Jacqueline M. Moore, *Cow Boys and Cattlemen: Class and Masculinities on the Texas Frontier, 1865-1900* (New York: New York University Press, 2010), 13-15.
2   Donna Haraway, *When Species Meet* (Minneapolis: University of Minnesota Press, 2008), 287.
3   "Stampede Winners List," *Kamloops Sentinel*, 12 September 1935, 3; Shirley Louis, *Q'sapi: A History of Okanagan People as Told by Okanagan Families* (Penticton: Theytus Books, 2002), 197; "Eleventh Stampede and Annual Gathering of the Cariboo, 1930," program, Stampede files, box 1, Williams Lake Library (WLL), Williams Lake.
4   "Diamond Stampede Draws Great Crowds," *High River Times*, 26 July 1934, 1; "Streeter Ranch Stampede," *High River Times*, 17 June 1937, 1.
5   "Raymond Stages Thrilling Rodeo," *Calgary Herald*, 5 July 1932, 13.
6   "Cowboys Win," *High River Times*, 17 July 1930, 1.
7   Clifford Putney, *Muscular Christianity: Manhood and Sports in Protestant America, 1880-1920* (Cambridge, MA: Harvard University Press, 2001); Thomas Winter, *Making Men, Making Class: The YMCA and Workingmen, 1877-1920* (Chicago: University of Chicago Press, 2002); Joy Parr, *The Gender of Breadwinners: Women, Men and Change in Two Industrial Towns, 1880-1950* (Toronto: University of Toronto Press, 1990); Philip Abbott, "Titan/Planners, Bohemians/Revolutionaries: Male Empowerment in the 1930s," *Journal of American Studies* 40,3 (2006): 463-85; Robert Nye, "Western Masculinities in War and Peace," *American Historical Review* 112,2 (April 2007): 428; Jeffery Vacante, "Evolving Racial Identity and the Consolidation of Men's Authority in Early Twentieth Century Quebec," *Canadian Historical Review* 88,3 (September 2007): 413-38; Steve Meyer, "Rough Manhood: The Aggressive and Confrontational Shop Culture of U.S. Auto Workers during World War II," *Journal of Social History* 36,1 (Fall 2002): 125-47; Colin Howell, "A Manly Sport: Baseball and the Social Construction of Masculinity," in *Gender and History in Canada*, ed. Joy Parr and Mark Rosenfeld (Toronto: Copp Clark, 1996), 187-210; Stacy L. Lorenz and Geraint B. Osborne, "'Talk about Strenuous Hockey': Violence, Manhood, and the 1907 Ottawa Silver Seven-Montreal Wanderer Rivalry," *Journal of Canadian Studies* 40,1 (Winter 2006): 125-56; Michael A. Robidoux, "Historical Interpretations of First Nations Masculinity and Its Influence on Canada's Sport Heritage," *International Journal of the History of Sport* 23,2 (March 2006): 267-84; Craig Heron, "The Boys and Their Booze: Masculinities and Public Drinking in Working-Class Hamilton, 1890-1946," *Canadian Historical Review* 86,3 (September 2005): 414; Christopher Breward, *The Hidden Consumer: Masculinities, Fashion and City Life, 1860-1914* (Manchester: Manchester University Press, 1999); Tom Pendergast, *Creating the Modern Man: American Magazines and Consumer Culture, 1900-1950* (Columbia and London: University of Missouri Press, 2000), 8-9; Jill Greenfield, Sean O'Connell, and Chris Reid, "Fashioning Masculinity: *Men Only*, Consumption and the Development of Marketing in the 1930s," *Twentieth Century Britain* 10,4 (1999): 457-76.

8   Laura McCall, "Introduction," in *Across the Great Divide: Cultures of Manhood in the American West*, ed. Matthew Basso, Laura McCall, and Dee Garceau (New York: Routledge, 2001), 1-24; J.A. Mangan and James Walvin, "Introduction," in *Manliness and Morality: Middle-Class Masculinity in Britain and America, 1800-1940*, ed. J.A. Mangan and James Walvin (Manchester: Manchester University Press, 1987), 4; John M. MacKenzie, "The Imperial Pioneer and Hunter and the British Masculine Stereotype in Late Victorian and Edwardian Times," in Mangan and Walvin, *Manliness and Morality*, 176-98; Michael S. Kimmel, *The History of Men: Essays in the History of American and British Masculinities* (Albany: State University of New York, 2005), 30, 32, 95.

9   McCall, "Introduction," 1-2; Mary Murphy, "Making Men in the West: The Coming of Age of Miles Cavanaugh and Martin Frank Dunham," in *Over the Edge: Remapping the American West*, ed. Valerie J. Matsumoto and Blake Allmendinger (Berkeley: University of California Press, 1999), 133-47; Cliff Kopas with Leslie Kopas, *No Path but My Own: Horseback Adventures in the Chilcotin and the Rockies* (Madeira Park, BC: Harbour, 1996).

10   Simon Evans, "Tenderfoot to Rider: Learning 'Cowboying' on the Canadian Frontier in the 1880s," in *Cowboys, Ranchers and the Cattle Business: Cross-Border Perspectives on Ranching History*, ed. Simon M. Evans, Sarah Carter, and Bill Yeo (Calgary: University of Calgary Press, 2000), 61-80; Clem Gardner, interview by Sheilagh Jamieson at Pirmez Creek, 24 November 1962, RCT 26-1, Glenbow Museum Archives (GMA), Calgary.

11   Quoted in Cliff Faulknor, *Turn Him Loose: Herman Linder, Canada's Mr. Rodeo* (Saskatoon: Western Producer Prairie Books, 1977), 7.

12   Quoted in ibid., 14.

13   McCall, "Introduction," 4; Kimmel, *The History of Men*, 32, 95.

14   Lucien M. Hanks and Jane Richardson Hanks, *Tribe under Trust: A Study of the Blackfoot Reserve of Alberta* (Toronto: University of Toronto Press, 1950); Esther Goldfrank, *Changing Configurations in the Social Organization of a Blackfoot Tribe during the Reserve Period (the Blood of Alberta, Canada)* (Seattle: University of Washington Press, 1966).

15   John C. Ewers, *The Horse in Blackfoot Indian Culture: With Comparative Material from Other Western Tribes*, Bureau of American Ethnology Bulletin 159 (1955; repr., Washington, DC: Smithsonian Institution, 1980), 227.

16   Hector Stewart, interview by author, Douglas Lake Reserve, 29 July 2003; "Memoirs of Harold Scheer," 1978, M-6659, GMA.

17   Allen, *Rodeo Cowboys*, 28; Garceau, "Nomads, Bunkies, Cross-Dressers and Family Men," in Basso, McCall, and Garceau, *Across the Great Divide*, 165.

18   Cariboo Stampede Association to the Liquor Control Board, 2 June 1931, Stampede files, box 1, WLL.

19   Hugh Dempsey, *Tom Three Persons: Legend of an Indian Cowboy* (Saskatoon: Purich, 1997), 90; see also Lucien Hanks's depiction of cowboy culture in Lucien Hanks, field notes, 19-21 July 1938, 20, Lucien Hanks and Jane Richardson Fonds, M-8458-20, GMA; Glen Campbell to the Hon. Thomas Crothers, 12 May 1913, Department of Indian Affairs (DIA), Black Series, RG 10, vol. 3826, file 60511, pt. 3, Library and Archives Canada (LAC), Ottawa.

20   "Cowboys' Association Meeting, Kelowna, BC," 3 September 1944, Canadian Professional Rodeo Association (CPRA), M-7072-1, GMA.

21   Jean Palmer, interview by author, Hudson's Hope, BC, 2 September 2002.

22   Clifford Westermeier, *Man, Beast, Dust: The Story of Rodeo* (1947; repr., Lincoln: University of Nebraska Press, 1987), 326.

23   Southwestern Saskatchewan Old Timers Association, "Our Pioneers," undated, Old Timers Museum Collection, acc. no. PC 0395.0001-0091, Esplanade Archives (EA), Medicine Hat.

24   Gwen Johansson, interview by author, Hudson's Hope, 1 and 3 September 2002; Jean Palmer, interview by author, 2 September 2002; Violet Pearl Sykes Legrandeur, "Memoirs of a Cowboy's Wife," undated, 18, Emery Legrandeur Family Fonds, M88.41.1-.2, EA.

25   Herman Linder, interview by George H. Gooderham, 14 November 1969, Linder Collection, M-3973, file 9, GMA; Allen, *Rodeo Cowboys*, 30-31.

26   Cyra McFadden, *Rain or Shine: A Family Memoir* (Lincoln: University of Nebraska Press, 1986), 16. Similar stories circulate about cowboy legend Pete Knight. See Darrell Knight, *Pete Knight: The Cowboy King* (Calgary: Detselig, 2004), 111.

27 Patrick (Paddy) Laframboise, interview, 11 May 1978, Laframboise Family Fonds, M78.52.2, box 33, file 6, EA. Laframboise self-identified as Métis, whereas Shuttleworth was well known as the son of an English immigrant and a Syilx woman.

28 "Cowboys Win," *High River Times*, 17 July 1930, 3.

29 Quoted in Faulknor, *Turn Him Loose*, 34.

30 "In 1929, Dave Twan Ran the Mountain Race and a Year Later Lost a Kidney to It," newspaper clipping, undated, Stampede files, box 1, WLL.

31 McFadden, *Rain or Shine*, 17, 19, 25.

32 Faulknor, *Turn Him Loose*, 91.

33 Canadian Professional Rodeo Hall of Fame, 1987 inductees, "Slim Dorin," Canadian Rodeo Historical Association, http://www.canadianprorodeohalloffame.com/.

34 McFadden, *Rain or Shine*, 19.

35 "High River Perspective," *High River Times*, 11 July 1929, 3.

36 McFadden, *Rain or Shine*, 16.

37 Jean Palmer, interview by author, 2 September 2002.

38 "Watrin Brothers Research Project," undated, Museum of the Highwood, High River Museum, High River.

39 Herman Linder, interview by George H. Gooderham, 14 November 1969, Linder Fonds, M-3973, file 9, GMA.

40 Mary-Ellen Kelm, "Manly Contests: Rodeo Masculinities at the Calgary Stampede," *Canadian Historical Review* 90,4 (December 2009): 711-51.

41 Guy Weadick to James B. Smith (Secretary-Treasurer, Cariboo Stampede Society), 22 February 1924, Stampede files, box 1, WLL.

42 "Old Timers Will Hold Picnic July 21 on Site of Fort Kipp," *Lethbridge Daily Herald*, 24 June 1935, 7. The roping event was open only to those men who were in livestock before 30 December 1900 and who were at least twenty years old at the time. Guy Weadick to CPRA executive, 23 May 1951, CPRA, M-7072-18, GMA.

43 Quoted in Donna Livingstone, *The Cowboy Spirit: Guy Weadick and the Calgary Stampede* (Vancouver: Douglas and McIntyre, 1996), 113.

44 Guy Weadick to Jim Maxwell, 19 November 1948, CPRA M-7072-13, GMA.

45 Livingstone, *Cowboy Spirit*, 122.

46 "Guy Weadick: Dean of Rodeo Producers," *Canadian Cattlemen*, June-September 1945, clipping, Horseman's Hall of Fame, M-211, file 100, GMA.

47 "Herman Linder to Ride Here – Champion Cowboy Passing Up Salt Lake Show to Enter Lethbridge Stampede," *Lethbridge Daily Herald*, 20 June 1935, 7.

48 "Stampedes and Sports Meets Will Be Features of South Alberta Celebrations July 1," *Lethbridge Daily Herald*, 30 June 1939, 7.

49 "Wild Bronks Featured as Stampede Opens Lethbridge Stampede," *Lethbridge Daily Herald*, 6 July 1939, 12; Faulknor, *Turn Him Loose*, 55, 88-89; "Rodeo Proves Success, Mammoth Crowds See Bigger, Better Show. – Linder Arena Director," *Cardston News*, 23 July 1940, 1, 4; "Report of the 2nd Annual Peach Festival and Rodeo," CPRA M-7072-12, 1948, GMA; N.D. McKerracher, Managing Director of the Penticton Peach Festival to Jim Maxwell, 24 August 1949, CPRA, M-7071-14, GMA.

50 "Cardston Golden Jubilee Souvenir Program," 1937, Manuscript Collection, acc. no. (UID) 19735123000, Galt Museum and Archives, Lethbridge; Faulknor, *Turn Him Loose*, 95.

51 Westermeier, *Man, Beast, Dust*, 152.

52 Joseph D. Horse Capture and George P. Horse Capture, *Beauty, Honor and Tradition: The Legacy of Plains Indian Shirts* (Minneapolis: National Museum of the American Indian, Smithsonian Institution, and the Minneapolis Institute of Arts, 2001), 22-23; Sheila McManus, *The Line Which Separates: The Making of the Alberta-Montana Borderlands* (Lincoln: University of Nebraska Press, 2005), 91; Hanks and Hanks, *Tribe under Trust*, 23-25, 88, 101; Loretta Fowler, *Shared Symbols, Contested Meanings: Gros Ventre Culture and History, 1778-1984* (Ithaca: Cornell University Press, 1987), 65; David W. Penney, "The Horse as Symbol: Equine Representations in Plains Pictographic Art," in *Visions of the People: A Pictorial History of Plains Indian Art*, ed. Evan M. Maurer (Minneapolis: Minneapolis Institute of Arts, 1993), 78; Loretta Fowler and Regina Flannery, "Gros Ventre," in

Handbook of North American Indians, vol. 13, *Plains,* ed. Raymond J. DeMallie (Washington, DC: Smithsonian Institution, 2001), 686.

53   Calgary Inspectorate, Northwest Territories, Department of Indian Affairs, "Annual Report, 1901," *Sessional Papers,* 1902, no. 13, 323.

54   Hanks and Hanks, *Tribe under Trust,* 23.

55   George H. Gooderham and Philip Godsell, *Northern Plains Tribes,* vol. 2, *Bloods* (Calgary: Glenbow Foundation, 1955), George H. Gooderham Fonds, M-4350, GMA; Esther Goldfrank, field notes, 7 July 1939, Esther Goldfrank Fonds, M-243, GMA.

56   Dempsey, *Tom Three Persons,* 29, 50-53, 64; Sarah Carter, *The Importance of Being Monogamous: Marriage and Nation Building in Western Canada to 1915* (Edmonton: University of Alberta Press, 2008), 13, 14, 115-22.

57   Gloria A. Young and Erik Gooding, "Celebrations and Giveaways," in DeMallie, *Handbook,* vol. 13, *Plains,* 1020; David Rodnick, *The Fort Belknap Assiniboine of Montana: A Study in Culture Change* (New York: AMS Press, 1978), 125; Ian Dyck, "Does Rodeo Have Roots in Ancient Indian Traditions?," *Plains Anthropologist: Journal of the Plains Anthropological Society* 41,157 (August 1996): 206.

58   W.J. Dilworth to Assistant Deputy and Secretary, 19 February 1917, DIA, Black Series, RG 10, vol. 3826, file 60511-4, pt. 1, LAC.

59   Dempsey, *Tom Three Persons,* 86, 88, 121; Untitled article, *Cardston News,* 22 July 1926, 3.

60   Guy Weadick to Tom Three Persons, 15 June 1932, Calgary Exhibition and Stampede Fonds, M-2160, GMA; Indian village prize list, 1 July 1924, Philip Godsell Fonds, M-433, box 15, file 18, GMA; Joe Medicine Shield, interview by Morgan Baillargeon, 17 August 1992, Legends of Their Times Fonds, V96-0459, Canadian Museum of Civilization Archives (CMC), Gatineau.

61   "Cardston Fair Big Financial Success," *Cardston News,* 19 August 1926, 1; "Cardston Stampede," *Cardston News,* 26 July 1928, 1.

62   Hanks and Hanks, *Tribe under Trust,* 56-57; Aileen Gladstone, interview by Pauline Dempsey, 12 March 1993, and Mary Black Kettle, interview by Pauline Dempsey, 4 March 1993, Interviews for Childhood Exhibit, M-9204-11, GMA; Esther Goldfrank, field notes, 7 July 1939, M-243, GMA.

63   Billy Strikes with a Gun, interview by Pauline Dempsey at the Elders Centre, Peigan Nation, Brocket, in Blackfoot translated by Dempsey, undated, Interviews for Childhood Exhibit, M-9204-33, GMA.

64   Quoted in Dempsey, *Tom Three Persons,* 84, 132.

65   "Police Notes," *Cardston News,* 23 June 1932, 3; Guy Weadick to Tom Three Persons, 15 June 1932, Calgary Exhibition and Stampede Fonds, M-2160, GMA; Lucien Hanks, field notes, 19-21 July 1938, M-8458-20, GMA.

66   Esther Goldfrank, field notes, 9 July 1939, M-243, GMA.

67   Lucien Hanks, field notebook, 9-21 July 1938, 11, M-8458-20, GMA; Jane Hanks, diary, 28 May-15 June 1939, 1, M-8458-48, GMA; Rodnick, *The Fort Belknap Assiniboine,* 89-90.

68   Rodnick, *The Fort Belknap Assiniboine,* 85.

69   Chester Bruisehead, Charlie Bear, and John Lefthand, interview by Morgan Baillargeon, undated, Legends of Our Times Fonds, V95-0103, CMC.

70   W.D. Murray to C.P. Schmidt, 24 July 1938, DIA, Black Series, RG 10, vol. 4010, file 253430, pt. 1, LAC.

71   Gooderham and Godsell, *Northern Plains Tribes,* 4 vols., George H. Gooderham Fonds, M-4350, GMA; Lynda Mannik, *Canadian Indian Cowboys in Australia: Representation, Rodeo and the RCMP at the Royal Easter Show, 1939* (Calgary: University of Calgary Press, 2006), 55.

72   Ewers, *The Horse in Blackfoot Indian Culture,* 227.

73   Canada, "Annual Report of the Department of Indian Affairs, 1910," *Sessional Papers,* 1911, no. 3, 572.

74   Louis, *Q'sapi,* 121-23; Canada, "Annual Report of the Department of Indian Affairs, 1910," *Sessional Papers,* 1911, no. 3, 572. See also "Metis as Stockmen," undated, Dorothy Calverley Collection, http://www.calverley.ca/.

75   Ken Mather, *Buckaroos and Mud Pups: The Early Days of Ranching in British Columbia* (Victoria: Heritage House, 2006), 55; John Sutton Lutz, *Makúk: A New History of Aboriginal-White Relations* (Vancouver: UBC Press, 2008), 146.

76 Canada, "Annual Report of the Department of Indian Affairs, 1905," *Sessional Papers*, 1906, no. 3, 14.

77 Mather, *Buckaroos and Mud Pups*, 47.

78 Harry Marriott, *Cariboo Cowboy* (Vancouver: Heritage House, 1994), 23, 43, 68, 72.

79 Canada, "Annual Report of the Department of Indian Affairs, 1913," *Sessional* Papers, 1914, no. 13, 53.

80 Louis, *Q'sapi*, 12; Mather, *Buckaroos and Mud Pups*, 64; Marriott, *Cariboo Cowboy*, 37; Jean Barman, *The West beyond the West: A History of British Columbia*, rev. ed. (Toronto: University of Toronto Press, 1996), 170-71; Jean Barman, "Lost Okanagan: In Search of the First Settler Families," *Okanagan History* 60 (1996): 9.

81 Louis, *Q'sapi*, 12; Peter Carstens, *The Queen's People: A Study of Hegemony, Coercion, and Accommodation among the Okanagan of Canada* (Toronto: University of Toronto Press, 1991), 70-72. Both Louis and Carstens argue that men such as O'Keefe married into Okanagan families precisely to gain access to land. Prior to the establishment of reserves, early ranchers also used provincial pre-emption processes as a means of gaining the best grazing land for themselves. When Gilbert Sproat visited these pre-emptions in 1877, he determined that they were illegal and attempted a land swap that would give ranchers adequate land but not that which was clearly and demonstrably claimed by Okanagan people. See Cole Harris, *Making Native Space: Colonialism, Resistance, and Reserves in British Columbia* (Vancouver: UBC Press, 2003), 125-27, 129, 135, 151.

82 Barman, "Lost Okanagan," 15-16; *Dictionary of Canadian Biography Online*, vol. 12, s.v. "Houghton, Charles Frederick," by Margaret A. Ormsby, http://www.biographi.ca/.

83 Carstens, *Queen's People*, 72.

84 Barman, "Lost Okanagan," 13-14.

85 Louis, *Q'sapi*, 156; Barman, "Lost Okanagan," 13-14, 16-19; Mather, *Buckaroos and Mud Pups*, 67-69; Jay Miller, ed., *Mourning Dove: A Salishan Autobiography* (Lincoln: University of Nebraska Press, 1990), xxvii.

86 Barman, "Lost Okanagan," 13-14.

87 Mather, *Buckaroos and Mud Pups*, 75; Eric D. Sismey, "Joseph Richter," *Okanagan History* 34 (1970): 13; Eliza Jane Swalwell, "Girlhood Days in Okanagan," *Okanagan History* 8 (1939): 36.

88 Barman, "Lost Okanagan," 15-16; Jean Barman and Mike Evans, "Reflections on Being, and Becoming, Métis in British Columbia," *BC Studies* 161 (Spring 2009): 76-81.

89 Mather, *Buckaroos and Mud Pups*, 69-76.

90 Louis, *Q'sapi*, 156; Barman and Evans, "Reflections," 78-81; British Columbia Cowboy Heritage Society, 2006 inductees, "William Twan," BC Cowboy Hall of Fame Archives, http://www.bcchs.com/.

91 See the correspondence between the Inspector of Indian Agencies and the Assistant Deputy and Secretary, Indian Affairs, 3, 4, 13, 19 April 1913, DIA, Black Series, RG 10, vol. 3867, file 87125, LAC.

92 "A List of Half-Breeds Living as Indians on Indian Reserves Belonging to This Agency," Report of the Kamloops Indian Agency, 1892, DIA, Black Series, RG 10, vol. 3867, file 87125, pt. 1, LAC.

93 Ibid.

94 Ibid.

95 Doug Cox, "Okanagan Roots," 1987, typescript, Oliver and District Heritage Society Archives, Oliver, BC.

96 "Fifth Annual Stampede, Williams Lake BC, June 30th, July 1st and 2nd, 1923," program, Stampede files, box 1, WLL.

97 Caroline Basil, "Report on Rodeo, Ranching of the Kutunaxa People," 1995, Legends of Their Times Fonds, E99.4, box 665, file 4, CMC; Patrick (Paddy) Laframboise, interview, 11 May 1978, Laframboise Family Fonds, acc. no. M78.52.2, box 33, file 6, EA.

98 "What You Can Expect to See," *Lethbridge Daily Herald*, 11 July 1918, 9; "News of the Big Stampede," *Lethbridge Daily Herald*, 24 July 1918, 7.

99 Mary Lou LeCompte, "Home on the Range: Women in Professional Rodeo: 1929-1947," *Journal of Sport History* 17,3 (Winter 1990): 318.

100 Westermeier, *Man, Beast, Dust*, 83.

101   Violet Pearl Sykes Legrandeur, "Memoirs of a Cowboy's Wife," 1952, 3, Emery Legrandeur Family Fonds, M88.41.1-.2, EA.
102   "Jenner Girl Rides Steer," *Lethbridge Daily Herald,* 22 July 1926, 2.
103   "4000 Past through Gates," *Lethbridge Daily Herald,* 16 August 1926, 2.
104   "Claresholm Girl Thrown from Horse at Stavely Races," *Lethbridge Daily Herald,* 27 June 1935, 3.
105   Nancy Young, "The Reins in Their Hands: Ranchwomen and the Horse in Southern Alberta, 1880-1914," *Alberta History* 52,1 (Winter 2004): 2-8.
106   "Champion Cowboy Sees Real Future for Local Rodeo," *Lethbridge Daily Herald,* 26 July 1935, 7.
107   Mary Lou LeCompte, *Cowgirls of the Rodeo: Pioneer Professional Athletes* (Urbana and Chicago: University of Illinois Press, 1993).
108   "The Winners," *Kamloops Sentinel,* 13 September 1935, 3.
109   Clayton Mack, *Bella Coola Man* (Madeira Park, BC: Harbour, 2002), 202.
110   Ollie (Curtis) Matheson, undated interview, newspaper clipping, undated, Stampede files, box 1, WLL.
111   Newspaper clipping, undated, Stampede files, box 1, WLL.
112   "Cariboo Stampede & 8th Annual Gathering Celebrating Canada's Diamond Jubilee June 30th and July 1st & 2nd 1927," program, Stampede files, box 1, WLL.
113   See "From Cradle to Cowboy to Working Cowboy – June Charlton," in "The Cowboy Times: Official Program of the 2001 Kamloops Cowboy Festival," 2.
114   Newspaper clipping, undated, Stampede files, box 1, WLL.
115   "Votes Are Piling Up for Queen Contestants," *Williams Lake Tribune,* 18 May 1933, 1; "Her Majesty the Queen," *Williams Lake Tribune,* 1 June 1933, 1; "Colorful Stampede Attended by Large Crowds," *Williams Lake Tribune,* 8 June 1933, 1; "Glorious Weather Favors Big Stampede," *Williams Lake Tribune,* 22 June 1933, 1.
116   "Queens of the Stampede Contest Results," *Williams Lake Tribune,* 21 June 1934, 1.
117   Elizabeth Furniss, *The Burden of History: Colonialism and the Frontier Myth in a Rural Canadian Community* (Vancouver: UBC Press, 1999), 169.
118   "Her Majesty the Queen," *Williams Lake Tribune,* 1 June 1933, 1.
119   "Glorious Weather Favors Big Stampede," *Williams Lake Tribune,* 22 June 1933, 1.
120   Beverly Stoeltje, "The Snake Charmer Queen: Ritual, Competition and Signification in an American Festival," in *Beauty Queens on the Global Stage: Gender, Contests, and Power,* ed. Colleen Ballerino Cohen, Richard Wilk, and Beverly Stoeltje (New York and London: Routledge, 1996), 14.
121   "Call of Rita, Queen of Lac LaHache," *Williams Lake Tribune,* 14 June 1934, 6.
122   "Future and Past Queens," *Williams Lake Tribune,* 28 April 1938, 8.
123   "Past and Future Queens," *Williams Lake Tribune,* 5 May 1938, 5.
124   "Cariboo Girls That Are Helping to Make the Stampede a Success," *Williams Lake Tribune,* 26 May 1938, 5.
125   "Programmes for Williams Lake Stampede Are Now on Hand," *Williams Lake Tribune,* 30 April 1936, 1; Hilary Place, *Dog Creek: A Place in the Cariboo* (Surrey: Heritage House, 1999), 134-41; Newspaper clipping, undated, Stampede files, box 1, WLL.
126   Colleen Ballerino Cohen, Richard Wilk, and Beverly Stoeltje, "Introduction: Beauty Queens on the Global Stage," in Cohen, Wilk, and Stoeltje, *Beauty Queens,* 4-7; Place, *Dog Creek,* 141.
127   George Pragnell to W.J. Ditchburn, 9 October 1931, DIA, Black Series, RG 10, vol. 7557, file 1120-1, pt. 1, LAC.
128   George Pragnell to W.J. Ditchburn, 13 October 1931, DIA, Black Series, RG 10, vol. 7557, file 1120-1, pt. 1, LAC.
129   "Finest Indian Exhibits in the Arena," *Kamloops Sentinel,* 29 September 1933, 7.
130   George Pragnell to W.J. Ditchburn, 15 August 1934, DIA, Black Series, RG 10, vol. 7557, file 1120-1, pt. 1, LAC.
131   Canada, "Annual Report of the Department of Indian Affairs, 1935," *Sessional Papers,* 1936, no. 13, 332.
132   Ibid.
133   R.A. Hoey, "Economic Problems of the Canadian Indian Today," in *The North American Indian Today,* ed. C.I. Loram and T.F. McIlwraith (Toronto: University of Toronto Press, 1943), 199-206.

Hugh Shewell argues that relief payments through Indian Affairs actually decreased during the 1930s. He writes that between 1931 and 1936, relief expenditures for those living on-reserve dropped from $790,672 in 1931 to $786,830 in 1936. Per capita relief expenditures for those living on-reserve diminished from $7.20 in 1931 to $6.01 in 1934, recovering slightly by 1936 to $6.85. That year, non-Native Canadians received relief at a per capita rate of $12.34, and total relief expenditures were $135 million in 1935. Hugh Shewell, "Jules Sioui and Indian Political Radicalism in Canada 1943-1944," *Journal of Canadian Studies* 34,3 (Fall 1999): 214.

134   Hoey, "Economic Problems," 204.

135   Ibid., 205.

136   Gerald R. McMaster, "Tenuous Lines of Descent: Indian Arts and Crafts of the Reservation Period," *Canadian Journal of Native Studies* 9,3 (1989): 211-15.

137   Horse Capture and Horse Capture, *Beauty, Honor and Tradition.*

138   Oscar Lewis, "Manly-Hearted Women among the North Piegan," *American Anthropologist* 43,2 (1941): 173-87.

139   Horse Capture and Horse Capture, *Beauty, Honor and Tradition,* 32; see also Mary Wright and Gerald Conaty, "Comments and Reflections: Economic Models and Blackfoot Ideology," *American Ethnologist* 22,2 (1995): 407; Penney, "The Horse as Symbol," 69-79.

140   George H. Gooderham and Philip Godsell, *Northern Plains Tribes,* vol. 2, *Bloods* (Calgary: Glenbow Foundation, 1955), unpaginated, George H. Gooderham Fonds, M-4350, GMA; Evan M. Maurer, "Visions of the People," in Maurer, *Visions of the People,* 44; Katie Labelle, "Profile of Outstanding Stonies of the Past," *Stoney Country,* newspaper clipping, M36 f1492, Whyte Museum of the Rockies, Banff, Alberta.

141   Mather, *Buckaroos and Mud Pups,* 131.

142   Vera Gully, interview on Fernley Gully, 1973, Fern Gully Fonds, RCT-120-1, GMA.

143   Esther Goldfrank, field notes, 16 August 1939, M-243, GMA; Hanks and Hanks, *Tribe under Trust,* 79.

144   Louise Lincoln, "The Social Construction of Plains Art, 1875-1915," in Maurer, *Visions of the People,* 47-59.

145   Gwen Johansson, interview by author, 1 and 3 September 2002.

146   Jean Palmer, interview by author, 2 September 2002.

147   John K. Thompson, *Cabin in the Pines* (Belleville, ON: Epic Press, 2001), 268.

148   *Simpcw Adaptation to Change 1930-1950* (Victoria: BC Ministry of Skills, Training and Labour, 1999), 27; Fred Gladstone, interview by Charles Ursenbach, 4 June 1975, Fred Gladstone Fonds, M-6049, file 18, GMA.

149   Marriott, *Cariboo Cowboy,* 131.

150   "Stampede Scores Another Success," *Williams Lake Tribune,* 25 June 1931, 8.

151   Rodnick, *The Fort Belknap Assiniboine,* 85, 89, 90; Hugh Dempsey, interview by author, Calgary, 21 August 2003.

152   David Wyatt, "Thompson," in *Handbook of North American Indians,* vol. 12, *Plateau,* ed. Deward E. Walker (Washington, DC: Smithsonian Institution, 1988), 191-200; Stephen Dow Beckham, "History since 1846," in Walker, *Handbook,* vol. 12, *Plateau,* 149-73, 165; Caroline Basil, "Report on Rodeo, Ranching of the Kutunaxa People," 1995, Legends of Their Times Fonds, E99.4, box 665, file 4, CMC.

153   Jim Webster, interview by Faith Moosang, 26 September 1998, in Faith Moosang, *First Son: Portraits of C.D. Hoy* (Vancouver: Presentation House/Arsenal Pulp Press, 1999), 141.

154   Thompson, *Cabin in the Pines,* 268.

155   Ollie (Curtis) Matheson, undated interview, newspaper clipping, undated, Stampede files, box 1, WLL.

156   Lenora Duce, interview by Frances Roback, 18 March 1993, Interviews for Childhood Exhibit, M-9204-11, GMA.

157   Garry Oker, interview by author, Fort St. John, BC, 12 December 2003.

158   H.M. Helmsing to Department, 27 December 1922, DIA, Black Series, RG 10, vol. 3827, file 60511-5, pt. 1, LAC.

159   Quoted in Moosang, *First Son,* 141.

160   Quoted in ibid., 136.
161   Place, *Dog Creek,* 118-19.
162   "Those Cariboo Stampedes," newspaper clipping, undated, Stampede files, box 1, WLL.
163   Dempsey, *Tom Three Persons,* 108.
164   Fred Gladstone, interview by Charles Ursenbach, 4 June 1975, Fred Gladstone Fonds, M-6049, file 18, GMA.
165   Lucien Hanks, field notebook, 9-21 July 1938, 20, M-8458-20, GMA; Jane Hanks diary, 28 May-5 June 1939, 11, M-8458-48, GMA.
166   Patricia C. Albers, "Santee," in DeMallie, *Handbook,* vol. 13, *Plains,* 775.
167   Gerald R. Desmond, *Gambling among the Yakima,* Catholic University of America Anthropological Series 14 (Washington, DC: Catholic University of America, 1952), 9.
168   Philip Deloria, *Indians in Unexpected Places* (Lawrence: University Press of Kansas, 2004), 55, 115.
169   Edna Mitchell, interview by Faith Moosang, 10 March 1999, in Moosang, *First Son,* 126.
170   Mourning Dove, *Cogewea, the Half-Blood: A Depiction of the Great Montana Cattle Range* (Lincoln: University of Nebraska, 1981), 62, 67.
171   Mary Black Kettle, interview by Pauline Dempsey, 4 March 1993, Interviews for Childhood Exhibit, M-9204-11, GMA; Aileen Gladstone, interview by Pauline Dempsey, 12 March 1993, Interviews for Childhood Exhibit, M-9204-11, GMA.
172   Esther Goldfrank, field notes, 16 August 1939, M-243, GMA.
173   Place, *Dog Creek,* 137-43; Joan (Palmantier) Gentles, interview by author, 12 May 2004.
174   Gooderham and Godsell, *Northern Plains Tribes,* vol. 2, *Bloods,* George H. Gooderham Fonds, M-4350, GMA.

Chapter 3: A Sport, Not a Carnival Act

1   Pete Knight's story is affectionately told by his grandnephew, Darrell Knight, in his biography *Pete Knight: The Cowboy King* (Calgary: Detselig, 2004).
2   Allen Guttmann, *From Ritual to Record: The Nature of Modern Sports* (New York: Columbia University Press, 1978).
3   Ibid., 32, 26, 18-19; Colin D. Howell, "Of Remembering and Forgetting: *From Ritual to Record* and Beyond," *Sport History Review* 32 (2001): 12-18; Douglas Booth, "*From Ritual to Record:* Allen Guttmann's Insights into Modernization and Modernity," *Sport History Review* 32 (2001): 19-27.
4   Howell, "Of Remembering and Forgetting," 16; see also Boria Majumdar, "The Vernacular in Sports History," *International Journal of the History of Sport* 20,1 (March 2003): 107-25.
5   "Kamloops Rodeo," *Kamloops Sentinel,* 14 September 1934, 7.
6   "Hundred Per Cent Better Than Last Year," *Kamloops Sentinel,* 10 September 1935, 1.
7   Cliff Faulknor, *Turn Him Loose: Herman Linder, Canada's Mr. Rodeo* (Saskatoon: Western Producer Prairie Books, 1977), 38.
8   Patrick (Paddy) Laframboise, interview, 11 May 1978, Laframboise Family Fonds, M78.52.2, box 33, file 6, Esplanade Archives (EA), Medicine Hat; Virginia Baptiste nomination for Rodeo Hall of Fame, Ethnology files 991, box 665, file 1, Canadian Museum of Civilization Archives, Gatineau; Shirley Louis, *Q'sapi: A History of Okanagan People as Told by Okanagan Families* (Penticton: Theytus Books, 2002), 197.
9   Clyde Ellis, "Five Dollars a Week to Be 'Regular Indians': Shows, Exhibitions and the Economics of Indian Dancing, 1880-1930," in *Native Pathways: American Indian Culture and Economic Development in the Twentieth Century,* ed. Brian Hosmer and Colleen O'Neill (Boulder: University Press of Colorado, 2004), 184-205; Lucien M. Hanks and Jane Richardson Hanks, *Tribe under Trust: A Study of the Blackfoot Reserve of Alberta* (Toronto: University of Toronto Press, 1950), 56; Ottawa Police Report, 27 July 1932, Department of Indian Affairs (DIA), Black Series, RG 10, vol. 3827, file 604111-4B, pt. 1, Library and Archives Canada (LAC), Ottawa; Scrapbook, Philip Godsell Fonds, M-433, box 4, Glenbow Museum Archives (GMA), Calgary; Gloria A. Young and Erik Gooding, "Celebrations and Giveaways," in *Handbook of North American Indians,* vol. 13, *Plains,* ed. Raymond J. DeMallie (Washington, DC: Smithsonian Institution, 2001), 1011-25; David Rodnick, *The Fort Belknap Assiniboine of Montana: A Study in Culture Change* (New Haven: privately printed, 1938; New York: AMS Press, 1978), 100-101, 135 (this work was originally presented as Rodnick's 1936 PhD dissertation in anthropology at the University of Pennsylvania, Philadelphia).

10 "Stampede Coverage," *Cardston News,* 18 June 1940, 3.

11 Donald G. Wetherell with Irene R.A. Kmet, *Useful Pleasures: The Shaping of Leisure in Alberta, 1896-1945* (Regina: Canadian Plains Research Center, 1990), 313.

12 Guy Weadick to James B. Smith (Secretary-Treasurer of the Cariboo Stampede Association), 22 February 1924, Stampede files, box 1, Williams Lake Library (WLL), Williams Lake.

13 "Stampede to Be Staged This Summer," *Lethbridge Daily Herald,* 21 May 1935, 6.

14 "The Stampede Rulebook, 1925," Horseman's Hall of Fame, M-2111, box 3, file 27, GMA; Calgary Stampede program, 1927, Calgary Exhibition and Stampede Fonds, M-2160-29a-5, GMA; Roberta J. Park, "Biological Thought, Athletics and the Formation of a 'Man of Character,' 1830-1900," in *Manliness and Morality: Middle-Class Masculinity in Britain and America, 1800-1940,* ed. J.A. Mangan and James Walvin (Manchester: Manchester University Press, 1987), 17. For examples of other stampedes that used the Calgary Stampede rules, see the advertisement for the Willow Creek Stampede, *High River Times,* 26 July 1934, 5, and "Program for Medicine Hat Stampede and Race Meet, June 23-25, 1937," Kelly Burbidge Papers, M86.29.1, box 29, file 509, EA.

15 "Program for Medicine Hat Stampede and Race Meet, June 23-25, 1937," Kelly Burbidge Papers, M86.29.1, box 29, file 509, EA.

16 Kristine Fredriksson, *American Rodeo: From Buffalo Bill to Big Business* (College Station: Texas A & M University Press, 1985), 22.

17 Ibid., 22-24.

18 "Cardston Golden Jubilee Souvenir Program," 1937, Manuscript Collection, acc. no. (UID) 19735123000, Galt Museum and Archives, Lethbridge; Raymond Stampede and Race Meet, official program, 1942, box 2743, Stockmen's Library and Archives (SLA), Cochrane, Alberta; "Medicine Hat Exhibition and Stampede," 1948, M83, file 1, EA; "Program for Medicine Hat Stampede and Race Meet, June 23-25, 1937," Kelly Burbidge Papers, M86.29.1, box 29, file 509, EA.

19 "Herman Linder Leads Cowboys' Special Prize: Update on Southern Alberta Championship Title," *Lethbridge Herald,* 19 July 1939, 6.

20 "Cardston Golden Jubilee Souvenir Program," 1937, Manuscript Collection, acc. no. (UID) 19735123000, Galt Museum and Archives.

21 Fredriksson, *American Rodeo,* 24; Faulknor, *Turn Him Loose,* 39-40.

22 Harry Shuttleworth to Guy Weadick, 15 May 1931, Stampede files, box 1, WLL.

23 Patrick (Paddy) Laframboise, interview, 11 May 1978, Laframboise Family Fonds, M78.52.2, box 33, file 6, EA.

24 Quoted in Faulknor, *Turn Him Loose,* 40.

25 Hugh Dempsey, interview by author, Calgary, 21 August 2003.

26 "Chuckwagon Entries Made," *Calgary Herald,* 20 June 1931, 13. In 1930 the Cariboo Stampede Committee announced the following judges for its events: racing judges: Jas Stewart, Riske Creek; A.W. McMorran, Gang Ranch; C. Spencer, Chilco Ranch; C. Moon, Deer Park Ranch; J. Hargreaves, Springfield Ranch; John L. Hill, Quesnel; George V. Copley, District Forester; Jas. J. Donnelly, Quesnel; arena judges: Leonard Palmantier, Gang Ranch; Dan Weir, Chilcotin; Darwin Bell, Williams Lake; chute judges: W. Smith, Williams Lake; E. Madden, Prince George; timekeeper: B.C. Barron, Riske Creek. "Eleventh Stampede and Annual Gathering of the Cariboo, 1930," program, Stampede files, box 1, WLL.

27 Stuie Stampede program, 9 July 1932, T.A. Tommy Walker Papers, Add. MSS 2784, box 24, file 13, British Columbia Archives (BCA), Victoria; "Stampede at Blood Indian Reserve," *High River Times,* 23 June 1938, 3.

28 Knight, *Pete Knight,* 80-81.

29 "Program for Medicine Hat Stampede and Race Meet, June 23-25, 1937," Kelly Burbidge Papers, M86.29.1, box 29, file 509, EA.

30 Fredriksson, *American Rodeo,* 37.

31 Faulknor, *Turn Him Loose,* 51.

32 Knight, *Pete Knight,* 95-96, 110-11.

33 Clifford Westermeier, *Man, Beast, Dust: The Story of Rodeo* (1947; repr., Lincoln: University of Nebraska Press, 1987), 149.

34 See the ad for the Raymond Stampede and Race Meet in Supplement to the *Raymond Recorder,* 19 August 1927, 3, and the ad for the Cardston Stampede in the *Cardston News,* 16 June 1936, 6.

35   Karen R. Merrill, "Domesticated Bliss: Ranchers and Their Animals," in *Across the Great Divide: Cultures of Manhood in the American West*, ed. Matthew Basso, Laura McCall, and Dee Garceau (New York: Routledge, 2001), 169-84; Lynette Tan, "The New Deal Cowboy: Gene Autry and the Antimodern Resolution," *Film History* 13 (2001): 89-101.

36   Quoted in Tan, "The New Deal Cowboy," 100.

37   Tom Dunsmore to A.D. Kean, 6 December 1932, and J. Wilson Cooper to A.D. Kean, 19 January 1934, A.D. Kean Papers, Add. MSS 2456, box 1, file 5, BCA.

38   Don Smith, Training School for Boys, to A.D. Kean, 15 September 1937, A.D. Kean Papers, Add. MSS 2456, box 1, file 5, BCA.

39   Westermeier, *Man, Beast, Dust*, 287-91.

40   See, for example, the coverage of Harry Knight's career in the *Crag and Canyon*, a Banff paper. "Harry Knight," *Crag and Canyon*, 26 July 1935, 3.

41   Scrapbook, Paddy Ryan, M-6974, GMA; Herman Linder, interview by George H. Gooderham, 14 November 1969, Linder Fonds, M-3973, file 9, GMA.

42   "Stampede Office Opened Monday," *Calgary Herald*, 22 June 1932, 3.

43   Fredriksson, *American Rodeo*, 31-33.

44   Ibid., 32-33.

45   Clifford Westermeier includes an apostrophe in "Cowboys' Turtle Association," though others delete it. A number of stories explain the choice of the name including that rodeo cowboys were so slow to organize, they were like turtles. Another story goes that cowboys did not want a "high-falutin' name" and so chose the turtle to represent them. See Westermeier, *Man, Beast, Dust*, 94, and Fredriksson, *American Rodeo*, 40.

46   Quoted in Fredriksson, *American Rodeo*, 42.

47   Ibid., 43-49.

48   Guy Weadick, "What Are Rodeos Doing?," *Hoofs and Horns* 7,7 (January 1938): 14-15.

49   Cyra McFadden, *Rain or Shine: A Family Memoir* (Lincoln: University of Nebraska Press, 1986), 118.

50   Faulknor, *Turn Him Loose*, 84.

51   Quoted in ibid., 83.

52   Ibid., 55.

53   "Champion Cowboy Sees Real Future for Local Rodeo," *Lethbridge Daily Herald*, 26 July 1935, 7.

54   Gerd von der Lippe, "Sportification Processes: Whose Logic? Whose Rationality?," *Sport History Review* 32 (2001): 42-55; Mary Lou LeCompte, *Cowgirls of the Rodeo: Pioneer Professional Athletes* (Urbana: University of Illinois Press, 1993); Herman Linder, interview by George H. Gooderham, 14 November 1969, Linder Fonds, M-3973, file 9, GMA; Fredriksson, *American Rodeo*, 16.

55   Adolf Hungry Wolf, *The Blood People: A Division of the Blackfoot Confederacy: An Illustrated Interpretation of the Old Ways* (New York: Harper and Row, 1977), 234-35.

56   "Thrilling Rides, Clever Roping Mark Opening Day of Stampede," *Lethbridge Daily Herald*, 23 July 1935, 10.

57   Raymond Stampede and Race Meet, official program, 1942, box 2743, SLA.

58   "Record Crowds and Ideal Weather Features Cardston's Big 2-Day Stampede," *Cardston News*, 25 July 1946, 1.

59   Wallace Mountain Horse, interview by Pauline Dempsey, Moses Lake, 15 May 1993, Interviews for Childhood Exhibit, M-9204-11, GMA.

60   J. Dillon to Blair Holland, 12 January 1945, Canadian Professional Rodeo Association (CPRA), M-7072-2, GMA; Fred Gladstone, interview by Frances Roback, 12 February 1993, Interviews for Childhood Exhibit, M-9204-11, GMA.

61   Lynda Mannik, *Canadian Indian Cowboys in Australia: Representation, Rodeo and the RCMP at the Royal Easter Show, 1939* (Calgary: University of Calgary Press, 2006). See, for example, the correspondence between Indian Agents and Secretary, Department of Indian Affairs, 1913 to 1930s, DIA, Black Series, RG 10, vol. 3826, file 60511-4, pt. 1, LAC; Norman Luxton to C.P. Schmidt, 1 September 1937, Luxton Fonds, M-707, box 22, file 151, GMA; and "Report of Conference Held at the Inspector's Office at Calgary, Alberta, January 24, 1938," Luxton Fonds, M-707, box 22, file 151, GMA.

62   Herman Linder, interview by George H. Gooderham, 14 November 1969, Linder Fonds, M-3973, file 9, GMA.

63   Westermeier, *Man, Beast, Dust,* 125.
64   J. Dillon to Blair Holland, 12 January 1945, CPRA, M-7072-2, GMA.
65   Summary of CPRA history in the CPRA finding aid, CPRA, M-7072, GMA, http://ww2.glenbow.
      org/.
66   Ibid.
67   Cowboys' Association meeting, Kelowna, 3 September 1944, CPRA, M-7072-1, GMA.
68   Minutes, CPRA executive, 13 July 1945, CPRA, M-7072-1, GMA.
69   Ibid.
70   Knight, *Pete Knight,* 143-45.

Chapter 4: Heavens No! Let's Keep It Rodeo!

1   Josef Reeve (director), *Hard Rider* (Ottawa: National Film Board of Canada, 1972). The website
      of the Okanagan First Nation gives Syilx as the appropriate name for the nation. Syilx: Okanagan
      Nation Alliance, "History and Culture," 2004, http://www.syilx.org/.
2   Reeve, *Hard Rider.*
3   Ibid.
4   James Fentress and Chris Wickham, *Social Memory* (1992; repr., Oxford: Blackwell, 1994); John R.
      Gillis, *Commemorations: The Politics of National Identity* (Princeton: Princeton University Press, 1996), 7.
5   Richard Slotkin, *Gunfighter Nation: The Myth of the Frontier in Twentieth-Century America* (New York:
      Atheneum, 1992). Slotkin's analysis of the iconic Hollywood western *High Noon* (1952), for example,
      neatly demonstrates the array of ideological functions that the westerns could play in an era of
      increasing political polarization and fear.
6   Scholarly work in film and television studies attests to the penetration of western characters into
      the childhood consciousness of baby boomers and to the transnational reach of the western genre.
      See Elliott West, "Shots in the Dark: Television and the Western Myth," *Montana: The Magazine of
      Western History* 38,2 (Spring 1988): 720-76; J.G. O'Boyle, "Be Sure You're Right, Then Go Ahead,"
      Journal of Popular Film and Television 24,2 (Summer 1996): 69-82; Ann McGrath, "Playing Colonial:
      Cowgirls, Cowboys and Indians," *Journal of Colonialism and Colonial History* 2,1 (2001), http://www.
      muse.jhu.edu/; and Roger L. Nicholas, "Western Attractions: Europeans and America," *Pacific
      Historical Review* 74,1 (2005): 1-17.
7   Kristine Fredriksson, *American Rodeo: From Buffalo Bill to Big Business* (College Station: Texas A &
      M University Press, 1985), 88-89.
8   Michael Allen, *Rodeo Cowboys in the North American Imagination* (Reno and Las Vegas: University of
      Nevada Press, 1998), 40-51. On *Cariboo Country,* see Mary Jane Miller, "'Cariboo Country': A
      Canadian Response to American Television Westerns," *American Review of Canadian Studies* 14,3
      (Fall 1984): 322-32. Miller argues that *Cariboo Country* was distinctive in part because of its strong
      Aboriginal characters. See Chapter 5 for more on *Cariboo Country.*
9   The Cowboys' Protective Association changed its name to the Canadian Rodeo Cowboys' Asso-
      ciation in 1965 and then to the present name, the Canadian Professional Rodeo Association, in
      1980. For the sake of simplicity, I've chosen to use the present name in this and subsequent
      chapters, regardless of which version was current at the time under discussion.
10   Secretary Blair Holland to O.L. Snider, Fort Worth, Texas, 26 May 1945, Canadian Professional
      Rodeo Association (CPRA), M-7072-1, Glenbow Museum Archives (GMA), Calgary.
11   Minutes, CPRA executive, 1 and 2 February 1946, CPRA, MicroCPRA/1, series 22, GMA.
12   William Hay to Blair Holland regarding the Edmonton show joining the CPRA lists, prize money,
      and entry fees, 13 August 1946, CPRA, M-7072-6, series 1, GMA; Minutes, CPRA executive, 7
      December 1950, CPRA, MicroCPRA/1, series 22, GMA.
13   CPRA to Mr. D.M. Dugas, Maple Creek, Saskatchewan, undated (1947), CPRA, M-7072-7, series
      1, GMA.
14   Minutes, CPRA executive, 12 December 1946, CPRA, M-7072; MicroCPRA/1, series 22, GMA.
15   This is confirmed by the minutes of the CPRA executive meetings. For example, with a single
      exception, the CPRA directors elected in 1964 all listed "farmer" or "rancher" as their occupation.
      The directors were Phil Doan of Halkirk, Alberta, Tom Bews of Longview, Keith Hyland of Turner
      Valley, Bud Van Cleave of Taber, Norman Edge of Cochrane, and Bud Butterfield of Ponoka. Only
      Rocky Rockabar of Medicine Hat reported that he was a rodeo contestant by occupation. Three

years later, the situation had improved: of the eight newly elected directors, five identified rodeo contestant as their primary occupation. Kenny McLean reported that he was both rancher and rodeo contestant, and Fred Gladstone stated only that he was a rancher. Minutes, CPRA executive, 11 December 1964 and 24 November 1967, CPRA, MicroCPRA/1, series 22, GMA.

16 Minutes, CPRA executive, 19 July 1947, CPRA, MicroCPRA/1, series 22, GMA.

17 Ibid.; J. Summers to CPRA, 20 January 1960, CPRA, M-7072-44, series, 1, box 7, file 44; Hospitalization claim forms submitted by Saskatoon City Hospital (10 April 1960), Royal Alexandria Hospital, Edmonton (16 April 1960), and Winnipeg General Hospital (19 April 1960) to CPRA, April 1960, CPRA, M7072-45, series 1, box 7, file 45, GMA; Gerald Dosch to CPRA, 6 June 1960, CPRA, M7072-46, series 1, box 7, file 46, GMA.

18 Minutes, CPRA executive, 10 July 1947 and 11 December 1947, CPRA, MicroCPRA/1, series 22, GMA; CPRA to Princeton Rodeo Association, 3 January 1949, CPRA, M-7072-12, series 1, GMA; Fred Gladstone, interview by Charles Ursenbach, 4 June 1975, Fred Gladstone Fonds, M-6049, file 18, GMA.

19 Cowboys began wearing protective gear, including helmets and vests, in the 1990s. The death of bull rider Lane Frost in 1989 prompted an increased acceptance of protective vests among rough-stock contestants. See Dale Butterwick and W.H. Meeuwisse, "Bull-Riding Injuries in Professional Rodeo," *Physician and Sports Medicine* 31,6 (June 2003): 37-41; see also Gavin Ehringer, "Protective Gear: Accident Victims and Experts Alike Make the Case for Wearing Protective Riding Gear," *Western Horseman,* http://www.troxelhelmets.com/.

20 Christopher Dummitt, *The Manly Modern: Masculinity in Postwar Canada* (Vancouver: UBC Press, 2007), 53-65.

21 Minutes, CPRA executive, 11 December 1947, CPRA, MicroCPRA/1, series 22, GMA.

22 H.E. Churchill (Falkland Rodeo) to CPRA executive, 13 May 1948, CPRA, M-7072-10, series 1, GMA; Jim Maxwell to H.E. Churchill, 14 June 1948, CPRA, M-7072-10, series 1, GMA.

23 Jim Maxwell to CPRA trophy committee (recipient illegible), 28 November 1952, CPRA, M-7072-24, series 1, GMA.

24 Minutes, CPRA executive committee, 27 November 1955, CPRA, M-7072, MicroCPRA/1, series 22, GMA.

25 Minutes, CPRA executive committee, 3 December 1963, CPRA, MicroCPRA/1, series 22, GMA.

26 Minutes, CPRA executive committee, 6 July 1964, CPRA, MicroCPRA/1, series 22, GMA.

27 Minutes, CPRA executive committee, 7, 8, and 9 December 1964, CPRA, MicroCPRA/1, series 22, GMA.

28 Minutes, CPRA executive committee, 27 November 1965, CPRA, MicroCPRA/1, series 22, GMA.

29 Minutes, CPRA executive committee, 11 July 1968, CPRA, MicroCPRA/1, series 22, GMA. Conflicts between hoteliers and rodeo cowboys could seriously affect the ability of small towns to put on rodeos. Gwen Johansson, a barrel-racer and rodeo promoter in Hudson's Hope and Fort St. John, credited the role played by various rodeo associations in punishing cowboys who trashed rooms or left town without paying their hotel bills for making it easier to convince hoteliers to support local rodeos. Gwen Johansson, interview by author, 1 and 3 September 2002.

30 Minutes, CPRA executive, 13 July 1966, and Minutes, special CPRA executive committee meeting with Reg Kessler, 8 July 1967, CPRA, MicroCPRA/1, series 22, GMA.

31 Craig Levitt, "On the Road: Cassady, Kerouac and Images of Late Western Masculinity," in *Across the Great Divide: Cultures of Manhood in the American West,* ed. Matthew Basso, Laura McCall, and Dee Garceau (New York: Routledge, 2001), 211-30; Allen, *Rodeo Cowboys,* 45-46.

32 Minutes, CPRA executive committee, 8 November 1959, CPRA, MicroCPRA/1, series 22, GMA.

33 Gwen Johansson, interview by author, 1 and 3 September 2002.

34 Minutes, CPRA executive committee, 21 November 1961, CPRA, MicroCPRA/1, series 22, GMA.

35 Minutes, CPRA executive committee, 25 November 1967, CPRA, MicroCPRA/1, series 22, GMA.

36 Mary-Ellen Kelm, "Manly Contests: Rodeo Masculinities at the Calgary Stampede," *Canadian Historical Review* 90,4 (December 2009): 714.

37 Cliff Faulknor, *Turn Him Loose: Herman Linder, Canada's Mr. Rodeo* (Saskatoon: Western Producer Prairie Books, 1977), 55; *Protection of Animals Act, 1934* (U.K.), 24 and 25 Geo. V, c. 21, s. 1.

38 Guy Weadick to Jim Maxwell, 13 May 1950, CPRA, M-7072-16, series 1, GMA.

39 Ed Bergeron, president of the Vancouver Island Kinsmen Club of Victoria, to Jim Maxwell (CPRA), 11 September 1954 and 14 September 1954, and Jim Maxwell to Ed Bergeron, 18 September 1954, CPRA, M-7072-32, series 1, box 5, file 32, GMA.

40 Wilf Hodgson, Lower Fraser Valley Exhibition Society, to Paddy Brown, Secretary, CPRA, 26 January 1967, CPRA, M-7072-276, series 1, GMA.

41 Heather Ann Thompson, *Speaking Out: Activism and Protest in the 1960s and 1970s* (Boston: Prentice Hall, 2010), 52-55.

42 Minutes, CPRA executive committee, 9 December 1948 and 14 July 1949, CPRA, M-7072, MicroCPRA/1, series 22, GMA; Herman Linder to Jim Maxwell regarding calf roping, 14 August 1950, CPRA, M-7072-17 and M-7072-18, series 1, GMA.

43 Minutes, CPRA executive committee, 21 November 1961, CPRA, MicroCPRA/1, series 22, GMA; Guy Weadick to CPRA executive committee, 21 May 1951, CPRA, M-7072-18, series 1, GMA.

44 Minutes, CPRA executive committee, 7 December 1950, CPRA, M-7072, MicroCPRA/1, series 22, GMA; Minutes, CPRA, annual general meeting, 11 December 1964, CPRA, MicroCPRA/1, series 22, GMA.

45 Minutes, CPRA executive committee, 4 December 1949, CPRA, MicroCPRA/1, series 22, GMA.

46 Minutes, CPRA executive committee,, 27 November 1956, CPRA, MicroCPRA/1, series 22, GMA.

47 Minutes, CPRA executive special meeting, 24 November 1962, CPRA, MicroCPRA/1, series 22, GMA.

48 Minutes, CPRA executive committee, 10 July 1964, CPRA, MicroCPRA/1, series 22, GMA.

49 F.H. Ougden, SPCA secretary, letter to the editor, *Canadian Rodeo News*, 1 August 1964, 3.

50 Ralph Loosmore to Jim Maxwell, undated [1960], and Jim Maxwell to Hank Willard, 2 July 1960, CPRA, M-7072-47, series 1, box 7, file 47, GMA.

51 Minutes, CPRA executive committee, 1 October 1966 and 24 November 1966, CPRA, MicroCPRA/1, series 22, GMA.

52 Minutes, CPRA board of directors meeting with stampede managers, 24 November 1966, CPRA, MicroCPRA/1, series 22, GMA.

53 Karen R. Merrill, "Domesticated Bliss: Ranchers and Their Animals," in Basso, McCall, and Garceau, *Across the Great Divide,* 169-84.

54 For example, see Clem Gardner's discussion of the effects of the die-off of 1907-08, when thousands of cattle died of exposure in late spring snowstorms in southern Alberta. Clem Gardner, interview by Sheilagh Jamieson at Pirmez Creek, 24 November 1962, RCT-26-1, GMA.

55 Wilfred E. Gray (director), *Land of the Overlanders* (Victoria: British Columbia, Department of Recreation and Conservation Photographic Branch, 1965).

56 Minutes, Executive committee, 5 May 1933, CS 99.106, box 1, Calgary Stampede Archives, Calgary, Alberta.

57 Fredriksson, *American Rodeo,* 149-59; see also the rules prepared and accepted by representatives of the Rodeo Cowboys Association, formerly the Cowboys' Turtle Association (renamed in 1945) and renamed the Professional Rodeo Cowboys Association in 1975; and the American Humane Association, undated, CPRA, M-7072-25, series 1, box 5, file 31, GMA.

58 Harold Mandeville, editorial, *Canadian Rodeo News*, 1 August 1964, 3.

59 Ibid.

60 "The Rodeo Cowboy: Why Does He Do It?" *United Farmer,* July 1970, 1, CPRA, M-7072-385, series 9, "Press Kit Material," GMA. This point came up in my interviews with small-town rodeo promoters and competitors. Al Byer, interview by author, Merritt, 26 January 2002; Deb Fleet, interview by author, Fort St. John, BC, 3 September 2002.

61 Untitled CPRA press release, undated (probably 1962), CPRA, M-7072-385, series 9, "Press Kit Material," GMA.

62 Ibid.

63 "The Rodeo Cowboy," undated (late 1960s), CPRA, M-7072-385, series 9, "Press Kit Material," GMA.

64 Jacqueline M. Moore, *Cow Boys and Cattle Men: Class and Masculinities on the Texas Frontier, 1865-1900* (New York: New York University Press, 2010), 3, 7, 13, 215.

65 Dummitt, *Manly Modern,* 23.

66　K.A. Cuordileone, "'Politics in the Age of Anxiety': Cold War Political Culture and the Crisis in American Masculinity, 1949-1960," *Journal of American History* 87,2 (September 2000): 515-45.

67　Sandra Shields, "Rodeo Side Show," *Canadian Geographic,* July-August 2003, 66-74.

68　Anonymous writer to Bert Shepperd, undated, Rodeo file, Stockmen's Library and Archives (SLA), Cochrane, Alberta.

69　"Lethbridge 60th Anniversary, 1891-1951, Programme, Lethbridge and District Exhibition and Rodeo," 1951, Manuscript Collection, P19640605000, Galt Museum and Archives, Lethbridge.

70　Larry Beany to Blair Holland, 16 April 1945, CPRA, M-7072-2, series 1, GMA.

71　Newspaper clipping, 1998, clipping files, Rodeo, Surrey Museum and Archives (SMA), Surrey.

72　"Ten Seconds – That's Half a Week's Work," undated, CPRA, M-7072-384, series 9, "Press Kit Material," GMA.

73　Kathleen Mullen Sands, "'Got a Hole in Your Trailer?': Metaphor as Boundary Marker in Cowboy Culture," *Western Folklore* 49 (July 1990): 239-59.

74　Elizabeth Atwood Lawrence, *Rodeo: An Anthropologist Looks at the Wild and the Tame* (Chicago: University of Chicago Press, 1982), 112, 113.

75　Ibid., 117.

76　Author, field notes, Whispering Pines Rodeo, 21 June 2004.

77　Ibid.

78　David A. Poulsen, *Wild Ride! Three Journeys Down the Rodeo Road* (Toronto: Balmur, 2000), 13.

79　Ibid., 19.

80　Cindy Nickerson, clipping from the *Okotoks Western Wheel,* 1 October 1997, Rodeo personalities file, SLA.

81　Peter Iverson, *Riders of the West: Portraits from Indian Rodeo* (Vancouver: Greystone Books, 1999), 61.

82　Ibid., 56; Doug Cuthand (director), *The Gift of the Grandfathers* (Ottawa: National Film Board of Canada, 1997).

83　Gottfriedson family, interview by author, 24 August 2004; Chester Bruisehead, Charlie Bear, and John Lefthand, interview by Morgan Baillargeon, Calgary Stampede, 1995, Legends of Our Times, V95-0103, Canadian Museum of Civilization Archives (CMC), Gatineau.

84　Gottfriedson family, interview by author, 24 August 2004.

85　Deb Fleet, interview by author, 3 September 2002.

86　Gwen Johansson, interview by author, 1 and 3 September 2002.

87　Iverson, *Riders of the West,* 63.

88　Author, field notes, Whispering Pines Rodeo, 21 June 2004.

89　Duke LeBourdais, interview by author, Whispering Pines Reserve, 23 August 2004.

90　"Isabella Miller," undated, Rodeo personalities file, SLA; Minutes, Canadian Girls Rodeo Association, 1962-64, Canadian Girls Rodeo Association, M-7073-1, file 1, GMA.

91　"Rodeo Line-Up," *Cardston News,* 21 July 1955, 1.

92　Minutes, Executive committee, 3 June 1958, Foothills Cowboys Association, M-8266, file 6, GMA.

93　"1962 Barrel Racing Results," Southern Alberta Rodeo Circuit, CPRA, M-7072-101, series 2, GMA.

94　"Fall Fair and Rodeo," *Alaska Highway News,* 12 July 1962, 3; Programs 1966, 1967, Fall Fair and Rodeo Programs, MS 049 2001.041, South Peace Historical Society Archives, Dawson City, BC.

95　Minutes, Canadian Girls Rodeo Association (CGRA), 12 May 1964, and Minutes, CGRA, 11 January 1965, Canadian Girls Rodeo Association (CGRA), M-7703-1, file 1, GMA.

96　Roger Earl Haugen, "Indian Rodeo in British Columbia: A Structural-Functional Analysis" (master's thesis, University of Victoria, 1971), 28.

97　"Lethbridge and District Exhibition and Rodeo. July 20th – 25th, 1964," Manuscript Collection, acc. no. (UID) 19750009000, Galt Museum and Archives.

98　Minutes, CGRA, 11 January 1965, CGRA, M-7703-1, file 1, GMA.

99　"The End: Isabella Miller Haraga, 1941-2007," *Maclean's,* 19 February 2007, http://www.macleans.ca/.

100　Mary Lou LeCompte, *Cowgirls of the Rodeo: Pioneer Professional Athletes* (Urbana and Chicago: University of Illinois Press, 1993), 158-59.

101　Final circuit standings, Girls' International Rodeo League (GIRL), 1969, CPRA, M-7072-148, series 3, GMA.

102   "The End," *Maclean's*.
103   "Isabella Miller," undated, Rodeo personalities file, SLA.
104   "The End," *Maclean's*.
105   "News from BC," *Canadian Rodeo News*, 1 April 1964, 5.
106   Joan Perry, Legends of Our Times, Ethnology, E99.5, box 665, file 6, pt. 6, CMC.
107   Brenda Green, "Joan Perry," *Canadian Cowboy Country,* undated, 19-20. Thanks to Joan Perry for providing a photocopy of this article.
108   Gottfriedson family, interview by author, 24 August 2004.
109   Joan Perry, Legends of Our Times, Ethnology, E99.5, box 665, file 6, pt. 6, CMC; Green, "Joan Perry."
110   Gottfriedson family, interview by author, 24 August 2004.
111   Ibid.
112   "Official Program of Canada's First All-Girl Championship Rodeo and Race Meet, July 7, 1962, High River," SLA.
113   Minutes, CGRA, 10 March 1965, CGRA, M-7703-2, file 2, GMA. For more on Vold, see Siri Stevens, "Harry Vold," *Rocky Mountain Rodeo News*, 26 October 2002, http://www.teamroper.com/.
114   Minutes, CGRA, 10 March 1965, CGRA, M-7703-2, file 2, GMA.
115   Clipping from *Western People*, 24 February 1994, Rodeo personalities file, SLA.
116   "Official Program of Canada's First All-Girl Championship Rodeo and Race Meet, July 7, 1962, High River," SLA.
117   Quoted in Poulsen, *Wild Ride!* 26-27.
118   Barrel racing results, 1962, CPRA, M-7072-101, series 2, GMA.
119   Clipping from *Western People*, 24 February 1994, Rodeo personalities file, SLA.
120   Ibid.
121   Joan (Palmantier) Gentles, interview by author, 12 May 2004.
122   "Kaila Mussell: Cowgirl Original," http://www.kailamussell.com/.
123   "BCRA and Ts'il?os Rodeo Presents the 32nd Annual Nemiah Valley Rodeo and Mountain Race," program, 1 August 2009, in author's possession.
124   Minutes, CGRA, 28 January 1963, CGRA, M-7703-1, file 1, GMA; Gwen Johansson, interview by author, 1 and 3 September 2002. Women were fined if their hats fell off during a race. See Minutes, CGRA, 28 April 1964, CGRA, M-7703-1, file 1, GMA.
125   Minutes, CGRA, 12 September 1970, CGRA, M-7703-7, file 7, GMA. In 1964 two women were fined for arguing with officials. Minutes, CGRA, 28 April 1964, CGRA, M-7073-1, file 1, GMA.
126   Minutes, CGRA, 12 May 1964, CGRA, M-7703-1, file 1, GMA.
127   Minutes, CGRA, 28 April 1964, CGRA, M-7703-1, file 1, GMA.
128   "Out of the Barrel," *Canadian Rodeo News*, 1 May 1965, 7.
129   "Out of the Barrel," *Canadian Rodeo News*, 1 June 1964, 7.
130   Allen Guttmann, *From Ritual to Record: The Nature of Modern Sports* (New York: Columbia University Press, 1978).
131   Iverson, *Riders of the West*, 51.
132   Cuthand, *The Gift of the Grandfathers*.
133   Morgan Baillargeon and Leslie Tepper, *Legends of Our Times: Native Cowboy Life* (Vancouver: UBC Press, 1998), 2.
134   Rosamond Norbury, *Behind the Chutes: The Mystique of the Rodeo Cowboy* (Vancouver: Whitecap Books, 1992), 7.
135   Poulsen, *Wild Ride!* 82.
136   Reeve, *Hard Rider.*
137   Quoted in Iverson, *Riders of the West*, 57-58.
138   Fred Gladstone, interview by Charles Ursenbach, 4 June 1975, Fred Gladstone Fonds, M-6049, file 18, GMA.
139   "Jim Gladstone," undated, Rodeo personalities file, SLA; "Canada's Newest Hero," *Rodeo Sports News*, 8 February 1978, 3.
140   Ron West, interview by Mark Sarrazin, 8 August 2003, in author's possession.
141   Duke LeBourdais, interview by author, 23 August 2003.

142   "Jim Gladstone," undated, Rodeo personalities file, SLA; Hyland quoted in "Canada's Newest Hero," *Rodeo Sports News*, 8 February 1978, 3; Joan (Palmantier) Gentles, interview by author, Williams Lake, 12 May 2004.

143   Quoted in Poulsen, *Wild Ride!* 83.

144   Joan Burbick, *Rodeo Queens and the American Dream* (New York: Public Affairs, 2002), 141.

145   Fred Gladstone, interview by Charles Ursenbach, 4 June 1975, Fred Gladstone Fonds, M-4211, file 18, GMA.

146   Gottfriedson family, interview by author, 24 August 2004.

147   Ibid.

148   Joan (Palmantier) Gentles, interview by author, Williams Lake, 12 May 2004.

149   Al Byer, interview by author, Merritt, 26 January 2002.

150   Linnell family, interview by Mark Sarrazin, 100 Mile House, 7 July 2002, in author's possession.

151   Lil and Bill Evans, interview by Lorna Townsend, Fraser Lake, 14 May 2004, in author's possession.

152   Haugen, "Indian Rodeo," 48-49.

153   Lawrence, *Rodeo.*

154   Author, field notes, VIP grandstand, Williams Lake Stampede, 2 July 2001.

155   Author, field notes, Chilcotin, 3 August 2002. In particular, one rancher said that catching and branding wild horses, as in the *Hard Rider* scene, would probably have resulted in the death of the colts who followed their mothers into the corral only to be kicked by the horses as they fought the ropes and brand.

156   Green, "Joan Perry," 19-20; Gottfriedson family, interview by author, 24 August 2004.

157   Quoted in Poulsen, *Wild Ride!* 67.

158   Rick Blacklaws and Diana French, *Ranchland: British Columbia's Cattle Country* (Madeira Park, BC: Harbour, 2001), 51.

159   Quoted in Poulsen, *Wild Ride!* 71.

160   Ibid., 76-80.

161   Quoted in ibid., 80.

162   Author, field notes, Whispering Pines, 21 June 2004.

163   Burbick, *Rodeo Queens,* 66-72.

164   Baillargeon and Tepper, *Legends of Our Times,* 22; Duke LeBourdais funeral bulletin, 26 August 2005.

Chapter 5: Going Pro

1   Paul St. Pierre, *Breaking Smith's Quarterhorse* (Toronto: Ryerson Press, 1966), 92, 106.

2   Elizabeth Furniss, *The Burden of History: Colonialism and the Frontier Myth in a Rural Canadian Community* (Vancouver: UBC Press, 1999), 49.

3   David Dinwoodie, *Reserve Memories: Power of the Past in a Chilcotin Community* (Lincoln and London: University of Nebraska Press, 2002), 17; John Sutton Lutz, *Makúk: A New History of Aboriginal-White Relations* (Vancouver: UBC Press, 2008), 269.

4   Paul Voisey, *High River and the Times: An Alberta Community and Its Weekly Newspaper* (Edmonton: University of Alberta Press, 2004), 180.

5   Clipping, *Calgary Herald,* undated (1949), Canadian Professional Rodeo Association (CPRA), M-7072-13, series 1, Glenbow Museum Archives (GMA), Calgary.

6   Herman Linder to CPRA, reporting results at Bassano Stampede, 4 July 1954, CPRA, M-7072-237, series 4, box 5, file 31, GMA.

7   "Cloverdale Rodeo," *Surrey/North Delta Leader,* 19 May 1999, unpaginated, Clipping files, Surrey Museum and Archives, Surrey.

8   Correspondence, 18 July 1946-30 April 1947, CPRA, M-7072-6, series 1, GMA.

9   Jake Twoyoungmen to CPRA, 15 June 1946, CPRA, M-7072-5, series 1, GMA.

10   CPRA, M-7072-231 to M-7072-316, series 4, GMA.

11   Michael Dawson, *Selling British Columbia: Tourism and Consumer Culture, 1890-1970* (Vancouver: UBC Press, 2004); Patricia Jasen, *Wild Things: Nature, Culture, and Tourism in Ontario, 1790-1914* (Toronto: University of Toronto, 1995); Ian McKay, *The Quest of the Folk: Antimodernism and Cultural*

Selection in Twentieth-Century Nova Scotia (Montreal and Kingston: McGill-Queen's University Press, 1994); Larry Nespar, "Simulating Culture: Being Indian for the Tourists in Lac du Flambeau's Wa-Swa-Gon Indian Bowl," *Ethnohistory* 50,3 (Summer 2003): 447-61; Michael Harkin, "Staged Encounters: Postmodern Tourism and Aboriginal People," *Ethnohistory* 50,3 (Summer 2003): 575-85; Patricia Nelson Limerick, "Seeing and Being Seen: Tourism in the American West," in *Over the Edge: Remapping the American West,* ed. Valerie J. Matsumoto and Blake Allmendinger (Berkeley: University of California Press, 1999), 15-32; Colleen O'Neill, "Rethinking Modernity and the Discourse of Development in American Indian History, an Introduction," in *Native Pathways: American Indian Culture and Economic Development in the Twentieth century,* ed. Brian Hosmer and Colleen O'Neill (Boulder: University Press of Colorado, 2004), 15; Daniel H. Usner, *Indian Work: Language and Livelihood in Native American History* (Cambridge, MA: Harvard University Press, 2009); Daniel J. Walkowitz and Lisa Maya Knauer, *Contested Histories in Public Space: Memory, Race and Nation* (Durham: Duke University Press, 2009); Philip J. Deloria, *Playing Indian* (New Haven and London: Yale University Press, 1998), 115; Paige Raibmon, *Authentic Indians: Episodes of Encounter from the Late-Nineteenth Century Northwest Coast* (Durham: Duke University Press, 2005), 6; Furniss, *Burden of History,* 15.

12 Dawson, *Selling British Columbia,* 161-64.
13 "Williams Lake: Heart of the Cariboo," *Beautiful British Columbia,* Summer 1961, 2, 6.
14 Ibid. The claim that contestants did not compete for money was inaccurate. By 1961 the Williams Lake Rodeo was a pro event with prizes set by the CPRA.
15 Ibid.
16 "Lethbridge and District Exhibition and Rodeo, Program, 1951," Manuscript Collection acc. no. (UID) P19640605000, Galt Museum and Archives, Lethbridge.
17 Ibid.; James Clifford, *Routes: Travel and Translation in the Late Twentieth Century* (Cambridge, MA: Harvard University Press, 1997), 218; Paul Gilroy, *The Black Atlantic: Modernity and Double Consciousness* (Harvard: Harvard University Press, 1993), 3; Kathleen Mullen Sands, "'Got a Hole in Your Trailer?': Metaphor as Boundary Marker in Cowboy Culture," *Western Folklore* 49 (July 1990): 239-59.
18 Voisey, *High River and the Times,* 191.
19 Guy Weadick to Jim Maxwell, 17 December 1946, CPRA, M-7072-10, series 1, GMA.
20 "They Did It!" (editorial), *High River Times,* 2 June 1966, 2; Dee Camp, "Stampede: 70 Years of Action and Counting," *Omak Chronicle,* 11 August 2003, 3.
21 "Corrals, Chutes, Fences Take Form," *High River Times,* 6 June 1946, 1; "Rodeo Promotes Volunteer Service for Advance Work," *High River Times,* 9 May 1946, 1; "Volunteer Help Getting Rodeo Grounds in Shape," *High River Times,* 30 May 1946, 1.
22 "Rodeo Planned," *Kamloops Sentinel,* 14 June 1950, 7.
23 Clipping, *Laketown News,* 30 June 1982, Stampede files, box 1, Williams Lake Library (WLL), Williams Lake.
24 John W. Bennett with Seena B. Kohl, "Photographs from the Northern Plains Cultural Ecology Project and the Maple Creek Regional Research Project, 1961-1975" (1977), 168-69, Esplanade Archives (EA), Medicine Hat; Voisey, *High River and the Times,* 193; "Bradley's Paces Alberta Growth; Business Reflects Way of West," *High River Times,* 3 May 1962, 1; High River program, 1946, Museum of the High Wood, High River.
25 Furniss, *Burden of History,* 169.
26 "Official Program, Williams Lake Centennial Stampede, June 28-30th-July 1st, 1958," Curatorial files, Museum of Ranching and Rodeo (MRR), Williams Lake.
27 Clipping, "The Life of the Pioneer," Fall Fair and Rodeo Programs, MS 049 2001.041, South Peace Historical Society Archives, Dawson Creek, BC.
28 "Rodeo Scheme Turned Down by Council," *Kamloops Sentinel,* 19 September 1945, 3.
29 High River Rodeo program, 1946, Museum of the High Wood, High River.
30 "Those Early Stampedes," Fall Fair and Rodeo Programs, MS 049 2001.041, South Peace Historical Society Archives.
31 "The Future of Stampedes" (editorial), *High River Times,* 3 August 1950, 3.
32 "Progress 1950," Kamloops and District special edition, *Kamloops Sentinel,* 28 June 1950, 1.

33   Mrs. Ollie Norberg (Williams Lake Stampede Association secretary) to CPRA, 5 March 1948, CPRA, M-7072-10, series 1, GMA.

34   "Competition Said Keen in Rodeo at Coleman," *Calgary Herald,* 11 July 1960, 18.

35   "Rodeo Results," *Cardston News,* 28 July 1955, 1; "District Cowboys Rating High in Rodeos to Date," *High River Times,* 9 June 1966, 1.

36   Correspondence, 1949-52, Cremona Stampede Fonds, M-5623, GMA.

37   Jim Maxwell to Dave Powell (Williams Lake Stampede Association secretary), 7 March 1960, CPRA, M-7072-315, series 4, box 7, file 44, GMA.

38   Gwen Johansson, interview by author, Hudson's Hope, 1 and 3 September 2002.

39   Jim Maxwell to Bert Gibb, Fort Macleod Stampede Association, 27 September 1955, CPRA, M-7072-258, series, 4, box 5, file 34, GMA.

40   Williams Lake Stampede Association to CPRA, 25 March 1948, CPRA, M-7072-10, series 1, GMA.

41   J. Dillon to Blair Holland, 12 January 1945, CPRA, M-7072-2, series 1, GMA.

42   Williams Lake Stampede Association to CPRA, 25 March 1948, CPRA, M-7072-10, series 1, GMA; Williams Lake Stampede Association to CPRA, saying that it will withdraw from the CPRA while it works to rebuild, 7 March 1949, CPRA, M-7072-13, GMA.

43   Taber Rodeo Committee to Blair Holland, 14 May 1945, CPRA, M-7072-2, series 1, GMA.

44   Secretary, Saskatchewan Rodeo Association (signature illegible), to CPRA, 23 May 1945, CPRA, M-7072-5, series 1, GMA.

45   Williams Lake Stampede Association to CPRA, 5 March 1948, CPRA, M-7072-10, series 1, GMA.

46   Swift Current Frontier Days to CPRA, 23 May 1945, CPRA, M-7072-2, series 1, GMA.

47   Henry Carson to CPRA, 28 January 1950, CPRA, M-7072-15, series 1, GMA.

48   Harry Shuttleworth to CPRA, 11 June 1947, CPRA, M-7072-8, series 1, GMA.

49   W.A. Palmer to CPRA, 30 January 1959, CPRA, M-7072-266, series 4, box 6, file 37, GMA.

50   Fort Macleod Rodeo Association to CPRA, 25 May 1945, CPRA, M-7072-5, series 1, GMA.

51   Jake Twoyoungmen to CPRA, 15 June 1946, CPRA, M-7072-5, series 1, GMA.

52   Mrs. Dave Powell to CPRA, 31 May 1960, CPRA, M-7072-315, series 4, box 7, file 45, GMA; CPRA to Henry Bowe, 29 July 1965, CPRA, M-7072-315, series 4, box 7, file 47, GMA.

53   Joe Young Pine to Jim Maxwell, CPRA, 20 January 1948, CPRA, M-7072-10, series 1, GMA.

54   Stampede program, 1967, Stampede files, box 1, WLL.

55   "Welcome from the High River Rodeo and Annual Fair Committee," *High River Times,* 1 July 1948, 1.

56   "About 7000 People Throng Town for Parade and Rodeo," *High River Times,* 10 July 1947, 1.

57   Guy Weadick, "Ensure Success of Rodeo with Generous Prize List, Well-Classified Contests," *High River Times,* 19 June 1947, 1.

58   Guy Weadick, "HR Rodeo on July 1-2, to Have New Features," *High River Times,* 13 May 1948, 1.

59   "Afternoon-Evening Rodeo Roping – Riding – Branding," *High River Times,* 14 July 1949, 7.

60   "Chuck Wagons, Challenge Branding Racing, Rodeo, Horse Show Are Tops," *High River Times,* 10 July 1952, 8.

61   See, for example, "Thursday Rodeo Events Bring Top Entertainment," *High River Times,* 16 July 1953, 7, and "Appaloosa Tops Annual High River Horse Sale," *High River Times,* 18 June 1959, 8.

62   "Great Crowd at Rodeo," *High River Times,* 6 July 1950, 3; "Two Day Rodeo Draws Large Crowds – Fine Show," *High River Times,* 5 July 1951, 3.

63   "Town Topics," *High River Times,* 14 July 1949, 3.

64   "See HR Rodeo in Television," *High River Times,* 15 June 1951, 3.

65   "New York Camera Men at Rodeo," *High River Times,* 15 July 1948, 3.

66   "Pin Money from Tourist Trade," *High River Times,* 15 July 1948, 1.

67   "Good Profits from Rodeo Will Be Well Distributed," *High River Times,* 13 August 1953, 1.

68   Minute books, High River Agricultural Society, 1909-65, High River Agricultural Society, M-6669, GMA.

69   "A Good Celebration," *High River Times,* 10 July 1952, 2.

70   "Locally-Produced Stage Show Each Night," *High River Times,* 24 June 1954, 3.

71   "Rodeo Notes," *High River Times,* 10 July 1947, 7.

72   "Prizewinners among Indians," *High River Times,* 13 July 1950, 7.

73   "About 8000 People Gather for Big Rodeo and Parade," *High River Times*, 7 July 1949, 5.

74   "The Parade" (editorial), *High River Times*, 11 July 1957, 2.

75   "Indian Dances Evening Rodeo Feature," *High River Times*, 10 June 1954, 1.

76   "Postponed H.R. Frontier Days Bring Parade and Many Rodeo Thrills," *High River Times*, 12 July 1956, 1, 3.

77   "Woman's Uprising" (editorial), *High River Times*, 1 July 1954, 2.

78   For example, the death of Nakoda Jonas Rider while seeking the skills of a faith healer in Calgary permitted High River residents to contemplate how the sixty-five-year old elder was simultaneously a traditionalist, a well-regarded ranch hand who had worked on the Bar U for over forty years, and a well-known rodeo competitor who took the 1923 calf-roping championship. "Jonas Rider Was Once Champion Rider," *High River Times*, 18 August 1955, 8; "Jonas Rider Dies in Calgary," *High River Times*, 11 August 1955, 7.

79   "District Gift Is Cherished," *High River Times*, 11 July 1946, 1; "Will You Join Big Parade, High River Rodeo on July 3?" *High River Times*, 20 June 1946, 1; Gissing's own work plays with this balance, portraying the Alberta landscape at various stages of development. His 1951 painting *Yesterday Today and Tomorrow* depicts a prairie schooner travelling toward the city of Calgary, which looms above it as it was in 1951. Roland Gissing: The People's Painter, http://www.rolandgissing.com/.

80   See, for example, "Herb Miller and Men with Whom He Rode the Range," *High River Times*, 26 June 1947, 1; "Meet Another Old Timer, Billy Henry Came in 1885," *High River Times*, 3 July 1947, 1.

81   Charles Clark, "The Old Timer," *High River Times*, 10 July 1947, 2.

82   "50 Years District Progress at Rodeo Days Here July 1-2," *High River Times*, 24 June 1948, 1.

83   "H. River Park Is Dedicated in Impressive Ceremony," *High River Times*, 5 July 1951, 1.

84   "Mrs. Ruth Hanson Is Honor Guest of Rodeo Days," *High River Times*, 24 June 1954, 1.

85   "Good Old Days," *High River Times*, 1 July 1948, 1.

86   Sarah Carter, "Transnational Perspectives in the History of Great Plains Women," *American Review of Canadian Studies* 33,4 (December 2003): 585; Nupur Chaudhuri and Margaret Strobel, "Introduction," in *Western Women and Imperialism: Complicity and Resistance*, ed. Nupur Chaudhuri and Margaret Strobel (Bloomington & Indianapolis: Indiana University Press, 1992), 3-5.

87   "I Rode with Weadick Eliciting Response," *High River Times*, 26 June 1958, 1; "Weadick's Work as a Showman," *High River Times*, 3 July 1958, 1.

88   "Roping Club Plans Weekly Practice Starting May 4th," *High River Times*, 1 May 1947, 8.

89   "Black Diamond Riding and Roping Club," *High River Times*, 20 May 1948, 6.

90   "First 'Little Britches' Rodeo Provides Thrills for Big Crowd," *High River Times*, 21 May 1959, 1; "Unique Little Britches Rodeo Slated for Monday," *High River Times*, 14 May 1959, 3.

91   "And Another Winner," *High River Times*, 28 May 1959, 6.

92   "Little Britches Ride High," *High River Times*, 26 May 1960, 1.

93   Minute book, High River Agricultural Association, 12 December 1964, High River Agricultural Association, M-6669, GMA.

94   "Little Britches" (editorial), *High River Times*, 6 May 1965, 2.

95   "They Did It!" (editorial), *High River Times*, 2 June 1966, 2.

96   "Little Britches 1966 Statement," *High River Times*, 9 June 1966, 7.

97   "Girl Rodeo Events Worth $3800," *High River Times*, 10 May 1962, 6.

98   "All-Girl Rodeo Here Will Kick Off Stampede," *High River Times*, 28 June 1962, 1.

99   "Town Co-operation Praised by CBRA," *High River Times*, 12 July 1962, 1.

100 The association's secretary in 1957, for example, was Mrs. Olive Matheson, the former Ollie Curtis, mountain-racer of the pre-war stampedes.

101 Mrs. Ollie Norberg to Jim Maxwell, 25 March 1948, CPRA, M-7072-10, series 1, GMA.

102 "Victim of Progress," clipping from unknown Calgary newspaper, 1948, CPRA, M-7072-13, series 1, GMA.

103 Harold Jordon (Williams Lake Stampede Association secretary) to CPRA, 7 March 1949, CPRA, M-7072-13, series 1, GMA; "Official Program, Williams Lake Stampede, Three Days of Fun, June 13, 14, 15, 1951," and "Williams Lake Stampede Program, June 12, 13, 14, 1952," MRR.

104 Clipping, *Vancouver Province*, 25 March 1948, Stampede files, box 1, WLL; Clipping (1956), Stampede files, box 1, WLL; CPRA to Mrs. Dave Powell, 13 June 1960, CPRA, M-7072-315, series 4, box

7, file 45, GMA; "Official Program, 31st Annual Williams Lake Stampede, June 28, 29th and July 1st 1957," MRR.

105   "Williams Lake 30th Stampede," 29 June 1956, MRR.
106   British Columbia, Department of Recreation and Conservation, *Princess in Wonderland* (Victoria: Department of Recreation and Conservation, Photographic Branch, 1958), B.C. Centennial Committee, GR1448, box 24, Williams Lake file, 1958, British Columbia Archives, Victoria.
107   "Williams Lake Centennial Stampede, June 28th-30th-July 1st, 1958," official program, MRR.
108   "Official Program – Williams Lake Stampede, 1967," Stampede files, box 1, WLL. The 1977 program stated that a "subtle change" occurred in post-1946 stampedes: "The days of it being a strictly Cariboo Stampede were over. Tourists and visitors began to make up the greater part of the spectators and professional rodeo circuit cowboys heard of Williams Lake and arrived to take part in the competition." "Official Program – Williams Lake Stampede, 1977," MRR.
109   See Blaine Allan, "CBC Television Series, 1952-1982," Queen's Film and Media, http://www.film.queensu.ca/.
110   "Official Program – Williams Lake Stampede, 1960," MRR.
111   Ibid.
112   "Official Program – Williams Lake Stampede, 1964," MRR.
113   "Official Program – Williams Lake Stampede, 1970," MRR.
114   Ibid.
115   "Official Program – Williams Lake Stampede, 1971," MRR; Bernice Prior, quoted in newspaper clipping, undated, Stampede files, box 1, WLL.
116   "Keys of Village Presented: Capacity Crowd at Arena Sees Queen Crowning," *Williams Lake Tribune,* 15 June 1950, 5.
117   "Crown Stampede Queens before Large Audience," *Williams Lake Tribune,* 21 June 1951, 1.
118   "Official Program – Williams Lake Stampede, 1958," MRR; Newspaper clipping, undated, Stampede files, box 1, WLL.
119   "Judy Groundwater White, Former Queen, Interviewed," *Williams Lake Tribune,* 1 July 1976, 13.
120   "Official Program – Williams Lake Stampede, 1958," MRR.
121   Mrs. A.G. Isnardy to editor, *Williams Lake Tribune,* 27 May 1964, 4.
122   Mrs. R. Ranniger to editor, *Williams Lake Tribune,* 10 June 1964, 4.
123   In 1972, for example, Aboriginal "nationalities" were listed for two contestants: Violet Boyd of Nazko was given as Carrier, and Helen Charlie of Soda Creek was described as Shuswap. The other eight contestants all appear to be white. "Official Program – Williams Lake Stampede, 1972," MRR.
124   Joan (Palmantier) Gentles, interview by author, Williams Lake, 12 May 2004; "Joan BC Indian Princess," newspaper clipping, undated, Personality Files, MRR; "Joan Crowned Canada's Best," *Williams Lake Tribune,* 2 August 1967, 1; "Friendship Centre Her First Project," *News of Williams Lake and the Cariboo,* 2 August 1967, 1.
125   "Official Program – Williams Lake Stampede, 1970," MRR; "Official Program – Williams Lake Stampede, 1973," MRR.
126   "Against the Rules: Queen Candidate Rapped for 'Illegal' Speech," *Williams Lake Tribune,* 26 June 1975, 1.
127   Colleen Ballerino Cohen, Richard Wilk, and Beverly Stoeltje, "Introduction: Beauty Queens on the Global Stage," in *Beauty Queens on the Global Stage: Gender, Contests, and Power,* ed. Colleen Ballerino Cohen, Richard Wilk, and Beverly Stoeltje (New York and London: Routledge, 1996), 8-11.
128   "Stampede Queen's Reign Had Its 'Ups and Downs,'" *Williams Lake Tribune,* 26 June 1975, 19; Beverly Stoeltje, "The Snake Charmer Queen: Ritual, Competition and Signification in an American Festival," in Cohen, Wilk, and Stoeltje, *Beauty Queens,* 13-30.
129   Michael Ames, "Fountain in a Modern Economy: A Study of Social Structure, Land Use and Business Enterprise in a British Columbia Indian Community" (BA essay, University of British Columbia, 1956), 2-4, 57.
130   Bridget Moran, *Stoney Creek Woman (Sai'k'uz Ts'eke): The Story of Mary John* (Vancouver: Tillicum, 1988), 111-22.
131   For a clear depiction of the antipathy between settlers and Tsilhquot'in, Secwepemc, and Dakelh in the Cariboo-Chilcotin in the 1970s, 1980s and 1990s, see Terry Glavin, *This Ragged Place: Travels*

across the Landscape (Vancouver: New Star Books, 1996), 122-70. On the same period, see Lorne Dufour, *Jacob's Prayer: Loss and Resilience at Alkali Lake* (Halfmoon Bay, BC: Caitlin Press, 2009). See also Furniss, *Burden of History,* 104-37.

132 Hilary Place, *Dog Creek: A Place in the Cariboo* (Surrey: Heritage House, 1999), 240-42.
133 "Official Program – Williams Lake Stampede, 1964," MRR.
134 Place, *Dog Creek,* 246-48.
135 "Official Program – Williams Lake Stampede, 1970," MRR.
136 "Official Program – Williams Lake Stampede, 1971," MRR.
137 Ibid.
138 Jean Barman, "Aboriginal Women on the Streets of Victoria: Rethinking Transgressive Sexuality during the Colonial Encounter," in *Contact Zones: Aboriginal and Settler Women in Canada's Colonial Past,* ed. Katie Pickles and Myra Rutherdale (Vancouver: UBC Press, 2005), 205-27.
139 "Official Program – Williams Lake Stampede, 1998," MRR.
140 "Official Program – Williams Lake Stampede, 1977," MRR; "Official Program – Williams Lake stampede, 1980," MRR.
141 "Official Program – Williams Lake Stampede, 1992," MRR.
142 "Official Program – Williams Lake Stampede, 1995," MRR.
143 Ibid.
144 Liz Twan, "Rodeo History: The Lady on Red," Williams Lake Stampede, http://www.williamslake stampede.com/.
145 St. Pierre, *Breaking Smith's Quarterhorse,* 37.

Chapter 6: Where the Cowboys Are Indians

1 *Wild Horses, Unconquered People* (Vancouver: Omni Film Productions, 2002).
2 Lauren Berlant, *The Female Complaint: The Unfinished Business of Sentimentality in American Culture* (Durham and London: Duke University Press, 2008), 10.
3 A reserve rodeo is one organized on reserve and that may or may not be associated with any rodeo organization. In this chapter, I apply the term "Indian" to rodeos and participants in rodeos that belong to the various Indian rodeo cowboy organizations, including the IRCA and the Western Indian Rodeo and Exhibition Association (WIREA). I continue to use "Aboriginal" in general references to indigenous people.
4 Ottawa determined Indian status patrilineally: For example, a status woman who married a non-status man lost her status, and their children did not acquire it. Contrarily, a non-status woman who married a status man gained it as did their children. Treaties in the Canadian West also encouraged record keeping regarding who was and who was not included in the treaty and hence who could receive treaty payments, thus providing a secondary system by which Indian status was determined.
5 Lil and Bill Evans, interview by Lorna Townsend, Fraser Lake, 5 May 2004, and Bill Evans Jr., interview by Lorna Townsend, Fraser Lake, 6 June 2004.
6 "Eden Valley Holds Stampede," *High River Times,* 10 August 1950, 7; Prize list for the 1953 Stoney Indian Rodeo, Canadian Professional Rodeo Association (CPRA), M-7072-301, series 4, file 27, Glenbow Museum Archives (GMA), Calgary; Prize list for the 1951 Stoney Indian Rodeo, CPRA, M-7072-301, series 4, file 17, GMA.
7 Anthony M. Millan to Jim Maxwell, 24 July 1946, CPRA, M-7072-6, series 1, GMA.
8 E. Cousineau to CPRA, 23 August 1952, CPRA, M-7072-24, series 1, GMA.
9 "Montana Rider Wins," *Calgary Herald,* 4 July 1956, 10; John Lefthand to Jim Maxwell, regarding the rodeo at Morley, 6 March 1953, CPRA, M-7072-25, series 1, GMA.
10 Leslie Tepper, interviews and field notes, Omak parade, Omak Stampede suicide race, undated, Legends of Our Times ethnology files, V97-0886, Canadian Museum of Civilization Archives (CMC), Gatineau; Doug Cox with the Keremeos Elks Lodge, no. 56, *Rodeo Roots: 50 Years of Rodeo in the Similkameen and Okanagan* (Penticton: Skookum, 1988), 46, 76; Clipping, *Williams Lake Tribune,* 1988, Stampede files, box 1, Williams Lake Library (WLL), Williams Lake; Roger Earl Haugen, "Indian Rodeo in British Columbia: A Structural-Functional Analysis" (master's thesis, University of Victoria, 1971).

11   Jim Maxwell to Buster Ivory of the Rodeo Cowboys Association, 6 June 1956, CPRA, M-7072-259, series 4, box 6, file 34, GMA; W.A. Palmer (Heffley Creek) to Jim Maxwell, CPRA, 30 January 1959, CPRA, M-7072-266, series 4, box 6, file 37, GMA; Minutes, executive committee, 9 November 1963 and 18 August 1965, Foothills Cowboys Association, M-8266, file 11, GMA; Minutes, executive committee, 13 February 1959, Foothills Cowboys Association, M-8266, file 7, GMA.

12   Patricia C. Albers and Beatrice Medicine, "Some Reflections on Nearly Forty Years on the Northern Plains Powwow Circuit," in *Powwow,* ed. Clyde Ellis, Luke Eric Lassiter, and Gary H. Dunham (Lincoln: University of Nebraska Press, 2005), 26-45.

13   Newspaper clipping, August 1971, Banff Indian Days collection, M62, Whyte Museum of the Rockies, Banff, Alberta.

14   Hugh Dempsey, "The Indians and the Stampede," in *Icon, Brand and Myth: The Calgary Stampede,* ed. Max Foran (Edmonton: University of Alberta Press, 2008), 47-72.

15   Elizabeth Furniss, *The Burden of History: Colonialism and the Frontier Myth in a Rural Canadian Community* (Vancouver: UBC Press, 1999), 170.

16   Author, field notes, meeting with elders, Douglas Lake Reserve, 12 July 2003.

17   Todd Buffalo, interview by Morgan Baillargeon, Hobbema, Alberta, undated [1992], Rodeo and Ranching collection (Legends of Our Times), V95-0478, CMC.

18   Monty Palmantier, interview by author, 25 August 2005.

19   Peter Iverson, *Riders of the West: Portraits from Indian Rodeo* (Vancouver: Greystone Books, 1999), 14-15.

20   Willard Martin, "The Williams Lake Indian Stampede Association," 1967, Stampede files, box 1, WLL.

21   Evans Daychief to Fred Gladstone, 17 March 1989, Fred Gladstone Fonds, M-6049, box 2, file 9a, GMA.

22   Fred Gladstone, interview by Charles Ursenbach, 4 June 1975, Fred Gladstone Fonds, M-6049, file 18, GMA; Haugen, "Indian Rodeo," 35.

23   "The 1981 Indian National Finals Rodeo," program, Fred Gladstone Fonds, M-6049, box 2, file 22, GMA.

24   Gottfriedson family, interview by author, 24 August 2004.

25   Willard Martin, "The Williams Lake Indian Stampede Association," 1967, Stampede files, box 1, WLL; quoted in Iverson, *Riders of the West,* 26.

26   Morgan Baillargeon and Leslie Tepper, *Legends of Our Times: Native Cowboy Life* (Vancouver: UBC Press, 1998), 200; Morgan Baillargeon, "Native Cowboys on the Canadian Plains: A Photo Essay," *Agricultural History* 69,4 (Fall 1995): 547-62.

27   Cecil Currie, interview by Morgan Baillargeon, Calgary, 1995, Rodeo and Ranching collection (Legends of Our Times), V95-0137, CMC.

28   "Indian Rodeo Cowboys' Association Looks Forward to Successful Season," *Kainai News,* 15 April 1970, 15. The current name of the organization is the Indian Rodeo Cowboy Association, which is what I am using.

29   See, for example, a 1968 ad giving dates for all-Indian rodeo in *Kainai News,* 15 July 1968, 15.

30   "New Rodeo Association," *Kainai News,* 17 June 1973, 8.

31   "Western Indian Rodeo Association," 1980, Ethnology files, Legends of Our Times, E99.5, box 665, file 5, CMC.

32   "The 1981 Indian National Finals Rodeo," program, Fred Gladstone Fonds, M-6049, box 2, file 22, GMA.

33   Indian Rodeo Cowboy Association, "1970 Rules and By-Laws," CPRA, M-7072-407, series 11, GMA; Baillargeon, "Native Cowboys," 547-62.

34   Indian Rodeo Cowboy Association, "1970 Rules and By-Laws," CPRA, M-7072-407, series 11, GMA.

35   Untitled, *Kainai News,* 15 May 1972, 8; Cecil Currie, interview by Morgan Baillargeon, Calgary, 1995, Rodeo and Ranching collection (Legends of Our Times), V95-0137, CMC.

36   Doug Cuthand (director), *The Gift of the Grandfathers* (Ottawa: National Film Board of Canada, 1997).

37   Baillargeon and Tepper, *Legends of Our Times,* 199.

38   Hugh Dempsey, interview by author, 21 August 2003.

39 Ruth Scalplock, interview by Pauline Dempsey at the Dempsey home, Calgary, 14 April 1993, Interviews for Childhood Exhibit, M-9204-11, GMA.

40 Jan Penrose, "When All the Cowboys Are Indians: The Nature of Race in All-Indian Rodeo," *Annals of the Association of American Geographers* 93,3 (September 2003): 699.

41 Gerry Attachie, speaking about the Doig River Rodeo. Dane Wajich, Dane-zaa Stories and Songs: Dreamers and the Land, *Contact the People* (Garry Oker, 2001) http://www.virtualmuseum.ca/.

42 Marilyn Burgess, "Canadian 'Range Wars': Struggles over Indian Cowboys," *Canadian Journal of Communication* 18,3 (1993): 355-72.

43 Quoted in David Campion, "Cowboys and Indians," 53 (Summer 2004), *Geist*, http://www.geist. com/.

44 Jack Krieberg, Leroy Philip, and Michael Whiteman, interview by Morgan Baillargeon, Cheyenne, Wyoming, 1996, Rodeo and Ranching collection (Legends of Our Times), V96-0658, CMC.

45 Homi K. Bhabha, *The Location of Culture* (New York and London: Routledge, 1994), 148.

46 Colleen O'Neill, "Rethinking Modernity and the Discourse of Development in American Indian History, an Introduction," in *Native Pathways: American Indian Culture and Economic Development in the Twentieth Century*, ed. Brian Hosmer and Colleen O'Neill (Boulder: University Press of Colorado, 2004), 11-12.

47 Cuthand, *The Gift of the Grandfathers.*

48 "The 1981 Indian National Finals Rodeo," program, Fred Gladstone Fonds, M-6049, box 2, file 22, GMA.

49 Bill Cohen, ed., *Stories and Images about What the Horse Has Done for Us: An Illustrated History of Okanagan Ranching and Rodeo* (Penticton: Theytus Books, 1998), 34-36; Baillargeon and Tepper, *Legends of Our Times*, 51-53.

50 Ron and Robin Johnson, interview by Morgan Baillargeon, Head-Smashed-In Buffalo Jump, 1995, Rodeo and Ranching collection (Legends of Our Times), V97-0148, CMC.

51 George Saddleman, interview by Leslie Tepper, undated, V97-0088, CMC.

52 *Wild Horses, Unconquered People.*

53 Garry Oker, interview by author, Fort St. John, BC, 12 December 2004; Author, field notes, Whispering Pines, 21 June 2004; Baillargeon and Tepper, *Legends of Our Times*, 28, 198.

54 Many who have written about Aboriginal involvement in the Williams Lake Stampede comment that most people from the Chilcotin travelled to the event on horseback or in horse-drawn wagons into the 1970s.

55 Nicholas Read, "B.C.'s Mustang Valley: Magnificent Wild Horses Roam Chilcotin's Brittany Triangle," *Vancouver Sun*, 16 November 2002, A11; *Wild Horses, Unconquered People.*

56 Duke LeBourdais, interview by author, Whispering Pines, 23 August 2004.

57 Joan (Palmantier) Gentles, interview by author, Williams Lake, 12 May 2004.

58 Gottfriedson family, interview by author, Kamloops, 24 August 2004.

59 Fred Gladstone, interview by Charles Ursenbach, 4 June 1975, Fred Gladstone Fonds, M-6049, file 18, GMA.

60 Cuthand, *The Gift of the Grandfathers.*

61 Joe Medicine Shield, interview by Morgan Baillargeon, Calgary Stampede, undated, Rodeo and Ranching collection (Legends of Our Times), V96-0459, CMC.

62 Cohen, *Stories and Images;* Shirley Louis, *Q'sapi: A History of Okanagan People as Told by Okanagan Families* (Penticton: Theytus Books, 2002).

63 Quoted in Cohen, *Stories and Images*, 14.

64 Cuthand, *The Gift of the Grandfathers.*

65 Author, field notes, Whispering Pines, 24 June 2004.

66 Brad Medicine Shield, Ted Nuce, Pete Standing Alone, Larry Bull, and Steve Headrunner, interview by Morgan Baillargeon, undated, and footage of events at Standoff Rodeo, Rodeo and Ranching collection (Legends of Our Times), V95-0308, CMC.

67 Lenore Layman uses the word "reticence" to describe such moments that challenge the interviewer's interpretation of events. Standing Alone's statement was much more self-assured than the word "reticence" implies, so I have used "rupture." Nonetheless, Layman's observations remain germane. She describes four types of reticence in oral histories: "when what was being said or asked did not

fit into the narrator's purpose in agreeing to the interview, that which did not fit within the narrator's bounds of social discourse, that which was painful or disturbing to discuss and that which
did not fit with the public, commemorative memory." I would argue that Standing Alone's comment falls into the latter category. Lenore Layman, "Reticence in Oral History Interviews," *Oral
History Review* 32,2 (Fall 2009): 214.

68   Louis, *Q'sapi.*
69   "Competitive Achievements: Gus Gottfriedson," in "The Cowboy Times: Official Program of the
     Kamloops Cowboy Festival, March 2001," 5.
70   Gottfriedson family, interview by author, 24 August 2004.
71   Iverson, *Riders of the West,* 55-71.
72   Quoted in Cuthand, *The Gift of the Grandfathers.*
73   WIREA, Cecil Louis, Director, Okanagan Band, interview by Leslie Tepper, Douglas Lake, BC,
     undated, Rodeo and Ranching collection (Legends of Our Times), V97-0088, CMC.
74   Haugen, "Indian Rodeo," 84.
75   Ron and Robin Johnson, interview by Morgan Baillargeon, Head-Smashed-In Buffalo Jump, un-
     dated, Rodeo and Ranching collection (Legends of Our Times), V97-0148, CMC.
76   Quoted in Caen Bly, "What Rodeo Life Is Really About," *Kainai News,* 15 September 1969, 14.
77   Fred Gladstone, interview by Charles Ursenbach, 4 June 1975, Fred Gladstone Fonds, M-6049,
     file 18, GMA.
78   Gottfriedson family, interview by author, 24 August 2004.
79   Duke LeBourdais, interview by author, 23 August 2004.
80   Wallace Mountain Horse, interview by Pauline Dempsey at Moses Lake, 15 May 1993, Interviews
     for Childhood Exhibit, M-9204-11, GMA.
81   Anne Lefthand and John Lefthand, interview by Morgan Baillargeon, undated, Rodeo and
     Ranching collection (Legends of Our Times), V96-0460, CMC.
82   Joan (Palmantier) Gentles, interview by author, 12 May 2004.
83   Cara Currie, interview by Morgan Baillargeon, undated, History of Indian Rodeo Association,
     personal recollections, V95-0137, CMC.
84   Haugen, "Indian Rodeo," 35.
85   Ibid., 74.
86   Ibid., 95.
87   Ibid., 85.
88   Larry Hodgeson and Todd Buffalo, interview by Morgan Baillargeon, undated, Rodeo and Ranching
     collection (Legends of Our Times), V95-0478, CMC.
89   Cardly Elmer and Merrill Yellowbird, interview by Morgan Baillargeon, Calgary Stampede and at
     Hobbema, undated, Rodeo and Ranching collection (Legends of Our Times), V96-0459, CMC.
90   George Saddleman, interview by Leslie Tepper, undated, Rodeo and Ranching collection (Legends
     of Our Times), V97-0088, CMC.
91   Fred Gladstone, interview by Charles Ursenbach, 4 June 1975, Fred Gladstone Fonds, M-6049, file
     18, GMA; Louis, *Q'sapi.*
92   WIREA, Cecil Louis, Director, Okanagan Band, interview by Leslie Tepper, Douglas Lake, BC,
     undated, Rodeo and Ranching collection (Legends of Our Times), V97-0088, CMC.

Conclusion

1   Elaine Dewar, *Bones: Discovering the First Americans* (Toronto: Vintage Canada, 2001), 2. For a fic-
    tional account of the power of culture to bring people together, see Tomson Highway, *Kiss of the
    Fur Queen* (Toronto: Doubleday, 1998).
2   Elizabeth Furniss, *The Burden of History: Colonialism and the Frontier Myth in a Rural Canadian
    Community* (Vancouver: UBC Press, 1999), 16-17, 171-72.
3   Andrea L. Smith, "Heteroglossia, 'Common Sense,' and Social Memory," *American Ethnologist* 1,2
    (May 2004): 251-69.
4   R.D. Theisz, "Putting Things in Order: The Discourse of Tradition," in *Powwow,* ed. Clyde Ellis,
    Luke Eric Lassiter, and Gary H. Dunham (Lincoln: University of Nebraska Press, 2005), 85.
5   Jenéa Tallentire, "Strategies of Memory: History, Social Memory and the Community," *Histoire
    sociale/Social History* 34,67 (May 2001): 199.

6   Furniss, *Burden of History;* W. Keith Regular, *Neighbours and Networks: The Blood Tribe in the Southern Alberta Economy, 1884-1939* (Calgary: University of Calgary Press, 2009); Terry Glavin, *This Ragged Place: Travels across the Landscape* (Vancouver: New Star Books, 1996), 122-69. Kerry Abel produces a more nuanced and comprehensive view of rural community building that challenges some of the dominant scholarship on small towns and their relations with First Nations. Kerry M. Abel, *Changing Places: History, Community and Identity in Northeastern Ontario* (Montreal and Kingston: McGill-Queen's University Press, 2006).

7   Julie Cruikshank, *The Social Life of Stories: Narrative and Knowledge in the Yukon Territory* (Lincoln and London: University of Nebraska Press, 1998), 159.

8   Ibid.

9   John Carlos Rowe, "Introduction," in *Culture and the Problem of the Disciplines,* ed. John Carlos Rowe (New York: Columbia University Press, 1998), 10.

10 Cara Currie, interview by Morgan Baillargeon, undated, History of Indian Rodeo Association, personal recollections, V95-0137, Canadian Museum of Civilization, Gatineau.

11 Jan Penrose, "When All the Cowboys Are Indians: The Nature of Race in All-Indian Rodeo," *Annals of the Association of American Geographers* 93,3 (September 2003): 687-705; R. Douglas Francis, review of *Legends of Our Times: Native Cowboy Life, Canadian Historical Review* 80,1 (March 2000): 129-30.

12 For two examples in which Aboriginal people express a desire not to mix with whites, see Michael Ames, "Fountain in a Modern Economy: A Study of Social Structure, Land Use and Business Enterprise in a British Columbia Indian Community" (BA essay, University of British Columbia, 1956), 2-4, and Joseph Vandale, interview by Victoria R. Racette, Debden, Saskatchewan, 4 March 1984, Indian History Film Project, IH-SD71, University of Regina Archives, Regina.

13 Tony Bennett, "The Politics of the 'Popular' and Popular Culture," in *Popular Culture and Social Relations,* ed. Tony Bennett, Colin Mercer, and Janet Wollacott (Philadelphia: Open University Press, 1986), 19.

14 Nicholas Thomas, *In Oceania: Visions, Artefacts, Histories* (Durham: Duke University Press, 1997), 227; David Nock and Celia Haig-Brown, "Introduction," in *With Good Intentions: Euro-Canadian and Aboriginal Relations in Colonial Canada* (Vancouver: UBC Press, 2006), 1-9; Thomas King, *The Truth about Stories: A Native Narrative* (Toronto: Anansi Press, 2003), 88-89; J. Edward Chamberlin, *If This Is Your Land, Where Are Your Stories? Finding Common Ground* (Toronto: Alfred A. Knopf, 2003).

Index

Page numbers in italics indicate illustrations.

sports culture: admiration of skill, 96, 97; masculinity, 13; modernity, 108; reinforcement of shared values, 98; sports organization and societal power structures, 128, 130. *See also* culture; popular culture; role models

Sproat, Gilbert, 256*n*81

spurs, 142

Squaw Hall, 195-96, 202, 203. *See also* Indian Open-Air Dance Hall

squaw-men, 84

squaw race, 36, 50, 60, 100

Squinahan, Lorraine, 197

Squinahan, Pierro, 60

Squiness, Peter (chief), 116

St. Eugene's Residential School, 55, 56-57

St. Pierre, Paul, 174, 196, 197, 204

stampede programs. *See* programs

stampede queen contests: Aboriginal contestants, 92, 103-4, 168, 195; Calgary Stampede, 162-64; CGRA, 162-63; Joan (Palmantier) Gentles, 104, 159, 168; local participation, 175; role in parades, 5; Williams Lake Stampede, 89-92, 168, 195, 197-201, 202. *See also* femininity; Indian queen contests

Stampede Ranch, 70

stampedes. *See* rodeo; *names of specific stampedes*

Standing Alone, Pete, 220, 274-75*n*67

standings, 138

Star, Johnny, 30

Starlight, Jim, 75, 81

status Indians, 207, 209, 272*n*4

steer decorating, 68, 138, 193

steer riding: CPRA sanction, 138; Dorothy Ion, 88; Harry Shuttleworth, 67; little britches rodeo, 190; overview of, 4; Paddy Laframboise, 67; picture of, *187*; Wilf Gerlitz, 181

steer wrestling, 4, 142

Stevens, Christine, 143

Stevenson, Jean, 197

Stewart, Jas, 260*n*26

Stewart McCall pageant, 106

Stoeltje, Beverly, 201, 240*n*5

Stoler, Ann Laura, 14-15

Stoney Indian Rodeo, *185*, 209

Stott, Jack, 159

Stott, Tracy, 158, 159

Stuart, James, 41

Stuie Stampede, 116

Sumas, Washington, Rodeo, *8*

sun dance, 9, 26, 35, 47, 109

Sydney, Australia, 81

Syilx cowboys, 109

Taber, Alberta, 35-36, 182

Tail Feathers, Fred (chief), 36, *37*

Tailfeathers, Ken, 211, 222

Tailfeathers, Tuffy, 211

Taillon, Cy, 67, 68, 122

Tallow, Cecil, 124

Taylor Flats, BC, 179

television: Canadian television, 118; *Cariboo Country*, 136, 196, 197, 204, 262*n*8; *Goldenrod*, 136; *Sails and Saddles*, 118; Westerns on, 136. *See also* Westerns

Tepper, Leslie, 165

Thode, Earl, 114

Thomas, Alex, 30

Thomas, Coreen, 201

Thomas, Larry, 201

Thomas, Nicholas, 15

Thompson, Don, 64

Thompson, John K., 96

Thomson, Ken, 126, 130

Thoreson, Julie, 163

Three Persons, Eliza, 81

Three Persons, Katie, *54*, 92

Three Persons, Tom: as Aboriginal, 75; accomplishments of, 105; best-dressed cowboy contest, 92; and Cardston Stampede, 32; career of, 78-81; discrimination, 116, 210; Dominion Indian Celebration, 57; Fort Macleod, 7, 76; and Fred Gladstone, 221; friendships with settler cowboys, 97; identity, 105; in Lethbridge Stampede, 31, *32*; mentorship, 79-80, 105; pictures of, *32, 54, 77, 79*; at southern Alberta rodeos, 59

Time magazine, 117

timed events: discrimination, 80, 116; goat tying, 151, 152, 153, *164*, 191, 221; overview of, 4; partnerships with horses, 171; steer wrestling, 4, 142. *See also* calf roping; roughstock events

tipi races, 36

Titley, Brian, 37

Togstead, Dave, 106

Tolmie, S.F. (premier), 47

Toronto, Ontario, 119

Toronto Star Weekly, 118

Touin, Charles, 85

tourism: automobile tourists, 39; British Columbia, 43-44; Canadian West, 176; community building, 38; competition for, 229; contact zones for tourists, 7; High River, 178, 185-86; *Land of the Overlanders*, 146; Nakoda people, 186; *Princess in Wonderland*, 194; rodeo as attraction, 177-78; small-town rodeos, 33, 178-79; Williams Lake, 194, 271*n*108. *See also* promotion

Printed and bound in Canada by Friesens

Set in Galliard and New Baskerville by Artegraphica Design Co. Ltd.

Copy Editor: Deborah Kerr

Proofreader: Grace Yaginuma

Cartographer: Eric Leinberger

Indexer: Natalie Boon